KU-383-847

LIVERPOOL JMU LIBRARY

3 1111 01355 9966

Advances in
COMPUTERS
VOLUME 83

Advances in
COMPUTERS

EDITED BY

MARVIN V. ZELKOWITZ

Department of Computer Science
University of Maryland
College Park, Maryland
USA

VOLUME 83

AMSTERDAM • BOSTON • HEIDELBERG • LONDON • NEW YORK • OXFORD
PARIS • SAN DIEGO • SAN FRANCISCO • SINGAPORE • SYDNEY • TOKYO
Academic Press is an imprint of Elsevier

ACADEMIC
PRESS

Academic Press is an imprint of Elsevier

32 Jamestown Road, London, NW1 7BY, UK
Radarweg 29, PO Box 211, 1000 AE Amsterdam, The Netherlands
225 Wyman Street, Waltham, MA 02451, USA
525 B Street, Suite 1900, San Diego, CA 92101-4495, USA

First edition 2011

Copyright © 2011 Elsevier Inc. All rights reserved

No part of this publication may be reproduced, stored in a retrieval system or transmitted in any form or
by any means electronic, mechanical, photocopying, recording or otherwise without the prior written
permission of the publisher Permissions may be sought directly from Elsevier's Science & Technology
Rights Department in Oxford, UK: phone (+44) (0) 1865 843830; fax (+44) (0) 1865 853333; email:
permissions@elsevier.com. Alternatively you can submit your request online by visiting the Elsevier web
site at http://elsevier.com/locate/permissions, and selecting *Obtaining permission to use Elsevier material*

Notice
No responsibility is assumed by the publisher for any injury and/or damage to persons or property as a
matter of products liability, negligence or otherwise, or from any use or operation of any methods,
products, instructions or ideas contained in the material herein

Library of Congress Cataloging-in-Publication Data
A catalog record for this book is available from the Library of Congress

British Library Cataloguing-in-Publication Data
A catalogue record for this book is available from the British Library

ISBN: 978-0-12-385510-7

ISSN: 0065-2458

For information on all Academic Press publications
visit our web site at elsevierdirect.com

Printed and bound in USA

11 12 13 14   10 9 8 7 6 5 4 3 2 1

Working together to grow
libraries in developing countries

www.elsevier.com | www.bookaid.org | www.sabre.org

ELSEVIER   BOOK AID
             International   Sabre Foundation

Contents

PREFACE   ix

The State of the Art in Identity Theft

Amit Grover, Hal Berghel, and Dennis Cobb

1. Introduction   2
2. What Sets Identity Theft Apart from Other Crimes   3
3. Statistical Data for Identity Theft and Associated Crimes   6
4. The Genesis of the Problem   11
5. How SSN Became the *De Facto* Primary Key for Most Databases . . .   12
6. The Ubiquitous Use of Fungible Credentials   13
7. Phishing   14
8. Modus Operandi   26
9. Inadequate Credential Management Procedures   31
10. Strategies for Defeating Identity Thieves   32
11. Conclusion   47
    References   47

An Overview of Steganography

Gary C. Kessler and Chet Hosmer

1. Introduction   52
2. Low-Tech Stego Methods   56

3. Digital Technology Basics 62
4. Steganography and Digital Carrier Files 67
5. Detecting Steganography 85
6. Steganography Detection Tools 93
7. Summary and Conclusions 100
   References 103

CAPTCHAs: An Artificial Intelligence Application to Web Security

José María Gómez Hidalgo and Gonzalo Alvarez

1. Introduction 110
2. Motivation and Applications 116
3. Types of CAPTCHAs 127
4. Evaluation of CAPTCHAs 146
5. Security and Attacks on CAPTCHAs 156
6. Alternatives to CAPTCHAs 171
7. Conclusions and Future Trends 173
   References 173

Advances in Video-Based Biometrics

Rama Chellappa and Pavan Turaga

1. Introduction 184
2. Video-Based Face Recognition 186
3. Video-Based Identification Using Gait 191
4. Conclusions 200
   Acknowledgments 201
   References 201

Action Research Can Swing the Balance in Experimental Software Engineering

Paulo Sérgio Medeiros dos Santos and Guilherme Horta Travassos

1. Introduction 206
2. Action Research Overview 210
3. The Use of Action Research in Software Engineering:
   A Preliminary Survey? 219
4. Using Action Research in Software Engineering: An *In Vivo* Study . . . 225
5. Applying Action Research to Software Engineering 254
6. Final Considerations 270
   Acknowledgments 270
   References 270

Functional and Nonfunctional Design Verification for Embedded Software Systems

Arnab Ray, Christopher Ackermann, Rance Cleaveland, Charles Shelton, and Chris Martin

1. Introduction 279
2. Background 281
3. Instrumentation-Based Verification 284
4. Quality Attribute-Based Reasoning 296
5. Integrated Functional and Nonfunctional Verification 300
6. Tool Support 313
7. Conclusion 318
   References 318

AUTHOR INDEX 323
SUBJECT INDEX 333
CONTENTS OF VOLUMES IN THIS SERIES 345

Preface

This is Volume 83 of the *Advances in Computers*, subtitled *Security on the Web*. This series, continuously published since 1960, is the oldest series covering the development of the computer industry. With the impact that the World Wide Web has on every facet of our lives today, this volume focuses on the security aspect of computing. How can we be sure that our computing needs are secure and reliable from intrusion by others? When we put most of our private, financial, and business information out there "on the Web," how can we be sure that the information is available when we need it and that unauthorized outsiders cannot gain access to that information? In this volume, we present six chapters. Four are directly related to the theme of Web security, whereas the other two are related to software engineering goals to produce correct software, a major precondition to obtaining Web security.

In the first chapter, "The State of the Art in Identity Theft," Amit Grover, Hal Berghel, and Dennis Cobb define one of the growing threats in using the World Wide Web—that of identity theft. What is the impact of others finding out your account password; personal identity number, such as a Social Security number in the United States; credit card number; or other Web site password? Using such information, thieves can easily empty bank accounts, charge thousands of dollars of goods to your account, and generally play havoc with your personal information. After reading this chapter for the first time, I quickly felt like I never wanted to see a credit card again—but using such "plastic" has become an unavoidable aspect of everyday life. This chapter explains many of the ways thieves gain access to your online information and provides a list of actions you can take both online and in your everyday life to minimize the possibility of unauthorized intrusion into your accounts.

Once we establish, as in the first chapter, that the risk of having an insecure computer system is real, the next three chapters discuss various ways to build that security back into the system. In the second chapter, "An Overview of Steganography," by Gary C. Kessler and Chet Hosmer, the authors discuss steganography, the use of hidden text to hide messages. Everyone is familiar with the concept of encryption using codes and ciphers that make messages unreadable unless one has the appropriate decryption information. The weakness of encryption is that anyone wanting to steal that information knows that it is there—all that is missing is the mechanism to extract the hidden information. With steganography, the goal is to hide even the fact that there is hidden information present so that thieves or others do not know where to look for that information. Steganography has been used for hundreds of years, but the advent of computers with complex data types makes the job easier. For example, a photograph encoded using the JPG format is quite large. Knowing that format allows one to add extra information to the JPG file without altering the picture, yet anyone knowing that there is hidden information there can easily extract it. In this chapter, many ways of hiding information in various computer file types is presented.

CAPTCHAs are the topic of the third chapter "CAPTCHAs: An Artificial Intelligence Application to Web Security" by José María Gómez Hidalgo and Gonzalo Alvarez. With the advent of the World Wide Web and the use of Web crawlers (Web robots or bots) that move from Web site to Web site gathering information, a new threat has emerged. Many Web sites depend upon the slow response rate of people to monitor behavior on that site. A bot can respond much quicker. Thus, for example, a bot can buy tickets for an event at a certain Web site within a few seconds or perhaps milliseconds. Such bots can buy all the tickets for a popular event quickly, and then these tickets can be resold at a much higher rate. To prevent this from happening, many sites want to make sure that a real human is accessing the site and not a preprogrammed bot. This is the goal of a CAPTCHA. Before submitting a transaction on this site, the user has to submit information into a box on the screen. Often it is the distorted text that the user has to understand and repeat. Any question that is easy for a person to understand and answer but extremely difficult for a computer to answer is appropriate. This chapter discusses these CAPTCHAs and gives a detailed taxonomy of the various forms of queries that have been implemented with a discussion of their reliability.

Rama Chellappa and Pavan Turaga in the fourth chapter "Advances in Video-Based Biometrics" discuss another aspect of the online security problem. Online identity recognition (see the first chapter) today mostly depends upon using the correct password. But if your password is stolen, anyone can gain access to your information. Rather than using "what you know" (i.e., a password) to gain access to private information, another approach is to use "who you are." While passwords can easily be used by anyone, physical attributes such as fingerprints or eye iris scans are harder to counterfeit. In this chapter, the authors discuss another aspect of who you are. In this case, they look at motion. How you walk is almost as indicative as how tall you are and how you look. (How often have you looked into the distance and recognized someone by their gait before they were close enough to actually make out who they were?) This chapter discusses these and related ways to use video-based biometrics.

The last two chapters discuss two approaches to software development that aid in building correct systems. One cannot have secure systems without trustworthy software. In the fifth chapter "Action Research Can Swing the Balance in Experimental Software Engineering" by Paulo Sérgio, Medeiros dos Santos, and Guilherme Horta Travassos, the authors discuss the problem of how new technology gets adopted by the software engineering community. They state, "In general, professionals still ignore scientific evidence in place of expert opinions in most of their decision-making." Why is this so? They discuss some of the problems of why technology transfer of new technology into the software development world is hard, and they explore Action Research and describe how it can be an aid in making new effective technology more available.

In the final chapter, "Functional and Nonfunctional Design Verification for Embedded Software Systems" by Arnab Ray, Christopher Ackermann, Rance Cleaveland, Charles Shelton, and Chris Martin, the authors look at model-based design. "The ability to perform verification in the design phase itself allows engineers to catch bugs early in the development lifecycle where they are cheaper and easier to fix," say the authors. The chapter discusses a graphically based tool where the execution behavior of the design is specified and various behavioral properties, such as safety and correctness, can be determined via simulation of the design. This has application, for example, in the automotive industry.

I hope that you find these chapters of interest. I want to say that I have enjoyed producing these volumes. I have been series editor of the *Advances in Computers* since 1993, and this volume is the last volume that I will produce in this series. Since 1993, I have helped to put out 44 volumes containing 266 chapters exploring new technology. When I started working on the series in 1993, the mainframe computer was still a viable concept, although rapidly becoming obsolete, and the desktop workstation was becoming the computer platform of choice. The "Web," initially a U.S. Defense Department research network called the *ARPANET* in the early 1970s, was just being introduced to the general public with the development of hypertext, HTML and Web browsing in the early 1990s. In the intervening two decades, the Web has taken over computing, with most computing problems today related to providing Web-based services that are efficient, secure, trustworthy, reliable, and fast to a worldwide audience. With the current development of "cloud" computing, we are again returning to our roots of providing centralized computing platforms, which we can connect to, much like the mainframes of an earlier generation. Only now we have an immense network of services providing this support rather than a single processor. I hope that I have adequately chronicled those changes in the approximately 13,000 pages of text that have appeared here over the past two decades.

Although I am stepping down as series editor, the *Advances in Computers* will continue to present the ever-changing face of computing. The series will continue uninterrupted with new leadership. I hope that you will continue to find this series of use to you in your work.

Marvin Zelkowitz
College Park, Maryland

The State of the Art in Identity Theft

AMIT GROVER

Identity Theft and Financial Fraud Research and Operations Center, UNLV School of Informatics, University of Nevada Las Vegas, Las Vegas, Nevada, USA

HAL BERGHEL

Identity Theft and Financial Fraud Research and Operations Center, UNLV School of Informatics, University of Nevada Las Vegas, Las Vegas, Nevada, USA

DENNIS COBB

Identity Theft and Financial Fraud Research and Operations Center

Abstract

This chapter examines in detail the various aspects of identity theft—the nation's fastest-growing crime—and its impact in today's world. The introduction section defines several meanings of "identity theft" as it is commonly used, while Section 2 explores the unique characteristics of identity theft as a crime. Sections 3 covers detailed analyses of statistical data for identity theft and associated crimes. Sections 4 through 9 discuss the core issues involved including the genesis of the problem, the misuse of Social Security Numbers, the ubiquitous use of fungible credentials, the role of phishing and strategies to minimize its effect, the problem of inadequate credential management procedures and its solution, and the impact of technological advances in the

Copyright © 2011 Elsevier Inc.
All rights reserved.

unprecedented rise of identity theft incidents. Section 10 discusses the strategy
of prevention as well as cure in the context of identity theft.

1. Introduction 2
2. What Sets Identity Theft Apart from Other Crimes 3
3. Statistical Data for Identity Theft and Associated Crimes 6
4. The Genesis of the Problem 11
5. How SSN Became the *De Facto* Primary Key for Most Databases 12
6. The Ubiquitous Use of Fungible Credentials 13
7. Phishing 14
    7.1.   Phenomenal Growth in the Number and Sophistication of Phishing Attacks   14
    7.2.   The Importance of Secure Online Transactions 15
8. Modus Operandi 26
9. Inadequate Credential Management Procedures 31
    9.1.   CardSleuth 31
10. Strategies for Defeating Identity Thieves 32
    10.1.   Precautions to Prevent ID Theft 33
    10.2.   Remediation 47
11. Conclusion 47
    References 47

1. Introduction

Technically, the term "identity theft" refers to two distinct, but interrelated,
crimes: the act of stealing another's identity and the use of that stolen identity in
committing a fraudulent act. In the first case, identity theft is similar in function to
"pretexting"—or the attempt to take on the persona of another individual for social
engineering purposes. In the second case, identity theft falls into the category of
digital crime, along with copyright infringement, espionage, phishing, financial
crimes, money laundering, and so forth. In many if not most cases, the first type
of identity theft is used as a means to the commission of the second type of identity
theft. In the fullest sense, identity theft is a strong candidate for the major crime of
the new millennium. Identity theft usually begins with a fraudulent document such
as that shown in Fig. 1.

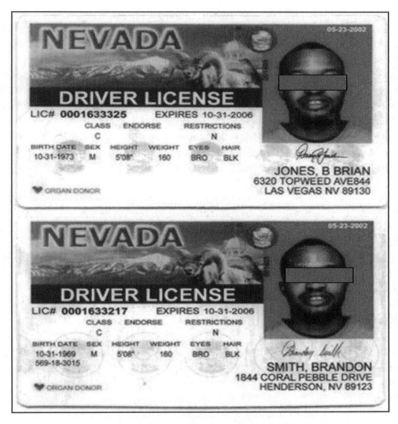

F_IG. 1. Example of Identity Theft. Source: The Identity Theft and Financial Fraud Research and Operations Center. www.itffroc.org.

2. What Sets Identity Theft Apart from Other Crimes

As per the U.S. Internal Revenue Service, "Most scams impersonating the IRS are identity theft schemes" [1]. The inherent dangers associated with Identity Theft as a crime-facilitator ensure that its potential for causing disasters can hardly be over-emphasized. The calamitous effect of identity fraud is perhaps best illustrated by the fact that the 9/11 hijackers successfully opened 35 U.S. bank accounts using fictitious Social Security numbers that the banks never bothered to countercheck. These accounts were used for international money—laundering and financing terrorist activities. As per a Department of Homeland Security report titled, "Identity and Security: Moving Beyond the 9/11 Staff Report on Identity Document Security" [2], "The 9/11 hijackers engaged in a travel operation that included fraudulently obtaining 17 driver's licenses (one in Arizona, two in California, and 14—four of which were duplicates—in Florida) and 13 state-issued identifications (five from Florida, one from Maryland, and seven from Virginia). All seven in Virginia were obtained fraudulently, and three of the hijackers presented those same identification cards on the morning of 9/11 at Dulles International Airport ticket counters."

Further, during a hearing on "Preserving the Integrity of Social Security Numbers and Preventing Their Misuse by Terrorists and Identity Thieves" as part of a testimony to the U.S. House of Representatives [3], Chris Jay Hoofnagle stated that "a terrorist suspect reportedly connected to the Al Qaeda network was recently charged with selling the SSNs of 21 people who were members of the Bally's Health Club in Cambridge, Massachusetts. The SSNs were sold in order to create false passports and credit lines for bank accounts."

The New York Times Square incident involving Faisal Shahzad in May 2010 which is the most recent terrorism attempt on U.S. soil was financed by international money laundering operations (known as "hawala") originating in Pakistan and made possible in part by identity theft [4]. The use of identity theft in facilitating cross-border crimes ranging from international espionage to illegal trafficking of weapons as well as narcotics is also well documented. The U.S. Treasury's Terrorist Financing Tracking Program (TFTP) focuses among other things to investigate identity theft involved in funding international terrorist activities [5].

Identity theft is unique in its spread across all demographics and apart from ordinary citizens, victims of identity theft or people whose personal information has been compromised in some way include high-profile individuals such as Warren Buffett, Bill Gates, Tom Cruise, Steven Spielberg, Oprah Winfrey, Danny DeVito, David Letterman, Jay Leno, Federal Reserve Chairman Ben Bernanke, Tiger Woods, Martha Stewart, Ted Turner, George Lucas, Ross Perot, Senator Norm Coleman of Minnesota, Will Smith, Steven Segal, Mel Gibson, Michael Ovitz, Sydney Pollack, Leonard Nimoy, Lawrence Tisch, Arsenio Hall, Lew Wasserman, Alan Ladd, former Vice President Al Gore's daughter, CEOs, senior corporate executives, high-ranking military officials, and top politicians along with thousands of Clinton administration staff members and White House visitors [6–8].

Identity theft is probably one of the only crimes that can ruin within days the sound financial health, good credit history as well as an impeccable reputation that a victim might have painstaking built over a lifetime. There have been cases where innocent identity theft victims have been arrested for crimes committed by others. Many identity theft victims have reported that apart from the financial loss, they had to endure a lot of stress and emotional challenges in their battle to get back their life. An identity theft often results in having a debilitating effect on the victim's potential for getting a new job or buying a new house.

The Social Security Administration has identified identity theft as one of the fastest-growing crimes in the nation [9] and the 2010 Identity Fraud Survey Report by Javelin Strategy & Research [10] states that while there were approximately 10 million victims of identity fraud in 2008, the number rose to *more than 11 million victims for 2009* with the associated *annual costs as high as $54 billion*. As per the Federal Trade Commission's 2006 Identity Theft Survey Report [11], the number of identity theft victims in 2005 was around 8.3 million. This steady increase in the number of victims of identity fraud over the years is charted in Fig. 2.

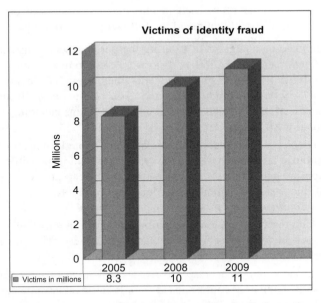

FIG. 2. Steady increase in the number of victims of identity fraud over the years.

3. Statistical Data for Identity Theft and Associated Crimes

Identity Theft and Financial Fraud Research and Operations Center (ITFF/ROC, www.itffroc.org) is a collaborative effort between the University of Nevada Las Vegas and law enforcement agencies such as the Las Vegas Metropolitan Police Department dedicated to effectively fight the problem of identity theft and associated crimes through a synergy between high-tech research and current law enforcement procedures. Established in 2004, the ITTFROC has worked with the Department of Justice on a number of projects using cutting-edge technology to fight digital crime.

For increasing social awareness, ITTFROC also highlights the most important data breaches relevant to identity theft and financial fraud on a weekly basis and archives the data for future reference in its "Reading Room" section [12]. The detailed statistics presented in this section are derived from 61 specific incidents representing all major data breaches from January 24, 2009 till June 24, 2010. It is important to note that the data represent the total number of compromised records and not the total number of verified identity theft victims. The data collection, analysis, and interpretation highlighted the following salient points:

- The combined data suggest that during the period under consideration, *more than 260 million (260,247,580) records* were compromised with almost 50% of the records attributed to a single incident—the largest U.S. Identity Theft case involving *130 million stolen credit and debit card numbers* from credit-card processor Heartland Payment Systems and retail chains including 7-Eleven Inc. and Hannaford Brothers Co.

- Figure 3 depicts a chart (derived from data from Table I) indicating the number of compromised records based on the type of incident responsible for information exposure and shows that apart from the Heartland Payment Systems incident, the maximum number of compromised records can be attributed to *failure in sanitizing hard disk drives before disposal.*

- Figure 4 represents a graphical distribution of the number of compromised records per incident which was spread over a very wide range from the humongous 130 million to the paltry 50.

- Figures 5 and 6 represent, respectively, a breakdown of the number of incidents and the number of compromised records based on the type of organization (derived from data from Table II and Table III respectively).

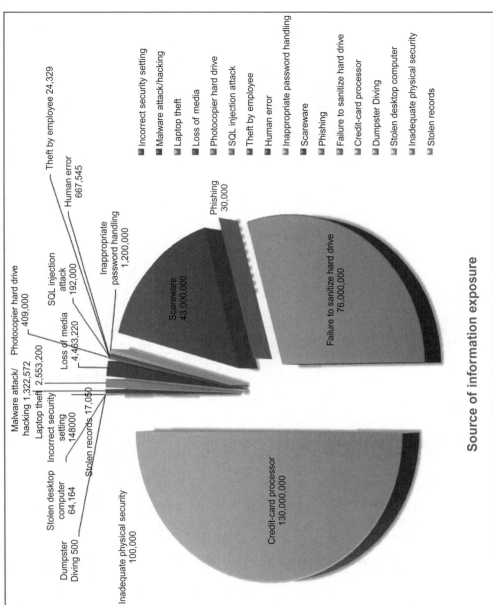

Fig. 3. Compromised records based on source of information exposure (data in Table 1).

TABLE I
COMPROMISED RECORDS BASED ON SOURCE OF INFORMATION EXPOSURE

Incorrect security setting	148,000
Malware attack/hacking	1,322,572
Laptop theft	2,553,200
Loss of media	4,463,220
Photocopier hard drive	409,000
SQL injection attack	192,000
Theft by employee	24,329
Human error	667,545
Inappropriate password handling	1,200,000
Scareware	43,000,000
Phishing	30,000
Failure to sanitize hard drive	76,000,000
Credit-card processor	130,000,000
Dumpster diving	500
Stolen desktop computer	64,164
Inadequate physical security	100,000
Stolen records	17,050

- While all individuals whose data have been compromised are at a high risk of becoming victims of identity theft, the actual number of victims would be substantially less.
- Since the data are derived from a large number of incidents spread over a 17-month period, it is very likely that data of some individuals have been compromised in more than one incident, thus reducing the actual number of distinct individuals affected.
- Even in a single incident such as the Heartland Payment Systems breach, the number of distinct people affected might be less than the number of records compromised as it is common for people to use a number of different credit/debit cards.
- There are instances when the identity theft victims do not file reports with law enforcement for various reasons, and hence the actual number of victims is more than what is reflected by the law enforcement records.

As per Privacy Rights Clearinghouse, a nonprofit consumer organization, the consolidated number of records breached based on 1728 data breaches made public since 2005 till September 20, 2010 is a staggering 510,547,119 [13].

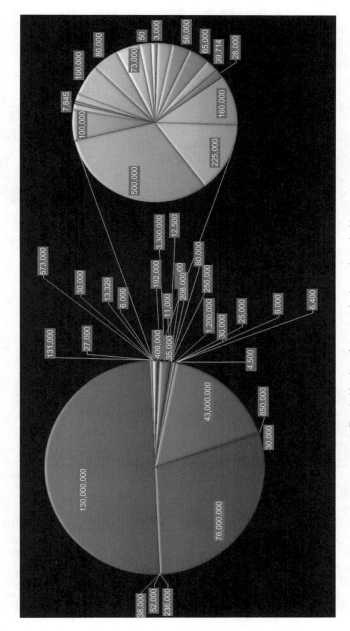

Fig. 4. Number of compromised records per incident.

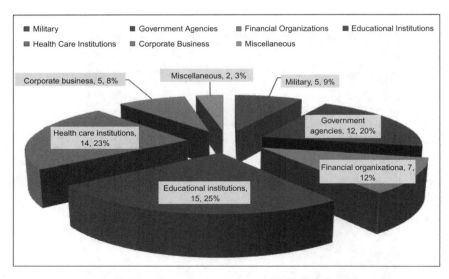

FIG. 5. Number of incidents based on type of organization (data in Table II).

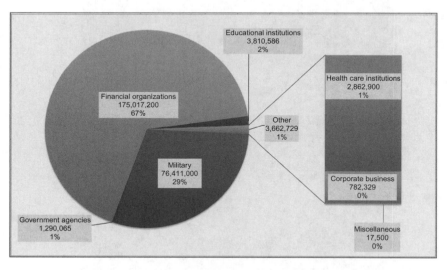

FIG. 6. Compromised records based on type of organization (data in Table III).

TABLE II
NUMBER OF INCIDENTS BASED ON TYPE OF ORGANIZATION

Organization type	Number of incidents
Military	5
Government agencies	12
Financial organizations	7
Educational institutions	15
Healthcare institutions	14
Corporate business	5
Miscellaneous	2

TABLE III
COMPROMISED RECORDS BASED ON TYPE OF ORGANIZATION

Organization type	Number of compromised records
Military	76,411,000
Government agencies	1,290,065
Financial organizations	175,017,200
Educational institutions	3,810,586
Healthcare institutions	2,862,900
Corporate business	782,329
Miscellaneous	17,500

4. The Genesis of the Problem

The primary components for a successful identity theft are name, Social Security Number, date of birth, address, and any other personally identifiable information such as driver's license information, passport details, account information, or online login credentials that can be used to generate counterfeit IDs or allow an identity thief to open a line of credit in the victim's name without the victim's knowledge [14] (Fig. 7). Once this information is compromised and is out in the public domain, it is very difficult to control the damage. The underground market for exploiting personally identifiable information is so efficient that stolen credit/debit card information has been used in many cases to perform fraudulent financial transactions in a matter of minutes rather than days from the time information was compromised [15].

The primary reasons that make identity theft the fastest-growing crime in the USA can be identified as:

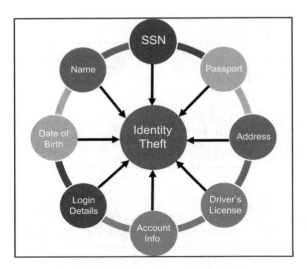

FIG. 7. Primary components of identity theft.

(a) The unprecedented and unregulated use of Social Security Number as a primary identifier for an entire range of transactions.
(b) The ubiquitous use of fungible credentials.
(c) Phenomenal growth in the number and sophistication of phishing attacks.
(d) Ease of making counterfeit IDs facilitated by an exponential growth in the technological prowess available to the masses.
(e) The inadequate and far-from-secure credential management procedures.

Each of these aspects is examined in detail in the following sections.

5. How SSN Became the *De Facto* Primary Key for Most Databases

The use of the Social Security Number was a by-product of the Social Security Act of 1935. This was extended to federal agencies other than the Social Security Administration by Executive Order 9397 in 1943. These restrictions were further relaxed in the Federal Privacy Act of 1974 to include state and local agencies. This resulted in the unprecedented and unregulated use of Social Security Number as a primary identifier for an entire range of transactions even when there was no logical/ legal requirement for using the SSN [16]. Now state governments are attempting to do damage control with what are known as "Security Breach Notification Laws." Generally, these laws require companies, and in some cases state agencies, to report to consumers if their computers have experienced a security breach resulting in important personal information being released to unauthorized parties. As per the National Conference of State Legislatures Web site, 46 states, District of Columbia, Puerto Rico, and the Virgin Islands had enacted such legislation as of April 12, 2010 [17]. Although the laws differ somewhat, they generally replicate California's breach protection law passed in 2003. At least two states, Michigan and Massachusetts, require businesses that collect SSNs to have an "information security program that specifically addresses SSN protection." The only states presently without such a law are Alabama, Kentucky, New Mexico, and South Dakota.

The good news is that the Federal and various state governments are now taking the issue of identity theft very seriously [18]. Of the 31 recommendations made in the President's Identity Theft Task Force Report [19], the top two recommendations are to decrease the unnecessary use of SSNs in the public sector including the establishment of a Clearinghouse for Agency Practices that Minimize Use of SSNs, and develop a comprehensive record of SSN use in the private sector. Other recommendations included increased prosecution of identity theft and the establishment of a National Identity Theft Law Enforcement Center to deal more effectively with various aspects of the crime.

6. The Ubiquitous Use of Fungible Credentials

The operative meaning of "fungible" in this context is "interchangeable" [20]. As we use the term, fungible documents include counterfeits (e.g., currency), forgeries (contracts, negotiable instruments, signatures), as well as a third category that we will call "quasi-verifiable" or "legitimized." Most fungible documents are created for criminal purposes, usually with the intent to defraud. "Legitimized" documents are those that are produced by legitimate issuing authorities based upon false information. One example is a driver's license that has been issued to an individual under a fictitious name. That is where the quasi-verifiable characteristic comes in. The driver's license corresponds to a Department of Motor Vehicle (DMV) database record—in that sense it is legitimate. However, the data fields do not correspond to the holder—both the credential and the credentialed are real; they just do not correspond to each other.

Fungible credentials are useful precisely because they simultaneously obscure the criminal's real identity and facilitate any authentication that may be required. The starting point of a legitimized credential remains the counterfeit document. However, the counterfeit is only the means to the end of obtaining a legitimized document.

A typical scenario might be to begin by ordering a counterfeit passport from people who linger about the dark side of swap meets. It is not uncommon nowadays for criminals to special order the passports by country, name, visas, and endorsements. The counterfeit passport is then used in the "credential amplification" phase to produce the tokens that will be actually used to defraud—e.g., a driver's license issued by DMV. The typical DMV has no means to validate passports, so the amplification is relatively straightforward. The driver's license may in turn be used to obtain a Social Security Number, county health card, etc. until the wallet is filled. It goes without saying that the variations on this theme seem endless.

7. Phishing

According to Microsoft [21], "Phishing (pronounced 'fishing') is a type of online identity theft. It uses e-mail and fraudulent Web sites that are designed to steal your personal data or information such as credit-card numbers, passwords, account data, or other information. Con artists might send millions of fraudulent e-mail messages with links to fraudulent Web sites that appear to come from Web sites you trust, like your bank or credit-card company, and request that you provide personal information. Criminals can use this information for many different types of fraud, such as to steal money from your account, to open new accounts in your name, or to obtain official documents using your identity."

Phishing attacks carried out using Short Messaging Service (SMS) or text messages on cell phones are referred to as *SMiShing*, while those that depend on voice communications especially using the Voice-over-Internet Protocol (VOIP) are termed as *Vishing*. A related term, "Pharming" refers to Web site redirection with an aim to carry out phishing attacks.

7.1 Phenomenal Growth in the Number and Sophistication of Phishing Attacks

A phenomenal growth in the number and sophistication of phishing attack is a major contributor to the exponential growth of identity theft and related crimes. As per the Anti-Phishing Working Group (APWG)—a global consortium of law enforcement agencies and private sector entities with a stake in secure online transactions that strives to eliminate identity theft and related fraud resulting from phishing, pharming, and e-mail spoofing—more brands are under attack today than ever before [22,23]. As per the Phishing Activity Trends Report, 4th Quarter/2009 [24], the number of hijacked brands rose to a record 356 in October 2009 up nearly 4.4% from the

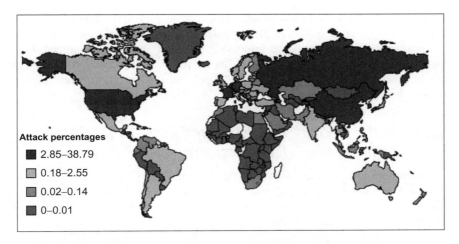

F<small>IG</small>. 8. Global phishing and crimeware map. Source: Anti-Phishing Working Group Web site, generated by Websense Security Labs.

previous record of 341 in August 2009. The report also states that "the United States continued its position as the top country hosting phishing sites in Q4, 2009."

Figure 8 shows a global distribution of Phishing and Crimeware (a term coined by Peter Cassidy, Secretary General of the APWG to refer to malware specifically designed to perpetrate cybercrime) attacks for a 12-month period from June 2009 to June 2010 [25].

7.2   The Importance of Secure Online Transactions

To effectively deal with phishing and other online threats, the best defense against identity theft is undoubtedly practicing a proactive policy of an "abundance of caution" based on awareness and a thorough understanding of the various threats and their countermeasures. Some of the salient points to remember before entering any sensitive personal or financial information on a Web site are discussed below.

7.2.1   Use of Hypertext Transfer Protocol Secure Instead of Hyper Text Transfer Protocol

The Hyper Text Transfer Protocol (HTTP), the backbone of the World Wide Web, is inherently insecure for sensitive transactions. To ensure secure transmission of data, HTTP is used in conjunction with Secure Socket Layer (SSL) or its successor

Transport Layer Security (TLS) in what is known as Hypertext Transfer Protocol Secure (HTTPS). SSL/TLS provide encryption of the data between endpoints as well as a mechanism to certify the authenticity of a web server. From an end-user's point of view, it is necessary to confirm that the protocol mentioned in the URL in the address bar of the browser should be "https" and not "http" when dealing with sensitive information.

7.2.2   Is the "Lock" Really Your "Key" to a "Safe and Secure" Transaction?

A prominent visual indicator of SSL has been the "lock" icon displayed on the right-hand side in most browsers' status bar as shown in Fig. 9. Many malicious sites have successfully fooled victims into believing that a Web site offers secure transactions just because it displays an image of a "lock" icon somewhere on its page even though the protocol in the address bar clearly states "HTTP" thereby signifying an inherently insecure connection. Similar to the real-estate industry, the location of the "lock" icon is of paramount importance to determine the reliability.

7.2.3   Encryption Versus Trust

Most online users wrongly interpret the lock icon in the status bar as an indication of a guarantee of a safe transaction. All that the lock icon denotes is that the connection between the web browser and the server uses encryption. It does not imply that the web server is a trusted source. Rouge Web sites set up with malicious intent will also display the lock icon as long as they use SSL, and the connection is

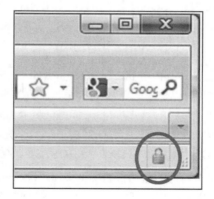

Fig. 9.   SSL "lock" icon displayed in browser's status bar.

encrypted. The authentication of a Web site as a trusted site is handled by the associated digital certificate. An expired, invalid, or revoked certificate is as bad as (if not worse than) the absence of a certificate but many users tend to skip the browser warnings and assume that as long as there is a certificate (even though invalid), the transaction is secure. The certificate contains the web server's identity information which needs to be authenticated and verified by an independent third party (known as Certification Authority) for a site to be considered as "trusted."

Figure 10 shows a comparison of a valid/authenticated digital certificate with an invalid certificate both issued to the same entity. The certificate on the left-hand side is invalid as it has not been authenticated by an independent trusted Root Certification Authority. The person it is issued to as well as the person it is issued by is one and the same (Amit Grover). The certificate on the right-hand side is valid as it has been authenticated by an independent trusted Root Certification Authority, and the certification path is clearly evident and verifiable.

It is interesting to note, however, that both certificates represent a public key in the PKI cryptography system and generated a corresponding private key for the user which can be used for encryption/decryption. Hence, the "Details" tab will not indicate anything unusual even with the invalid certificate as shown in Fig. 11.

Another important precaution is to ensure never to trust a site whose certificate has been revoked. RFC 5280 specifies 10 different reasons for certificate revocation including private key compromise and fraudulent or erroneous issuance of the digital certificate [26]. A high-profile example was when VeriSign revoked two digital certificates issued to Microsoft after discovering that an individual had obtained them fraudulently by falsely claiming to be Microsoft's representative. As per the VeriSign advisory [27], "The certificates were VeriSign Class 3 Software Publisher certificates and could be used to sign executable content under the name 'Microsoft Corporation.' The risk associated with these certificates is that the fraudulent party could produce digitally signed code and appear to be Microsoft Corporation. In this scenario, it is possible that the fraudulent party could create a destructive program or ActiveX control, then sign it using either certificate and host it on a Web site or distribute it to other Web sites." Figure 12 shows the revoked certificates.

7.2.4 Visual Indicators

The foregoing discussion underlines the critical importance of correctly analyzing and interpreting the visual indicators during an online session. Thus, ensuring a secure connection requires verifying the validity of the digital certificate as well as the location of the "lock" icon. The lock icon in the status bar was used to signify a level of trust in the Web site for a number of years till it was successfully

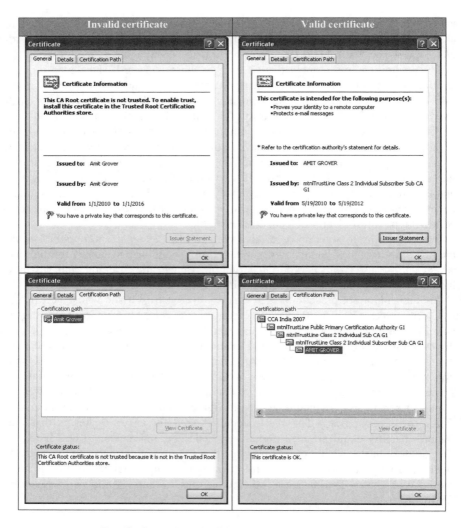

FIG. 10. Comparison of valid and invalid digital certificates.

demonstrated that the status bar in a browser can be faked and JavaScript can be used to manipulate the fake status bar in real time to falsely display the lock icon even when the connection was not encrypted [28]. This prompted many browsers to move the location of the "lock" icon to the Navigation/Address bar and depict the presence

Fig. 11. "Details" tab of an invalid digital certificate.

of SSL/TLS with a different color of either the text or the background of the Navigation/Address bar. This is considered extremely difficult to spoof, and there are no reported claims to break this security feature as yet.

7.2.4.1 Trusted Sites with a Secure and Authenticated Connection.
Figures 13–16 show the different visual indicators for a trusted HTTPS connection with an authenticated certificate in four popular browsers, viz., Mozilla Firefox v 3.6.3, Apple Safari v 5, Microsoft Internet Explorer v 8, and Google Chrome v 5, respectively.

7.2.4.2 Sites with Invalid Certificate Warning.
Figures 17–20 show the different visual indicators for an untrusted HTTPS connection with an invalid/unauthenticated certificate in four popular browsers, viz., Mozilla Firefox v 3.6.3, Apple Safari v 5, Microsoft Internet Explorer v 8, and

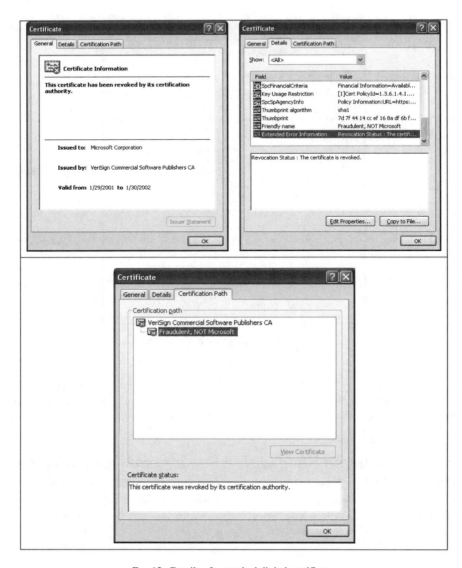

FIG. 12. Details of a revoked digital certificate.

FIG. 13. Visual indicators for a trusted HTTPS connection in Firefox v 3.6.3.

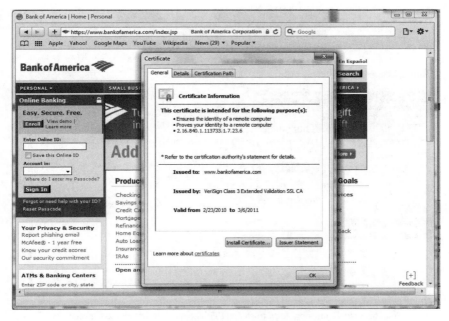

FIG. 14. Visual indicators for a trusted HTTPS connection in Safari v 5.

Fig. 15. Visual indicators for a trusted HTTPS connection in Microsoft Internet Explorer v 8.

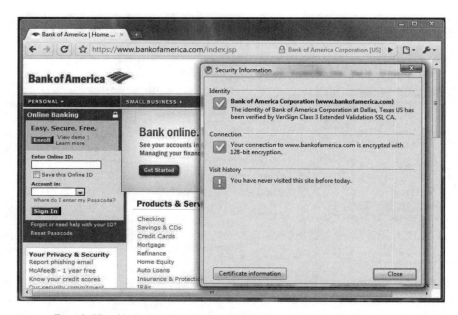

Fig. 16. Visual indicators for a trusted HTTPS connection in Google Chrome v 5.

FIG. 17. Visual indicators for an untrusted HTTPS connection in Firefox v 3.6.3.

FIG. 18. Visual indicators for an untrusted HTTPS connection in Safari v 5.

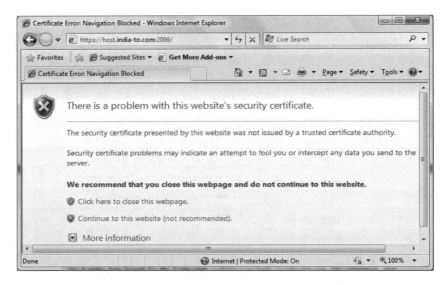

Fɪɢ. 19. Visual indicators for an untrusted HTTPS connection in Microsoft Internet Explorer v 8.

Fɪɢ. 20. Visual indicators for an untrusted HTTPS connection in Google Chrome v 5.

Google Chrome v 5, respectively. In this specific example, the certificate has not been verified by a trusted root Certificate Authority.

7.2.5 Favicon Spoof to Undermine the "Lock" Icon Visual Indicator

With many popular browsers moving the location of the SSL "lock" icon to the Navigation/Address bar and specifically to the right side of the URL, an exploit emerged that puts the "lock" icon in the Navigation/Address bar but on the left side of the URL as opposed to the right side. This is done by replacing the Favicon—short for "favorites" icon that generally displays the logo of the Web site—with a "lock" symbol. This exploit banks on creating sufficient confusion in the mind of the unsuspecting victim as a vast majority of the online users are not savvy enough to appreciate the difference between a favicon placed by a malicious user and an SSL lock icon placed by the browser. Figure 21 shows numerous examples of sites—all displaying a "lock" icon (of various styles) in the Navigation/Address bar—and none of them actually using SSL as is evident from the "HTTP" in the URL. It is also noteworthy that the lock icon in the status bar is missing (as highlighted in Fig. 22) even though the browser used is Mozilla Firefox v 3.6.3 which uses the status bar to display the visual indicator for an SSL/TLS connection.

7.2.6 Domain Validation Versus Extended Validation Certificates

To make things more complicated, all valid digital certificates do not offer the same level of trustworthiness. Entry level certificates known as Domain Validation Certificates are issued after minimal verification, and request are honored as long as the person requesting the certificate is the registered owner of the domain name. However, Extended Validation (EV) Certificates are issued after thorough vetting of credentials of the applicant by the Certificate Authority and thus offer the highest industry standard for authentication and trustworthiness. The examples shown in figures through are for EV Certificates. When viewed in Firefox, a Domain Validation Certificate will use blue color as the visual indicator as opposed to green that is used for representing EV certificates as shown in Fig. 23.

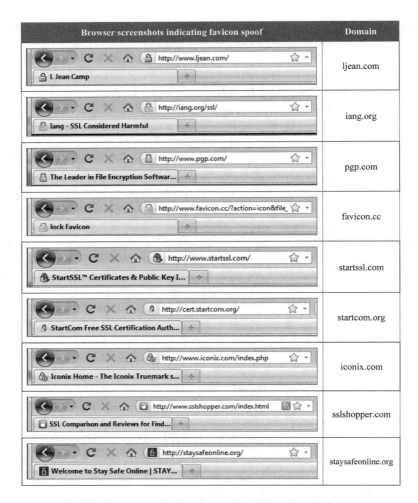

Browser screenshots indicating favicon spoof	Domain
http://www.ljean.com/ — L Jean Camp	ljean.com
http://iang.org/ssl/ — Iang - SSL Considered Harmful	iang.org
http://www.pgp.com/ — The Leader in File Encryption Softwar...	pgp.com
http://www.favicon.cc/?action=icon&file_ — lock Favicon	favicon.cc
http://www.startssl.com/ — StartSSL™ Certificates & Public Key I...	startssl.com
http://cert.startcom.org/ — StartCom Free SSL Certification Auth...	startcom.org
http://www.iconix.com/index.php — Iconix Home - The Iconix Truemark s...	iconix.com
http://www.sslshopper.com/index.html — SSL Comparison and Reviews for Find...	sslshopper.com
http://staysafeonline.org/ — Welcome to Stay Safe Online	STAY...	staysafeonline.org

FIG. 21. Favicon spoof undermines the "lock" icon visual indicator.

8. Modus Operandi

One of the primary factors that have fueled the unprecedented rise in identity theft incidents is the easy and relatively cheap availability of computing resources including the necessary hardware and software required for counterfeiting fungible credentials. An entire set of high-quality counterfeit driver's licenses can be made at home with just

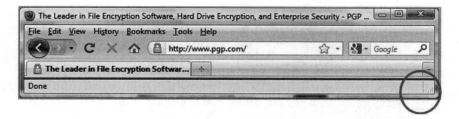

Fig. 22. Favicon spoof with the missing "lock" icon visual indicator in the status bar.

Fig. 23. Visual indicators for a trusted HTTPS connection with a DV certificate in Firefox v 3.6.3.

a regular computer, card printer, credential management software, magnetic stripe writer, and card stock/lamination supplies that are easily available at a cost that is minimal as compared to the potential return on investment (ROI) that such an operation promises. It is therefore understandable as to why obtaining multiple counterfeit IDs with fictitious or stolen identities such as those shown in Fig. 24 is so easy.

Easy accessibility to the Internet compounds the problem by facilitating the identity thief to carry out the crime while being located in a geographical location outside the jurisdiction of the victim's country, thereby dramatically reducing the risk of facing any legal consequences. Identity thieves use the Internet to "safely and efficiently" sell the stolen personally identifiable information of victims through

FIG. 24. Near-perfect counterfeit IDs with different fictitious or stolen identities being used by a single individual. Source: The Identity Theft and Financial Fraud Research and Operations Center, www.itffroc.org.

organized crime broker sites which are commonly known as "dumpsites." The name comes from the word "dump" which in the credit-card industry parlance refers to an electronic copy of the magnetic stripe data of a credit/debit card [29]. What is shocking is that this underground black market for stolen card information is highly organized and thrives openly on the Internet from Web sites hosted in countries with a poor track record of law enforcement.

On a professionally run dumpsite based in Russia, called Golden Dump (registered to a certain Alexey A Potapov from Moskow), the prices of stolen dumps ranged from $23 to $200 as shown in the screenshot taken on June 25, 2010 (Fig. 25) [30]. The prices depend on how detailed the stolen information is and

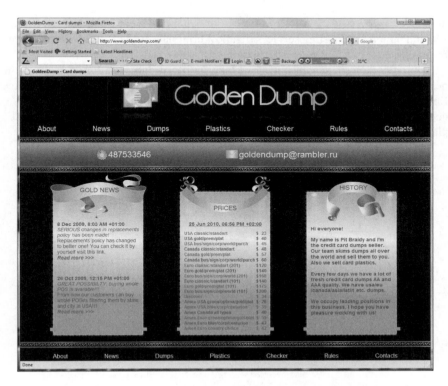

Fig. 25. A professionally run Russia-based dumpsite selling dumps ranging from $23 to $200.

the extent of financial gain a Fin-Av stands to make by purchasing a particular dump. The communication is generally done using the anonymous instant messaging service; ICQ or e-mail and the preferred route for money transfer are services such as Western Union, Moscow-based WebMoney Transfer, or the Caribbean Island-based e-Gold Ltd. As per a report in the New York Times [31], "A user by the nickname Sirota is peddling account information so detailed, and so formatted, that it clearly came from a credit report. He is asking $200 per dump on accounts with available balances above $10,000, with a minimum order of five if the buyer wants accounts associated with a particular bank. 'Also, I can provide dumps with online access,' he wrote. 'The price of such dumps is 5% of available credit.'"

To make matters worse, trends indicate that the underground prices of dumps are only decreasing and as per the RSA Online Fraud Report for August 2010 on "Prices of Goods and Services offered in the Cybercriminal Underground," Fin-Avs can buy CVV2 data sets for as low as $1.50, "Fulls" data sets for as low as $5, and Track 2 data dumps for as low as $15. A DDoS Attack Service for 24 h can be purchased for just $50 and bulletproof hosting services (to allow criminals evade law enforcement) can be purchased for as low as $87 per month [32].

Figure 26 shows a screenshot of a Malaysia-based dumpsite forum with all the necessary details to produce counterfeit credit/debit cards or use the data for online financial transactions as the 3-digit Card Verification Value also known as the CVV code (required for completing Card-Not-Present or CNP transactions) is also displayed [33].

Fig. 26. A screenshot of a Malaysia-based dumpsite with stolen credit-card details.

9. Inadequate Credential Management Procedures

Another important factor responsible for the exponential rise in identity theft incidents is the inadequate and far-from-secure credential management procedures used during all the typical phases of credential management including creation, validation, authentication, and storage.

A recent news report on CNN revealed that two different women sharing the same birthday and the same name—Alyssa Green—with one living in Albany, New York (SSN issued in Florida) and the other in Minneapolis (SSN issued in Illinois) have been allotted the same Social Security Number by the Social Security Administration making life difficult for both of them [34]. As mentioned in Section 5, the inadequate credential validation procedures allow quasi-verifiable IDs to be used for "credential amplification," thereby legitimizing counterfeit credentials. The over-reliance on "look and feel" authentication despite the fact that typical credentials such as the driver's license are inherently fungible indirectly gives a boost to the business of producing counterfeit credentials. The far-from-secure storage proce-dures were highlighted by a 2005 incident where identity thieves stole around 1700 blank driver's licenses along with laminated covers and the entire license-making equipment including a digital license camera, a camera computer, and a license printer from a Nevada Department of Motor Vehicles office in North Las Vegas [35]. The operation was conducted in a very professional manner, and the thieves were out of the DMV office with all the necessary equipment in less than 20 min. Given this background, it is hardly surprising to come across news headlines such as, "Teens can get fake IDs in a few keystrokes on Web" [36]. CardSleuth is a unique solution that provides the next generation of credential management and control.

9.1 CardSleuth

CardSleuth is a secure, ephemeral, self-referential mobile credential system developed at ITFF/ROC to solve the abovementioned problems in a traditional credential management system. It is FIPS compliant and supports a layered-security approach toward managing credentials. As shown in Fig. 27, it is ideal for various types of credentials including employee ID, Hotel room key, driver's license, event ID, and financial transactions card. CardSleuth offers encrypted ID information as well as photo encoded in standard 2D barcode symbologies such as PDF 417 and the QR Code. Additional security is provided by means of detailed access and validation logs. It is compatible with standard encoding technologies including magnetic stripes, common 2D barcode symbologies, RFIDs, and smart cards.

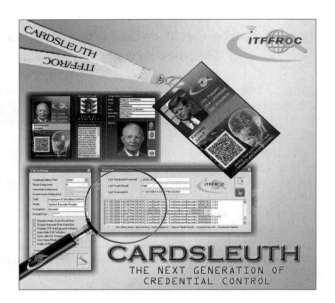

Fɪɢ. 27. CardSleuth: The next generation of credential management and control.

A typical ID scan as shown in Fig. 28 indicates complete badge holder information including normal and photographs, visual indication of the scan result, the encrypted data stream, multilevel security with two separate barcode symbologies being used simultaneously and support for biometrics or future enhancements.

10.   Strategies for Defeating Identity Thieves

This section discusses in detail the finer points of the two-pronged strategy of prevention and cure. The first part deals with the precautions that can effectively prevent a person from becoming a victim of identity fraud, while the other part focuses on the measures to be taken if a person's identity has already been compromised. While prevention is always better than cure, the key to surviving an identity theft is taking effective steps to minimize the damage by carrying out specific actions in a timely manner. The importance of keeping one's presence of mind

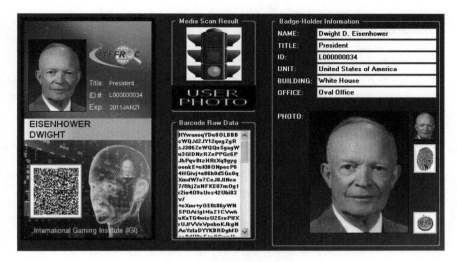

FIG. 28. CardSleuth features at a glance.

and acting swiftly to effectively defeat one's identity thief is perhaps best demonstrated by Seattle-based 23-year-old Michelle McCambridge who helped authorities not only to catch her identity thief but also to bust an active ring of Identity thieves who had stolen at least 39 identities [37].

10.1 Precautions to Prevent ID Theft

The precautions that should be taken to prevent being a victim of identity theft can broadly be classified into two categories based on the type of transaction: offline transactions and online transactions, both of which are described in detail in the following sections.

10.1.1 Precautions for Offline Transactions
10.1.1.1 Document and Information Handling.
- Be vigilant whenever dealing with sensitive personal or financial information.
- Shred all unnecessary documents that contain personally identifiable or financial information before disposing them off as dumpster diving is a very big source of identity theft.

- Do not carry your Social Security card in your wallet unless required for a specific purpose.
- Be extremely cautious about providing your SSN to non-governmental agencies and do so only if it is absolutely necessary.
- Do not leave checks in your car and avoid carrying your check book with you unless required for a specific reason. The Fed Chairman, Ben Bernanke became a victim of identity theft when his wife left her purse carrying personalized checks in a restaurant [38,39].
- Do not carry all your credit cards and debit cards in your wallet—if your wallet is lost or stolen, you stand to lose all your cards.
- Prefer using credit cards over debit cards as a fraudulent use of a stolen debit card number would result in immediate withdrawal of funds from your checking account as opposed to a financial transaction on the credit card that can be disputed more easily with the banks.

10.1.1.2 Monitoring Financial Accounts and Records.

- Monitor your credit reports thoroughly and regularly.
- Federal law allows one free credit report from each of the three nationwide consumer credit reporting companies: Equifax, Experian, and TransUnion every year by going to www.annualcrditreport.com. It's a good practice to stagger the reports from the three different agencies thereby allowing a free credit report every 4 months.
- One can also utilize free services at www.Quizzle.com that offer free credit reports as well as free credit score twice a year to monitor the credit reports more effectively. Call the three major credit reporting bureaus—Equifax, Experian, and TransUnion and ask them verbally as well as in writing to correct any discrepancies in your credit report with immediate effect.
- Track the possible misuse of your identity at the free service My ID Score, www.myidscore.com.
- Be wary of tall claims by companies offering services to repair bad credit history or guaranteeing protection from identity theft. Just a few months back, identity theft prevention service LifeLock was fined $12 million for making inaccurate identity theft prevention claims and in fact failing to secure its own customer data adequately [40].
- Scrutinize credit card and bank account statements closely. Even small amounts that look suspicious should be followed up and reconciled. The need for this is

highlighted by the recent incident where FTC revealed that fraudsters have stolen millions of dollars in a highly sophisticated scheme that fraudulently charged 1.35 million credit cards and ran successfully for about 4 years [41]. The scammers escaped detection for such a long time by charging very small amounts per transaction (usually between $0.25 and $9.00 per card).

10.1.1.3   ATM Transactions.

- While using ATM machines, make sure that the machine does not look suspicious as many identity thieves install card skimmers to capture the information from the magnetic stripes and hidden cameras to capture the PIN.
- If an ATM appears to be altered, there is a high possibility that it has been equipped with a skimming device.
- Cover the keypad while entering the PIN on an ATM.
- Be aware that stand alone ATMs in convenience stores may be more susceptible to fraud than bank-based ATMs.

10.1.2   Precautions for Online Transactions

10.1.2.1   Defense in Depth.   It is important to use a multilayered approach to security so that a single failure does not translate into a complete breakdown of security. This involves using tools like antivirus, antimalware (to detect keyloggers, crimeware, etc), firewalls, and security plug-ins in addition to ensuring that system updates and security patches are always up-to-date. A free personal firewall, ZoneAlarm, is a very effective tool that gives real-time online protection from malicious attackers. Figure 29 shows the yellow colored visual warning produced by ZoneAlarm when a user tries to access a site with suspicious activity.

FIG. 29. Visual warning produced by ZoneAlarm.

Most browsers support a wide range of browser plug-ins and add-ons, and at the time of writing, there were almost 700 different add-ons available covering an entire gamut of privacy and security issues for Firefox as shown in Fig. 30. It is a good idea to use verified add-ons to make one's online experience more secure.

FIG. 30. Privacy and security add-ons for Firefox.

10.1.2.2 Anti-Phishing Measures.

Most popular web browsers use phishing filters to warn users about known phishing sites based on global blacklists. Thus, for example, when a user tries to access a known phishing site such as http://www.kinova.net/PayPal.com/index.php, which hosts a perfectly spoofed PayPal site as shown in Fig. 31, most browsers display adequate visual warnings.

Figures 32–36 show the different visual indicators when an attempt is made to access a known dangerous Web site in Phishing and other malicious activities in four popular browsers, viz., Mozilla Firefox v 3.6.3, Apple Safari v 5, Microsoft Internet Explorer v 8, and Google Chrome v 5, respectively.

In case the browser does not support phishing filters, the defense-in-depth strategy would pay off as ZoneAlarm would step in and issue a warning as indicated in Fig. 37.

FIG. 31. Perfectly spoofed PayPal site on www.kinova.net.

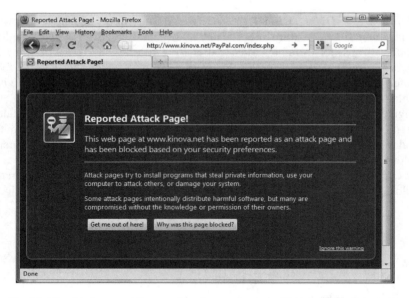

Fɪɢ. 32. Visual indicators while accessing a known dangerous Web site in Firefox v 3.6.3.

Fɪɢ. 33. Visual indicators while accessing a known dangerous Web site in Firefox v 3.6.3.

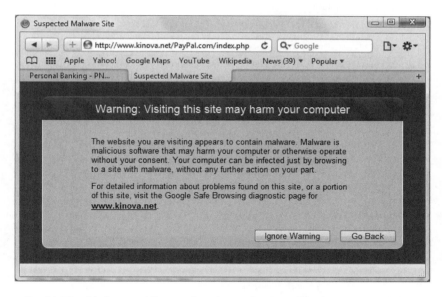

FIG. 34. Visual indicators while accessing a known dangerous Web site in Apple Safari v 5.

FIG. 35. Visual indicators while accessing a known dangerous Web site in Internet Explorer v 8.

Fɪɢ. 36. Visual indicators while accessing a known dangerous Web site in Google Chrome v 5.

Fɪɢ. 37. Visual warning issued by ZoneAlarm while accessing a known dangerous Web site.

Since these warning are based on global blacklists and whitelists and new threats keep emerging every day, it is possible that a particular filter may not detect all known bad sites. In case one requires specific information about a suspected site, one can manually check the details by entering the corresponding URL. A good example is *PhishTank* <www.phishtank.com>—a collaborative clearinghouse for information about phishing that provides a free service for verifying suspected phishing sites as shown in Fig. 38. As per statistics as of September 19, 2010, PhishTank had verified 591,862 phishes as valid out of a total of 1,021,375 submissions received [42].

10.1.2.3 Anti-Spoofing Measures.

SpoofStick is another free browser extension that works well with Internet Explorer and prominently displays the most relevant part of the domain name, thus making the process of manually detecting a spoofed Web site easy. The example in Fig. 39 shows a fabricated URL deliberately made lengthy to obfuscate the real domain name http://www.customer_service.trusted.secure.server.bestandmostsecureonlinebankinamerica.myfavoritebank.com.berghel.com/home.php and using a number of words that

FIG. 38. A free service for verifying suspected phishing sites.

FIG. 39. SpoofStick in action.

make it look like a genuine, trusted and secure customer service site of a standard bank to an unsuspecting Internet user. However, the SpoofStick add-on gives a very prominent visual indication of the actual domain www.berghel.com which is certainly not that of a bank.

Iconix www.iconix.com offers a professional service that visually identifies messages from over 1500 senders—one can instantly recognize who the message is from and whether it is been verified as coming from the claimed sender or not [43]. They support most major web-based e-mail providers such as Gmail, Yahoo, Hotmail, AOL, etc., as well as POP3 e-mail clients like MS Outlook. Figure 40 shows a screenshot where verified messages are identified by an Iconix Truemark icon.

10.1.2.4 *Trust indicators.*

As mentioned earlier, trust is different from encryption, and a malicious Web site can legitimately display the SSL lock icon if its uses encryption. A very popular add-on for indicating the trustworthiness of Web sites is the WOT (Web of Trust) add-on that relies on community feedback to rate Web sites on aspects such as trustworthiness, vendor reliability, privacy, and child safety. The rating scale has five grades: very poor, poor, unsatisfactory, good, and excellent, and these are available as visual indicators with five distinct colors ranging from red (very poor) to green (excellent) as shown in Fig. 41. Figure 42 shows a screenshot displaying WOT in action.

URLVoid www.Urlvoid.com, started in May 2010, offers a free service to facilitate detection of malicious Web sites by giving users the ability to scan any URL with multiple scanning engines such as Google Diagnostic, McAfee SiteAdvisor, Norton SafeWeb, and MyWOT simultaneously.

In-built trust indicators in browsers should act as the first line of defense. Table IV gives a summary of the visual indicators used by Firefox for Web site identification along with their interpretation.

The vast majority of the Web sites will display the "no identity information" icon (Fig. 43) as most Web sites do not deal with sensitive information exchange and hence do not require the additional safety offered by HTTPS. It is perfectly safe to visit these sites as long as you are not entering any sensitive information.

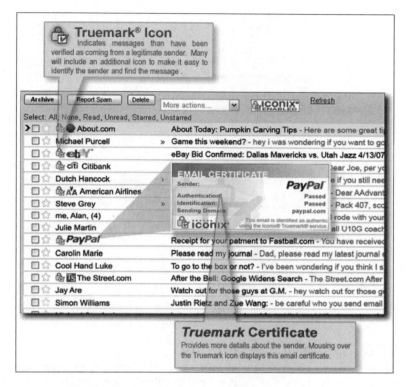

FIG. 40. Iconix in action. Source: http://www.iconix.com/index.php.

10.1.2.5 Financial Transactions.

- Use virtual credit cards that are generated online for one-time use to limit the extent of damage even if the card details are compromised.

- Keep one credit card exclusively for online use with a small credit limit and monitor that account vigorously.

- Use virtual keyboards if possible to enter passwords for sensitive Web sites such as online trading and brokerage accounts as this is a good defense against keyloggers.

- Remember that while SSL is reasonably safe, nothing is foolproof as Man-In-The-Middle (MITM) attacks have been demonstrated to compromise even SSL connections [44–47].

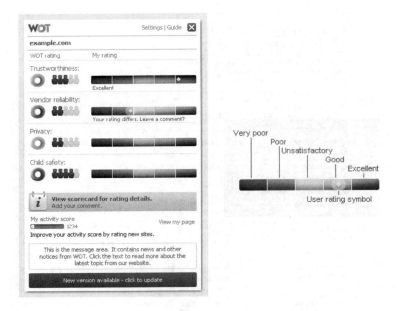

F<small>IG</small>. 41. Visual indicators used in WOT. Source: http://www.mywot.com.

10.1.2.6   *General Precautions.*

- Phishing e-mails generally evoke either a sense of urgency or a certain amount of fear of consequence to elicit people to submit their sensitive information. These scams can also take the form of IRS scams, fake traffic ticket scams, fake Jury summons, 4-1-9 Nigerian scams, or lottery scams involving trans-national money transfer.
- When you get e-mails asking you to go to some site for entering information, do not click on the link, type the URL instead.
- Follow safe password formulation guidelines.
- Do not reuse passwords.
- Copy machines store images of all documents—be careful of using public machines for making copies of highly sensitive data.
- Wipe hard disks before disposing off old computers.
- Remember that FTP and telnet sessions are inherently insecure and transmit passwords in clear-text.
- Be careful about the information you provide on online social networking sites such as Facebook, LinkedIn, MySpace, and Twitter.

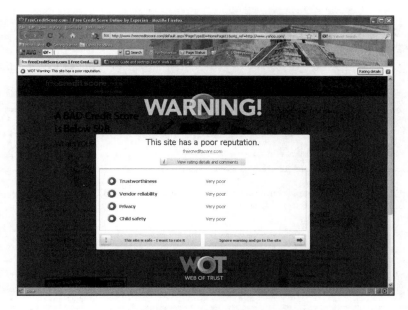

Fig. 42. A screenshot displaying WOT in action.

Table IV
Visual Indicators Used by Firefox for Site Identification

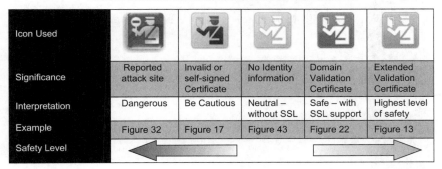

Icon Used					
Significance	Reported attack site	Invalid or self-signed Certificate	No Identity information	Domain Validation Certificate	Extended Validation Certificate
Interpretation	Dangerous	Be Cautious	Neutral – without SSL	Safe – with SSL support	Highest level of safety
Example	Figure 32	Figure 17	Figure 43	Figure 22	Figure 13
Safety Level					

- Use virtualization—Using the freely available VMware Player along with the VMware Browser Appliance will add an additional layer of security and even if malware attacks compromise the OS of the Browser Appliance, the native operating system will remain insulated. Figure 44 shows a VMware Browser Appliance running on Ubuntu as the virtual operating system and Windows XP as the native operating system.

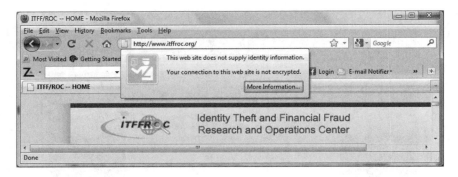

Fig. 43. Visual indicators while accessing a neutral Web site over HTTP in Firefox v 3.6.3.

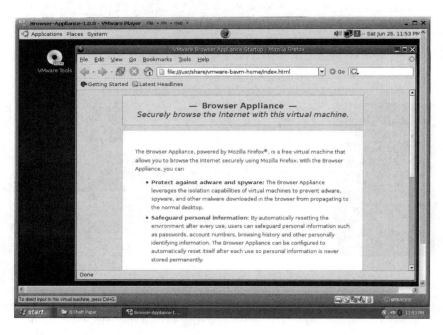

Fig. 44. VMware Browser Appliance with Windows XP as the native operating system.

10.2   Remediation

- The FACT (Fair and Accurate Credit transactions) Act of 2003 which amended the Fair Credit Reporting Act allows individuals to put a fraud alert on their credit reports—Call any of the three major credit reporting bureaus—Equifax, Experian, and TransUnion and ask them to place a fraud alert on your file so that no new credit line is opened in your name without an explicit confirmation from you [48].
- Lodge a complaint with the FTC and use the ID Theft affidavit available on their Web site [49].
- File a police report as that will help expedite the reconciliation of any discrepancies in your credit reports.
- Close all the tainted accounts with immediate effect.
- Make full use of state-sponsored programs to support victims of identity theft such as Ohio's *Identity Theft Verification Passport Program* [50].
- If the identity theft was a result of a cybercrime [9], then also file an online complaint with the Internet Crime Complaint Center (IC3)—a partnership between the FBI and other agencies—at www.ic3.gov.

11.   Conclusion

The fight against identity theft is an ongoing battle wherein the key to victory lies in inculcating a professional attitude with an enduring persistence to guard your sensitive information from being compromised. In the unfortunate eventuality where actions beyond your control have resulted in an information breach, it is imperative to proactively pursue all legal remedies as outlined in the preceding sections and limit the damage to yourself and claim back your life. Further, the inherently dynamic nature of the Internet results in generation of new exploits almost on a daily basis and the only way to fully protect oneself is by aggressively monitoring emerging threats and taking timely countermeasures. The need to have a defense-in-depth approach toward online security and make optimum use of the strategies and tools mentioned in this chapter to stay one step ahead of the bad guys can thus hardly be overemphasized.

REFERENCES

[1] http://www.irs.gov/newsroom/article/0,,id=217794,00.html (accessed 28.11.2010).
[2] Department of Homeland Security report titled, 'Identity and Security: Moving Beyond the 9/11 Staff Report on Identity Document Security'. http://www.homelandsecurity.org/journal/Default. aspx?oid=153&ocat=1 (accessed 28.11.2010).

[3] Testimony of Chris Jay Hoofnagle during the Hearing on Preserving the Integrity of Social Security Numbers and Preventing Their Misuse by Terrorists and Identity Thieves at the U.S. House of Representatives. http://epic.org/privacy/ssn/ssntestimony9.19.02.html (accessed 28.11.2010).

[4] Three held in Times Square probe face immigration charges. http://www.cnn.com/2010/CRIME/05/14/times.square.investigation/index.html?iref=allsearch (accessed 28.11.2010).

[5] Security Brief: To track terrorists follow the money—if you can. http://news.blogs.cnn.com/2010/05/14/security-brief-to-track-terrorists-follow-the-money-if-you-can/ (accessed 28.11.2010).

[6] ID thief to the stars tells all. http://www.msnbc.msn.com/id/5763781/ (accessed 28.11.2010).

[7] 250,000 White House Staffers, Visitors Affected by National Archives Data Breach. http://www.wired.com/threatlevel/2010/01/national-archives-data-breach/ (accessed 28.11.2010).

[8] Apple's Worst Security Breach: 114, 000 iPad Owners Exposed. http://gawker.com/5559346/apples-worst-security-breach-114000-ipad-owners-exposed (accessed 28.11.2010).

[9] Identity Theft and Your Social Security Number, SSA Publication No. 05-10064, August 2009, ICN 463270. http://www.ssa.gov/pubs/10064.html (accessed 28.11.2010).

[10] 2010 Identity Fraud Survey Report: Consumer Version, Javelin Strategy & Research.

[11] Federal Trade Commission's 2006 Identity Theft Survey Report.

[12] www.Itffroc.org (accessed 28.11.2010).

[13] http://www.privacyrights.org/data-breach#CP (accessed 28.11.2010).

[14] Hal Berghel, Ph.D., Identity Theft and Financial Fraud for the New Millennium.

[15] http://cardcops.com/press/nbc_dateline_20070327.htm (accessed 28.11.2010).

[16] Hal Berghel and Bob Aalberts, Identity Theft FAQs. http://www.itffroc.org/faqs/index.php (accessed 28.11.2010).

[17] http://www.ncsl.org/default.aspx?tabid=13489 (accessed 28.11.2010).

[18] http://www.idtheft.gov/ (accessed 28.11.2010).

[19] The President's Identity Theft Task Force Report, September 2008.

[20] Hal Berghel, Ph.D., Fungible Credentials and 'Next Generation Fraud'.

[21] http://www.microsoft.com/protect/yourself/phishing/faq.mspx (accessed 28.11.2010).

[22] http://www.antiphishing.org/ (accessed 28.11.2010).

[23] Global Phishing Survey: Trends and Domain Name Use 2H2009, APWG, May 2010.

[24] Phishing Activity Trends Report, 4th Quarter/2009, APWG, p. 2.

[25] http://www.antiphishing.org/crimeware.html (accessed 28.11.2010).

[26] http://www.ietf.org/rfc/rfc5280.txt (accessed 28.11.2010).

[27] http://www.verisign.com/support/advisories/authenticodefraud.html (accessed 28.11.2010).

[28] Eileen Zishuang Ye, Yougu Yuan, Sean Smith, Web Spoofing Revisited: SSL and Beyond, p. 7, Section 4.6.

[29] http://www.creditcards.com/glossary/term-dump.php (accessed 28.11.2010).

[30] http://www.goldendump.com/ (accessed 28.11.2010).

[31] Black Market in Stolen Credit Card Data Thrives on Internet. http://www.nytimes.com/2005/06/21/technology/21data.html?#59;partner=rssuserland&38=&_r=1&en=c06809a02406a9f8&ex=1277006400; ei=5090;emc=rss&pagewanted=print (accessed 28.11.2010).

[32] RSA Online Fraud Report, Prices of Goods and Services offered in the Cybercriminal Underground, August 2010, p. 3.

[33] http://www.topix.com/forum/my/kuala-lumpur/TGVDR9ASS6C8BNDNT (accessed 28.11.2010).

[34] Women share same SSN. http://www.cnn.com/video/#/video/us/2010/06/24/dnt.women.same.ss.number.KARE.WNYT?hpt=T2 (accessed 25.06.2010).

[35] Identity Theft: Blank licenses stolen from DMV. http://www.reviewjournal.com/lvrj_home/2005/Mar-08-Tue-2005/news/26018927.html (accessed 28.11.2010).

[36] Teens can get fake IDs in a few keystrokes on Web. http://www.csmonitor.com/2001/0829/p1s4-ussc.html/%28page%29/2 (accessed 28.11.2010).

[37] Identity-theft victim meets her identity thief. http://seattletimes.nwsource.com/html/businesstechnology/2009818847_idtheft07m.html (accessed 28.11.2010).

[38] Bernanke Victimized by Identity Fraud Ring, Newsweek. http://www.newsweek.com/2009/08/24/bernanke-victimized-by-identity-fraud-ring.html (accessed 28.11.2010).

[39] Federal Reserve Chairman Hit by High-Tech Pickpocket Ring, Wired.com. http://www.wired.com/threatlevel/2009/08/cannon-to-the-wiz/ (accessed 28.11.2010).

[40] LifeLock fined $12 million over lack of life-locking ability. http://arstechnica.com/tech-policy/news/2010/03/lifelock-cant-guarantee-id-theft-prevention-after-all-settles-with-ftc.ars (accessed 28.11.2010).

[41] FTC Says Scammers Stole Millions, Using Virtual Companies. http://news.yahoo.com/s/pcworld/20100628/tc_pcworld/ftcsaysscammersstolemillionsusingvirtualcompanies (accessed 28.11.2010).

[42] http://www.phishtank.com/stats.php (accessed 28.11.2010).

[43] http://www.iconix.com/index.php (accessed 28.11.2010).

[44] New Tricks For Defeating SSL In Practice, Moxie Marlinspike. http://www.blackhat.com/presentations/bh-dc-09/Marlinspike/BlackHat-DC-09-Marlinspike-Defeating-SSL.pdf (accessed 28.11.2010).

[45] Researcher Hacks Twittter Using SSL Vulnerability, Brian Prince. http://www.eweek.com/c/a/Security/Researcher-Demonstrates-SSL-Vulnerability-on-Twitter-291904/ (accessed 28.11.2010).

[46] Renegotiating TLS, Marsh Ray, Steve Dispensa, PhoneFactor, Inc. http://extendedsubset.com/Renegotiating_TLS.pdf (accessed 28.11.2010).

[47] Hackers Forge SSL Certificate, Anastasia Tubanos. http://www.thewhir.com/web-hosting-news/123008_Hackers_Forge_SSL_Certificate (accessed 28.11.2010).

[48] http://www.onguardonline.gov/topics/identity-theft.aspx (accessed 28.11.2010).

[49] Filing a complaint with the FTC. http://www.ftc.gov/bcp/edu/microsites/idtheft/consumers/filing-a-report.html (accessed 28.11.2010).

[50] http://www.ohioattorneygeneral.gov/About/FAQ/Identity-Theft-Passport-FAQs (accessed 28.11.2010).

ABOUT THE AUTHOR

Hal Berghel is currently professor and director of the School of Informatics and associate dean of the Howard R. Hughes College of Engineering, and professor and past director of the School of Computer Science, all at the University of Nevada, Las Vegas. He is also founding director of the Center for Cybersecurity Research, and the founding co-director of the Identity Theft and Financial Fraud Research and Operations Center (www.itffroc.org (accessed 28.11.2010)). Berghel has held a variety of research and administrative positions in industry and academia during his 30-year career in computing. His current research focuses on computing and network security, digital forensics, and digital crime. Berghel is a fellow of both the Institute for Electrical and Electronics Engineers and the association for Computing Machinery, and serves as an ACM Distinguished Lecturer and an IEEE Distinguished Visitor. He holds a Ph.D. from the University of Nebraska–Lincoln.

Dennis Cobb is retired from the Las Vegas Metropolitan Police Department Deputy Chief and now president of DCC Group, Inc. assisting public and private organizations with critical communications technology, processes, and capabilities. Dennis is a founding co-director in the UNLV/LVMPD Identity Theft and Financial Fraud Research and Operations Center. Dennis served as Nevada's Interoperable Communications Coordinator and chaired Nevada's Communications Steering Committee, and as a member of USDHS SAFECOM Emergency Response Council. He assisted in developing the U.S. National Emergency Communications Plan and assists with radio interoperability issues in National Institute of Justice Technology Working Groups. Dennis Cobb holds a BA in political science and MS in crisis and emergency management from the University of Nevada, Las Vegas. He is a graduate of the FBI National Academy, a 1992 Fulbright Fellow, and 1994 White House Fellow.

Amit Grover has 14 years of experience in information technology and has played an instrumental role in the development, implementation and commissioning of a wide variety of defense-related IT applications. He has had the opportunity of designing and implementing INFOSEC policies in military units and has worked on interfacing information systems on board warships, submarines and UAVs (Unmanned Aerial Vehicles). Amit holds a Master of Science degree in Computer and Information Science from East Tennessee State University and a Bachelor's degree in Mechanical Engineering. Presently, he is the Project Manager of the Identity Theft and Financial Fraud Research and Operations Center at Las Vegas where he contributes to the development of comprehensive secure credentialing systems.

An Overview of Steganography

GARY C. KESSLER

Gary Kessler Associates, Burlington, Vermont, USA

CHET HOSMER

Allen Corporation, Conway, South Carolina, USA

Abstract

Steganography is the art of *covered*, or *hidden*, *writing*. The purpose of stegano-graphy is covert communication—to hide the existence of a message from a third party. Knowledge of steganography is of increasing importance to indivi-duals in the law enforcement, intelligence, and military communities. This chapter provides a high-level introduction to methods and tools for both hiding information (steganography) and detecting hidden information (steganalysis). This chapter is technical, in that it uses many examples using the current tools of the trade, without delving into the deeper mathematics, although references are provided to some of the ongoing research in the field. While this chapter provides a historical context for stego, the emphasis is on digital applications, focusing on hiding information in digital image or audio files. Examples of software tools that employ steganography to hide data inside of other files as well as software to detect such hidden files will also be presented.

1. Introduction 52
    1.1. A Brief History 53
    1.2. Terms, Concepts, and Classifications of Steganography 53
    1.3. Steganography Versus Digital Watermarking 55
    1.4. "Time-Sensitive" Steganography 55
2. Low-Tech Stego Methods 56
    2.1. Semagrams 56
    2.2. Concealment Ciphers 58
    2.3. Other Methods 61

ADVANCES IN COMPUTERS, VOL. 83
ISSN: 0065-2458/DOI: 10.1016/B978-0-12-385510-7.00002-3

51

Copyright © 2011 Elsevier Inc.
All rights reserved.

3. Digital Technology Basics 62
   3.1.   Digital Images and Color 62
   3.2.   Digital Audio 64
   3.3.   Payload Compression and Steganography 66
4. Steganography and Digital Carrier Files 67
   4.1.   Least-Significant Bit Overwriting 68
   4.2.   Encoding Algorithm Modification 71
   4.3.   Grammar Selection 71
   4.4.   Data Appending 73
   4.5.   Color Palette Modification 75
   4.6.   Format Modification 79
   4.7.   Covert Communication Channels 80
   4.8.   Conclusion and Summary 84
5. Detecting Steganography 85
   5.1.   The Prisoner's Problem 85
   5.2.   Steganalysis Overview 86
   5.3.   Steganalysis of JPEG Images 88
6. Steganography Detection Tools 93
   6.1.   Steganography Detection Tools 93
   6.2.   Stego Carrier File Detection 96
7. Summary and Conclusions 100
   References 103

1. Introduction

Steganography is the art of *covered*, or *hidden*, *writing*. The purpose of steganography is *covert communication* to hide a message from a third party. This differs from *cryptography*, the art of *secret writing*, which is intended to make a message unreadable by a third party but does not necessarily hide the very existence of the secret communication. While steganography is separate and distinct from cryptography, there are many analogies between the two and, in fact, some authors categorize steganography as a form of cryptography, as *hidden* communication certainly is a form of *secret* writing [1]. Nevertheless, this chapter will treat stego as a separate and independent field of study.

Steganography has been—and continues to be—used for the purpose of hiding the fact that two parties are communicating. Aside from an interesting research problem, stego has a number of nefarious applications, however, most notably hiding records of illegal activity, financial fraud, industrial espionage, and communication among members of criminal or terrorist organizations [2]. As such, stego is of interest—either for the purpose of transmitting covert messages or detecting them—to the diplomatic, military, intelligence, criminal, terrorist, and law enforcement communities.

1.1   A Brief History

Although the term *steganography* was only coined at the very end of the fifteenth century, the use of stego dates back several millennia. Soon after humans could write (approximately 2000 BC), we learned how to write in secret codes and, soon thereafter, how to communicate covertly. In ancient times, messages were hidden on the back of wax-writing tables, written on the stomachs of rabbits, or tattooed on the scalp of slaves. Invisible ink has been in use for centuries—for fun by kids and students, for serious espionage by spies and terrorists. Microdots and microfilm, a staple of war and spy movies, came about after the invention of photography [3–6].

Steganography hides the covert message but not necessarily the fact that two parties are communicating with each other. As will be discussed below, messages can be hidden in an e-mail message, a photograph posted on a Facebook page, or a drawing given to a friend. While there are many high-technology methods of hiding information, low-tech methods may work just as well for a period of time.

1.2   Terms, Concepts, and Classifications of Steganography

The stego process generally involves placing a *hidden message* within some transport medium, called the *carrier*. The hidden message is embedded within the carrier to form the *stego medium*. The use of a *stego key* may be employed for encryption of the hidden message and/or as a randomization seed for the stego algorithm. In summary:

stego_medium = hidden_message + carrier + stego_key

Figure 1 shows a common taxonomy of steganographic techniques [1,3]:

- *Technical steganography* uses scientific methods to hide a message, such as the use of invisible ink or microdots and other size reduction methods. This chapter will not address technical steganography methods.

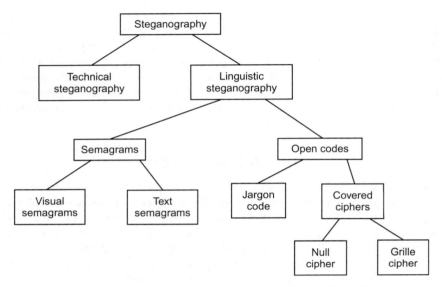

FIG. 1. Classification of steganography techniques (adapted from [1]).

- *Linguistic steganography* hides the message within the carrier in some nonobvious ways and is further categorized as *semagrams* or *open codes*.
- *Semagrams* hide information by the use of symbols or signs. A *visual semagram* uses innocent-looking or everyday physical objects to convey a message, such as doodles, the positioning of items on a desk or Web site, or the placement of a flag on a balcony (à la Deep Throat of Watergate fame). A *text semagram* hides a message by modifying the appearance of the carrier text, such as subtle changes in font size or type, adding extra spaces, or different flourishes in letters or handwritten text.
- *Open codes* hide a message within a legitimate carrier message in ways that are not obvious to an unsuspecting observer. The carrier message is sometimes called the *overt communication*, while the hidden message is the *covert communication*. This category is subdivided into *jargon codes* and *covered ciphers*.
- *Jargon code*, as the name suggests, uses language that is understood by a group of people but is meaningless to others. Jargon codes include warchalking (symbols used to indicate the presence and type of wireless network signal [7]), underground terminology, or an innocent conversation that convey special meaning because of facts known only to the speakers. A subset of jargon codes is *cue codes*, where certain prearranged phrases convey meaning. Jargon codes are not addressed further in this chapter.

- *Covered, or concealment, ciphers* hide a message openly in the carrier medium so that it can be recovered by anyone who knows the secret for how it was concealed. A *grille cipher* employs a template that is used to cover the carrier message; the words that appear in the openings of the template are the hidden message. A *null cipher* hides the message according to some prearranged set of rules, such as "read every fifth word" or "look at the third character in every word."

As an increasing amount of data is stored on computers and transmitted over networks, it is no surprise that steganography has entered the digital age. On computers and networks, stego applications allow for someone to hide any type of binary file into many other types of binary files, although image and audio files are today's most common carriers.

1.3 Steganography Versus Digital Watermarking

Steganography provides some very useful and commercially important functions in the digital world, most notably *digital watermarking*. In this application, an author can embed a hidden message in a file so that he/she can later assert their ownership of intellectual property and/or ensure the integrity of the content. An artist, for example, could post some original artwork on a Web site. If someone else should "steal" the file and claims the work as his/her own, the artist can later prove ownership because only he/she can recover the watermark [3,8,9]. While conceptually similar to stego, digital watermarking usually has different technical goals, namely:

- Generally, the watermark is a small amount of repetitive information that is inserted into the carrier,
- It is not always necessary to hide the watermarking information from the viewer, and
- It is useful if the watermark can be removed while maintaining the integrity of the carrier file.

Regardless of how one looks at it, however, watermarking is not the same as steganography; the two methods use different algorithms, have different purposes, and provide different levels of threat [10].

1.4 "Time-Sensitive" Steganography

As a slight aside to the art and science of steganography, it is worth noting that no covert channel needs to remain covert forever. While some academics eschew the thought of using any stego method that has not been shown to be immune from many types of attack, most practitioners recognize that most secret messages have a finite lifetime. For this reason, a stego method is sufficient for its task if it can hold the secret long enough to suit the aims of the covert communicators. Stated another way, even a poor stego method may be of use if it can hold a secret longer than it takes an adversary to detect and decode the covert channel.

Time-sensitive steganography refers to the criteria in the design or selection of a stego method. A practitioner needs a stego scheme that has usability and implementation criteria that meet the following:

$$T_{CRITICAL} < T_{DETECT} + T_{DECODE}$$

As stated above, a stego method needs to be strong enough so that the time to detect the covert channel (T_{DETECT}) plus the amount of time to decode the covert channel (T_{DECODE}) is greater than the required lifetime of the channel ($T_{CRITICAL}$). $T_{CRITICAL}$ is up to the user; in some cases, one only needs to keep the secret for a few days or weeks; in other cases, one would want the covert channel to be kept secret for years or decades.

2. Low-Tech Stego Methods

A variety of low-technology stego methods are presented in this section. While some of the methods described here employ computers in one way or another, they all require some form of human intelligence to prepare and interpret. Low-tech methods, therefore, are often difficult to detect using only automated methods and, indeed, may be improvisational. This section will discuss various forms of semagrams, concealment ciphers, and other methods.

2.1 Semagrams

Semagrams hide information using special symbols or signs. These signs can be in the form of pictures or objects (visual semagram), or subtlety altered written documents (text semagrams). A visual semagram conveys a message using items that can be seen, such as articles of clothing or the placement of items in a room. Pictures and images on a Web site can also convey information, such as the position of items on a particular Web page or the order of pages at a site. The orientation of photographs on a Web page might also convey meaning (Fig. 2). Of course, any such arrangement of items requires an *a priori* agreement between the communicating parties.

FIG. 2. Screen shots of LATimes.com Web site. The real screen shot is on the left and the altered site is on the right.

FIG. 3. Drawing of the San Antonio River.

Another form of visual semagram is to hide a code within a picture. Figure 3 shows a well-known drawing of the San Antonio River [1]. This drawing was created by a group of government censors in San Antonio to commemorate the visit of their commander, Col. Harold Shaw, in May 1945.

The reader should pay particular attention to the grass along the river; each clump of grass represents a single Morse code character, with the short blades representing a dot and a long blade representing a dash. The complete message says:

> Compliments of CPSA MA to our chief Col Harold R Shaw on his visit to San Antonio May 11th 1945

2.2 Concealment Ciphers

Concealment ciphers are an old method of hiding messages. These type of ciphers hide a message openly in the carrier medium so that it can be recovered by anyone who knows the secret for how it was concealed. A grille cipher, for example, employs a template that reveals the message once applied to the original carrier. One well-known example is that of a letter written by British Lt. General Sir Henry Clinton to General John Burgoyne in August 1777 (Fig. 4).

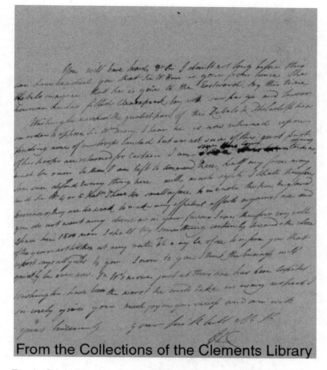

From the Collections of the Clements Library

FIG. 4. Original letter written by Henry Clinton to John Burgoyne [11].

The text of the letter reads [11]:

You will have heard, Dr Sir I doubt not long before this
can have reached you that Sir W. Howe is gone from hence. The
Rebels imagine that he is gone to the Eastward. By this time
however he has filled Chesapeak bay with surprize and terror.
Washington marched the greater part of the Rebels to Philadelphia
in order to oppose Sir Wm's. army. I hear he is now returned upon
finding none of our troops landed but am not sure of this, great part
of his troops are returned for certain. I am sure this countermarching
must be ruin to them. I am left to command here, half of my force may
I am sure defend everything here with much safety. I shall therefore
send Sir W. 4 or 5 Bat [talio] ns. I have too small a force to invade the New England
provinces; they are too weak to make any effectual efforts against me and
you do not want any diversion in your favour. I can, therefore very well

spare him 1500 men. I shall try some thing certainly towards the close
of the year, not till then at any rate. It may be of use to inform you that
report says all yields to you. I own to you that I think the business will
quickly be over now. Sr. W's move just at this time has been capital.
Wahingtons have been the worst he could take in every respect.
sincerely give you much joy on your success and am with
great Sincerity your [ ]
HC

Clinton's letter was intended to be read by Burgoyne using a grille (Fig. 5). Once
the grille is applied, the letter reads [11]:

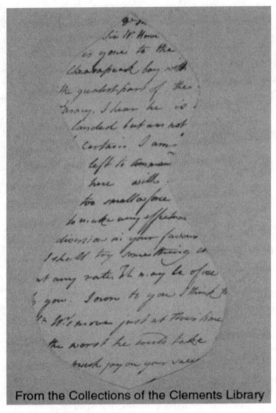

From the Collections of the Clements Library

FIG. 5. Grille applied to letter written by Henry Clinton to John Burgoyne [11].

Sir. W. Howe
is gone to the
Chesapeak bay with
the greatest part of the
army. I hear he is
landed but am not
certain. I am
left to command
here with
too small a force
to make any effectual
diversion in your favour.
I shall try something
at any rate. It may be of use
to you. I own to you I think
Sr W's move just at this time
the worst he could take.
Much joy on your success.

A null cipher also hides a message openly in the carrier text according to some prearranged agreement. One of the simplest null ciphers is shown in the classic examples below:

PRESIDENT'S EMBARGO RULING SHOULD HAVE IMMEDIATE NOTICE. GRAVE SITUATION AFFECTING INTERNATIONAL LAW. STATEMENT FORESHADOWS RUIN OF MANY NEUTRALS. YELLOW JOURNALS UNIFY-ING NATIONAL EXCITEMENT IMMENSELY.

APPARENTLY NEUTRAL'S PROTEST IS THOROUGHLY DISCOUNTED AND IGNORED. ISMAN HARD HIT. BLOCKADE ISSUE AFFECTS PRETEXT FOR EMBARGO ON BYPRODUCTS, EJECTING SUETS AND VEGETABLE OILS.

The German Embassy in Washington, DC sent these messages in telegrams to their headquarters in Berlin during World War I [5]. Reading the first character of every word in the first message or the second character of every word in the second message will yield the following hidden text, referring to US General John Pershing:

PERSHING SAILS FROM N.Y. JUNE 1

2.3 Other Methods

It is important to note that one does not need any special tools or skills to hide messages in digital files using other variances of these low-tech methods. An image or text block can be hidden under another image in a PowerPoint file, for example.

Messages can be hidden in the properties of a Word file. Messages can be hidden in comments within Web pages or in other formatting vagaries that are ignored by browsers [12]. Text can be hidden as line art in a document by putting the text in the same color as the background and placing another drawing in the foreground; the recipient could retrieve the hidden text by changing its color (J. Seward, personal communication, January 2004). These are all decidedly low-tech mechanisms—but can be very effective.

3. Digital Technology Basics

Most of today's most commonly used digital steganography techniques employ graphical images or audio files as the carrier medium. It is instructive, then, to review image and audio encoding before discussing how steganography and steganalysis work with these carriers.

3.1 Digital Images and Color

The Red–Green–Blue (RGB) color cube (Fig. 6) is a common means with which to represent a given color by indicating the relative intensity of its three component colors—red, green, and blue—each with their own axis. The absence of all colors

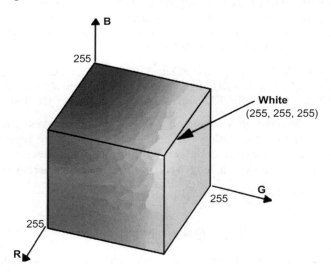

Fig. 6. The RGB color cube [13]. (For interpretation of the references to color in this figure legend, the reader is referred to the Web version of this chapter.)

yields black, shown as the intersection of the zero point of the three-color axes (not visible in the figure). The mixture of 100% red, 100% blue, and the absence of green form magenta (255, 0, 255); cyan is 100% green and 100% blue without any red (0, 255, 255); and 100% green and 100% red with no blue combine to form yellow (255, 255, 0). White is the presence of all three colors (255, 255, 255).

Figure 7 shows the RGB intensity levels of some given color. Each RGB component is specified by a single byte, so that the values for each color intensity can vary from 0 to 255. This particular shade is denoted by a red level of 191 (hex 0xBF), a green level of 29 (hex 0x1D), and a blue level of 152 (hex 0x98). One picture element (pixel, or pix) of the color shown in the "new" block in the dialog box in the figure, then, would be encoded using 24 bits as 0xBF1D98. This 24-bit encoding scheme supports 16,777,216 (2^{24}) unique colors [14,15].

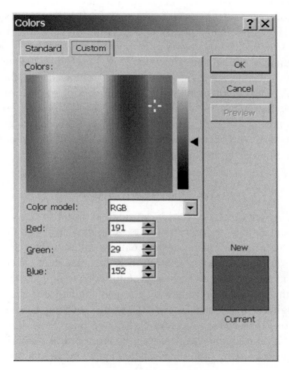

FIG. 7. This color selection dialog box shows the red, green, and blue (RGB) levels of this particular color. (For interpretation of the references to color in this figure legend, the reader is referred to the Web version of this chapter.)

Most digital image applications today support 24-bit True Color, where each pixel is encoded in 24 bits, comprising the three RGB bytes described above. Other applications encode color using 8 bits/pix. These schemes also use 24-bit true color but employ a palette that specifies which colors are used in this image file. Each pix is encoded in 8 bits, where the value points to a 24-bit color entry in the palette. This method limits the unique number of colors in a given image to 256 (2^8). The choice of color encoding obviously affects image size. A 640×480 pixel image using 8-bit color would occupy approximately 307 KB ($640 \times 480 = 307,200$ bytes), while a 1400×1050 pix image using 24-bit true color would require 4.4 MB ($1400 \times 1050 \times 3 = 4,410,000$ bytes).

Color palettes and 8-bit color are commonly used with Graphics Interchange Format (GIF) and Bitmap (BMP) image formats. GIF and BMP are generally considered to offer *lossless compression* because the image recovered after encoding and compression is bit-for-bit identical to the original image [15].

The Joint Photographic Experts Group (JPEG) image format uses discrete cosine transforms (DCTs) rather than a pix-by-pix encoding. In JPEG, the image is divided into 8×8 blocks for each separate color component. The goal is to find blocks where the amount of change in the pixel values (the *energy*) is low. If the energy level is too high, the block is further subdivided into 8×8 subblocks until the energy is low enough. Each 8×8 block (or subblock) is transformed into 64 DCT coefficients that approximate the luminance (brightness, darkness, and contrast) and chrominance (color) of that portion of the image. JPEG is generally considered to be *lossy compression* because the image recovered from the compressed JPEG file is a close approximation of, but not identical to, the original [15–17].

3.2 Digital Audio

Audio encoding involves converting an analog signal to a bit stream. Analog sound—voice and music—is represented by sine waves of different frequencies. The human ear can hear frequencies nominally in the range of 20–20,000 cycles/second (Hertz, or Hz). Sound is analog, meaning that it is a continuous signal. Storing the sound digitally requires that the continuous sound wave be converted to a set of samples that can be represented by a sequence of zeroes and ones [18].

Analog-to-digital conversion is accomplished by sampling the analog signal (with a microphone or other audio detector) and converting those samples to voltage levels. The voltage, or signal, level is then converted to a numeric value using a scheme called pulse code modulation (PCM). The device that performs this conversion is called a *coder–decoder*, or *codec* [18].

PCM provides only an approximation of the original analog signal (Fig. 8). If the analog sound level, for example, is measured at a 4.86 level, it would be converted to

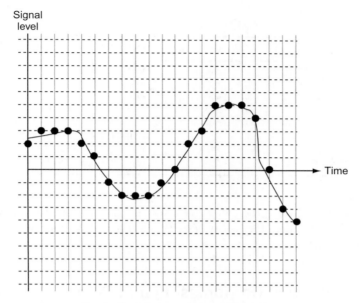

FIG. 8. Simple pulse code modulation (PCM).

a 5 in PCM; this is called *quantization error*. Different audio applications define a different number of PCM levels so that this "error" is nearly undetectable by the human ear. The telephone network converts each voice sample to an 8-bit value (255 PCM levels), while music applications generally use 16-bit values (65,535 PCM levels) [18,19].

Analog signals need to be sampled at a rate of twice the highest frequency component of the signal so that the original can be correctly reproduced from the samples alone. In the telephone network, the human voice is carried in a frequency band 0–4000 Hz (although only about 400–3400 Hz is actually used to carry voice); therefore, voice is sampled 8000 times per second (an 8 kHz sampling rate). Music audio applications assume the full spectrum of the human ear and generally use a 44.1 kHz sampling rate [18,19].

The bit rate of uncompressed music can be easily calculated from the sampling rate (44.1 kHz), PCM resolution (16 bits), and number of sound channels (2) to be 1,411,200 bits per second. This would suggest that a 1-minute audio file (uncompressed) would occupy 10.6 MB (1,411,200 × 60/8 = 10,584,000). Audio files are, in fact, made smaller by using a variety of compression techniques. One obvious method is to reduce the number of channels to 1 or to reduce the sampling rate, in

TABLE I
COMMON DIGITAL AUDIO FORMATS (FROM [19])

Audio type	File extension	Codec
AIFF (Mac)	.aif, .aiff	PCM (or other)
AU (Sun/Next)	.au	μ-law (or other)
CD audio (CDDA)	n/a	PCM
MP3	.mp3	MPEG Audio Layer III
Windows Media Audio	.wma	Microsoft proprietary
QuickTime	.qt	Apple Computer proprietary
RealAudio	.ra, .ram	Real Networks proprietary
WAV	.wav	PCM (or other)

some cases as low as 11 kHz. Other codecs use proprietary compression schemes. All these solutions reduce the quality of the sound. Table I lists some of the common digital audio formats.

3.3   Payload Compression and Steganography

There are two fundamental reasons for steganography algorithms compressing payloads prior to embedding, namely, to reduce the size of the payload or to create a more randomized payload.

By reducing the size of the payload through compression, the overall impact on the carrier file is also reduced (Fig. 9). This is quite obvious, although not all steganography programs provide this capability automatically. For example, the F5 algorithm—one of the best JPEG embedding algorithms, developed by Andreas Westfeld of Technische Universität Dresden—leaves *a priori* payload compression up to the user. Since compression of documents, spreadsheets, and other noncompressed files can significantly reduce the size of the payload, the ability to embed more information safely (without detection) improves as the payload size is reduced. For some steganography applications, such as S-Tools, the program provides both information regarding the maximum size of the payload and the ability to control the compression method.

The second and less obvious reason for applying compression is to create a more randomized payload (Fig. 10). This is particularly important when embedding text or simple messages into a carrier file. Clearly, encryption can be used for the same purpose. The underlying rationale behind the randomization of the payload is to ensure the 50% rule; since most steganography makes slight alterations to the least significant bit (LSB; RGB values, Palette Colors, JPEG DCT coefficients, etc.),

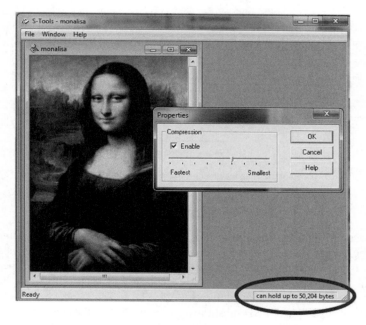

FIG. 9. S-Tools showing the potential payload capacity of this carrier file.

there is a 50/50 chance that the bit you are modifying will already be in the correct state if the data being embedded is random. In this case, there is a 50% chance that no actual alteration would be made, making the carrier an even better approximation of the original, unmodified carrier.

4. Steganography and Digital Carrier Files

This section will discuss the major classifications of steganography methods that operate on digital carriers. Image and audio files are the easiest and most common carrier media because of the plethora of potential carrier files already in existence, the ability to create an infinite number of new carrier files, and the easy access to stego software that will operate on these carriers. For that reason, most of the examples below operate on image and audio files. That said, digital carriers also include network traffic, so methods operating over Transmission Control Protocol/ Internet Protocol (TCP/IP) packets will also be addressed, including stego in digital voice.

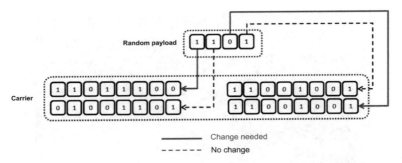

FIG. 10. A compressed payload being used to add randomization to the carrier.

4.1   Least-Significant Bit Overwriting

LSB overwriting (or substitution) is a common stego method when using audio and image carrier files. The term LSB comes from the numeric significance of the bits in a byte. The high-order, or most significant, bit is the one with the largest arithmetic value (i.e., $2^7 = 128$), while the low-order, or least significant, bit is the one with the smallest arithmetic value (i.e., $2^0 = 1$).

As a simple example of LSB substitution, imagine hiding the character "G" across the following eight bytes of a carrier file (the LSBs are underlined):

```
10010101  00001101  11001001  10010110
00001111  11001011  10011111  00010000
```

A "G" is represented in the American Standard Code for Information Interchange (ASCII)/International Alphabet 5 (IA5) as the binary string 01000111. These 8 bits can be written to the LSB of each of the 8 carrier bytes as follows:

```
10010100  00001101  11001000  10010110
00001110  11001011  10011111  00010001
```

In the sample above, note that only half of the LSBs were actually changed (shown above in *italics*). This actually makes some sense since there should only be about a 50% mismatch when substituting one set of zeroes and ones with another set of zeroes and ones.

LSB substitution can be used to overwrite legitimate RGB color encodings or palette pointers in GIF and BMP files, coefficients in JPEG files, and PCM levels in audio files. By overwriting the LSB, the numeric value of the byte changes very little and is least likely to be detected by the human eye or ear. (Imagine how unlikely the reader would be to detect a red level change from 191 to 190, a green level change from 29 to 28, and/or a blue level change from 152 to 153 in the color in Fig. 7.)

LSB substitution is a simple, albeit common, technique for steganography. Its use, however, is not necessarily as simplistic as the method sounds. Only the most naive stego software would merely overwrite every LSB with hidden data; almost all use some sort of means to randomize the actual bits in the carrier file that are modified. This is one of the factors that makes stego detection so difficult.

One example of hiding information in a digital carrier uses a program called S-Tools. In this example, an 11,067-byte GIF image of the Burlington, Vermont airport (Fig. 11) will be hidden in a WAV audio file.

S-Tools is a program, written by Andy Brown, which can hide information inside GIF, BMP, and WAV files. S-Tools uses LSB substitution in files that employ lossless compression, such as 8- or 24-bit color image and PCM audio files. S-Tools employs a password for LSB randomization and can encrypt data using the Data Encryption Standard (DES), International Data Encryption Algorithm (IDEA), Message Digest Cipher (MDC), or Triple-DES [6,15,20,21]. Figure 12 shows a signal level comparison between a WAV carrier file before (left) and after (right) the airport map was hidden. The original WAV file is 178,544 bytes in length, while the stego WAV file is 178,298 bytes in length. Although the relatively small size of the figure makes it hard to see details, some differences are noticeable at the beginning and end of the audio sample; that is, during periods of silence. (Some stego tools have built-in intelligence to avoid the low-intensity portions of the signal.) Audio files are well suited to information hiding because they are usually relatively large, making it relatively easy to hide, but difficult to find, small volumes of hidden data.

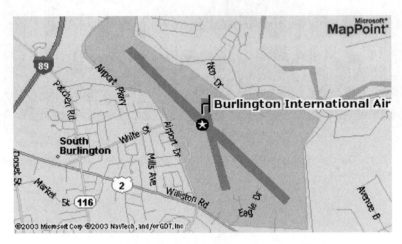

FIG. 11. A GIF image file of the map of the Burlington, VT airport.

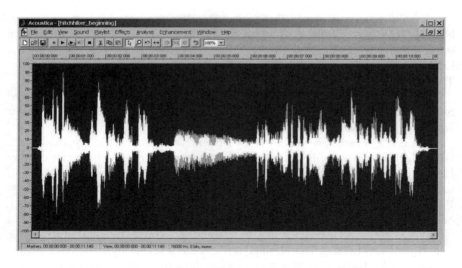

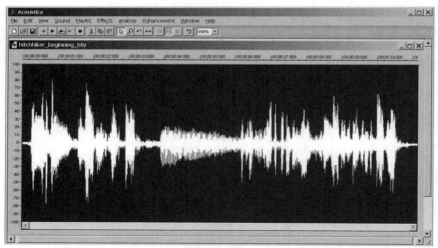

FIG. 12. The signal level comparisons between a WAV carrier file before (above) and after (below) the airport map is inserted.

4.2 Encoding Algorithm Modification

JP Hide-&-Seek (JPHS) by Allan Latham is designed to be used with JPEG files and lossy compression. JPHS alters the DCT coefficients used by the JPEG algorithm. The Blowfish crypto algorithm is used for LSB randomization and encryption [20,21]. Figure 13 shows an example of JPEG file with the airport map embedded in it. The original carrier file is 207,244 bytes in size and contains 224,274 unique colors; the stego file is 207,275 bytes in size and contains 227,870 unique colors. There is no color palette to look at because JPEG uses 24-bit color coding and DCT.

4.3 Grammar Selection

Another way in which to hide a message in plain sight employs grammar-based mimicry [6]. In this scheme, the communicating parties have a prearranged set of phrases and text clauses that convey meaning. The bit string that represents the hidden message dictates the phrases and clauses that will appear in the carrier text.

An example of grammar-based stego hides a message in a carrier that otherwise looks like spam, such as the following:

Dear Friend, This letter was specially selected to be sent to you! We will comply with all removal requests! This mail is being sent in compliance with Senate bill

Fɪɢ. 13. A JPEG carrier file containing the airport map.

1621; Title 5; Section 303! Do NOT confuse us with Internet scam artists. Why work for somebody else when you can become rich within 38 days! Have you ever noticed the baby boomers are more demanding than their parents & more people than ever are surfing the web! Well, now is your chance to capitalize on this! WE will help YOU sell more & SELL MORE. You can begin at absolutely no cost to you! But don't believe us! Ms Anderson who resides in Missouri tried us and says "My only problem now is where to park all my cars". This offer is 100% legal. You will blame yourself forever if you don't order now! Sign up a friend and your friend will be rich too. Cheers! Dear Salaryman, Especially for you - this amazing news. If you are not interested in our publications and wish to be removed from our lists, simply do NOT respond and ignore this mail! This mail is being sent in compliance with Senate bill 2116, Title 3; Section 306! This is a legitimate business proposal! Why work for somebody else when you can become rich within 68 months! Have you ever noticed more people than ever are surfing the web and nobody is getting any younger! Well, now is your chance to capitalize on this. We will help you decrease perceived waiting time by 180% and SELL MORE. The best thing about our system is that it is absolutely risk free for you! But don't believe us! Mrs Ames of Alabama tried us and says "My only problem now is where to park all my cars". We are licensed to operate in all states! You will blame yourself forever if you don't order now! Sign up a friend and you'll get a discount of 20%! Thanks! Dear Salaryman, Your email address has been submitted to us indicating your interest in our briefing! If you no longer wish to receive our publications simply reply with a Subject: of "REMOVE" and you will immediately be removed from our mailing list. This mail is being sent in compliance with Senate bill 1618, Title 6, Section 307. THIS IS NOT A GET RICH SCHEME. Why work for somebody else when you can become rich within 17 DAYS! Have you ever noticed more people than ever are surfing the web and more people than ever are surfing the web! Well, now is your chance to capitalize on this! WE will help YOU turn your business into an E-BUSINESS and deliver goods right to the customer's doorstep! You are guaranteed to succeed because we take all the risk! But don't believe us. Ms Simpson of Wyoming tried us and says "Now I'm rich, Rich, RICH"! We assure you that we operate within all applicable laws. We implore you - act now! Sign up a friend and you'll get a discount of 50%. Thank-you for your serious consideration of our offer.

This message looks like the spam that most Internet users receive every day, which are generally ignored and discarded. This message was created at *spammimic. com*, a Web site that converts a short text message into a text block [22]. The reader will learn nothing by looking at the word spacing or misspellings in the message; the zeroes and ones are encoded by the very choice of the words.

The hidden message in the spam carrier above is:

Meet at Main and Willard at 8:30

The algorithm from *spammimic.com* takes the message above, deciphers it into a bit stream, and then selects phrases from a database based upon the combination and order of bits in the stream. This is the essence of grammar-based steganography.

Text files are not the only type of carrier on which a grammar-selection type of method can be employed; other file types also have characteristics that can be exploited for information hiding. Hydan, for example, can conceal text messages in OpenBSD, FreeBSD, NetBSD, Red Hat Linux, and Windows executable files. Developed by Rakan El-Khalil, Hydan takes advantage of redundancies in the i386 instruction set and inserts hidden information by defining sets of functionally equivalent instructions, conceptually like a grammar-based mimicry (e.g., where ADD instructions are a zero bit, and SUB instructions are a one bit). The program can hide approximately one message byte in every 110 instruction bytes and maintains the original size of the application file. Blowfish encryption can also be employed [23,24].

4.4   Data Appending

Data appending is an almost obvious way of hiding data in a digital carrier. In this method, the data to be hidden is merely piggybacked to the carrier file. This method actually will only work with files that have both a file header (signature) and trailer, because these will demarcate the beginning and, more importantly, end of the carrier.

Figure 14 shows two JPEG files; the original carrier file on the left (61,289 bytes in length) and the carrier file with hidden data on the right (73,211 bytes). The two files look identical, and from the perspective of any JPEG image viewer application, they are.

Fɪɢ. 14. A JPEG original (left) and carrier (right) file containing the airport map.

The hidden data was inserted into this JPEG carrier file using a program called Camouflage. Camouflage works by encrypting the data file to be hidden in the carrier (which adds randomization) and then appending it to the original carrier file's data.

The example shown here employs a JPEG file as the carrier. The first 4 bytes of a JPEG file are the file signature (header), comprising the byte pattern FF D8 FF E0 (ÿØÿà) [the byte pattern 4A 46 49 46 (JFIF) can also be found starting at byte offset 6]. JPEG files also have a two-byte trailer with the byte pattern FF D9 (ÿÙ) [25]. A hex view of the portion of the carrier file with the JPEG trailer (at bytes 0xEF67-EF68) clearly shows data after the end of the JPEG image (Fig. 15). Note also that the size of the carrier file with hidden text is roughly the sum of the original carrier file and that of the file containing the image to be hidden.

Inch [26] describes a low-tech method of information hiding using data appending and a file compression application such as RAR or ZIP. Consider an example where one wishes to use a JPEG file as a carrier and wants to hide one or more other files. First, create a ZIP archive of the files that are to be hidden. Then, using the DOS copy command with the /b (binary) switch, append the ZIP file to the JPEG carrier, as follows:

    copy /b original.jpg+hidden.zip stego.jpg

The size of the resultant JPEG file with the hidden data (stego.jpg) will be approximately the sum of the size of the original carrier file (original.jpg) and the

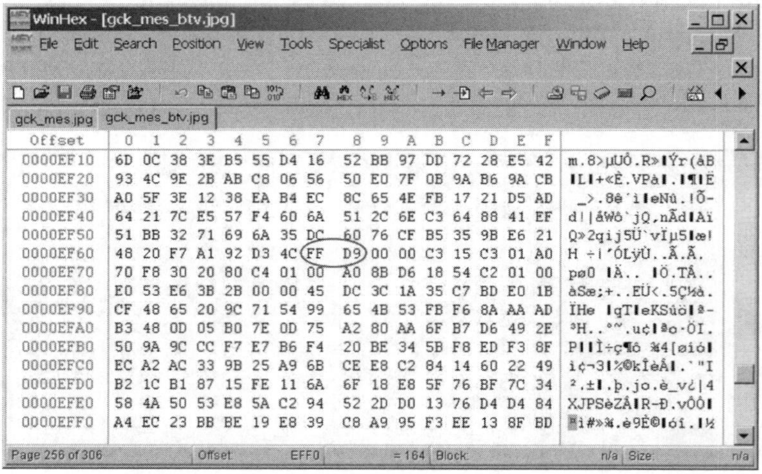

FIG. 15. A hex dump of a portion of the JPEG carrier file, showing the JPEG trailer.

ZIP archive file (hidden.zip). This method is simple and works for two reasons. First, the file has a JPEG extension and will, therefore, be associated with an image viewer. Since JPEG has a file trailer, the image viewer will stop displaying when it finds the trailer. Second, one can open the stego.jpg file directly from the ZIP program. Since this application starts to process the archive from the end of the file, it will find the archived information and not be confused by the presence of anything before the ZIP archive header. This method is not perfect and will not stand against analysis for very long, but it can work for a sufficient amount of time for the two parties.

4.5 Color Palette Modification

One other way to hide information in a paletted image is to alter the order of the colors in the palette or use LSB encoding on the palette colors rather than on the image data. These methods are potentially weak, however. Many graphics software tools order the palette colors by frequency, luminance, or other parameter, and a randomly ordered palette stands out under statistical analysis [27].

Gif-It-Up is a Nelsonsoft program that hides information in GIF files using color palette modification (and includes an encryption option). Figure 16 shows a GIF image of the Washington, DC mall at night where Gif-It-Up has been used to insert the Burlington airport map image from above. The original carrier file is 632,778 bytes in length and uses 249 unique colors, while the stego file is 677,733 bytes in

Fig. 16. A GIF carrier file containing the airport map.

length and uses 256 unique colors. The file size is larger in the stego file because of a color extension option used to minimize distortion in the stego image; if color extension is not employed, the file size differences are slightly less noticeable.

Figure 17 shows the carrier file's palettes before and after message insertion. Like all palette modification programs that act on 8-bit color images, Gif-It-Up modifies the color palette and generally ends up with many duplicate color pairs. Note that the original palette (on the left in the figure) appears to be slightly more ordered in terms of color organization than the palette from the stegoed image; this is one of the results of palette modification.

Color palette modification is one area of steganalysis that is sometimes overlooked, largely due to the general opinion that these palette-based carrier files have minimal payload carrying capabilities. This is caused first by the nature of palette images and second due to the compression that is applied to GIF and other palette types. In addition, the sophistication of algorithms that have been traditionally created for palette image types is far less than those applied to JPEG images, for example.

Figure 18 shows another view of a carrier file before and after data is hidden, using the program Gif-It-Up, where the image on the left is the original (unmodified) file and the image on the right is the one with stego data. (Note in this case that the process started with a GIF image to produce a new GIF image, whereas a more effective method would be to start with a True Color image to produce a GIF from

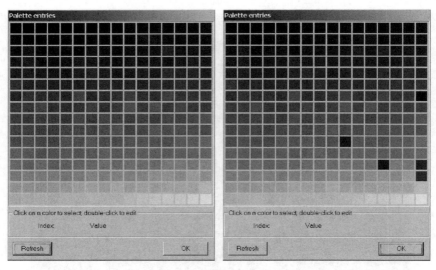

FIG. 17. The palette from the Washington mall carrier file before (left) and after (right) the map file was hidden.

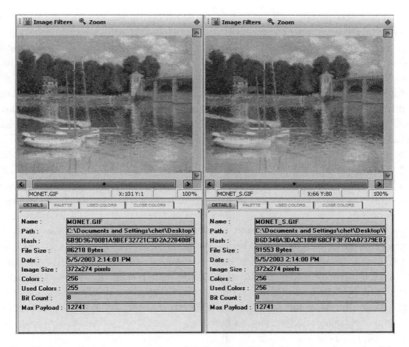

Fig. 18. Palette-based steganography; original carrier of the left, stego carrier on the right.

the True Color image while embedding the payload during the conversion. As it happens, very few, if any, stego programs offer this option for palette images).

Examining the basic properties of each image, we see the two files differ in one parameter, namely *file size*. The reason for this difference, however, may not be the expected one. The most common approach used to perform steganography on palette images is to create close color pairs, or *color buddies*, that can be used to encode a binary value into the pixel data. This common technique makes alterations (not additions) to the palette and alters the pixel data values to correspond with the new palette. Once again, however, this does not increase the number of pixel entries.

If the palette does not change in size and the number of pixel entries remains the same, why then does the file size change? The answer is compression. GIF images are compressed using the lossless Lempel–Ziv–Welch (LZW) compression [28]. As the pixel data has changed based on stego-based palette modification, the compression can be either less or more efficient and thus impacts the resulting file size.

GIF and other palette-based images are generally lower quality images due to the reduced color availability. Common palette images contain a fixed palette of 256 colors (extended palettes are available in some formats). While each of paletted color can be any one from the 24-bit RGB array (~ 16.8 million), a single image can only contain 256 unique colors. For this reason, any rendering of the image will have reduced color resolution. For this reason, GIF images are grainier than other image types. When stego is applied, the graininess is exaggerated. As shown in Fig. 19, graininess is present in both the original (left) and stego (right) carrier images but is much more predominant in the stego image (making the image appears pixelated). This is caused by the further reduction in colors that takes place through the stego process that replaces unique colors in the palette with close pairs.

These palette-based anomalies can be easily detected through algorithmic analysis of the palette. The simplified concept is to examine the distance between colors in the palette; as only 256 colors are available, the standard encoding algorithms will not naturally select close colors since humans cannot distinguish close color pairs. The encoding algorithms instead select a wider range of colors to populate the palette. When stego is applied and the palette is modified using the close color pair process, the close pairs can be easily identified. The first trick in this visual identification is to sort the palette by color (as the palette is not normally ordered this way), which allows rapid identification of the distribution of colors present in the palette. This is shown in Fig. 20, with the original palette on the left and the stego image palette on the right. The greater diversity of colors that exist in the original versus the stego modified version is obvious.

Close color pairs can be further illustrated by examining the binary values of adjacent palette color entries in the stego image (Fig. 21). Note in this example that the only difference between these two palette entries is the least significant bit of the red color value (the first byte of the 24-bit RBG value). This is anomalous to any known palette encoding method and is attributed directly to palette modification for data hiding.

FIG. 19. GIF image enlargement reveals distorsion in stego carrier image (right).

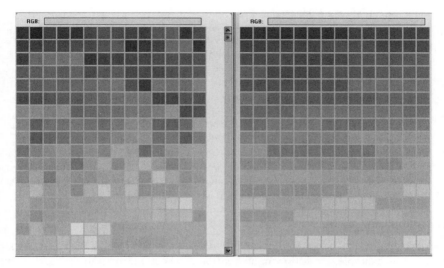

FIG. 20. Sorted palette before (left) and after (right) stego has been applied.

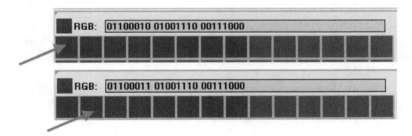

FIG. 21. Binary color values of adjacent palette entries in the stego image.

One caution in very small palette images that are used on the Web where only a handful of colors are used to display an icon-like object is that close color pairs can occur naturally. These images, however, would not be suitable for carrying hidden payloads of any size or value.

4.6 Format Modification

Format modification methods are a form of text semagram, where simple modifications are made to the carrier file containing the hidden text. Consider, for example, the following portion of text:

Enriched Air Nitrox (Wikipedia)
Nitrox refers to any gas mixture composed (excluding trace gases) of nitrogen and
oxygen; this includes normal air which is approximately 78% nitrogen and 21%
oxygen, with around 1% inert gases, primarily argon. However, in SCUBA diving,
nitrox is normally differentiated and handled differently from air. The most common
use of nitrox mixtures containing higher than normal levels of oxygen is in SCUBA,
where the reduced percentage of nitrogen is advantageous in reducing nitrogen take up
in the body's tissues and so extending the possible dive time, and/or reducing the risk of
decompression sickness (also known as the bends).
Nitrox is mainly used in scuba diving to reduce the proportion of nitrogen in the
breathing gas mixture. Reducing the proportion of nitrogen by increasing the proportion of oxygen reduces the risk of decompression sickness, allowing extended dive
times without increasing the need for decompression stops. Nitrox is not a safer gas
than compressed air in all respects: although its use reduces the risk of decompression
sickness, it increases the risk of oxygen toxicity and fire, which are further discussed
below.

A program called Snow can be used to hide a short text string into a text carrier
file. In this example, the following text string has been placed into the carrier text
file above:

We need to meet ASAP

Using a program called Snow to hide this string into the text block above would
result in the file shown in Fig. 22, as seen in Word using *show* mode. Note all the
extraneous space and tab characters; it is in these white space characters that the
message is hidden.

4.7   Covert Communication Channels

Steganography itself forms a covert communication channel since, presumably,
only the sender and receiver know where the hidden messages have been placed and
how they can be retrieved. Some forms of stego actually employ covert communication channels within real-time data and network communications by exploiting the
protocols themselves.

4.7.1   Stego and Communication Protocols

As the plethora of communication protocols evolves, the ability to embed (hide)
information in these data streams in order to either leak information or to covertly
communicate using these streams is possible. As with other forms of steganography,
the first key to identifying the covert channels is to be looking for them.

FIG. 22. Resultant text file after hiding a text string into a text file using the program Snow.

It is important to remember that individuals would use this method to leak information or covertly communicate when proven cryptography methods do not exist. Consider that the primary purpose for crypto is to deliver private and confidential communication between users that possess the proper credentials and keying material. The purpose or intent of steganography, however, is to hide the very existence of the communication channel.

Given this distinction, covert channels attempt to circumvent organization security policies by exploiting legitimate communication channels [29]. Organizations today have large, complex network and communications infrastructures. Each provides a point of attack for insiders or infected systems to communicate covertly. Utilizing compromised images and multimedia files in conjunction with Internet, e-mail, and other common infrastructure services to push files that contain hidden content represents the simplest form of this attack. More complex forms involve the modification of the communication channel itself in order to exploit unused spaces and attributes of the channels.

Even wireless local area networks (WLANs) are susceptible to such attacks [30]. One such example is the Frame Control (FC) field of IEEE 802.11 WLAN frame header. Manipulating rarely used bits in the FC field, such as More Frag, Retry, PwrMgt, or More Data, can provide single or multiple bit alterations in every frame and, thus, a low-bandwidth side communication channel.

The method of modifying communication packets to embed hidden information is not new. Covert TCP by Craig Rowland [31], for example, forms covert communication channels using the Identification field in IP packets or the Sequence Number field in TCP segments [4,32]. As new protocols are developed, rarely used fields or fields that contain limited value offer new applications for steganography. Whether these protocols are TCP, IP, or User Datagram Protocol (UDP) based, or whether the application is client/server or peer-to-peer, exploitation opportunities exist.

4.7.2 Streaming Channels

With the advent of multimedia streaming data for audio, video, or Voice-over-IP (VoIP), several researchers theorized that embedding steganography in such streams would be difficult, if not impossible. The reason most often given is that these protocols assume data loss as a normal part of the protocol; thus, loss of data is not only tolerated, it is expected. Missing a couple of packets or discarding corrupted packets has limited, and only momentary, effects on the experience of the listener or viewer of digital communication streams. Indeed, this is something that we are all familiar with, as with a momentary burst of static on a voice channel or a frozen or pixilated picture on a digital movie, viewing or communicating over streams.

One could jump to the conclusion that an effective jamming attack against both static steganography (images and audio files) as well as within streaming media would be to routinely inject steganography noise into the data stream using similar techniques defined above. If done properly, there would be little impact on the resulting data stream. This argument holds true for nonlossy compressed images and audio types. Injecting noise into lossless data types such as JPEG and MP3 carriers, however, noticeably degrades the carrier file quite quickly because each time an image is re-encoded, the quality is affected.

Some experiments conducted at WetStone Technology with a range of sample images show that degradation begins to become visible to the naked eye after 200–500 cycles, depending on image and noise insertion characteristics. Larger images (3 MB and larger) of outside scenery with high color counts can sustain up to a 1000 injections before noticeable distortion is apparent. However, if you have embedded a compressed, encrypted steganography payload within the data stream and data loss or corruption occurs, it is likely that all information after either of these events will be lost.

4.7.3   VoIP-Based Steganography

An increasing threat today—hiding data in an IP-based voice or video call—is an outcome of the natural evolution of steganography [33]. The Real-time Transport Protocol (RTP), described in RFC 1889, is a transport protocol for real-time applications [34]. A successful RTP environment provides an end-to-end transport with the ability to transmit real-time data such as audio and video. RTP uses UDP as its end-to-end transport protocol. Within VoIP environments, RTP provides the channel for call traffic. Therefore, there are three likely candidates for embedding steganography within the VoIP model:

1. UDP datagram headers: Exploitation of unused or rarely used header fields.
2. RTP packet headers: Exploitation of unused or rarely used header fields.
3. Voice payload: When making VoIP calls, the analog voice signals are transformed into digital content using a coder/decoder (codec), which is responsible for the analog-to-digital (and reverse) conversion. The digitized voice is then compressed and, in most environments, encrypted. The voice compression method, much like JPEG compression described previously, is lossy; therefore, modifications due to steganography must be made after the lossy compression stage and prior to any encryption.

All these general approaches suffer from potential data loss, a condition that must be overcome prior to implementing steganography within any of these channels. The first option is to employ error correction methodologies that will automatically correct a small number of lost or corrupted packets. These methods work quite well for normal channel traffic provided the payload is broken into multiple pieces. For example, it would not be wise to attempt transmission of a large compressed encrypted document over anything less than a perfect VoIP connection unless the payload was first broken into small discrete components. Error correction methodologies can be successfully applied to VoIP-based steganography, especially if the embedding takes place in the unused or rarely used bits in the packet header (this is because only a handful of bits are transmitted with each packet header). However, if voice payload steganography methods are employed, error correction techniques are less useful due to the amount of information embedded within each packet and the dependence on multiple consecutive packets being delivered without error.

A second method to overcome the data loss and corruption issue is to use encoded voice content to transfer data that is also resilient to data loss. For example, if audio or video information is embedded into the VoIP channel, then losing a small percentage of packets will have limited impacts on the hidden payload. Some of the voice or video content might be lost, much like normal calls, but the message can still be communicated.

With the almost ubiquitous proliferation of VoIP, the ability to covertly communicate over these channels is quickly becoming a reality. With Android phones being delivered ready for custom application development, along with a growing Open Source VoIP community, the ability for both the good guys and the bad guys to exploit these devices for their own purposes is endless. The detection, cracking, and jamming of steganography laced covert communication channels are not at the end of a life-cycle, but rather just at the beginning. With the almost limitless number of VoIP calls, streaming audio and video content, and connected mobile devices, our ability to overtly or covertly communicate to anyone, anywhere, anytime is upon us. The question is what we will choose to do with it.

4.8   Conclusion and Summary

Gif-It-Up, JPHS, Snow, and S-Tools are used above, for example, purposes only; they are free, easy to use, and perform their tasks well. There are many other programs that can be used to hide information in BMP, GIF, JPEG, MPEG-1 Audio Layer 3 (MP3), Paintbrush (PCX), Portable Network Graphics (PNG), Tag Image File Format (TIFF), WAV, and other carrier file types. The StegoArchive. Com Web site has a good list of more than 400 freeware, shareware, and commercial steganography software for DOS, Linux/Unix, MacOS, Windows, and other operating systems [35].

There are many other ways in which messages can be hidden in digital media. Digital forensic examiners are very familiar with data that remains in file slack or unallocated space as the remnants of previous files and, of course, programs can be written that can access slack and unallocated space directly. Small amounts of data can also be hidden in the unused portion of file headers [14].

Information can also be hidden on a hard drive in a secret partition. A hidden partition will not be seen under normal circumstances although disk configuration and other tools might allow complete access to the hidden partition [4]. This theory has been implemented in a steganographic ext2fs file system for Linux. A hidden file system is particularly interesting because it protects the user from being inextricably tied to certain information on their hard drive. This form of *plausible deniability* allows a user to claim to not be in possession of certain information or to claim that certain events never occurred. Under this system, users can hide the number of files on the drive, guarantee the secrecy of the files' contents, and not disrupt nonhidden files by the removal of the stego file driver [12,36,37].

There are also several characteristics of sound that can be altered in ways that are indiscernible to human senses, and these slight alterations—such as tiny shifts in phase angle, speech cadence, and frequency—can transport hidden information [14].

Newer, more complex, steganography methods continue to emerge. *Spread spectrum steganography* methods are analogous to spread spectrum radio transmissions (developed in World War II and commonly used in data communication systems today) where the energy of the signal is spread across a wide frequency spectrum rather than focused on a single frequency, in an effort to make detection and jamming of the signal harder. Spread spectrum stego has the same function; avoid detection. These methods take advantage of the fact that little distortions to image and sound files are least detectable in the high-energy portions of the carrier; that is, high intensity in sound files or bright colors in image files. Even when viewed side by side, it is easier to fool human senses when small changes are made to loud sounds and/or bright colors [6].

5. Detecting Steganography

This section will discuss issues related to the detection of steganography software that hides information in digital files and carrier files that contain hidden information. Stego will be described in terms of the Prisoner's Problem. Steganalysis methods and tools will then be discussed.

5.1 The Prisoner's Problem

The Prisoner's Problem [38] is sometimes used to explain steganography in practice although it was originally introduced to describe a cryptography scenario. The problem involves two prisoners, Alice and Bob, who are locked in separate prison cells and wish to communicate with each other. Alice and Bob are allowed to exchange messages but William, the warden, can read all of the messages. Alice and Bob know that William will terminate the communications if he discovers the secret channel [39,40].

William can act in either a passive or active mode. In the *passive warden* model, William examines each message and determines whether to forward the message or not based upon his ability to detect a hidden message. In the *active warden* model, William can modify messages if he wishes. A conservative, or malicious, warden might actually modify all messages in an attempt to disrupt any covert channel so that Alice and Bob would need to use a very robust stego method [39,40].

The difficulty of the warden's task will depend largely on the complexity of the steganography algorithm and the amount of William's *a priori* knowledge [17,39,40]:

- In a *pure steganography* model, William knows nothing about the steganography method employed by Alice and Bob. This is a poor assumption on Alice and Bob's part as "security through obscurity" rarely works and is particularly disastrous when applied to cryptography. This is, however, often the model of the digital forensics analyst searching a Web site or hard drive for the possible use of steganography.
- *Secret key steganography* assumes that William knows the stego algorithm but does not know the secret stego/crypto key employed by Alice and Bob. This is wholly consistent with the assumption that a user of cryptography should make, per Kerckhoff's Principle; that is, "the security of the crypto scheme is in key management, *not* secrecy of the algorithm" [5]. This may also be too strong of an assumption for practice, however, as complete information would include access to the carrier file source.

5.2   Steganalysis Overview

Steganalysis, the detection of steganography by a third party, is a relatively young research discipline with few articles appearing before the late-1990s. The art and science of steganalysis is intended to detect (or estimate) hidden information based upon observing some data transfer, making no assumptions about the stego algorithm [39]. Detection of hidden data may not be sufficient; the steganalyst may also want to extract the hidden message, disable the hidden message so that the recipient cannot extract it, and/or alter the hidden message to send misinformation to the recipient [41]. Stego detection and extraction is generally sufficient if the purpose is evidence gathering related to a past crime, although destruction and/or alteration of the hidden information might also be legitimate law enforcement goals during an ongoing investigation of criminal or terrorist groups.

Steganalysis techniques can be classified in a similar way as cryptanalysis methods, largely based upon how much *a priori* information is known [14,20]:

- *Stego-only attack:* The stego medium is the only item available for analysis.
- *Known carrier attack:* The carrier and stego media are both available for analysis.
- *Known message attack:* The hidden message is known.
- *Chosen stego attack:* The stego medium and algorithm are both known.

- *Chosen message attack:* A known message and stego algorithm are used to create stego media for future analysis and comparison.
- *Known stego attack:* The carrier and stego medium, as well as the stego algorithm, are known.

Stego methods for digital media can be broadly classified as operating in the *image domain* or *transform domain*. Image domain tools hide the message in the carrier by some sort of bit-by-bit manipulation, such as LSB insertion. Transform domain tools manipulate the stego algorithm and the actual transformations employed in hiding the information, such as the DCT coefficients in JPEG images [20].

It follows, then, that steganalysis broadly follows the way in which the stego algorithm works. One simple approach is to visually inspect the carrier and stego media. Many simple stego tools work in the image domain and choose message bits in the carrier independently of the content of the carrier; while it is easier to hide the message in the area of brighter color or louder sound, the program may not seek those areas out. Thus, visual inspection may be sufficient to cast suspicion on a stego medium [6].

A second approach is to look for structural oddities that suggest manipulation. LSB insertion in a palette-based image often causes a large number of "duplicate" colors, where identical (or nearly identical) colors appear twice in the palette and differ only in the LSB. Stego programs that hide information merely by manipulating the order of colors in the palette cause structural changes, as well. The structural changes often create a signature of the stego algorithm that was employed [6,41].

Steganographic techniques generally alter the statistics of the carrier and, obviously, longer hidden messages will alter the carrier more than shorter ones [27,42–44]. Statistical analysis is commonly employed to detect hidden messages, particularly when the analyst is working in the blind [41]. There is a large body of work in the area of statistical steganalysis.

Statistical analysis of image and audio files can show whether the statistical properties of the files deviate from the expected norm [42,44,45]. These so-called first-order statistics—means, variances, chi-square (χ^2) tests—can measure the amount of redundant information and/or distortion in the medium. While these measures can yield a prediction as to whether the contents have been modified or seem suspicious, they are not definitive [6].

Statistical steganalysis is made harder because some stego algorithms take pains to preserve the carrier file's first-order statistics to avoid just this type of detection. Encrypting the hidden message also makes detection harder because encrypted data generally has a high degree of randomness, and ones and zeroes appear with equal likelihood [42,45].

Recovery of the hidden message, of course, adds another layer of complexity compared to merely detecting the presence of a hidden message. Recovering the message requires knowledge or an estimate of the message length and, possibly, an encryption key and knowledge of the crypto algorithm [40].

Carrier file type-specific algorithms can make the analysis more straightforward. JPEG, in particular, has received a lot of research attention because of the way in which different algorithms operate on this type of file. JPEG is a poor carrier medium when using simple LSB insertion because the modification to the file caused by JPEG compression eases the task of detecting the hidden information [27]. There are several algorithms that hide information in JPEG files and all work differently; JSteg sequentially embeds the hidden data in LSBs, JPHS uses a random process to select LSBs, F5 uses a matrix encoding based on a Hamming code, and OutGuess preserves first-order statistics [17,45–49].

More advanced statistical tests using higher-order statistics, linear analysis, Markov random fields, wavelet statistics, and more on image and audio files have been described [42–44,50]. Detailed discussion is beyond the scope of this chapter, but the results of this research can be seen in some steganography detection tools.

Most steganalysis today is signature-based, similar to anti-virus and intrusion detection systems; anomaly-based steganalysis systems are just beginning to emerge. While the former systems are accurate and robust, the latter will be more flexible and better able to quickly respond to new stego techniques. One form of so-called blind steganography detection distinguishes between clean and stego images using statistics based on wavelet decomposition, or the examination of space, orientation, and scale across subsets of the larger image [41,42].

This type of statistical steganalysis is not limited to image and audio files. The Hydan program retains the size of the original carrier but, by using sets of functionally equivalent instructions, employs some instructions that are not commonly used. This opens Hydan to detection when examining the statistical distribution of a program's instructions.

The law enforcement, intelligence, and military communities do not always have the luxury of knowing either when and where stego has been used or the algorithm that has been employed. Generic tools that can detect—and classify—steganography is where research is still in its infancy but methods are already becoming available in software tools, some of which are described in the Section 5.3 [51].

And the same cycle is recurring as seen in the crypto world—steganalysis helps find embedded stego but also shows writers of new stego algorithms how to avoid detection.

5.3 Steganalysis of JPEG Images

Steganalysis can have a wide range of meanings depending upon whom you might be talking with, and there is certainly no single method or process. To explore some of the ways that steganalysis is actually performed, the discussion needs to narrow in a carrier type so as to move from the general to the specific. In this section, a presentation will be made about detailed analysis of JPEG files.

Figure 23 shows the most common method of applying stego to an existing JPEG file by making modifications to the quantized DCT values. These values are, in essence, the result of the lossy compression stage and provide the input to the final lossless compression stage. Making careful and slight alterations to these values can deliver visually indistinguishable changes to the resulting image when decoded, although this does not mean they are undetectable.

Figure 24 depicts two JPEG images; the one on the left is the original carrier file and the one on the right is the same image where data have been hidden using the JPEG Hilde&Seek (JPHS) stego software. When performing steganalysis, the examiner most likely will have only one image (assuming that the suspect is a professional and has been careful to keep the original image secluded); to illustrate the challenge, however, two images will be employed.

Examining the properties of the two images immediately shows several differences, namely, file size, used colors, and maximum payload. Figure 25 shows the JPEG headers and shows additional modifications that have occurred; in the stego image, in particular, the JPEG header information has been stripped out. There are two schools of thought on this from the steganographer's perspective. The first, and predominant, view is to strip the headers to eliminate any pedigree information that might be present in the header, such as identity, camera, photo source, etc. The second school of thought says to leave the header information intact so as to make the stego image look as conventional as possible.

The primary goal of any stego program is to ensure that the image, audio file, movie, or data stream looks, sounds, and behaves as close to normal as possible. Thus, visually examining a JPEG image may seem futile. However, by rendering the resulting JPEG with certain filters, anomalies caused by the stego process may

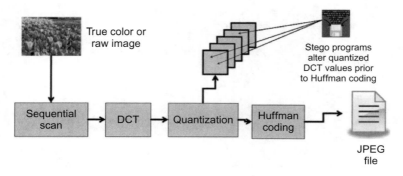

FIG. 23. JPEG encoding.

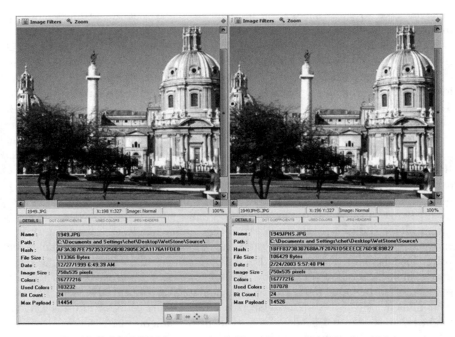

FIG. 24. Original JPEG image carrier (left) and image with hidden data (right).

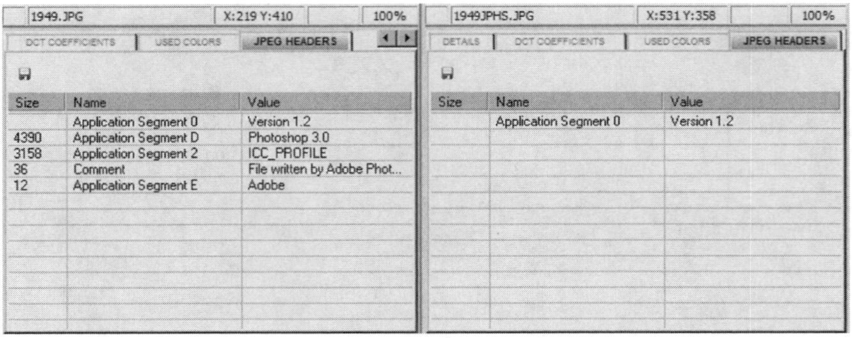

Size	Name	Value		Size	Name	Value
	Application Segment 0	Version 1.2			Application Segment 0	Version 1.2
4390	Application Segment D	Photoshop 3.0				
3158	Application Segment 2	ICC_PROFILE				
36	Comment	File written by Adobe Phot...				
12	Application Segment E	Adobe				

FIG. 25. JPEG header analysis (original carrier on left, stego image on right).

emerge. Figure 26, for example, shows the result when rendering the JPEG images using a hue filter. The reader can clearly see the distortion effect in the stego image on the right versus the original on the left, particularly in the area of the sky. Similar results would occur when filtering based on saturation or intensity.

These artifacts are caused by the modification of the quantized DCT values during the stego insertion. When the image is rendered (i.e., decoded from JPEG to RGB), the hue angles have been distorted from the normal state found in the original image. The amount of distortion is directly related to how much information is embedded; in other words, the size of the hidden payload in relationship to the content in the original image. This effect is a second-order artifact since these resulting RGB effects are caused by alterations that have been made to the quantized DCT values.

Direct examination of the quantized DCT values is also possible. Figure 27 shows a histogram of the discrete coefficients (DC) of both the original (left) and stego (right) image. At first glance, the two histograms look similar in shape. Closer examination, however, shows very discernable and measurable differences.

Figure 28 narrows the focus of the analysis to the peak areas of the two histograms, in this case, DC value is 169. Notice that the value 169 occurred as a DC coefficient 874 times in the original image (left), with the adjacent values of 168 and 170 occurring 25 and 0 times, respectively. Knowing that a key element of JPEG compression is the preparation of the quantized DC value to aid in the lossless Huffman compression that follows this type of statistical distribution makes sense, especially near the peak values. However, the examination of the stego image (right) shows that the 169 value has been decreased to only 423 occurrences, while the 168 value has increased to 426. This change is the equivalent of a least significant bit

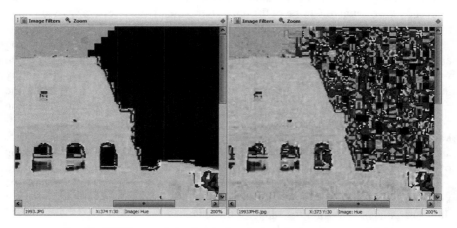

Fɪɢ. 26. JPEG hue rendering (original carrier on left, stego image on right).

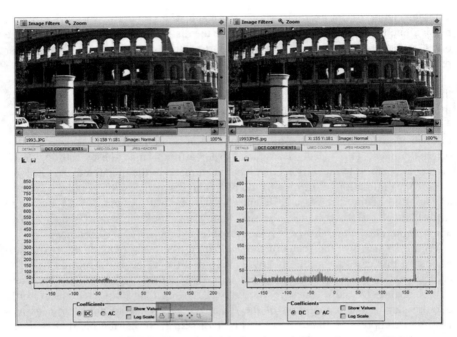

Fig. 27. Quantized DCT histogram (original carrier on left, stego image on right).

change used to hide bits of the hidden payload. This slight change has minimal impact on the normal rendering of the image but is clearly visible here as an anomaly that is a direct indicator that stego may be in play.

Even in a simple analysis of an image, the process can be both time consuming and may change or vary based on each result. It is important to point out that even when employing steganography detection algorithms to identify high probability images, several of the examination steps above must be applied to validate the results or rule out possible false positives. It is true that some signature detection capabilities do exist for stego where we can identify specific characteristics of well-known stego embedding programs, but for the more advanced methods where anomaly detection methods must be employed, human analysis and examination of the resulting images is an important step to confirm the presence of hidden evidence. Of course, the ultimate confirmation comes from the cracking of the known stego and the ultimate recovery of the hidden payload. Detailed analysis of those techniques is beyond the scope of this chapter.

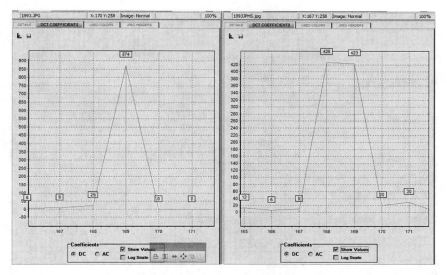

FIG. 28. Quantized DCT analysis (original carrier on left, stego image on right).

6. Steganography Detection Tools

This chapter has a stated focus on the practicing computer forensic examiner rather than the researcher. This section, then, will show some examples of currently available software that can detect the presence of stego programs, detect suspect carrier files, and disrupt steganographically hidden messages. This is by no means a survey of all available tools, but an example of available capabilities; StegoArchive. com lists many steganalysis programs [35], and Hayati et al.[52] provide an overview of over 100 different stego and steganalysis software packages.

6.1   Steganography Detection Tools

The detection of stego software on a suspect computer is important to the subsequent forensic analysis. Many stego detection programs work best when there are clues as to the type of stego that was employed in the first place. Finding stego software on a computer would give rise to the suspicion that there are actually stego files with hidden messages on the suspect computer. Further, the type of stego software found will directly impact any subsequent steganalysis; for example,

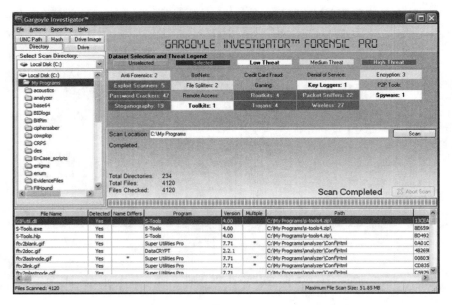

FIG. 29. The output from Gargoyle when aimed at one of the directories on author Kessler's hard drive.

S-Tools might direct one's attention to GIF, BMP, and WAV files while JPHS might direct the analyst to look more closely at JPEG files.

WetStone Technologies' Gargoyle software [53] can be used to detect the presence of stego software and other forms of malware. Gargoyle employs a proprietary hash set of all the files in the known stego software distributions, comparing them to the hashes of the files subject to search. Figure 29 shows the output when Gargoyle was directed to target one of the directories on the author's systems where stego programs are stored. Gargoyle data sets can also be used to detect the presence of cryptography, instant messaging, key logging, Trojan horse, password cracking, and other malicious software. WetStone's Stego Hunter, part of WetStone's Stego Suite [54], is designed to detect remnants of steganography programs. Stego Hunter can be directed to examine a local hard drive, or mount and examine an E01 (EnCase), AD1 (AccessData), dd, ISO, or other image file (Fig. 30).

Similar functionality can be found in the Steganography Analyzer Artifact Scanner (StegAlyzerAS) from Steganography Analysis and Research Center (SARC) [55] (Fig. 31). StegAlyzerAS uses SARC's Steganography Application Fingerprint Database (SAFDB) to detect the presence of stego application artifacts.

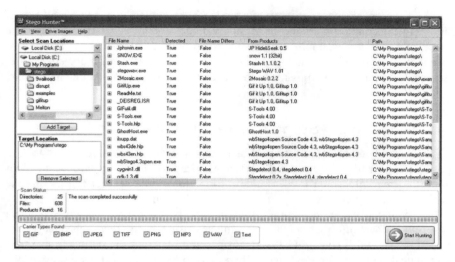

Fɪɢ. 30. The output from Stego Hunter when aimed at one of the directories on author Kessler's hard drive.

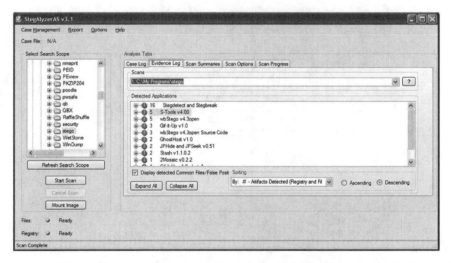

Fɪɢ. 31. The output from StegAlyzerAS when aimed at one of the directories on author Kessler's hard drive.

The detection of steganography software is a hard problem due to the small size of the software coupled with the increasingly large storage capacity of removable media. S-Tools, for example, requires less than 600 KB of disk space and can be executed directly, without additional installation, from a USB memory key. Under those circumstances, no remnants of the program would be found on the hard drive.

6.2   Stego Carrier File Detection

The second important function of steganography detection software is to find possible carrier files. Ideally, the detection software would also provide some clues as to the stego algorithm used to hide information in the suspect file so that the analyst might be able to attempt recovery of the hidden information.

One commonly used detection program is Niels Provos' stegdetect. Stegdetect can find hidden information in JPEG images using such stego schemes as F5, Invisible Secrets, JPHide, and JSteg [56]. Figure 32 shows the output from xsteg, a graphical interface for stegdetect, when used to examine two files on one of the author's hard drive—the original carrier file and one containing the Burlington

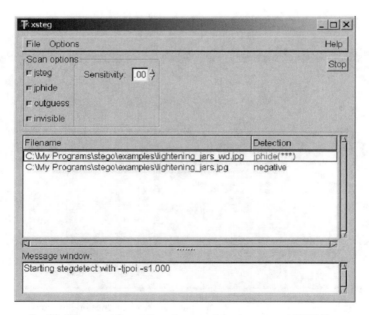

FIG. 32. The output from xsteg when examining two suspect JPEG files.

airport map. Note that the stego file is not only flagged as containing hidden information, but the program also suggests (correctly) the use of the JPHide stego scheme.

WetStone Technologies' Stego Suite [54] comprises four program that do the following:

- *Stego Hunter:* Detects remnants of steganography programs (described above)
- *Stego Watch:* Anomaly-based, blind stego detection software
- *Stego Analyst:* Imaging and analysis tool, providing visual clues that steganography may have been used in both image and audio files
- *Stego Break:* A password cracker for stego carrier files

Stego Watch analyzes a set of files and provides a probability about which are stego media and the likely algorithm that was used for hiding information; this metric, in turn, provides clues as to the most likely software employed. The analysis uses a variety of user-selectable statistical tests that are based upon the carrier file characteristics that might be altered by the different stego methods. Knowing the stego software that is available on the suspect computer will, obviously, help the analyst in selecting the most likely statistical tests. Figure 33 shows the output from

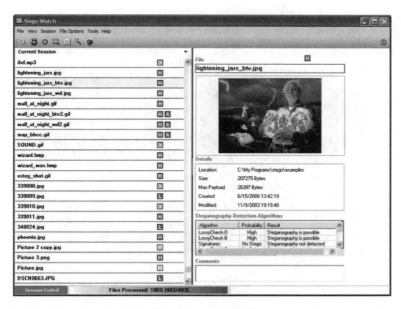

FIG. 33. Information from Stego Watch about a JPEG file suspected to be a stego carrier.

Stego Watch when aimed at the JPEG carrier file containing the airport map. Note that the Stego Detection Algorithms section in the display shows the statistical algorithms that were employed for analysis and the ones that bore fruit for this image; in this case, Stego Watch's LossyCheck-B and LossyCheck-D tests are highly suggestive of the use of the JPHide stego method which, in turn, suggests the use of the JPHide&Seek (JPHS) software.

Stego Analyzer provides a number of detailed analysis tools that allow the examination of image files for clues that something has been altered in the file. Alteration of an image can be suggestive of many things, including the possibility that data has been hidden. Stego Analyst can display many aspects of an image file, such as the palette, intensity, saturation, and hue of paletted images, or the DCT coefficients (Fig. 34), color set, and headers of JPEG files.

The SARC Steganography Analyzer Signature Scanner (StegAlyzerSS) [57] examines possible carrier files using three tests: a stego application signature scan (Fig. 35), a search for image file trailers to detect stego by appending hidden data, and an analysis searching for possible LSB overwriting methods.

Finding steganography in a file suspected to contain it is relatively easy compared to the extraction of the hidden data. Most stego software uses passwords for secrecy, randomization, and/or encryption. Stegbreak, a companion program to stegdetect,

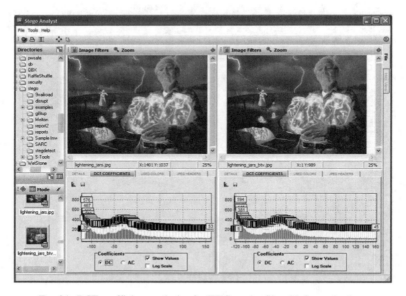

Fig. 34. DCT coefficient analysis of a JPEG carrier file with Stego Analyst.

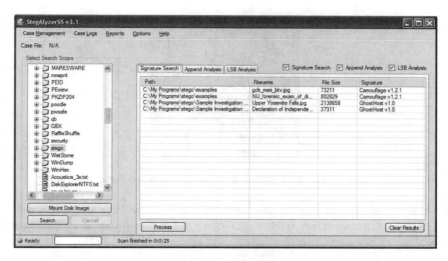

FIG. 35. Signature search display from StegAlyzerSS.

uses a dictionary attack against JSteg-Shell, JPHide, and OutGuess algorithms to find the password of the hidden data but, again, this is only applicable to JPEG files [56]. Similarly, Stego Break, a component part of WetStone's Stego Watch, uses a dictionary attack on suspect files in an attempt to extract and recover hidden data [54]. Steganography detection schemes do not directly help in the recovery of the password; finding appropriate clues is where the rest of the investigation and computer forensics comes into play.

The Prisoner's Problem suggests that a steganalyst may or may not want to disrupt the hidden data in a known carrier file. A computer forensic examiner looking at evidence in a criminal case probably has no reason to alter any evidence files. However, an examination that is part of an ongoing terrorist surveillance might well want to disrupt the hidden information even if it cannot be recovered. Hidden content, such as steganography and digital watermarks, can be attacked in several ways so that it can be removed or altered [58,59], and there is software specifically designed to attack digital watermarks. Such attacks have one of two possible effects: they either reduce the stego carrying capacity of the carrier (necessary to avoid the attack) or fully disable the capability of the carrier as a stego medium.

Although this subject is also beyond the scope of this chapter, one interesting example of stego disruption software can be used to close this discussion. 2 Mosaic, by Fabien Petitcolas, employs a so-called "presentation attack" primarily against images on a Web site. 2 Mosaic attacks a digital watermarking system by chopping

FIG. 36. A portion of the JPEG image with the hidden airport map, created by 2Mosaic.

an image into some number of smaller subimages. On the Web site, the series of small images are positioned next to each other and appear the same as the original large image [60].

Figure 36 shows an example of 2 Mosaic when used against the JPEG image from Fig. 13. In this case, the carrier file is split into 165 subimages, as shown in the figure (11 rows of 15 subimages). The 2 Mosaic approach of course is obvious when used; the viewer of the altered image knows immediately that something is amiss.

7. Summary and Conclusions

Consider the following hypothetical scenario. By preagreement among members of a terrorist organization, the leader puts an item for sale on an Internet auction site every Monday morning and posts a photo of the item. The item for sale is legitimate; bids are accepted, money is collected, and the item is dutifully delivered. At some prearranged time during the week, a version of the photo is posted that contains a hidden message. The cell members know when that time is and download the weekly message—and sometimes even bid on the item. As time goes on, the leader gets good ratings on the site and receives thousands of visitors each week; even if this site was under active surveillance, it is unclear that the few members of the cell can be distinguished from the thousands of legitimate bidders.

This scenario—or one like it—is a viable method for terrorists or criminals to communicate, but is it real? In the aftermath of 9/11, a number of articles appeared suggesting that al Qaeda terrorists employ stego [51,61–63] and alleged Russian spies arrested in the United States in the summer of 2010 reportedly hid communications in images on public Web sites [64,65]. In partial response to the earlier reports, several attempts have been made to ascertain the presence of stego images on the Internet. One well-known study searched more than three million JPEG images at eBay and USENET archives; using stegdetect, 1–2% of the images were found to be "suspicious," but no hidden messages were recovered using steg-break [17,45]. Another study examined several hundred thousand images from a random set of Web sites and, also using stegdetect and stegbreak, obtained similar results [66].

While these projects do provide a framework for searching a Web site for stego images, no conclusions can be drawn from them about stego images on the Internet. First and foremost, stegdetect only looks at JPEG images; other image types were never examined. Second, a very limited number of Web sites were examined, too few to make any definitive statements about the Internet as a whole. It is also interesting to note that several stego researchers are purposely not publishing information about what Internet sites they are examining or what they are finding [51,62].

There appear to be few hard statistics about the frequency with which steganography software or media are discovered by law enforcement officials in the course of computer forensic examinations. Anecdotal evidence suggests, however, that many computer forensic examiners do not routinely search for stego software and many might not recognize such tools if they found them. In addition, the tools that are employed to detect stego software are often inadequate, frequently relying solely on hash sets or the stego tools themselves [67]. A thorough search for evidence of steganography on a suspect hard drive that might contain thousands of images, audio files, and video clips could take days [2].

Indeed, many digital forensic examiners consider the search for stego tools and/or stego media to be a routine part of every examination. But what appears to be lacking is a set of guidelines providing a systematic approach to stego detection; even the U.S. Department of Justice search and seizure guidelines for digital evidence barely mention steganography [68,69]. Steganalysis will only be one part of an investigation, however, and an investigator might need clues from other aspects of the case to point them in the right direction. A computer forensic examiner might suspect the use of stego because of the nature of the crime, books in the suspect's library, the type of hardware or software discovered, large sets of seemingly duplicate images, statements made by the suspect or witnesses, or other factors. A Web site might be suspect by the nature of its content or the population that it serves. These same items might give the examiner clues to passwords, as well. And searching for steganography is not only necessary in criminal investigations and intelligence gathering operations; forensic accounting investigators are realizing the need to search for stego as this becomes a viable way to hide financial records [2,70].

It is impossible to know for sure at this point how widespread the use of steganography is by criminals and terrorists [2]. Today's truth, however, may not even matter; the use of stego is sure to increase and will be a growing hurdle for law enforcement and antiterrorism activities. Ignoring the significance of stego because of the lack of statistics is "security through denial" and not a good strategy.

Stego will certainly not be found if it is not being looked for. And as the number of potential carriers grows, the opportunity for these covert channels rises exponentially.

Appendix A.   Additional Web Sites

Computer Forensics, Cybercrime and Steganography Resources Web site, "Steganography & Data Hiding—Articles, Links, and Whitepapers" page (http://www.forensics.nl/steganography).

GCK's steganography links (http://www.garykessler.net/library/securityurl.html#crypto).

Neil Johnson's Steganography & Digital Watermarking page (http://www.jjtc.com/Steganography/).

Appendix B.   Companion Downloads to this Chapter

The hidden, carrier, and stego files mentioned in this chapter can be downloaded from *http://www.garykessler.net/download/stego.zip*. Use the password *tyui* to recover the hidden file from the stego files. The contents of the ZIP file include:

- Figure 11, Airport image: *btv_map.gif*
- Figure 12a, Original WAV carrier file: *hitchhiker_beginning.wav*
- Figure 12b, Stego WAV file: *hitchhiker_beginning_btv.wav*
- Figure 13, JPEG carrier file: *lightening_jars.jpg*
- Figure 13, Stego JPEG file: *lightening_jars_btv.jpg*
- Figure 14, Original and stego JPEG file: *gck_mes.jpg* and *gck_mes_btv.jpg*
- Figure 16, Original GIF carrier file: *mall_at_night.gif*
- Figure 16, Stego GIF file: *mall_at_night_btv2.gif*
- Figure 36, Disrupted stego JPEG file: *disrupt/lighte~1.html*

The noncommercial software employed in the examples in this chapter can be downloaded from the following mirror site:

- 2 Mosaic (*http://www.garykessler.net/download/2Mosaic_0_2_2.zip*)
- Camouflage (*http://www.garykessler.net/download/Camou121.exe*)
- Gif-It-Up (*http://www.garykessler.net/download/Gif-it-up.exe*)
- JPHS for Windows (*http://www.garykessler.net/download/jphs_05.zip*)
- Snow (*http://www.garykessler.net/download/snow.zip*)
- Stegdetect (*http://www.garykessler.net/download/stegdetect-0.4.zip*)
- S-Tools (*http://www.garykessler.net/download/s-tools4.zip*)

REFERENCES

[1] F.L. Bauer, Decrypted Secrets: Methods and Maxims of Cryptology, fourth ed., Springer-Verlag, Berlin, 2007.

[2] C. Hosmer, C. Hyde, Discovering covert digital evidence, Digital Forensic Research Workshop (DFRWS) 2003, (2003, August). Retrieved April 16, 2010, from http://www.dfrws.org/2003/presentations/Paper-Hosmer-digitalevidence.pdf

[3] M. Arnold, M. Schmucker, S.D. Wolthusen, Techniques and Applications of Digital Watermarking and Content Protection, Artech House, Norwood, MA, 2003.

[4] N.F. Johnson, Z. Duric, S.G. Jajodia, Information Hiding: Steganography and Watermarking—Attacks and Countermeasures, Kluwer Academic Publishers, Norwell, MA, 2001.

[5] D. Kahn, The Codebreakers: The Story of Secret Writing, revised ed., Scribner, New York, 1996.

[6] P. Wayner, Disappearing Cryptography—Information Hiding: Steganography & Watermarking, third ed., Morgan Kaufmann, Burlington, MA, 2009.

[7] Warchalking, Wikipedia, the Free Encyclopedia. Retrieved April 16, 2010, from http://en.wikipedia.org/wiki/Warchalking. 2010, January 31.

[8] M. Barni, C.I. Podilchuk, F. Bartolini, E.J. Delp, Watermark embedding: hiding a signal within a cover image, IEEE Commun. 39 (8) (2001, August) 102–108.

[9] S.H. Kwok, Watermark-based Copyright Protection System Security, Commun. ACM 46 (10) (2003, October) 98–101.

[10] M. Duren, M. Davis, C. Hosmer, Steganography vs. Digital Watermarking, in: The Science of Digital Investigation blog, (2008, September 24). Retrieved April 16, 2010, from http://www.wetstonetech.com/blogs/blog1.php/2008/09/24/test-post

[11] H. Clinton, Letter to John Burgoyne. Spy Letters of the American Revolution, from the Collection of the Clements Library, Retrieved April 17, 2010, from http://www.clements.umich.edu/Spies/letter-1777august10-1.html, 1777, August 10.

[12] D. Artz, Digital steganography: hiding data within data, IEEE Internet Comput. 5 (3) (2001, May/June) 75–80. Retrieved April 17, 2010, from http://www.cc.gatech.edu/classes/AY2003/cs6262_fall/digital_steganography.pdf

[13] The MathWorks, RGB Color Cube for uint8 Images. Retrieved April 18, 2010, from http://www.mathworks.com/access/helpdesk/help/toolbox/images/color7.gif, 2010.

[14] K. Curran, K. Bailey, An evaluation of image based steganography methods, Int. J. Digital Evidence 2 (2) 2003, Fall. Retrieved April 17, 2010, from http://www.utica.edu/academic/institutes/ecii/ publications/articles/A0AD276C-EACF-6F38-E32EFA1ADF1E36CC.pdf

[15] N.F. Johnson, S. Jajodia, Exploring steganography: seeing the unseen, IEEE Computer 31 (2) (1998, February) 26–34. Retrieved April 17, 2010, from http://www.jjtc.com/pub/r2026.pdf

[16] Monash University (n.d.). JPEG Image Coding Standard. Retrieved April 17, 2010, from http:// www.ctie.monash.edu.au/emerge/multimedia/jpeg/.

[17] N. Provos, P. Honeyman, Hide and seek: an introduction to steganography, IEEE Security Privacy 1 (3) 2003, May/June. Retrieved April 17, 2010, from http://niels.xtdnet.nl/papers/practical.pdf

[18] R.F. Rey (Ed.), Engineering and Operations in the Bell System, AT&T Bell Laboratories, Murray Hill, NJ, 1983.

[19] B. Fries, M. Fries, The MP3 and Internet Audio Handbook, Tacoma Books, Burtonsville, MD, 2000.

[20] N.F. Johnson, S. Jajodia, Steganalysis of images created using current steganography software, D. Aucsmith (Ed.), in: Proceeding of the Second International Workshop on Information Hiding (IH '98), Lecture Notes in Computer Science, vol. 1525, Springer-Verlag, New York, 1998, April, pp. 273–289.Portland, OR. Retrieved April 19, 2010, from http://www.jjtc.com/ihws98/jjgmu.html

[21] G.C. Kessler, An overview of cryptography, GaryKessler.net Web site. Retrieved April 19, 2010, from http://www.garykessler.net/library/crypto.html, 2010, March 16.

[22] spam mimic, Spam Mimic. 2009.Web site. Retrieved April 17, 2010, from http://www.spammimic. com/

[23] R. El-Khalil hydan. Retrieved April 19, 2010, from http://www.crazyboy.com/hydan/

[24] R. El-Khalil, A.D. Keromytis, Hydan: Hiding Information in Program Binaries, Proceedings of the 6th International Conference on Information and Communications Security, 2004, pp. 187–199. Retrieved April 19, 2010, from http://www1.cs.columbia.edu/~angelos/Papers/hydan.pdf

[25] G.C. Kessler, File signatures table, GaryKessler.net Web site. Retrieved April 19, 2010, from http:// www.garykessler.net/library/file_sigs.html, 2010, April 15.

[26] S. Inch, A simple image hiding technique: what you may be missing, J. Digital Forensic Pract. 2 (2) (2008, April) 83–94.

[27] J. Fridrich, R. Du, Secure steganographic methods for palette images, Proceedings of the 3rd Information Hiding Workshop, Lecture Notes in Computer Science, vol. 1768, Springer-Verlag, New York, 1999, September, pp. 47–60. Dresden, Germany. 2000. Retrieved April 15, 2010, from http://www.ws.binghamton.edu/fridrich/Research/ihw99_paper1.dot.

[28] T.A. Welch, A technique for high-performance data compression, IEEE Computer 17 (6) (1984) 8–19. Retrieved June 7, 2010, from http://www.cs.duke.edu/courses/spring03/cps296.5/papers/ welch_1984_technique_for.pdf

[29] R.C. Newman, Covert Computer and Network Communications, in: Proceedings of the 4th Annual Conference on Information Security Curriculum Development 2007, September 28–29, 2007.

[30] C. Krätzer, J. Dittmann, A. Lang, T. Kühne, WLAN steganography: a first practical review, Proceedings of the 8th Workshop on Multimedia and Security (MM&Sec '06), 2006, pp. 17–22. September 26–27, 2006, Geneva, Switzerland.

[31] C.H. Rowland, Covert channels in the TCP/IP protocol suite, First Monday 2 (5) 1996. Retrieved April 15, 2010, from http://131.193.153.231/www/issues/issue2_5/rowland/index.html

[32] S.J. Murdoch, S. Lewis, Embedding covert channels into TCP/IP, in: Proceedings of the 7th Information Hiding Workshop, 2005, June. Barcelona, Italy. Retrieved April 15, 2010, from http://www.cl.cam.ac.uk/~sjm217/papers/ih05coverttcp.pdf

[33] W. Mazurczyk, K. Szczypiorski, Steganography of VoIP Streams, in: R. Meersman, Z. Tari (Eds.), Proceedings of On the Move to Meaningful Internet Systems: OTM 2008, 2008, pp. 1001–1018. Part II, LNCS 5332.

[34] H. Schulzrinne, S. Casner, R. Frederick, V. Jacobson, RTP: A Transport Protocol for Real-Time Applications, Internet Engineering Task Force, Request for Comments (RFC) 1889, January.

[35] StegoArchive.com, Stego Archive Web site. Retrieved April 15, 2010, from http://home.comcast. net/~ebm.md/stego.html, 2005.

[36] R. Anderson, R. Needham, A. Shamir, The Steganographic File System, in: D. Aucsmith (Ed.), Proceedings of the Second International Workshop on Information Hiding (IH '98), Portland, OR, Lecture Notes in Computer Science, vol. 1525, Springer-Verlag, New York, 1998, April, pp. 73–82. Retrieved April 15, 2010, from http://www.cl.cam.ac.uk/~rja14/Papers/stego-fs.pdf

[37] A.D. McDonald, M.G. Kuhn, StegFS: a steganographic file system for Linux, A. Pfitzmann (Ed.), Proceedings of the Third International Workshop on Information Hiding (IH '99), Lecture Notes in Computer Science, vol. 1768, Springer-Verlag, New York, 1999, September-October, pp. 462–477. Dresden, Germany. Retrieved April 15, 2010, from http://www.cl.cam.ac.uk/~mgk25/ih99-stegfs. pdf

[38] G.J. Simmons, The prisoners' problem and the subliminal channel, in: D. Chaum (Ed.), Advances in Cryptology: Proceedings of CRYPTO 83, Santa Barbara, CA, Plenum Press, New York, 1984, pp. 51–67.

[39] R.A. Chandramouli, Mathematical approach to steganalysis, in: E.J. Delp III, P.W. Wong (Eds.), Proceedings of SPIE Security and Watermarking of Multimedia Contents IV, 2002, April, pp. 14–25. San Jose, CA, January 2002. Retrieved April 15, 2010, from http://www.ece.stevens-tech.edu/~mouli/spiesteg02.pdf

[40] J. Fridrich, M. Goljan, D. Hogea, D. Soukal, Quantitative steganalysis of digital images: estimating the secret message length, ACM Multimedia Syst. J. 9 (3) (2003, September) 288–302. Special issue on Multimedia Security, Retrieved April 15, 2010, from http://www.ws.binghamton.edu/fridrich/ Research/mms100.pdf

[41] J.T. Jackson, G.H. Gunsch, R.L. Claypoole, G.B. Lamont, Blind steganography detection using a computational immune system: a work in progress, Int. J. Digital Evidence 1 (4) 2003, Winter. Retrieved April 19, 2010, from http://www.utica.edu/academic/institutes/ecii/publications/articles/ A04D31C4-A8D2-ADFD-E80423612B6AF885.pdf

[42] H. Farid, Detecting Steganographic Messages in Digital Images, Technical Report TR2001-412 Dartmouth College, Computer Science Department, Hanover, NH, 2001. Retrieved April 19, 2010, from http://www.cs.dartmouth.edu/~farid/publications/tr01.pdf

[43] J. Fridrich, M. Goljan, Practical steganalysis—state of the art, in: E.J. Delp III, P.W. Wong (Eds.), Proceedings of SPIE Security and Watermarking of Multimedia Contents IV, 2002, April, pp. 1–13. San Jose, CA, January 2002. Retrieved April 15, 2010, from http://www.ws.binghamton.edu/ fridrich/Research/steganalysis01.pdf

[44] H. Özer, İ. Avcıbaş, B. Sankur, N. Memon, Steganalysis of Audio Based on Audio Quality Metrics, in: E.J. Delp III, P.W. Wong (Eds.), Proceedings of SPIE Security and Watermarking of Multimedia Contents V, 2003, June, pp. 55–66. Santa Clara, CA, January 2003. Retrieved April 18, 2010, from http://www.busim.ee.boun.edu.tr/~sankur/SankurFolder/Audio_Steganalysis_16.doc

[45] N. Provos, P. Honeyman, Detecting Steganographic Content on the Internet, Center for Information Technology Integration, University of Michigan, 2001, August 31.CITI Technical Report 01–11. Retrieved April 17, 2010, from http://www.citi.umich.edu/techreports/reports/citi-tr-01-11.pdf

[46] J. Fridrich, M. Goljan, R. Du, Steganalysis based on JPEG compatibility, in: A.G. Tescher, B. Vasudev, V.M. Bove Jr. (Eds.), Proceedings of SPIE Multimedia Systems and Applications IV,

2001, November, pp. 275–280. Denver, CO, August 2001. Retrieved April 19, 2010, from http://www.ws.binghamton.edu/fridrich/Research/jpgstego01.pdf

[47] J. Fridrich, M. Goljan, D. Hogea, Steganalysis of JPEG images: breaking the F5 algorithm, 5th Information Hiding Workshop, 2002, October. Noordwijkerhout, The Netherlands. Retrieved April 19, 2010, from http://www.ws.binghamton.edu/fridrich/Research/f5.pdf

[48] J. Fridrich, M. Goljan, D. Hogea, Attacking the OutGuess, Proceedings of the ACM Workshop on Multimedia and Security 2002, 2002, December. Juan-les-Pins, France. Retrieved April 19, 2010, from http://www.ws.binghamton.edu/fridrich/Research/acm_outguess.pdf

[49] J. Fridrich, M. Goljan, D. Hogea, New methodology for breaking steganographic techniques for JPEGs, in: E.J. Delp III, P.W. Wong (Eds.), Proceedings of SPIE Security and Watermarking of Multimedia Contents IV, 2003, June, pp. 143–155. Santa Clara, CA, January 2003. Retrieved April 19, 2010, from http://www.ws.binghamton.edu/fridrich/Research/jpeg01.pdf

[50] H. Farid, S. Lyu, Higher-order wavelet statistics and their application to digital forensics, IEEE Workshop on Statistical Analysis in Computer Vision, 2003, June. Madison, WI. Retrieved April 19, 2010, from http://www.cs.dartmouth.edu/~farid/publications/sacv03.pdf

[51] D. McCullagh, Secret Messages Come In .Wavs, WIRED News 2001, February 20. Retrieved April 15, 2010, from http://www.wired.com/news/politics/0,1283,41861,00.html

[52] P. Hayati, V. Potdar, E. Chang, A survey of steganographic and steganalytic tools for the digital forensic investigator, in: Proceedings of the Workshop of Information Hiding and Digital Watermarking, 2007, July Moncton, New Brunswick, Canada.

[53] WetStone Technologies, Gargoyle Investigator, Retrieved April 20, 2010, from http://www.wetstonetech.com/cgi-bin/shop.cgi?view,2, 2010.

[54] WetStone Technologies, Stego Suite, Retrieved April 20, 2010, from http://www.wetstonetech.com/cgi-bin/shop.cgi?view,1, 2010.

[55] Steganography Analysis and Research Center (SARC), StegAlyzerAS. Retrieved April 20, 2010, from http://www.sarc-wv.com/products/stegalyzeras.aspx, 2010.

[56] OutGuess, Steganography Detection with Stegdetect. Retrieved April 20, 2010, from http://www.outguess.org/detection.php, 2004.

[57] Steganography Analysis and Research Center (SARC), StegAlyzerSS. Retrieved April 20, 2010, from http://www.sarc-wv.com/products/stegalyzerss.aspx, 2010.

[58] J.R.H. Martin, M. Kutter, Information retrieval in digital watermarking, IEEE Commun 39 (8) (2001, August) 110–116.

[59] S. Voloshynovskiy, S. Pereira, T. Pun, J.J. Eggers, J.K. Su, Attacks on digital watermarks: classification, estimation-based attacks, and benchmarks, IEEE Commun. 39 (8) (2001, August) 118–126.

[60] F.A.P. Petitcolas, 'mosaïc' attack, Retrieved April 20, 2010, from http://www.petitcolas.net/fabien/watermarking/2mosaic/index.html, 2009, June 20.

[61] J. Kelly, Terror groups hide behind Web encryption, USA Today Online 2001, February 5. Retrieved April 20, 2010, from http://www.usatoday.com/tech/news/2001-02-05-binladen.htm

[62] G. Kolata, Veiled messages of terror may lurk in cyberspace, The New York Times Online 2001, October 30.Retrieved April 20, 2010, from http://www.nytimes.com/2001/10/30/science/physical/30STEG.html?pagewanted=1.

[63] F. Manoo, The Case of the Missing Code, Salon.com. Retrieved April 20, 2010, from http://www.salon.com/tech/feature/2002/07/17/steganography/, 2002, July 17.

[64] D. Montgomery, Arrests of alleged spies draws attention to long obscure field of steganography, The Washington Post 2010, June 30. Retrieved September 6, 2010, from http://www.washingtonpost.com/wp-dyn/content/article/2010/06/30/AR2010063003108.html

[65] N. Shactman, FBI: spies hid secret messages on public Websites, WIRED Magazine Online 2010, June 29. Retrieved September 6, 2010, from http://www.wired.com/dangerroom/2010/06/alleged-spies-hid-secret-messages-on-public-websites/

[66] J. Callinan, D. Kemick, Detecting Steganographic Content in Images Found on the Internet, Department of Business Management, University of Pittsburgh at Bradford, 2001. Retrieved April 20, 2010, from http://www.chromesplash.com/jcallinan.com/publications/steg.pdf

[67] B. Nelson, A. Phillips, F. Enfinger, C. Steuart, Guide to Computer Forensics and Investigations, third ed., Thomson Course Technology, Boston, 2008.

[68] U.S. Department of Justice, Forensic Examination of Digital Evidence: A Guide for Law Enforcement. Office of Justice Programs, National Institute of Justice, 2004, April. NCJ 199408. Retrieved April 20, 2010, from http://www.ncjrs.org/pdffiles1/nij/199408.pdf

[69] U.S. Department of Justice, Searching and Seizing Computers and Obtaining Electronic Evidence in Criminal Investigations. Criminal Division, Computer Crime and Intellectual Property Section, 2009. Retrieved April 20, 2010, from http://www.cybercrime.gov/ssmanual/ssmanual2009.pdf

[70] J. Seward, The debtor's digital reckonings, Int. J. Digital Evidence 2 (2) 2003, Fall. Retrieved April 17, 2010, from http://www.utica.edu/academic/institutes/ecii/publications/articles/A0AE0A62-D73A-CB30-B0C1363FC9B1E185.pdf

ABOUT THE AUTHOR

Gary C. Kessler is the president of Gary Kessler Associates, a digital forensics and information security consulting and training firm in Burlington, Vermont. Gary holds a B.A. in Mathematics, an M.S. in Computer Science, and a Ph.D. in Computing Technology in Education. He is a Certified Computer Examiner (CCE) and Certified Information Systems Security Professional (CISSP). Gary is also an adjunct associate professor at Edith Cowan University in Perth, Western Australia and a member of the Vermont Internet Crimes Against Children (ICAC) Task Force. In addition, he is the editor in-chief of the *Journal of Digital Forensics, Security and Law*. His e-mail address is *gck@garykessler.net*.

Chet Hosmer is Senior Vice President, Chief Scientist, and co-founder of WetStone Technologies, Inc., now a subsidiary of Allen Corporation of America. Chet, currently located in Conway, South Carolina, received his B.S. in Computer Science from Syracuse University and Utica College where he now serves as a visiting professor. Chet serves on multiple digital forensic editorial boards and speaks around the globe on steganography, malware and live investigation methodologies, and a plethora of other cyber security related issues. His e-mail address is *chet@wetstonetech.com*.

CAPTCHAs: An Artificial Intelligence Application to Web Security

JOSÉ MARÍA GÓMEZ HIDALGO

Optenet, R&D Department, C/José Echegaray 8, edificio 3, Parque Empresarial Alvia, 28230 Las Rozas, Madrid Spain

GONZALO ALVAREZ

Instituto de Física Aplicada, Consejo Superior de Investigaciones Científicas, Serrano 144, Madrid, Spain

Abstract

Nowadays, it is hard to find a popular Web site with a registration form that is not protected by an automated human proof test which displays a sequence of characters in an image, and requests the user to enter the sequence into an input field. This security mechanism is based on the Turing Test—one of the oldest concepts in Artificial Intelligence—and it is most often called Completely Automated Public Turing test to tell Computers and Humans Apart (CAPTCHA). This kind of test has been conceived to prevent the automated access to an important Web resource, for example, a Web mail service or a Social Network. There are currently hundreds of these tests, which are served millions of times a day, thus involving a huge amount of human work. On the other side, a number of these tests have been broken, that is, automated programs designed by researchers, hackers, and spammers have been able to automatically serve the correct answer. In this chapter, we present the history and the concept of CAPTCHAs, along with their applications and a wide review of their instantiations. We also discuss their evaluation, both from the user and the security perspectives, including usability, attacks, and countermeasures. We expect this chapter provides to the reader a good overview of this interesting field.

ADVANCES IN COMPUTERS, VOL. 83
ISSN: 0065-2458/DOI: 10.1016/B978-0-12-385510-7.00003-5

Copyright © 2011 Elsevier Inc.
All rights reserved.

1. Introduction 110
    1.1.   The Turing Test and the Origin of CAPTCHAs 111
2. Motivation and Applications 116
    2.1.   General Description of CAPTCHAs 116
    2.2.   Desirable Properties of CAPTCHAs 117
    2.3.   Implementation and Deployment 119
    2.4.   Applications and the Rise of the Robots 121
3. Types of CAPTCHAs 127
    3.1.   OCR 130
    3.2.   Image 135
    3.3.   Audio 143
    3.4.   Cognitive 144
4. Evaluation of CAPTCHAs 146
    4.1.   Efficiency 147
    4.2.   Accessibility Problems 152
    4.3.   Practical Considerations 154
5. Security and Attacks on CAPTCHAs 156
    5.1.   Attacks on CAPTCHAs 158
    5.2.   Security Requirements on CAPTCHAs 169
6. Alternatives to CAPTCHAs 171
7. Conclusions and Future Trends 173
    References 173

1. Introduction

During more than 60 years, the purpose of Artificial Intelligence (AI) has been to design and build a machine able to think as a human person. The term AI was coined by John McCarthy in the summer of 1956, during a historic meeting held at the Dartmouth College by him and other leaders of this field over decades. While first works in AI were surprising, and some of these and other researchers believed this problem would be solved in 20 years, it was not. Evaluating how far we are today from meeting this ambitious goal is out of the scope of this chapter, but no one can deny that this field has provided hundreds of ideas that have been at the heart of Computer Science, and often driven it.

For instance, Semantic Networks emerged as a mechanism to formalize the semantics of Natural Languages to enable Machine Translation and to, ultimately, make computers understand and express through human languages. While machines still do not have this ability, Semantic Networks are a representation language that has for instance evolved to languages used to describe software models, like class diagrams in Object Oriented Programming. Semantic Networks are also the underlying mechanism to the Semantic Web and several other technologies. Computer Science is plagued with subproducts of AI, and Information Technologies (IT) Security is not an exception—modern spam filters include Machine Learning and Natural Language Processing techniques; Machine Learning is also used in antivirus research, intrusion detection, etc.; and there are many other examples.

In 1950, Alan Turing, one of the fathers of AI, faced the question: "Can machines think?" He conceived a test to evaluate it, the Turing Test. Theoretically, using this test it is possible to decide if a machine has reached the human levels of communication and reasoning. Current computers are still not able to pass that test, but as with Semantic Networks, other applications of this test have emerged.

Perhaps the most prominent application of the Turing Test to the field of Information Security is the concept of CAPTCHA. This word, which stands for Completely Automated Public Turing test to tell Computers and Humans Apart,[1] makes reference to an automated test aimed at confirming that the user of an application is a human being instead of a robot, that is, a program which would probably misuse a service or resource. The concept, often named also reverse Turing test or Human Interactive Proof, has emerged in the context of Web security. This can be explained by the huge and ever-increasing popularity of Web-based services that range from low level ones like online data and information storage, to more complex and extremely popular ones like Web-based e-mail, word processors, image processors, etc., and ultimately, Social Networks as the ultimate communication platform for hundreds of millions of users. However, the concept can be applied to any other kind of IT service or tool.

1.1 The Turing Test and the Origin of CAPTCHAs

The Turing Test was conceived by Alan Turing and presented in a rather philosophical paper [124] discussing the properties of a machine able to think like a human being. The test is based in the "imitation game," described as follows: given a man and a woman, an interrogator (the player or judge) has to guess who is who by

---

[1] The word (and concept) of CAPTCHA has been registered as a Trade Mark held by Carnegie Mellon University in 2004, but it seems abandoned at the current moment.

addressing questions to them. The goal of one of them is make the interrogator fail, while the other has to help the player to make a correct guess. The experiment or game is done using typewritten text, so the voices may not help the player. Questions made by the interrogator may include, for example, "Will you please tell me the length of your hair?" but the answers may be absolutely correct, partly false, etc. To answer the question "Can machines think?" Turing proposed to substitute the man or the woman by a computer. If after the game, the player makes a wrong guess, then we can deduce that the machine has reached the human levels of performance at communication and intelligence.

This test has been considered as a real "think proof" for many years, but not exempt of criticism as human intelligence is still hard to define (e.g., Refs. [99,101]). Moreover, no machine has yet passed the test, although a public contest, The Loebner Prize in AI [75], is yearly carried out since 1991, and computers and programs have greatly evolved since Turing posed his question. However, a number of systems have been inspired by this test, Eliza [135] being the most popular one. Weizenbaum's Eliza is a relatively simple pattern-matching program able to simulate the conversation of a therapist or psychoanalyst. For instance, given a sentence by a person: "I believe I do not love my mother," the program might answer: "Please tell me more about your mother," based on an rule that fires when the person writes the word "mother." Conversational programs have evolved to commercial products that are used for, for example, Customer Relationship Management [128].

The first mention of ideas related to Automated Turing Tests seems to appear in an unpublished manuscript by Moni Naor [85], who in 1996 proposed a theoretical framework that would serve as the first approach in testing humanity by automated means. In Naor's humanity test, the human interrogator from the original Turing Test was substituted by a computer program. The original goal of his proposal was to present a scheme that would discourage computer software robots from misusing services originally intended to be used by humans only, much in the same sense of stopping an automation based attack though human identification. Basically, he proposed an adaptation of the way identification is handled in cryptographic settings to deal with this situation. In cryptography, when one party A wants to prove its identity to another party B, the process is a proof that A can effectively compute a (keyed) function that a different user (not having the key) cannot compute. The identification process consists of a challenge selected by B and the response computed by A. What would replace the keyed cryptographic function in the proposed setting would be a task where humans excel, but machines have a hard-time competing with the performance of a 3 year old. By successfully performing such a task, the user proves that he or she is human.

In Naor's work, the collection of problems should possess the following properties:

1. It is easy to generate many instances of the problem, together with their unambiguous solution, without requiring human intervention at all.
2. Humans can solve a given instance effortlessly with very few errors. Providing the answer should also be easy.
3. The best known programs for solving such problems fail on a nonnegligible fraction of the problems, even if the method of generating instances is known. The number of instances in a challenge will depend on this fraction.[2]
4. An instance specification is succinct both in the amount of communication needed to describe it and in the area it takes to present it to the user.

Naor suggested a number of areas from vision and natural language processing as possible candidates for such problems: gender recognition, facial expression understanding, finding body parts, deciding nudity, naive drawing understanding, handwriting understanding, speech recognition, filling in words, and disambiguation. As will be seen later in this chapter, many of his suggestions have been applied throughout years to develop automated Turing Tests. Luis von Ahn et al. would later formalize and substantiate Naor's conceptual model in what would be known as CAPTCHA [129].

Major differences between the Turing test and Naor's proposal include:

- In a Naor test, the judge is also a computer, and the goal is not to verify that the other part in the communication is a computer as proficient as a person, but to confirm that he or she is actually a person. That is the reason why these tests are often called reverse Turing tests.
- In the Turing test, the communication is conversational. However, Naor's proposal involves a variety of sensory inputs.
- In the Turing test, the conversation lasts until the player is able to take a (possibly wrong) decision. However, in these reverse Turing tests, the player has only a chance (posing a challenge to the user and screening their answer) to take the decision. The challenge may be very difficult to verify that only a person can solve it, but not as difficult as an average human user is unable to solve it.

The first known application of reverse Turing tests (named CAPTCHAs from now on) was developed by a technical team at the search engine AltaVista. In 1997, AltaVista sought ways to block or discourage the automatic submission of URLs to their search engine. This free "add-URL" service was important to AltaVista since it broadened its search coverage. Yet some users were abusing the service by

---

[2] Rather than asking the prover to solve the problem once, he or she can be asked to solve the problem twice. If the prover gets good at solving the problem twice, she can be asked to solve the problem three times, etc. If for example the best computer program has a success 0.1 against a given problem, when asked to pass it twice in a series, the best computer program's success probability will be reduced to 0.01, etc.

automating the submission of large numbers of URLs, in an effort to skew AltaVista's importance ranking algorithms. Andrei Broder, Chief Scientist of AltaVista, and his colleagues developed a filter. Their method is to generate an image of printed text randomly so that machine vision (optical character recognition, OCR) systems cannot read it but humans still can. In January 2002, Broder stated that the system had been in use for "over a year" and had reduced the number of "spam add-URL" by "over 95%." A U.S. patent was issued in April 2001.

In September 2000, Udi Manber of Yahoo! described this "chat room problem" to researchers at Carnegie Mellon University (CMU): "bots" were joining online chat rooms and irritating the people there by pointing them to advertising sites. How could all bots be refused entry to chat rooms? CMU's Prof. Manual Blum, Luis A. von Ahn, and John Langford developed a (hard) GIMPY CAPTCHA, which picked English words at random and rendered them as images of printed text under a wide variety of shape deformations and image occlusions, the word images often overlapping. The user was asked to transcribe some number of the words correctly. A simplified version of GIMPY (EZ-GIMPY), using only one word-image at a time, was installed by Yahoo!, and was used in their chat rooms to restrict access to only human users. A sample of several GIMPY CAPTCHA images are shown in the Fig. 1.

Other researchers were stimulated by this particular problem, and the Principal Scientist of Palo Alto Research Center, Henry Baird, leaded the development of PessimalPrint, a CAPTCHA that uses a model of document image degradations that approximates ten aspects of the physics of machine-printing and imaging of text. This model included spatial sampling rate and error, affine spatial deformations, jitter, speckle, blurring, thresholding, and symbol size. Their paper [32] was the first refereed technical publication on CAPTCHAs.

These works and many others discussed in this chapter have been widely used by the World Wide Web-related industry, from search engines like Yahoo! or Google, to Web e-mail providers (Gmail, Hotmail, etc.), and ultimately, nearly all major Social

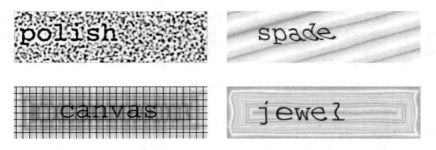

Fig. 1. Examples of EZ-GIMPY CAPTCHAs.

Networking sites like Facebook or MySpace, to prevent automated subscription, posting, and in general, automated misuse of their services to human users. CAPTCHAs have evolved to become a commodity, as they are integrated as plugins in Content Management Systems (CMSs), for example, Drupal, or even as Web Services. A major instance of a reverse Turing test provided as a Web Service is reCAPTCHA [47] (shown in the Fig. 2), started by the previously mentioned researcher Louis von Ahn. This service can be integrated in any Web page to typically protect a Web form, and it has become very popular, serving more than 30 million instances of the challenge every day. Now this service is provided by Google.

Moreover, the popularity of CAPTCHAs is so big that companies have emerged to take advantage of it, by using them as a platform for serving ads to the consumers [117], as shown in Fig. 3. A very interesting feature of CAPTCHA ads is that it is the very user who writes the brand message into the text field provided, so they effectively read and even learn the message.

On the opposite side, the popularization of CAPTCHA technologies has pushed a number of (quite often successful) attempts to circumvent these kinds of challenges. Attacks include automated bots able to understand the CAPTCHA itself, attacks to the programming structure of the form to avoid solving the CAPTCHA, and crowd sourcing. These attacks are further discussed in the Section 5.1.

FIG. 2. Examples of reCAPTCHA.

FIG. 3. Examples of advertising CAPTCHAs.

2. Motivation and Applications

2.1 General Description of CAPTCHAs

The general goal of a CAPTCHA is to defend an application against the automated actions of undesirable and malicious bot programs on the Internet. To achieve this goal, CAPTCHAs are programs designed to generate and grade tests that most humans can pass, but current computer programs cannot. A CAPTCHA works as a simple two-round authentication protocol as follows [141]:

S(ervice) → C(lient): a CAPTCHA *challenge*
C → S: *response*

Such challenges are based on hard, open AI problems [129]. It is important to remark that in this context "hard" is defined in terms of the consensus of a community: an AI problem is said to be hard if the people working on it agree that it is hard [129]. This notion is very similar to that of computational complexity theory, in which a problem is regarded as inherently difficult if solving the problem requires a large amount of resources, whatever the algorithm used for solving it. The security of most public key cryptosystems is based on assumptions agreed upon by the community, such as the existence of one-way functions. For instance, RSA's security relies on the assumption that 1024-bit integers are impossible to factor with today's available computing resources and number theory advances, although it has not yet been proven that any function exists for which no such reverse algorithms exist.

For all practical purposes, it is assumed that the adversary creating the malicious bot cannot solve the underlying AI problem proposed by the CAPTCHA with higher accuracy than what is currently known to the AI community. Given that at present there is no way to prove that a program cannot pass a test which a human can pass, all CAPTCHAs can do is to present evidence that with the current state of the art in AI it is hard to write a program that can pass the test, just as it happens with many cryptographic primitives.

Such hard AI problems are hypothesized to include [100]:

- Computer vision and subproblems such as object recognition. Actually, these problems are used in many CAPTCHAs, as will be covered in Sections 3.1 and 3.2.
- Natural language understanding and subproblems such as text mining, machine translation, and word sense disambiguation. This type of problems is also used in many CAPTCHAs, as will be explained in Section 3.4.

- Dealing with unexpected circumstances while solving any real world problem, whether it is navigation or planning or even the kind of reasoning done by expert systems.

However, as with computational problems used in public key cryptography, not all hard AI problems yield usable CAPTCHAs: there are some restrictions to be imposed upon the AI problems that can be applied to construct a CAPTCHA. Most importantly, since CAPTCHAs must work unattended to protect an application from malicious bots, there needs to be an automated way to generate problem instances along with their solution without any human supervision.

As noted in Ref. [130], it also makes practical sense to search for AI problems that are useful because then the CAPTCHA will imply a win–win situation: either the CAPTCHA is not broken and there is a way to differentiate humans from computers or the CAPTCHA is broken and a useful AI problem is solved. To some extent, this symbiosis is similar to that between cryptography and number theory: as an example, it is worth noting the tremendous algorithmic progress that has been made in factoring numbers since RSA was invented.

Summing up, an ideal CAPTCHA could be considered as a function whose input parameters take random values, and which produces a challenge and an answer, in a way that they cannot be related automatically, but is easy for a human being to relate them [51]:

$$f(\text{random}) \Rightarrow (\text{challenge, answer})$$

2.2 Desirable Properties of CAPTCHAs

A CAPTCHA is not just an isolated hard AI problem to be solved. In real world scenarios, CAPTCHAs are to be deployed in Internet environments subject to heavy load by the use of thousands or even millions of users, and most likely under attack by hackers when the protected resource is appealing enough. As a consequence, choosing an interesting AI problem is not enough to make for a good CAPTCHA.

A usable CAPTCHA for security purposes should satisfy most, if not all, of the following properties:

1. *Efficient*: It should be taken quickly and easily by human users. While it would be ideal to have 100% recognition accuracy for human users, it would be safe to assume that human users would tolerate some lack of CAPTCHA ease. For instance, a human user might not be overly concerned with having to retry a CAPTCHA once in 10 attempts. This fact can be exploited while designing CAPTCHAs: some human recognition performance can be deliberately

sacrificed if it degrades machine performance by a considerable amount. However, it must have very low false negatives—false negative takes place when a legitimate human user is flagged as a bot. It should reject very few human users.

2. *Usable*: It should accept all human users with high reliability, without any discrimination based on mental or physical disabilities, race, language, genre, nor age. This property might require the combined use of different AI problems.

3. *Economical*: It is also desirable that its generation consumes a small amount of network and computational resources in the client and that the area it takes to present it to the user is small to allow for hand-held devices.

4. *Secure*: Virtually no machine should be able to solve it. The only way to pass the CAPTCHA should be to solve the underlying AI problem. A secure implementation should avoid side-channel attacks, described later in Section 5.1.4. It should have very few false positives—a false positive takes place when a bot is flagged as a legitimate human user. It should reject virtually all machine users.

5. *Transparent*: It should be difficult to write a computer program that can solve the AI problem posed by a CAPTCHA even if its algorithm and its data are known: the only hidden information is a small amount of randomness used to generate the tests. As opposed to the "security through obscurity" principle, in cryptography, this transparency is often referred to as Kerckhoffs' principle: a cryptosystem should be secure even if everything about the system, except the key, is public knowledge [81]. Another argument for disclosure is that, like cryptographic systems, CAPTCHAs benefit from peer review as well, which is usually successful at identifying weaknesses. This public scrutiny also allows researchers to compete with each other in an attempt to find CAPTCHAs with increasing levels of security, thus making the field advance.

6. *Robust*: The test should resist automatic attack for many years even as technology advances. Depending on the actual implementation, changing a CAPTCHA might be a costly and time-consuming process, leaving the application unprotected in the meantime. Such upgrades should happen rarely, if at all.

7. *Automated*: It must be generated and evaluated automatically. Obviously, a CAPTCHA that requires human supervision to evaluate answers would be impractical for large-scale deployment. A computer program should be able both to generate the challenges and mark the answers as qualifying or not.

8. *Random*: The random piece of information used to create the CAPTCHA should be generated in a truly random, unpredictable way. Otherwise, an adversary might attack the sequence generator instead of solving the AI puzzle.

9. *Large space*: It should be immune to brute force guessing attacks. This means that the CAPTCHA solution must occupy a space large enough so that both

simple dictionary attacks and exhaustive search attacks become impractical. Good CAPTCHAs rely on a completely random system of generation based on creating random word images or choosing files from a database consisting of many names, images, and other files. This database should be large enough to deter efforts to mine it all. The database used to create the CAPTCHA should not contain the solutions, because hackers could break into the database and obtain the solutions to the tests.

10. *Human cost*: A CAPTCHA is successful if the cost of answering challenges with a machine is higher than the cost of soliciting humans to perform the same task.

During their history, a number of CAPTCHAs have been proposed that do not fit some of these requirements, and depending of their popularity, they have been broken (automatically solved) quite often. Moreover, the security requirement, that is, the premise in CAPTCHA design that being able to build an automated system that solves a CAPTCHA should involve giving a fundamental step on solving a relevant AI problem, has been violated in practice, with no relevant contribution to AI [77]. This is due to the fact that, for the most part, the challenges in question are largely artificial, having little basis in the real world of an AI problem.

2.3 Implementation and Deployment

When Web designers want to install a CAPTCHA to protect a Web form, they have three main possibilities:

- Programming their own CAPTCHA. This is the most costly approach, as the designer has to program all the software (probably reusing existing graphic and voice libraries), ensuring that the challenge fits all previous features, and intensively testing it.
- Installing an available CAPTCHA software, or activating one available at the CMS he or she is using. Many commercial and open source CMSs currently include either their own CAPTCHAs or allow to insert them as plugins. For instance, the open source Java-based OpenCMS [2] includes CAPTCHAs as a part of the system; the open source systems Drupal (PHP-based) [39] and the Plone (Python-based) [90] admit CAPTCHAs as plugins; the proprietary IBM WebSphere server that powers Lotus Web Content Management solution [62] allows also CAPTCHA plugins, etc. Plugins and software packages include Securimage [89], WebSpamProtect [134], or WP Captcha-Free [138].

- Subscribing to an external CAPTCHA service and integrating it in the CMS/ Web server [116]. The generation and validation of the CATPCHA is done in a separate server (the service provider's one), and it is needed to include small pieces of code into the Web site to be protected. Example services include reCAPTCHA [47], captchas.net [20], or the WebSpam-Protect service cited above.

Implementing a CAPTCHA from scratch is not a trivial task. First of all, it is needed to implement all the steps of the Generalized Classical CAPTCHA algorithm [76]:

1. Computer generates a test instance.
2. Test is shown to the human/bot.
3. Human/bot attempts to solve the test.
4. Human/bot reports supposed solution to the computer.
5. Computer evaluates the submitted solution.
6. Computer reports the result of evaluation to the human/bot and allows or blocks access to a resource based on the result.

For the generation of the test instance, all previous desirable properties must be considered. Libraries and Application Programming Interfaces that help a programmer to write the test generation are very scarce. Moreover, while most of the programmers focus on the test generation, the rest of steps allow the programmed CAPTCHA to fail easily, making it vulnerable to the side-channel attack. If the user fails a CAPTCHA, the processing must be performed carefully to keep all the data he or she has already entered in the Web form, as it is very annoying for them to type these data again and again.

The design and implementation of CAPTCHAs by nonexperts is typically weak, because they are not aware of the current methods of CAPTCHA solving, and of the typical flaws present in CAPTCHA design. Instead of inventing a new CAPTCHA, it is a better security decision to use one whose robustness has been already tested. Installing existing CAPTCHA software comes with the same considerations as installing any packaged security control, like a firewall or antivirus. To be effective, the software makers have to update the software frequently to patch vulnerabilities in previous versions and to combat cracks.

The integration of an existing and tested CAPTCHA service in a Web server can be a relatively simple task. For instance, reCAPTCHA offers an e-mail address protection service named Mailhide, intended to hide an e-mail address in a Web page until the user demonstrated he or she is a human being. The integration of the Mailhide service implies including few lines of simple HTML/JavaScript code in the Web page, as shown in the Fig. 4. The code shown includes a hyper link ($<$a$>$) for a

```
<html>
  <title>
    Example of using reCAPTCHA Mailhide
  </title>
  <body>
    <p>
      Click on the link below to discover my email address:
    </p>
    <p>
      you
      <a href="http://www.google.com/recaptcha/mailhide/d?..."
        onclick="window.open(
          'http://www.google.com/recaptcha/mailhide/d?...',
          '',
          'toolbar=0,scrollbars=0,location=0,statusbar=0,
          menubar=0,resizable=0,width=500,heightt=300'
        );
        return false;"
        title="Reveal this e-mail address">
      ...</a>@example.com
    </p>
  </body>
</html>
```

FIG. 4. Mailhide reCAPTCHA Service HTML code.

part of the e-mail address to hide (. . .) which leads to the execution of a script when the action is clicking on it (onClick). The script opens a window (window.open ()) with a number of parameters (the address at which the CAPTCHA is generated, the parameters of CAPTCHA view, the size and outlook of the window, etc.), in which the CAPTCHA is shown, and after solved, the complete e-mail address is displayed, as shown in the Fig. 5.

2.4 Applications and the Rise of the Robots

Today CAPTCHAs are vastly applied in Internet environments to prevent resource abuse by bots, although marginally there exist some other applications, which will be described later in Section 2.4.2. Usually, Web sites are designed and intended for human use. According to Basso and Sicco [14], Web robots, or bots for

Click on the link below to discover my email address:

myad_...@example.com

Fig. 5. Web page displaying the Mailhide example.

short, can be defined as computer programs that run automated tasks over the Internet without the need of human interaction. Typically, bots perform tasks that are both simple and structurally repetitive, at a much higher rate than would be possible for a human alone.

From the point of view of the Web server, it is impossible to tell whether a Web request originated from a human user or from a bot: HTTP (Hypertext Transfer Protocol) requests look exactly the same. However, a bot can repeatedly perform Web-related activities, which have been thought and created as prerogatives of human beings, much more rapidly than a human user. As will be seen later in Section 6, these differences in behavior can become alternative ways to distinguish between human and machine users over Internet.

Provided that it is impossible to distinguish human users from machine users based solely on the HTTP protocol, CAPTCHAs provide a security barrier by posing a puzzle that human users can pass but machine users cannot. To be able to go ahead, first the CAPTCHA must be solved. It works as the gatekeeper to the Web resource coveted by the attacker.

In an effort to defeat all attempts to stop the proliferation of bots, automated tools are evolving toward the development of more complex and sophisticated programs, which posses an always increasing intelligence and can reproduce human actions with a high degree of fidelity.

The actions of bots can be driven by legitimate purposes or can rely on malicious plans. Therefore, robots can accomplish two opposite goals [14]:

- Help human beings in carrying out repetitive and time-consuming operations.
- Undertake hostile or illegal activities, becoming a serious threat to Web application security.

2.4.1   Legitimate Purposes of Robots

Currently, there are several situations in which using automated tools is mandatory, due to large amount of data to process. Some examples are:

- Web spidering or crawling [53]. A Web crawler is a computer program that browses the World Wide Web in a methodical, automated manner or in an orderly fashion. Many sites, in particular, search engines, use spidering as a means of providing up-to-date data. Web crawlers are mainly used to create a copy of all the visited pages for later processing by a search engine that will index the downloaded pages to provide fast searches. Crawlers can also be used for automating maintenance tasks on a Web site, such as checking links or validating HTML code. Legitimate Web bots identify themselves by the User-agent field of an HTTP request when they make a request to a Web server; for instance, Yahoo!'s Web crawler Slurp is identified with the following string: `Mozilla/5.0 (compatible; Yahoo! Slurp; http://help.yahoo.com/help/us/ysearch/slurp)`. Legitimate Web spiders usually respect the resources of Web servers according to the robots exclusion protocol, also known as the robots.txt protocol [93], that is, a standard for administrators to indicate which parts of their Web servers should not be accessed by crawlers.
- Web site mirroring [63]. For instance, the Internet Archive is a nonprofit that was founded to build an Internet library. Its purposes include offering permanent access for researchers, historians, scholars, people with disabilities, and the general public to historical collections that exist in digital format. The Internet Archive includes texts, audio, moving images, and software as well as archived Web pages in their collections, and it features a crawler named Heritrix and identified with the user agent field `archive.org_bot`.
- Vulnerability assessment [49]. This is the process of performing a security review of a Web application by searching for design flaws, vulnerabilities, and inherent weaknesses. It can be automated by using a software that retrieves Web site pages and builds specific requests to find unvalidated inputs, improper error handling, cross site scripting, etc. An example of an automated Web site vulnerability assessment tool is White-Hat Sentinel [136].
- Chat and instant messaging system management. For instance, an Internet relay chat (IRC) bot is a set of scripts or an independent program that connects to IRC

as a client, to perform automated functions that include preventing malicious users from taking over the channel, logging what happens in an IRC channel, giving out information on demand, creating statistics, hosting trivia games, etc.

Unfortunately, not always previous uses are legitimate. For instance, Web crawlers can be used to gather specific types of information from Web pages, such as harvesting e-mail addresses (most often for spamming). These bots identify themselves as legitimate users or as search engine bots to disguise their ultimate goal. Another example is malicious IRC bots [19], designed for the purpose of infecting other users with viruses, sending spam, or controlling botnets for spamming and Denial of Service attacks.

There are also some activities in the fringes of legality. For instance, gaming bots can be used for fair purposes (e.g., as competitors or collaborators in a game, featuring week AI functions), or for unfair purposes (like those used as a help to the user for collecting resources, increasing player's avatar experience, etc.). As another example, automated trading systems help stock brokers to, for example, make sells or purchases under certain conditions. However, they can also be used for artificially manipulating stock prices.

2.4.2 CAPTCHA Applications: Malicious Activities of Robots

Automation based attacks are those which do not actually violate a specific security rule; they simply use (or misuse) a legitimate system in a superhuman way, performing requests to the system repeatedly and in a high rate, to achieve some objective that goes against the initial goals of the systems designer. Some computer systems are designed with the assumption that only humans will use them, factoring human limitations as a part of the systems security policy. This way, such computer systems do not worry about imposing restrictions on, for example, an excessive high rate of requests per second, because this is simply not humanly possible. The problem happens when superhumans, or computer software robots, enter in action. They can repeat the same request several times every second, disrupting the original intent of the vulnerable computer system. Thus, a simple electronic mailing server, while being under an automation based attack, may become a disgusting spam relayer.

However, most uses associated to the action of bots are malicious: they are created to abuse Internet services intended only for human interaction. The motivation behind bots is usually financial profit. Some of the illegitimate purposes they are used for include, although are not limited to, the following:

- Free e-mail account registration: these are later used to massively send spam; to send phishing messages to harvest credentials of financial and e-commerce sites; to send scam messages to defraud a person or group by gaining their confidence; to distribute malware, usually in the form of banking trojans, again for financial gain; etc. For instance, spam sent using shortened URLs used in microblogging services like Twitter has reached up to 18.0% of spam some days, and while most of this spam is generated from botnets, and it is believed that the 28% of it may be connected with other nonbotnet sources of spam, such as Webmail accounts that have been created using CAPTCHA-breaking tools [121].
- Systematical database mining: buying event tickets to resell them at a higher price; downloading and archiving an entire Web site or FTP server, with pseudo-public files such as research papers, picture repositories, and shareware programs; etc.
- Massive voting in opinion polls, best product contests, product recommendation systems, popularity contests, etc. The very famous 1999 online poll proposed by slashdot.com about the best graduate school in computer science soon degenerated into a contest between voting bots written by Carnegie Mellon and MIT students [130]. IP address recording and blocking is not enough to protect against ingeniously designed bots. In general, bots can be used to abuse usage policies based on given thresholds, and to violate rate limiting in Web-based services.
- Brute force and dictionary attacks on password based Web authentication systems: the cracking program can sequentially submit every possible login/ password combination until a match is found. This process might go on for days, weeks, and even months without the Web site noticing that no detecting measures are into place. Many mechanisms exist to prevent and/or detect cracking, such as account or IP address blocking after a threshold of failed login attempts is exceeded, or log reviewing, but they pose their own problems, sometimes discouraging their use.
- Comment and Web spam [8]: they can be inserted in virtually every site which reflects the comments so that other users can see them, such as in blogs, forums, newsgroups, product reviews in consumer groups, etc. These comment fields are thus used usually for the purpose of raising search engine ranks of some Web site by getting backlinks, or to announce fraudulent products, divert traffic to malware distributing Web sites, etc. Comment and Web spam can include not only commercial promotions but also harassment and vandalism.

- Operations in online social networks: due to the increasing popularity of professional and general-purpose online social networks among Internet users, they are becoming a preferred attack target. Certain actions can be automated to the advantage of the attacker, such as sending requests to add new contacts in an effort to expand the social network and reach more victims, sending private messages with spam or malware, etc.
- Massive multiplayer online role-playing games (MMORPG): to farm for resources that would otherwise take significant time or effort to obtain [141].

CAPTCHAs can be used against all previous illegitimate usage of bots, in Web environments. Moreover, CAPTCHAs can also be used in other non-Web abuses. For instance, CAPTCHAs also offer a plausible solution against e-mail worms and spam; a user may only accept an e-mail if they know there is a human behind the other computer (e.g., Ref. [115]). This kind of antivirus and antispam technique can be called "human postage," as the sender of the e-mail is forced to invest a part of their time (i.e., money) in solving a CAPTCHA. Also, CAPTCHAs can be used to prevent bots joining IRC channels, as they may be intended to make illegitimate operations like gaining operator privileges at the channels. This technique has been further extended to SMS spam [110].

2.4.3 Other Applications

While the general application of CAPTCHAs is providing protection against all previous automated abuses of resources, they have a collateral benefit. As abusers are highly (and most often economically) motivated to pursue CAPTCHA violation, if the implemented versions of CAPTCHA are secure, they are forced to design and implement systems able to solve the underlying AI problem (accurately recognizing text in images, etc.). It is a win–win situation:

- The CAPTCHA is able to resist all attacks by posing a complex challenge, thus providing a reliable security service to protect an application.
- The CAPTCHA is broken at the cost of solving a complex, AI problem, thus pushing the state of the art in a particular AI area.

However, CAPTCHAs provide a security service at the expense of a lot of time wasted by human users to solve them. For instance, von Ahn et al. [132] estimate that humans around the world type more than 100 million CAPTCHAs every day, in each case, spending a few seconds typing the distorted characters. In aggregate, this amounts to hundreds of thousands of human hours per day.

To avoid wasting such human effort, CAPTCHAs can provide alternative usages of it by including a collateral application. Examples of these collateral applications include:

- Helping to digitalize books and newspapers. For instance, the system reCAPTCHA presents two words to the users, a random one and another coming from a book or newspaper. When the human writes both words, he or she is transcribing the second word, that is, acting as a human OCR system. By using several voting and testing mechanisms, von Ahn et al. demonstrate that this effort leads to an OCR quality over 99%, much over automated OCR programs (83.5%). Moreover, according to the system's popularity, the rate of transcription currently exceeds 4 million suspicious words per day, which is equivalent to about 160 books per day.

- Promoting pet adoption. Initially conceived and presented by Oli Warner in the form of KittenAuth [87], and further developed by Microsoft in Asirra [41], this CAPTCHA presents the user a number of pictures and he or she has to identify which of them are cats, as shown in the Fig. 6. Cat pictures are taken from database of a pet adoption promotion Web site (petfinder.com), hopefully improving the number of adoptions. In the Asirra Fig. 7, it is shown how moving the pointer over one of the pictures shows it in a larger size, with the promoted site and a link to adopt it.

- Serving advertisements, as discussed above with the example of the advertising company Solve Media [117], and as shown in the Fig. 3.

Obviously, the latest examples of collateral applications of CAPTCHAs do not explicitly exploit the huge amount of human effort that reCAPTCHA does. The idea behind reCAPTCHA can be framed into the concept of human computation or crowd sourcing, sketched by Louis von Ahn [131] and currently offered in the cloud-services market by companies like Amazon with their Amazon Mechanical Turk [3].

3. Types of CAPTCHAs

There are many possible classifications of CAPTCHAs. For the sake of clarity, we divided them into two broad categories, represented in the Fig. 8: visual and Nonvisual. Among the first group, visual, there are in turn two main categories: OCR-based and image-based. Among the second group, nonvisual, there are again two main categories: audio-based and cognitive-based. In the following sections, the main proposals in each category are reviewed.

FIG. 6. The KittenAuth CAPTCHA.

An important issue regarding this classification is that some authors are proposing combinations of CAPTCHAs to strengthen the verification test, by chaining several challenges that can be of the same type or of mixed types. For instance, Olumide et al. propose the multiple challenge-response system (M-CR CAPTCHA) [76], in which the user is presented with two CAPTCHAs: a mathematical one (type: cognitive) and a letter recognition one (type: OCR). If each test can be solved by a bot with a one over a hundred probability, the bot will only able to solve both tests in one over 10,000 times. However, the underlying tests fit into several classes in this taxonomy.

Please select all the cat photos:

Score Test

Fig. 7. The Asirra CAPTCHA when one picture is being pointed.

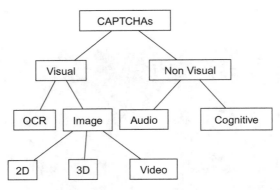

Fig. 8. Different types of CAPTCHAs.

3.1 OCR

The majority of CAPTCHAs used on the Web today rely on the difficulty of OCR, that is, the difficulty of automatically reading distorted text. Their challenges are created as follows: pick a word, pick a typeface, render the word using the typeface into an image, and degrade the image. The choices of word, typeface, and degradation must be engineered to yield images which are easy for humans to recognize but baffling to all OCR systems now and, one hopes, for years to come.

As a general comment, these choices can be:

- *Word choice*: Words can be chosen from a predefined dictionary (usually from a language dictionary or from a number of texts in a database), or they can be randomly generated as sequences of characters that may include letters (usually in an Western language) and/or numbers. The experience in evaluating CAPTCHA simplicity for humans say that this selection can be critical. For instance, words or letters from a Western language may pose special difficulties for Eastern-language countries citizens (e.g., China). Also this selection is important for making CAPTCHAs robust against dictionary attacks.

- *Typeface choice*: Two main options are choosing the same typeface or font for all the characters in the string, or mixing several typefaces. Again, mixing fonts is more robust and secure, but it may affect human readability. Different character sizes can also be chosen.

- *Degradation algorithms*: There are many degradation algorithms used in the bibliography below. These algorithms are intended to make current OCR programs failing on automatically reading the rendered text, so they somehow exploit current OCR difficulties. These difficulties include separating the letters to be recognized from the background, segmenting the input string into characters, etc. There are specific difficulties that may affect humans much less than computers, like mixing text in positive and in negative on a plain background, but others may even affect more humans than bots, leading to poor CAPTCHAs.

The first CAPTCHA of this type [72], used by AltaVista to block automated upload of URLs to their search engine, is based on the following process:

1. Utilization of a random string generator that selects ASCII characters able to be rendered, one by turn, and builds a target string.
2. Using a random appearance module that changes the orientation and position of each character but keeping the overall character string sorted from left to right.
3. Using a random background module that generates a noisy background such as a maze.
4. Rendering the distorted string on the generated background, and sending it to the client side (the user browser) in a HTML form that allows to enter an answer to the challenge.

Eventually, CAPTCHAs are being defeated by automated systems (either conceived by abusers or by researchers), and other researchers and service providers provide modifications of the generation modules above to make the challenge secure again, mostly following the previous steps. For instance, GIMPY [130] CAPTCHA was the fruit of collaboration between Yahoo! and CMU where the term "CAPTCHA" was first used. The developed algorithm picks English words at random from a subset of 850 words in the Ogden dictionary, and transforms them into an image after severe deformation and image occlusion with some overlapping. The user is challenged to read some number of words correctly (not necessarily all displayed words). An example is shown in the Fig. 9. It was found that users experienced difficulties with this type of CAPTCHA due to its complexity; so, the algorithm was quickly replaced by EZ-Gimpy which uses only one English word, which was better tolerated by users (Fig. 1).

Yahoo! used this CAPTCHA until it was broken by Mori et al. [83] using object recognition algorithms based on shape context matching, and by Moy et al. [84] using distortion estimation techniques [84]. The problem of identifying words in such severe clutter provides valuable insight into the more general problem of object recognition in scenes.

Coates et al. have proposed PessimalPrint [32], whose lexicon contains only 70 common English word which are between 5 and 8 characters. The algorithm uses the

Fɪɢ. 9. A Gimpy CAPTCHA image.

Baird degradation model [9] simulating physical defects caused by copying and scanning of printed text. An example of degradation includes salt and pepper noise, condensed fonts, and skewed characters. The algorithm is usually easy to beat as it uses a very small dictionary and is vulnerable to brute force attacks.

Chew and Baird have further proposed BaffleText [28], in which the challenge is generated by producing a pronounceable character string not present in a dictionary, choosing a font, rendering the string on an image without degradation, generating a mask image using circles and ellipses, and applying a masking operation to combine the image and the mask. Experiments with humans demonstrate that the difficulty of this CAPTCHA is highly correlated with the density and size of the circles and ellipses: the more dense and smaller, the more difficult to read it is, as it can be seen in the Fig. 10. This work has been continued with ScatterType [11–13], in which the base image with the string is splitted into several parts with random rotation values, and random lines are drawn on a grid background. Lines are in the same color with the CAPTCHA text and they provide a distortion of image with grid background [60]. User studies demonstrated that some characters were specially difficult for humans (e.g., a "C" and a "G" can be easily confused when small parts of the character disappear—the right tail in "G").

Most previous CAPTCHAs have been broken by a process of removing background noise and applying segmentation algorithms to separate the individual characters that make the string to be entered by the CATPCHA user [26]. It is obvious that the ability of image processing techniques has been quite underestimated by CAPTCHA designers. To make segmentation difficult for bots, Simard et al. [116] have proposed to add arcs that randomly break and join the separation among characters in the input string of the CAPTCHA image generator, along with using random distortion in letter rendering and improving the randomness of the function to generate the string (i.e., true random string generation instead of phonetic rules, selection from limited dictionaries, etc.). The arcs used must also be random in thickness, length, etc., as shown in the Fig. 11. This CAPTCHA techniques have been used by Microsoft registration servers (e.g., the Hotmail Web e-mail service).

FIG. 10. Examples of BaffleText CAPTCHAs with different densities and circle sizes.

FIG. 11. Examples of adding random arcs to make segmentation difficult.

To make character edge detection difficult for computer, Ferzli et al. [43] have further proposed on the masking characteristics of the human visual system (HVS). The visual CAPTCHA is formed by adding (Gaussian) noise and texture throughout the image in different amounts To control the masking so that letters (or patterns) can be made visible or invisible depending on the amount of masking. So, in some places,

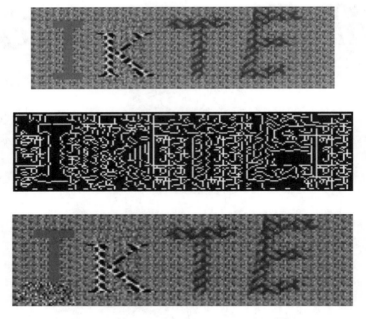

FIG. 12. Adding noise and textures to make edge detection difficult.

the noise is masked by texture while, in other places, the noise is itself masking edges. The machine can see the unseen and can detect both masked and unmasked edges and noise. This makes it harder for the machine to estimate the amount of injected noise and to predict what the human observer can see or not see. For instance, in the Fig. 12 it is shown how edge detection is difficult, but even more, while the machine is able to detect one of the characters (the "I"), it is not able to predict that the user will be able to see it, thus adding complexity to the CAPTCHA. Moreover in the third image, this property in strengthened by adding more noise to the detected character.

To improve all previous methods, and in addition to introducing noise to the background and the text characters, distorting the letters, etc., Gupta et al. [50,91] have proposed to add small disguised numbers to the letters to request the user to enter the recognized letters sorted according the attached numbers to them, as shown in the Fig. 13. This feature makes what is called a sequenced tagged captcha, and it adds a combinatorial difficulty to the proposed CAPTCHA, although no human studies prove that these CAPTCHAs are successful enough with human users.

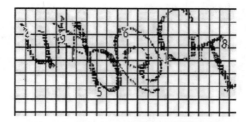

FIG. 13. The Sequenced Tagged Captcha adds numbers to the letters and requests the user to follow the resulting order.

It is known that humans reading familiar text perform better than on unfamiliar text. Computer vision systems also can exploit some kinds of linguistic context: many OCR systems can use known lexica. While human readers can exploit a range of degrees of familiarity, OCR technologies for exploiting such constraints (absent a fixed, known lexicon) are immature. This gap in ability between humans and machines may allow us to design stronger CAPTCHAs by exploiting trade offs between familiarity of challenge strings and degradation of the image [133].

In the work by Rusu et al. [96,97,123], a new improvement is proposed in the generation of the text string before applying disguising transformations. Instead of generating the string by a random-, phonetic-, or lexicon-driven model, samples of handwritten text and their corresponding electronic versions are collected (e.g., from postal applications). Moreover, the distortion algorithms are based on the ability gap between humans and machines in handwriting recognition using Gestalt laws of perception, by adding strokes, mirroring, and other features as shown in the Fig. 14. The authors demonstrate that the generated CAPTCHAs are robust against automated word recognizers, while keeping enough human readability.

There are some other proposals regarding OCR-based Human Interactive Proofs (e.g., Ref. [71]), but all of them mostly follow the previous schema.

3.2   Image

3.2.1   2D Images

In contrast to previous OCR-based reverse Turing tests, in which there is a clear and simple model for the generation of the challenge, the rest of visual tests is much more heterogeneous. However, some regularities exist:

- These challenges are in general based on the human ability to "semantically" interpret pictures. Given the current state-of-the-art in computer vision, we are

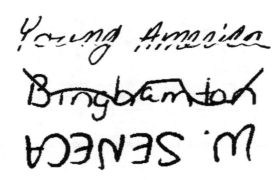

Fig. 14. Handwritten texts can be used to generate CAPTCHAs.

still far away from building systems able to describe a picture in terms of the objects, persons, actions, feelings, etc., present in it.

- Although simpler CAPTCHAs are based on selection procedures, these are generally improved by adding specific complex actions, like effects on the images (rotation, blurring, etc.), or requesting more advanced actions by the user (drag and drop, match pictures with labels, clicks on objects, etc.).

A major drawback of these challenges is that most of them have not been tested widely in the real world, while OCR CAPTCHAs are widely spread and tested; and sometimes, broken.

CAPTCHAs based on 2D-images request the users to work with 2D relations on the images, that is, they do not request the user to actively employ 3D abilities like "choose the object behind the tree" or "read the background text."

Selection CAPTCHAs are a major class among the family of image challenges. In these class, the user is required to choose one or several images from a table according to their properties. For instance, the previously mentioned KittenAuth and Asirra CAPTCHAs [41] rely on the problem of distinguishing images of cats from other animals. Asirra stands for "Animal Species Image Recognition for Restricting Access," and the challenge consists of 12 images, each of which is of either a cat or a dog. To solve the CAPTCHA, the user must select all the cat images, and none of the dog images. This is a task that humans are very good at. According to Elson et al. [41], Asirra "can be solved by humans 99.6% of the time in under 30 seconds." The usability of Asirra is a significant advantage compared to CAPTCHAs based on recognizing distorted strings of letters and numbers. The security of Asirra is based on the presumed difficulty of classifying images of cats and dogs automatically, but it has been broken in Ref. [45] with success probability 10.3%.

Another picture selection test are Collage CAPTCHAs [105,106,108]. In this method, some pictures are chosen randomly and after effecting some changes such as rotating, all of them are shown on the screen. Then we ask the user to choose a specific object. If the user chooses the right object we can guess that the user has been a human being not computer software.

In Implicit CAPTCHAs [10], the user has to make a simple click. For example, the picture of a mountain is shown to the user and he is asked to click on its top or a number of words are shown in an image and the user asked to click on a specific word, as in the Fig. 15. This method is expected to be easier for the users, although it has more cost for computers. Moreover, images can be reused as there are a lot reference points to be chosen for other instances of the CAPTCHA, highlighted in green on the picture. On the other side, creating these challenges involves a rather costly human task of selecting areas in the pictures and labeling them.

The idea of semantically exploiting real pictures is further developed in the PIX family of CAPTCHAs [23]. In this method, usual pictures, a library of pictures with different subjects is prepared and a number of these pictures that have a similar subject is selected and shown to the user while asking the user to select the subject of the picture from among the subjects shown, like in the Fig. 16. However, this method requires a large space for keeping the pictures and the library should also be very extensive, which in turn requires large expenses. This problem can be solved by developing free games in which the players label the images, as described in Ref. [131].

FIG. 15. In Implicit CAPTCHAs, the user is requested to click on a semantically labeled area.

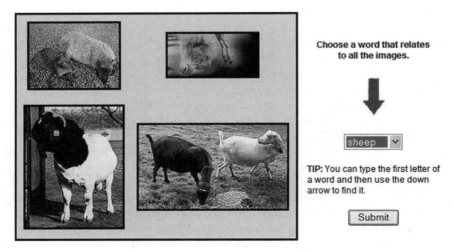

FIG. 16. An example of a PIX CAPTCHA.

Another proposal is the Bongo CAPTCHA [22], which asks the user to solve a visual pattern recognition problem. It displays two series of blocks, the left and the right. The blocks in the left series differ from those in the right, and the user must find the characteristic that sets them apart. A possible left and right series is shown in the Fig. 17. After seeing the two series of blocks, the user is presented with a single block and is asked to determine whether this block belongs to the left series or to the right. The user passes the test if he or she correctly determines the side to which the block belongs. As this can be solved by a bot by randomly choosing one of the two sides, the user can be requested to determine what makes both series different, from a set of options.

Further developments of previous ideas include:

- *The naming CAPTCHA* [29]: the user is shown a group of object pictures and is required to identify the common theme among the pictures and type it as an answer.

- *The sequenced picture CAPTCHA* [65]: it presents several object pictures, each of which is accompanied by a tag. The user is required to determine the logical sequence of the displayed object pictures based on the tags. Hence, the user is required to identify both the object pictures and the tags, and thus, it introduces two levels of security.

- *The anomaly CAPTCHA* [29]: the user is required to click the anomalous picture from among a group of object pictures.

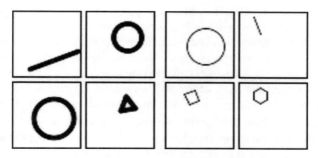

FIG. 17. An example of a Bongo challenge.

- *IMAGINATION* [37]: the system produces controlled distortions on randomly chosen images and present them to the user for annotation from a given list of words. The distortions are performed in a way that satisfies the incongruous requirements of low perceptual degradation and high resistance to attack by content-based image retrieval systems. Word choices are carefully generated to avoid ambiguity as well as to avoid attacks based on the choices themselves.

Other related CAPTCHAs in this family include the activity recognition CAPTCHA [127], facial expressions [126], or face recognition CAPTCHAs [82].

While previous CAPTCHAs do not request complex actions (but cognitive power) from the users, other methods have been proposed to exploit manipulation abilities. For instance:

- The drawing CAPTCHA [103] is designed for devices using light pen like PDA (personal digital assistant). In this method, numerous dots are drawn on a screen with noisy background and the user is asked to connect certain dots to each other. In view of the problems that computers face in recognizing the dots from the noise, only a human user can easily identify the special dots and connect them to each other. Unlike the other CAPTCHA methods, the users of any language in any age group can use this program and run it on devices with more limited resources than the computer.

- Zhangs CAPTCHA [146] is based on intelligent interaction, and it includes two lines of defenses against various types of attacks. The first line is constructed on rich client-side via Flex through intelligent interaction such as actions of drag–drop similar to computer games. The second line is constructed on the server side by comparing random state parameters such as Session-ID and Hidden-data between rich client-side and server-side to prevent automated programs to circumvent CAPTCHA and directly attack the server.

- The highlighting CAPTCHA [102] is proposed for touch-screen devices such as PDAs and mobile phones, and it is a combination of both OCR and non-OCR methods. In this system a random word is generated and drawn in a random place on the screen. Then various pictorial effects are applied to it and some noises are added to screen. Then the user is asked to highlight this word by the stylus. Due to the limitations of the PDA and mobile phone, OCR programs on these devices cannot recognize the shown word and only a human user can highlight the word.
- The Drag and Drop [38] challenge uses mouse actions for the distinction between human and computers. It uses familiar action of dragging and dropping items into specific regions. In this test, the user has to solve a normal CAPTCHA image, but he or she cannot type the answer of the test into text box. Instead, the user has to drag and drop character blocks into their respective blank spaces as they appear in the image.
- The rotCAPTCHA [48] is based on identifying an image upright orientation. To be strong, only images that are difficult to be automatically set upright are chosen, by the use a suite of automated orientation detectors. The user is requested to put the image upright by using a slider.
- The MosaHIP [14] proposes a mosaic-based Human Interactive Proof, in which the user is requested to drag and drop the resource to be accessed (e.g., a MPEG video) on to a picture in a blurred mosaic, which is in turn described in terms of cognitive hard features. For instance, the user can be requested to drag and drop on "something existing" and "laying upon" the rest of the images that make the mosaic.

Additional works which request the user relatively complex manipulation tasks include generating 2D CAPTCHAs from 3D Models [57], exchanging image blocks [70], Tree and Shape CAPTCHAs [95], and using facial features as in ARTiFA-CIAL [94].

3.2.2   3D Images

The previous concepts can be developed from a 2D scenario into a 3D one. For instance, the 3D CAPTCHA [58] consists of the alphanumeric characters which are letters and numbers. The text is composed of six characters, and each of which has its own axis and rotation angle. Each character is rotated in a certain angle ranging from $-45°$ to $45°$ by using standard randomization function. In consequence, adding the 3D component makes the CAPTCHA harder for OCR programs, while keeping visual usability for humans.

Another instance of 3D Image CAPTCHAs is the Cube CAPTCHA [59]. This test shows randomly selected characters and numbers on each cube faces to the end users. Users were requested to type in each character on the face of cube to input boxes properly. This model cannot be solved by OCR programs because the cube shows only a few faces at the same time and hides the remaining faces. Therefore any kind of image recognition programs cannot see the CAPTCHA text as a whole. Another significant feature of this model is the rotator which is used to move the cube. Moving the cube by this feature is intuitive to the users who are experienced in 3D graphic user interfaces.

It is remarkable that 3D CAPTCHAs have entered into production. For instance, the site YUNiTI.com [145] is making use of a 3D-CAPTCHA which offers the users three boxes, and the user has to select the appropriate 3D-object in each box while keeping the order in which the objects are rendered in the challenge image. An example of this CAPTCHA is shown in the Fig. 18.

As a final comment on 3D CAPTCHAs, it is clear that using 3D images make attack techniques harder, but none of the previously mentioned ones really exploits the concept of 3D in a cognitive fashion. For instance, in a 3D scenario, a user may be requested to select a particular object which is behind a different one, thus using not only 3D image recognition abilities but also the knowledge about 3D relations in a picture.

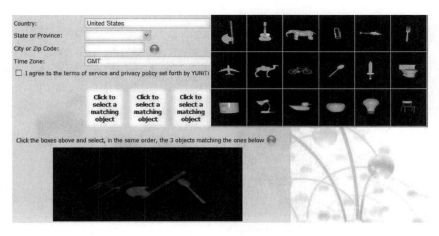

FIG. 18. The YUNiTI 3D CAPTCHA.

3.2.3   Video

In video CAPTCHAs, humans are intended to exploit their perception abilities regarding movement to solve them. The state-of-the-art in video recognition is still far from reaching human levels of competence regarding the identification of semantic items in videos.

Some basic approaches make use of video as an additional challenge disguising technique. For instance, the three-layer dynamic CAPTCHA [34] presents a character layer, a background interference layer, and a foreground interference layer. To further enhance security, the characters are overlapped partially. The three layers are animated and trajectories of characters in each CAPTCHA image are different, further increasing the difficulty of attack.

Animating text is being exploited commercially. For instance, NuCaptcha [86] offers the users an animated video with some highlighted letters to be typed into a box. The video includes an advertisement, much in the same fashion as Solve Media challenges. The system is offered as a service that acts as an ad delivery platform. An example of a Nucaptcha challenge is shown in the Fig. 19.

However, other, more sophisticated approaches try to involve semantics of video scenes to make the challenge resolution harder. For instance, the 3D animation [33] non-OCR-based CAPTCHA method in the form of 3D animation and based on the recognition of moving objects in videos. Another example, the Motion CAPTCHA [109] is based on describing a person's action. A movie is shown to the user and he or she should select the sentence which describes the motion of the person in the

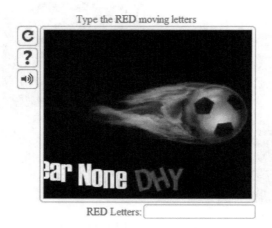

FIG. 19. The NuCaptcha challenge.

movie from a list of sentences. For implementing this method, a database of movies, which are described by natural language sentences, is needed.

In the video CAPTCHA presented by Kluever and Zanibbi [68], a user must provide three words (tags) describing a video taken from a public database. Words may be submitted as the video plays, that is, the user does not have to wait for the video to finish before submitting her three words. In its simplest form, a challenge is passed if any of the three submitted tags match an author-supplied tag associated with the video. This challenge is similar to the image labeling game known as ESP created by von Ahn et al. [131], in which people are randomly paired up and then try to guess a common tag for an image. The video CAPTCHA is similar to playing a game of ESP using videos, but where one player's responses (the ground truth set) are automatically generated from tags associated with videos in the database.

Athanasopoulos and Antonatos have presented an animated CAPTCHA [5] that displays several randomly moving items (apples, tigers, etc.) on a noisy background that is randomly changing also. The users are requested to click on one of the moving objects according to a text (e.g., click on the red apple). As it can be seen, this challenge also forces the user to have manual abilities apart from cognitive ones.

A major problem in the semantic video CAPTCHAs is that a database of samples (videos plus labels, actions, etc.) has to be collected to build the system. This database must be very large for disallowing sampling attacks, which have been successful with a number of previous challenges. The construction of such a database requires a huge human work. On the other side, the free-game framework proposed by von Ahn can solve this problem, although it is not clear if malicious users may poison the database. A more imaginative solution may be combining the ideas behind the tagging games and the reCAPTCHA techniques for human OCR, by requesting several tags from the users, and using some of them as answers to the challenge, and others for augmenting the database with the appropriate quality checks (e.g., inter-indexer consistency, etc.). Exactly this approach is proposed by Chew and Tygar [30].

3.3   Audio

Audio CAPTCHAs are based on delivering the user a sound and requesting him or her to recognize it. The audio provided is most often a sequence of letters or numbers said by different speakers on different noisy environments, to exploit the weaknesses of current audio recognition systems. The audio CAPTCHAs can be used in two ways:

- For offering impaired people with an alternative way to solve a main CAPTCHA. Several of the previously described tests do provide an audio alternative, represented as a button showing an speaker (see e.g., reCAPTCHA in the Fig. 2, Solve Media in the Fig. 3, or the NuCaptcha in the Fig. 19).

- For interaction channels in which is impossible to offer an image or video. The most evident utilization of CAPTCHAs is stopping SPIT (Spam over Internet Telephony), that is, automatic callers that abuse current Voice over IP (VoIP) systems.

One of the first works in this area was done by Kochanski et al. [36], who proposed a speech reverse Turing test by using the Bell Labs English text-to-speech system with the default male voice to generate sequences of five digits, and then distorting the signal. An exhaustive analysis of why persons and speech-to-text systems fail to recognize the sequence has been performed in the paper, providing valuable insights on how to design the test to separate humans from bots based on speech recognition. Exactly a 5-digit voice CAPTCHA has been proposed and a prototype for Skype has been developed by Markkola and Lindqvist [79].

Soupionis and Girtzalis [118] have performed a rather intensive evaluation of audio CAPTCHAs available in free services like reCAPTCHA, or in sites like MSN, Google, eBay, etc. They have defined the audio CAPTCHA production as an staged process quite similar to the previous one for OCR CAPTCHAs, which involves the selection of a vocabulary/character set, the utilization of noise, the utilization of several speakers, the composition of the final audio file (whether it is a sequence of files or just one), etc. Moreover, they have used open source software and their own bot to evaluate the security of previous tests with considerable success. Soupionis and Girtzalis propose their own audio CAPTCHA for detecting SPIT, which uses a four-digit pronounced CAPTCHA that uses seven different speakers, background noise, and intermediate noise like a sound between characters to make the file segmentation difficult. In their work, a good increase of security against the bots that defeat previous CAPTCHAs is shown, but a usability study is not performed.

3.4   Cognitive

A wide range of challenges have also been proposed in the literature, based on the semantic interpretation of texts and images. Although some of the previous CAPTCHAs rely on cognitive abilities (e.g., distinguishing a cat from a dog), the tests reviewed in this section take the challenge to a higher level. Most of them are based on the reading abilities of human beings, yet far from Natural Language Processing or Understanding systems. Also, most of them present variations of choosing the appropriate word in a context, facing the problem of human language ambiguity.

In consequence, a CAPTCHA in the text domain would draw the inner workings from AI problems that could be found within text constructs and would require only plain text to be assembled. Besides granting new possibilities to the CAPTCHA paradigm, a CAPTCHA in the text domain would be specially suitable for devices with low accessibility capabilities and for visually impaired users, since it would not require any advanced graphical screens and no multimedia features [139].

A first instance can be the Text-CAPTCHA [44]. In this challenge, a word from a piece of text taken from a data source of human-written text is randomly selected and substituted by another word selected at random, in the hope that it would be easy for humans to pick that word (because it did not fit in the context), but difficult for computers. However, it is demonstrated also in Ref. [44] that it was possible to write a program that had considerable success-rates in "cheating" the test by taking into account statistical characteristics of natural language.

In Ref. [15], it is proposed the use of lexical semantics to construct a test that draws its security from the problem of word-sense ambiguity, that is, the phenomenon that a single word can have different meanings, and that different words can have the same meaning, depending on the context in which a word is used. Despite the fact that indeed this CAPTCHA proposes a task difficult for computers and easy for humans, it violates Kerckhoff's principle that is present in the CAPTCHA paradigm, as the efficacy of the test is based on the secrecy of the database that holds the "secret annotations," which are mappings necessary for the disambiguation process, which is all it is necessary to solve the test.

An alternative can be the KK Joke CAPTCHA [139], which consists basically of a challenge that would present a set of Knock Knock Joke-like structures to the user. Despite all of the presented structures would be built upon the same general linguistic structure, only one of them would make sense as a real KK joke. The user would have to identify the correct joke within the set to prove his human condition.

What if for a specialized resource, we require that the human is also a professional with knowledge about the field of the resource? Exam HIP [114] is a proposal in this line. The CAPTCHA shows a picture of a multiple-choice question. This multiple-choice question is related to some protected information in the field of user's profession. As the picture of the question is viewed, the computer cannot answer it. On the other hand, only experts and professional people, or people related to the concerned subject, can answer the question and have access to the requested information because of the professional nature of the question.

The question-based CAPTCHA proposed in Ref. [107] is a combination of OCR-based and non-OCR-based methods. In this test, a mathematical question based on a predesigned pattern is shown as a combination of text and image of objects as a single image. The only thing the user has to do is to enter the answer only as a number. Considering the computer's difficulty in recognition of the text of the question, in recognition of question image, understanding of the problem, and solving the problem, it is assumed that only a human user can answer this question.

A rather different approach, but closely related, is exploiting the particular lack of quality of Machine Translation. The SS-CAPTCHA [140] detects an automated program by checking if a user can distinguish natural sentences created by humans from machine-translated sentences. To be more precise, a system simultaneously presents P natural sentences created by humans and Q garbage sentences generated from a natural sentence by a machine translator to a user. These $(P+Q)$ sentences are placed in random order. The user is then required to select P natural sentences from the $(P+Q)$ sentences. If the user can correctly select all P natural sentences, she is certified to be human.

A test that further exploits semantic interpretation is SemCAPTCHA [78], which consists of a distorted picture, on which three words are presented. One word differs from the other two in its meaning. The task is to recognize this word and point it by a mouse click. It has to be stressed that the words do not differ substantially as for their graphical properties (e.g., length): the difference is of semantic character. However, given that current OCR systems and image processing techniques can be quite successful in detecting the boundaries of the words, a bot's random attach could guess the correct answer with a 33% of likelihood.

CAPTCHAs in the text domain have also been deployed in practical settings. For instance, a text based CAPTCHA has been provided as a Web service by Rob Tuley [92]. This CAPTCHA offers a wide sample of simple logic questions (over 180 millions), like the following ones:

- 39, 29, and 34: the 3rd number is?
- Which of these is a color: yellow, rice, bank, shirt, or restaurant?
- How many letters in "fattest"?
- Knee, tongue, head, or chin: which is below the waist?
- If the shirt is brown, what color is it?

In the previous list of questions, there is not a clear pattern, and all of them can be easily solved by an English-speaking person. However, the author does not state which patterns are used for generating the question, and this is critical to assess the security of the challenge.

4. Evaluation of CAPTCHAs

CAPTCHAs have been proposed as a security mechanism to prevent automated systems to abuse services intended only for human users. So far, we have presented a number of CAPTCHA proposals that make use of a wide range of techniques for obscuring an underlying message (most often, a sequence of characters) for making its deciphering hard for bots, while trying to keep it solvable by humans. As a consequence, there is a clear trade-off between making things hard for bot while keeping them easy for humans. This trade-off has lead Chellapilla et al. [25] to define a line between the point of making challenges too easy for computers and the point of making them too hard for humans, in which there is a middle region, the "sweet spot," in which tests are still feasible by humans but too hard for automated systems.

How to ensure that the proposed challenge is in this sweet spot? This is the goal of evaluating CAPTCHAs. However, on one side there has been a number of successful attacks to CAPTCHAs that do not rely on trying to solve the underlying AI problem, like the side-channel attack (which targets the implementation of the system, exploiting, e.g., the possibility of reusing sessions), or the sampling attack (e.g., collecting and manually solving samples of a CAPTCHA that selects the challenge from a small number of inputs). On the other side, many CAPTCHAs result into too hard problems to be solved by humans, or just unfeasible for users with disabilities. In consequence, we believe that it is very important to evaluate all test proposals according to the desirable properties presented in Section 2.2. Those requirements can be divided into three main groups:

- Usability—efficient and usable.
- Security—secure, transparent, robust, random, large space, and human cost.
- Practicality—economical and automated.

In this section, we focus on Usability and Practicality, while we left Security for Section 5.

4.1 Efficiency

The design of current CAPTCHA systems makes humans find certain challenges hard to solve, annoying, and irritating. Some CAPTCHAs are not human-friendly and force some users to abandon a site for another resulting to financial loss to the site in question. Even simple challenges can drive away a substantial number of potential customers. Usability aspects are very important as CAPTCHAs cannot engage too much of the user's attention and cannot consume too much of her time.

To simplify the study, we decouple the problem of making the challenge hard for bot from the problem of making it easy for humans, and focus on the latter one. This is due to the fact that testing the security of a CAPTCHA is more complex in terms of a quantitative analysis, as there is no way to cover all the possibilities to attack a CAPTCHA, like in other security problems. However, evaluating user problems for solving the challenge can be done in terms of quantitative measures. Examples of those measures include:

- The False Negative Rate, or number of challenges failed by human users over the number of challenges issued. An optimal value for this measure is 0, that is, no test is unsolvable for a human user.

- The number of reloads required to solve the challenge, when the CAPTCHA allows to reload a new challenge if the current one is found too difficult by a human user. The optimal number of retries should also be 0.

- The time required for solving the challenge. Obviously, the less the better, while a 0 time cannot be expected.

- The user satisfaction/usability judgment as collected in an appropriate evaluation form.

The most appropriate way to ensure that a CAPTCHA is well designed in terms of human solvability is conducting a user study and using the previous measures as guidelines for success. However, making a good user study is not an easy task, as a representative population of users must be collected, and some variables must be suitably decoupled.

The representativeness of the user sample is a complex issue, as potential users of a service may vary a lot. For instance, it is clear that users can come from different countries and use different languages, and proficiency in a particular language should not be a requirement for a CAPTCHA to work. Moreover, the alphabet is not the same in different languages (not even on Western countries, which include, e.g., Greece). Also, CAPTCHAs can be a limiting barrier for persons with disabilities—a visual CAPTCHA for a blind person. We discuss this issue in the next section, about accessibility.

In a user study, a particular user should test a challenge several times. It is obvious that, for a new CAPTCHA design, the users will find the first challenges harder than the latest ones, and experience will help them to be more effective when solving other challenges of the same type. This effect or variable should also be considered when deriving measures and conclusions about the challenge efficiency.

Moreover, the solving time measure described above is extremely relative. For instance, let us say that a particular CAPTCHA takes an average time of around 15 s to be solved, while our new design takes nearly 20. To what extent is our new CAPTCHA worse than the previous one? For instance, our new CAPTCHA can have a higher coverage (more people will be able to solve it), smaller False Negative Rate, etc. On the other side, the effect of the solving time in user acceptability is not known—perhaps going from 10 to 12 s is acceptable, but from 12 to 14 s is not.

Another issue regarding the solving time is that the CAPTCHA is most often embedded into a Web form and delivered through the network. In consequence, the time used for filling the form, along with the time used for network transmission of the challenge and reception of the answer should be subtracted from the time used to solve the CAPTCHA.

Probably because of previous reasons, most user studies in CAPTCHA proposals, when available, are very limited. In particular, many of them forget about non-English speakers. Moreover, they are conducted on laboratory settings (e.g., persons of the same corporation, students in the same school, etc.) that allow to extract limited conclusions. Even more, many times these studies are just not performed.

On the other side, only really widespread challenges can be tested in real settings. A prominent example of a wide-coverage user study in a real setting is the evaluation of reCAPTCHA as discussed in Ref. [132]. This particular CAPTCHA has been deployed in more than 40,000 sites, with thousands of challenges served every day. In 1 year, approximately 1.2 billions of challenges have been served. On the basis of the information accumulated in the reCAPTCHA servers, the following conclusions can be drawn:

1. The CAPTCHA is quite easy to be solved by its users. The overall success rate for reCAPTCHA is 96.1%, and some of the errors may just be typing mistakes.
2. The ability for solving the challenge depends on the mother tongue of the user. Based on the IP address, it can be stated that users from English-speaking countries are more successful (97.1–97.4%) than users from non-English-speaking countries (92.6–96.9%).
3. The success rate is proportional to the length of the control word: Four-character words have a success rate of 93.7%; five-character words, 95.7%; six-character words, 96.4%; seven-character words, 96.7%; etc. This can be explained by longer words providing more context for the users.

Regarding time, a user study has been conducted in the captcha.net Web site, on a thousand users, demonstrating that there is not statistical difference between solving an ordinary seven-letter CAPTCHA (that takes 13.59 s in average) and solving a two-word reCAPTCHA (that takes 13.06 s in average).

However, a major drawback of the previous study is that no information about the evaluation of the audio alternative or reCAPTCHA is provided. Moreover, and according to Wilkins [137], versions of reCAPTCHA that draw a line to avoid character segmentation seem to be weak to relatively advanced OCR systems, leading to automated success rate that ranges from 5% to 17.5%. However, these results have been questioned by Baecher et al. [7], and reCAPTCHA has evolved, in certain environments, to a more difficult challenge that uses circles and ellipses with a part of the words in negative, as shown in the Fig. 20.

Unfortunately, there are few other studies with this strong statistical support. A major example is the work by Bursztein et al. [18], who collected CAPTCHA samples from each of the 13 most used image schemes and 8 most used audio

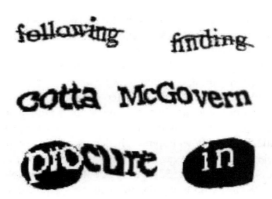

FIG. 20. The evolution of the reCAPTCHA challenge.

schemes, for a total of over 318,000 challenges. Using Amazon's Mechanical Turk, users were requested to solve the CAPTCHAs, leading to over 5000 challenges for each image scheme and 3500 challenges for each audio scheme, each annotated by at least three different humans from Amazons Mechanical Turk. Studying the accuracy of human responses, the following conclusions can be obtained:

- Despite their goals, CAPTCHAs are often hard for humans. When image challenges are presented to three different humans, all three agreed only 71% of the time on average.
- Audio challenges are much harder than image CAPTCHAs. It is found perfect agreement by three humans only 31% of the time for audio challenges.
- Some CAPTCHA schemes are clearly harder for humans than others. For example, three humans agreed on 93% of *authorize* service image captchas, but only 35% of mail.ru image captchas.

This study is extended to eBay CAPTCHAs, and the authors have collected the answers for 14 million challenges solved in a week. Using these answers and comparing to the previous analysis:

- The Mechanical Turk assessment of eBay image CAPTCHAs is lower than eBays measured success rate: data show 93.0% accuracy, compared to eBays measured success rate of 98.5% on 14,000,000 eBay site captchas.
- Evaluating the utility of audio challenges is important as they account for almost 1% of all captchas delivered.

Moreover, the authors of this study have analyzed human variations along a number of demographic lines, and found some interesting trends:

- Non-native speakers of English take longer to solve challenges, and are less accurate on CAPTCHAs that include English words.
- Humans become slightly slower and slightly more accurate with age.

As there is an obvious difficulty to engage users in usability evaluations of CAPTCHAs, Ho et al. [55] have proposed an arcade game named DevilTyper, in which users must defeat devils by typing the associated CAPTCHAs, as shown in the Fig. 21. A comparison with a similar job at the Mechanical Turk demonstrates that the rate of efficiency is similar, and in consequence, the results obtained about CAPTCHA usability using this game are trustful.

As an orthogonal method for evaluating CAPTCHA usability and efficiency, and given the difficulty of making sound user studies, Yan and Salah El Ahmad [144] have proposed an evaluation framework that focuses on three dimensions:

- Distortion. This dimension examines the form of distortions employed by a CAPTCHA and their impact on usability.
- Content. This dimension examines contents embedded in CAPTCHA challenges (or tests) and their impact on usability. For example, how should the content be organized, and is the content appropriate?
- Presentation. This dimension examines the way that CAPTCHA challenges are presented and its impact on usability.

Fig. 21. The DevilTyper game screen for evaluating CAPTCHA usability.

The authors of this proposal argue that the framework can be applied to most CAPTCHA designs, and make a systematic evaluation of a number of OCR challenges according to it, finding that they may be difficult for foreigners, and that colors and letter sizes can strongly affect the usability of the challenge design. Far from quantitative, this framework is rather heuristic and a usability expert must perform the evaluation.

Although some other works stress usability of CAPTCHAs (e.g., Refs. [25,31,68,98]), the provided evaluations are rather limited and do not allow to extract very general conclusions. Moreover, only hints of usability and general guidelines are provided. Some studies focus on specific aspects of CAPTCHAs, and although performed on small sets of users (below a hundred) and of challenges (below a hundred per user), the restricted scope allows to get relatively sound conclusions. As a matter of instance:

- Chellapilla et al. [25] have performed a limited study on how specific text distortions (e.g., location, rotation, warp, arcs, etc.) affect OCR challenges solvability by humans. Not only solving times and accuracy are collected but also user's subjective opinion about the difficulty of the challenge.

- Wang et al. [133] have evaluated the difficulty of OCR challenges according to two dimensions: the readability of the CAPTCHA text (e.g., an English word, a pronounceable word, etc.), and the degree of (ScatterType) distortion. Again efficiency is considered, but the subjective opinion of humans as well.

As an overall conclusion, we believe that the problem of evaluating CAPTCHAs efficiency is still lacking of a comprehensive approach.

4.2   Accessibility Problems

It is quite evident that CAPTCHAs can be a limiting barrier for Web service usage by impaired people [80]. The use of CAPTCHAs to prevent automation comes at a huge price to users: they fail to properly recognize users with disabilities as human, thus outrageously violating the property of low False Negative Rate. The types of disabilities most affected by CAPTCHAs when accessing a Web site are:

- *Visual*: Visual impairments including blindness, various common types of low vision and poor eyesight, various types of color blindness. All OCR- and visual-based CAPTCHAs reviewed in Sections 3.1 and 3.2 are inaccessible for visually impaired users.

- *Auditory*: Deafness or hearing impairments, including individuals who are hard of hearing. Audio-based CAPTCHAs reviewed in Section 3.3 are inaccessible for hearing impaired users.

- *Cognitive*: Developmental disabilities, learning disabilities (dyslexia, dyscalculia, etc.), and cognitive disabilities of various origins, affecting memory, attention, developmental "maturity," problem-solving and logic skills, etc. Language barriers might be included here, due to the global access to most Web sites. Cognitive-based CAPTCHAs reviewed in Section 3.4 are inaccessible for cognitive deficient users.

Most CAPTCHAs deployed today rely on the user being able to see an image. However, since there are many visually impaired people using the Web, CAPTCHAs based on sound are necessary for accessibility. Unfortunately, images and sound alone are not sufficient: there are people who use the Web that are both visually and hearing impaired. It is extremely important to have CAPTCHAs based on a variety of sensory abilities. The construction of a CAPTCHA based on a text domain such as text understanding or generation is an important open problem for research in CAPTCHAs.

Moreover, usage contexts should be added to disabilities. Some technological or environmental contexts cause similar access limitations in users with no disability whatsoever: for instance, excessive ambient noise; lack of sound card, loudspeakers, or appropriate plugins; smoke-filled environments; exceedingly small screens or deficient lightning conditions; foreign languages; etc. Therefore, CAPTCHAs might raise an accessibility barrier not only to disabled users, but to much wider user groups as well.

However, disabilities and usage context have not lost attention. On one side, most popular CAPTCHAs nowadays, based on visual input, also provide an audio alternative for visually impaired users. On the other, specific disabilities and environments are receiving more and more attention from researchers, who evaluate current proposals and improve them to help these users enjoying a nondiscriminative Web experience. Examples of these proposals, along with the target disabilities and environments, are reviewed below.

Blind users: This is probably the group that has attracted more attention, with works like the following ones:

- Bigham and Canvender [16] have performed an study that demonstrates that existing audio CAPTCHAs are clearly more difficult and time-consuming to complete as compared to visual CAPTCHAs for both blind and sighted users. They have developed and evaluated a new interface for solving CAPTCHAs optimized for nonvisual use that can be added in-place to existing audio CAPTCHAs. In a subsequent study, the optimized interface increased the success rate of blind participants by 59% on audio CAPTCHAs, showing a broadly applicable principle of accessible design: the most usable audio interfaces are often not direct translations of existing visual interfaces.

- Alternatively but in the same line, Shirali-Shahreza and Shirali-Shahreza [104] have proposed a cognitive challenge that exploits human ability for generalization, with questions like: "There are 5 cats, 3 apples, and 4 dogs on a table. How many pets are there on the table?" The questions can be read by a speech synthesizer, and the answers are always number, quite easy to enter. However, no evaluation is provided. This concept is also presented by Holman et al. [56].

Limited input devices: Specific devices like cell phones have limited input capabilities, that can discourage users from using a Web service. Chow et al. [31] have presented a visual CAPTCHA in which the user is requested to select a number of valid English words over a panel showing nine distorted strings. The valid words are selected using the numbers in the cell phone keyboard, thus simplifying user interaction with a such a limited device.

Language dependence: Shirali-Shahreza and Shirali-Shahreza [112] have proposed a language-independent CAPTCHA, which is based on two ideas: the language for showing the text that explains the challenge can be chosen by the user and the challenge itself consists of choosing a described item from a collage of pictures (e.g., a banana, a car, etc.).

Illiteracy and age problems: Developing the previous concept, the same authors have presented a proposal that address cognitive and age problems. Instead of writing the text that describes the CAPTCHA, it is played in the language of the user, and as a consequence, it is argued that it addresses problems of illiteracy [111] and age [113].

4.3   Practical Considerations

In this section, we address two of the required properties of CAPTCHA challenges, automated and economical. To make a challenge practical, the process of generating it has to be fully automated, that is, it should not involve human resources in real time (neither in the generation nor in the answer testing), and it should involve an small amount of network and computational resources.

The generation of a CAPTCHA test involves several steps which depend on the kind of challenge:

- In OCR challenges, the typical process includes defining the text to be displayed (random sequence of characters, pronounceable words according to phonetic or heuristic patterns, e.g., consonant-vowel-consonant, words taken from a dictionary), rendering the text (font and size choose, character separation), adding noise (background noise, arcs and segments, etc.), delivering the final image, and testing the answer against the text defined.

- In image CAPTCHAs, most often based on labeled images, the process includes: randomly choosing the images for the answer according to sharing the same label (e.g., instruments, animals, etc.); randomly choosing the rest of images (ensuring that they do not share the selected label); eventually choosing other labels randomly; eventually adding noise and distortion; building and delivering a collage; and testing the answer against the correct label.
- In video challenges, most often displaying texts or images, the process roughly involves a mix of previous techniques.
- In audio CAPTCHAs, the typical process includes: choosing the sequence of characters (letters or digits); generating the corresponding sounds (either by randomly choosing them from a database or using a speech synthesizer); eventually adding noise and distortion to each sound or to the full sequence; delivering the sounds to the user; and testing the answer against the chosen sequence.
- In text challenge CAPTCHAs, the process involves: generating the question and answer (either by randomly choosing it from a database or by using a randomly selected pattern); generating alternative answers (if needed and not included in the question); delivering the challenge; and testing the answer against the correct one.

In many cases the individual steps can overlap. For instance, in audio CAPTCHAs, the stored sounds that will make the test can include background noise, as in image CAPTCHAs.

A number of common properties arise in the previous processes:

- The CAPTCHA and the correct answer must be stored together in the server. This correspondence cannot be stored forever, as it would represent a potential security risk, and it represents a load for the server.
- Many of them rely on a database that has to be previously built or reused. Not only building such a database can be costly, but storing it also.
- The process involves server-side steps and client-side steps. The server-side load must be controlled to avoid Denial of Service attacks, but the client-side load is much more difficult to assess, as more and more types of devices are being used to access the Web.

Building databases is a major problem in many CAPTCHA proposals. For this task, several proposals emerge:

- In specific CAPTCHAs, the harder work (e.g., labeling the image) can be reused. For instance, in handwritten text CAPTCHAs (e.g., Ref. [97]), it is proposed to reuse postal services to match location names with their handwritten correspondences. Alternatively, Jain et al. [65] propose to build CAPTCHAs with images resulting from search engines queries.

- A previously discussed approach is making use of free crowd sourcing approaches like the ESP game proposed by Ahn et al. [131], or combining labeled and unlabeled data in CAPTCHAs to collect more instances of the problem [30].
- Another possibility is making use of paid crowd sourcing services, although this is obviously the more costly approach.

A complementary approach used in advertisement-based CAPTCHAs (e.g., Solve Media [117], NuCaptcha [86], or Ads Captcha [1] is making the clients responsible for designing the CAPTCHA.

There are not extensive evaluations regarding the practicality of CAPTCHAs. However, it is clear that the type of challenge clearly affect the resource needed to generate and serve it to the users. Also, the time required to solve it by the user affects the server load in terms of the resources needed to store the correspondence between the challenge and the correct answer. Regarding these issues:

- OCR challenges involve serving low quality images, which involve limited server and client load in terms of generation and traffic consumption.
- Image and video CAPTCHAs involve much more resources both in the server and the client sides, and the database construction and storage is a major problem.
- Audio and video challenges also involve waiting longer for a user response, depending on the length of the video or audio sequence served.
- Question-based CAPTCHAs are most often based on the selection of an stored question, so the storage problem is very relevant but the challenge generation is relatively simple and efficient, and few resources are needed in terms of bandwidth and client side computational power.

5. Security and Attacks on CAPTCHAs

CAPTCHAs are a mechanism to protect Web resources against massive access. Therefore, the security of a CAPTCHA solution relies not only on the hardness of the underlying AI problem, but on the implementation and other details. As discussed in Section 2.2, relevant properties about CAPTCHA security include the ability to make robots fail, to be based in an open algorithm, to implement a challenge able to resist for many years, to be based on really random generators, and to employ large databases to resist brute force attacks.

It is quite complex to measure some of these features. The most straightforward evaluation metric for security is the false positive rate or machine recognition rate, defined as the number of times that a bot solved the challenge over the number of times the challenge was issued. While this quantitative measure is quite useful, it is highly complex to obtain it, as there is not a repository of bots for testing CAPTCHAs. Another measure that can help to evaluate the security of a CAPTCHA is the size of the database employed in the generation. This applies to, for example, handwritten OCR CAPTCHAs, natural-audio-based tests, image collage and video challenges, and cognitive text CAPTCHAs based on questions. For instance, the database of questions employed in the text CAPTCHA available at Ref. [92] is claimed to have more than 180,243,205 different questions. Some features can be simply impossible to endure, like the potential lifetime of a challenge according to the AI difficulty to solve it, or the strength of the implementation. However, in the latter case, there is an increasing number of Web testing platforms that can help to check the CAPTCHA as a Web application, for example, Rational AppScan [61].

Other features can be easy to test; for instance, is the algorithm for challenge generation public? Also the random generative process can be manually inspected.

For suitable use in a cybersecurity scenario, we must ensure that the human recognition rate stays high when compared to machine recognition rates (which should ideally be 0). Even a seemingly low recognition rate for machines (say, $<0.001\%$), would not necessarily mean that a given cybersecurity application can be considered bot-proof. We must bear in mind that a recognition rate of $x\%$ means that, statistically, x out of every 100 attempts will be successful. Since it is possible to have distributed attack networks, repeatedly trying to gain access to a secured application, the shear volume of attacks would render the low recognition rate itself irrelevant.

This means that a human verification system using CAPTCHAs needs to ensure that additional checks and measures are in place to handle the rapid repeated attacks on the verification service. A simple test would be to check from where the verification requests are originating. Requests arriving within t seconds of each other, from the same IP address can be denied. In practice, t would be set to a small value to discourage Web bots that try to repeatedly access a CAPTCHA protected site. Each IP can only be allowed n number of authentication requests in some predetermined time period. These and other methods need to be used in conjunction with CAPTCHAs, while designing effective automated human verification systems. As AI algorithms get better everyday, and given the superior processing capabilities of machines, a 0% recognition rate cannot be guaranteed.

According to Basso and Sicco [14], a protection scheme is secure against massive access if programming and using a bot to massively download Web resources is an inconvenient task in terms of time, human resources, and process efficiency. From the above definition, it comes out that a CAPTCHA does not have to be 100% resistant to computer attack to be considered secure. If it is at least as expensive for an attacker to break the challenge by machine than it would be to pay a human to take the CAPTCHA, the test can be considered secure [29]. Generically, a CAPTCHA is effective as long as the cost of using a software robot remains higher than the cost of using a human, even when the spammers use cheap labor to solve CAPTCHA (see Section 5.1.3).

However, even what may seem a good figure (e.g., 0.01% success rate for bots) can be very dangerous. For instance, with a 10,000 machine botnet (which would be considered relatively small these days), given broadband connections and multi-threaded attack code, even with only 10 threads per machine, a 0.01% success rate would yield 10 successes every second, which would provide the attacker with 864,000 new accounts per day if they were attacking a registration interface [137].

5.1   Attacks on CAPTCHAs

In this section, a number of approaches that have been used to attack CAPTCHAs are discussed. These attacks can be grouped into blind guessing, AI attacks, relay attacks, and side-channel attacks.

5.1.1   Blind Guessing

Blind guessing attacks can be roughly classified into brute force and dictionary attacks. A brute force attack is a random guess of the answer to the CAPTCHA. As many challenges are based on letter or digit sequences, it can be performed as a brute force or a dictionary attack. In a brute force attack, all possible sequences are tested against the CAPTCHA. For instance, in a three digit code, all sequences "000," "001," ..., and "999" would be tried. However, as failing the answer makes the system generate another different challenge, the probability of randomly guessing the code 0.001. Obviously, making the code longer implies less probability, and this attack is not practical in general.

In a dictionary attack, it is assumed that the challenge code is generated according to some guidelines to make it easier for humans, and the bot answers are generated according to the same guidelines. For instance, using real words or pronounceable sequences highly reduces the search space for the bot, as there are less valid combinations. If a random sequence of 4 letters can be randomly guessed with a probability of $(1/26)^4 = 0.000002$, there are only about 5200 valid English words, leading a dictionary attack having a probability of success of around 0.0002 (100 times higher).

While these attacks may seem doomed to fail, they can be surprisingly effective. For instance, in image collage CAPTCHAs, users are often requested to choose an image from a table. In the simplest case, a user can be requested to choose one picture (e.g., a particular object, animal, or so) from a set of two images. A random guess leads to a success chance of 0.5 (!). This is why CAPTCHAs like ASIRRA and KittenAuth request users to choose several pictures among a bigger table of possibilities. For instance, choosing 3 objects over a table including 9 leads to a random guess success rate of $1/84 = 0.01$, and choosing 4 objects among 12 leads to success rate of $1/495 = 0.002$. This can also be applied to any CAPTCHAs in which the user is requested to choose answers from a predefined set, like in text challenges using multiple-choice questions, or image collage CAPTCHAs that request users to choose the appropriate label for a number of displayed pictures. For instance, the ESP-PIX challenge [23] offers 72 labels; if users were requested to use two labels, the probability of a random guess would be 0.0001 instead of 0.01.

The same kind of reasoning can be applied in sequence CAPTCHAs [50,65,91]. Let us suppose that a challenge has $1/10 = 0.1$ probability of success for a random guess robot. Forcing the same bot to solve three CAPTCHAs leads to a probability of 0.001, transforming a quite trivial CAPTCHA into an effective one (at the expense of usability).

Dictionary attacks are based on the existence of a database of possible responses. For instance, a form of dictionary attack oriented to replicate the challenge issuer database is described by Jain et al. [65], and it is named the Pictionary attack. In this attack, the bot maintains a picture dictionary (Pictionary) or a look-up table of object pictures along with their object names and any associated information useful in picture matching. Hence, whenever the bot comes across a picture, it searches for the picture in its table. If a match occurs that is the picture was old, the bot simply looks up the answer. If there is no match, that is the picture is new, this picture gets added in the table for future look-up. Pictionary-based attack exploits the fact that some pictures may be repeated in CAPTCHA rounds after some initial rounds. This assists the hacker by boosting the average CAPTCHA-breaking success rate. Of course, if images are altered (e.g., by adding noise to make recognition difficult), the bot table can include and use properties like color/intensity, edge detected pattern, pixel pattern, etc. This attack has been successful for, for example, KittenAuth.

While most of the time blind guessing is not a concern, it can alternatively support other attacks. For instance, if an OCR CAPTCHA is generated from real words, a bot could use a dictionary after processing the image with, for example, an OCR program.

5.1.2   AI Attacks

An AI attack is a method that tries to solve the challenge served in the CAPTCHA. For instance, in an OCR test, an AI attack should try to guess the correct answer by processing the included image featuring the text; in an audio CAPTCHA, the AI attack should analyze the audio files provided; etc. In other words, an AI attack should duplicate the human function. This is a key point in CAPTCHA development, as the correct challenge selection can make a test either secure or it may represent a noticeable step ahead in the solution of a complex AI problem, as stated by von Ahn et al. [130].

In consequence, the question is whether automatically solving the challenge is making an step in AI or not. In words of Daniel Lopresti [77]:

> We note with some irony that a fundamental premise behind the design of most CAPTCHA's has been that decades of research have failed to provide solutions to the pattern recognition problems in question. Yet, in a matter of months, certain types of challenges have been met in ways that are effective for the task at hand, but not particularly relevant to the original problem that motivated the CAPTCHA in the first place. Instead of helping to solve the general OCR problem for degraded text, which remains open, they can be viewed as specialized routines that are only useful for breaking CAPTCHA's. This is due to the fact that, for the most part, the challenges in question, (...), are largely artificial, having little basis in the real world of character recognition. (Daniel Lopresti, p. 99)

In other words, many of the attacks below, even successful, may not represent any significant advance in AI, because of the very design of the challenge.

Another issue regarding an AI attack to CAPTCHAs is that it is highly dependent on the type of challenge. Some of the challenges have common properties (e.g., how letters and sounds are chosen in OCR and audio CAPTCHAs), but most of the attacking techniques are specific to the type of CAPTCHA, and to the way it is generated as well.

By far, the most attacked CAPTCHAs are the OCR tests. This is of course due to the fact that they are most often used. The way a typical attack works is by reversing the steps followed in generating the challenge: deleting the noise, isolating the characters, trying to identify them, and using dictionaries to make an educated guess of the string to be answered. The work by Naor and Malik [83] is canonical in this sense. The concrete process they have followed to break the EZ-Gimpy challenge used by Yahoo! is represented in the Fig. 22, and it comprised of the following steps:

1. The first step is to hypothesize a set of candidate letters in the image. This is done using shape matching techniques that essentially look at a bunch of points

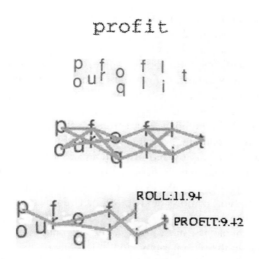

FIG. 22. The steps followed to break EZ-Gimpy, taken from Ref. [83].

in the image at random, and compare these points to points on each of the 26 letters of the alphabet. The comparison is done in a way that is very robust to background clutter and deformation of the letters. The process usually results in 3–5 candidate letters per actual letter in the image, as shown in the figure at the step (2).

2. Next, the method analyzes pairs of letters to see whether or not they are "consistent," or can be used consecutively to form a word. In the figure at step (3), green lines are drawn between pairs of letters that could be chained together to form a complete word.

3. Finally, plausible words are built. There are many possible paths through the graph of letters constructed in the previous step. However, most of them do not form real words. For example, the string "pfql" is a path through the graph, but meaningless. Words are selected according to three-letter sequences probabilities at the used dictionary. In the figure, at step (4), two complete words are found, "roll" and "profit." The word "profit" gets a better (lower in terms of distance) score than "roll."

This method allows to break the EZ-Gimpy challenge a success rate of 83% (158 over 191 test cases, picking the top matching word). In this particular example, the authors have employed rather sophisticated shape recognition techniques in the first step, which were at the top of the state-of-the-art in that moment. While not representing a substantial step in AI, it is clear that the approach involved a noticeable research aspect in AI.

The noise reduction step in the previous work was not needed for the particular example. This also happens with, for example, reCAPTCHA, as demonstrated in Ref. [137], and with many others. In many cases, the noise reduction step can be just applying a binarization algorithm. For instance, if the background colors used are different from the text color (which may be, e.g., in black), this binarization just turns to white all pixels in the image apart from black ones.

In general, the noise reduction step involves applying specific image filters. For instance, Lin et al. [73] employ bio-inspired image filters intended to separate background and foreground, which include a luminance-based and a chrominance-based filter. Also, Hindle et al. [54] apply erosion/dilation, thresholding (a generalized form of binarization), and lone pixel removal to delete background noise.

The isolation of characters, most often called segmentation, is ,however, much more heterogeneous in the bibliography, and it depends on the presence or absence of connecting lines, character distortion and rotation, character overlapping, etc. Of course, it depends also on the results of the previous step. For instance:

- Chandavale et al. [24] make use of a simple segmentation algorithm consisting of checking continuous black pixels.
- Lin et al. [73] just find connected sections and discard those which have not suitable shapes, proportions, etc. Finding connected regions is also done by Chellapilla and Simard [26].
- Yan and Salah El Ahmad [142,143] have defined an algorithm for vertically slicing the target picture according to color differences.
- Moy et al. [84] employ mesh nodes between the characters.

The final step consists of identifying the individual characters. This is a pure problem of OCR, that can be approached using different features, many often automatically learned on a manually tagged collection. The process involves collecting images for the possible characters and finding the values of the features for these characters, and then comparing each target character with them using the defined characters. For instance:

- Characters can be identified in terms of the number of holes they have, the height of the character, the maximum number of white-black transitions in vertical intersection, and the position of the vertical stroke (left or right) [24].
- Characters can also have unique pixel counts (depending on the fonts used, and when normalized in size) [142].

- Distortion can be approached by detecting the border points and estimating the number of changes needed to arrive to a template of the training characters [84].
- Rotation can be detected, for example, using skeletonization, that is, detecting the connected structure of a continuous block of pixels by keeping the main points of interest in the picture (a character) including sharp end points of the object, intersections, etc., and keeping the object connected (used, e.g., in Ref. [54]).

The results from the previous steps are lists of candidate letters and/or numbers that are sometimes compared to a dictionary of available words to make a better guess, leading to automated challenge recognition rates that go, for example, from 27% to 99% depending on the CAPTCHA attacked in Ref. [54].

Image CAPTCHAs have also been subject of AI attacks. Two prominent examples are the work of Zhu et al. [147] against the IMAGINATION challenge, and the Golle attack on ASIRRA [45]. A main difference between targeted challenges is that while ASIRRA keeps the pictures separated and fairly unprocessed, the IMAGINATION challenge mixes and distorts the images, leading to a quite specific and advanced attack. Golle attack on ASIRRA is as simple as using two learning stages on color features and texture features, reaching to a cat versus dog recognition rate of 82.7% and an ASIRRA solving rate of 10.3% (more than enough to consider it broken).

The IMAGINATION CAPTCHA proposes several types of tests, being the collage of images the most challenging one. As seen in the Fig. 23, the system issues a mix of images with added noise to make difficult to separate them. The goal is to click on the requested image as described with a label (e.g., man, car, etc.). As the number of images is relatively small, once separated, a random guess attack can lead to a solving rate over 5%. Zhu et al. [147] apply customized techniques that include edge detection, rectangle enumeration, and inconsistency detection (overlaps, etc.) to detect the individual images. As the authors are able to detect the correct rectangles 74.31% of the times, a random guess attack on a maximum of 15 images in the collage leads to a success rate of 4.95%.

In the case of audio CAPTCHAs, it is possible to use relatively standard Automated Speech Recognition techniques, as done by Tam et al. [122]. They make use of quite standard audio features (e.g., frequency bands) to make sound recognition independent of the speaker and robust against the background noise, leading to recognition rates that range from 67% in Google audio CAPTCHAs, to 45% in reCAPTCHA audio challenges. What makes this attack more threatening is that audio challenges are routinely provided as an alternative for persons with visual disabilities, and that the techniques used are nearly off-the-shelf.

Cognitive CAPTCHAs can also be solved, even if employing relatively hard questions. For instance, Hernandez-Castro and Ribagorda [51] have proposed a method to solve the Quantum Random Bit Generator Service MathCAPTCHA,

FIG. 23. The IMAGINATION collage challenge.

which features questions like "Find the smallest zero of $p(x) = (x - 5)(x - 4)(x + 6)$ $(x + 2)(x - 5)$." The method is highly customized to the kind of tests served, and involves determining the kind of challenge with a simple algorithm, and applying the mathematical solution depending on the type. For instance, in the previous question, it would be enough to find the biggest number among those preceded by the plus sign, as they correspond to negative zeros of the polynomial. Doing just these on these type of challenges and answering 0 for the rest of types leads to a recognition rate over 20%.

As a concluding remark, the recognition rate of standard software packages, for example, OCR like the open source OCRopus [64] or speech recognition like the open source package Sphinx [21], is not known. We must recall that if widely available software is able to solve a CAPTCHA in one over a hundred times, it may perfectly be considered broken.

5.1.3 Relay Attacks

CAPTCHAs have been developed to deal with the specific case of machines trying to masquerade as humans. Web services that require human verification only focus on differentiating between machines and humans. Such types of Web services are very vulnerable to attacks from humans itself. This fact has led to some concern of having CAPTCHAs broken by humans in what is known as the relay attack.

Jeff Yan [141] presents an interesting discussion about different ways in which relay attacks can be perpetrated in the context of MMORPGs cheating:

- *Man in the middle (MITM) attack*: It has been alleged that a spammer could make use of the MITM attack, shifting the load of solving CATPCHA challenges to porn site visitors [17]: the CAPTCHA challenge encountered by a Web-bot is forwarded to human users on some high traffic Web site (e.g., a pornographic Web site); the human users are required to decode the CAPTCHA to get access to pornographic images; the decoded responses are relayed back to the Web bots who supply the response to the Web service and gains access to the service.

- *Outsourcing attack*: Bot users can outsource both their game play and the task of solving CAPTCHA challenges to people in low-paying countries.

- *Housewife attack*: A key observation is that it is often possible for a bot to differentiate each CAPTCHA challenge from other game events. Thus, a human can be alerted by the bot to answer the challenge in time. Bot attending in MMORPGs could then become an attractive profession for housewives, who would make money by attending their bots occasionally (i.e., upon each alert), while looking after their household business as usual.

- *Collusion attack*: Bots can be made to communicate with each other, and then each alert can be propagated across the bot network. Therefore, a CAPTCHA challenge can be attended by either a cheater or one of his friends, whoever is available.

From a security point of view, if an attacker needs to hire a human "recognizer" to break the CAPTCHA, it can be assumed that the CAPTCHA generating tool is perfect. After all, CAPTCHAs try to distinguish humans from machines and they are doing well their job. The CAPTCHA mechanism is able to ensure that there is a human behind a computer, although he or she might not be the "right" human.

There are strong evidences that there are companies dedicated to break CAPTCHAs on demand, as stated by Dancho Danchev in his blog at ZDNet [35]. Such companies present themselves with introductions like:

> I have a team of 7 people, willing to do captchas at $2 per 1000 entries. Please consider my bid. We can definitely provide 50 K captchas per day.

Regarding relay attacks, we come back to the cost-effectiveness issue. To make these attacks unpractical, it is needed to make manual CAPTCHA solving task more resource consuming. These involves not only previous considerations about IP address recording and so on but also computational and time cost. However, it seems not easy to defeat this kind of underground economy. On the other side, applying data mining to CAPTCHA server logs can give helpful insights as time and rate anomalies may be detected.

5.1.4   Side-Channel Attacks

A side-channel attack is one that solves the CAPTCHA but not the AI problem it is based on, therefore not improving the state of the art on AI [52]. It is named side-channel, thus, as it solves the problem using a method that does not follow the intended attacking path.

It can be claimed that side-channel attacks can include random guess and relay attacks, as they do not try to solve the underlying AI problem. However, in this section, we consider only those attacks that target the implementation of the CAPTCHA. For instance, we leave apart the work by Hernandez-Castro et al. [52], who solve the ASIRRA challenge by applying a publicly available statistical tool to process the images (without really trying to understand if they are from cats or dogs), and then several Machine Learning classifiers.

The implementation of a CAPTCHA service relies on a server (which provides the challenge and validates the answer), and a client (the user browser, which displays the challenge and allows to enter the answer). The most simple weakness that can be found in a CAPTCHA is to deliver the validation code directly to the user. For instance, the code of a (freely available) mathematical CAPTCHA that is validated on the user side is shown in the Fig. 24. This simple CAPTCHA requests the user to enter the result of adding two numbers as shown in the Fig. 25, and it features two JavaScript functions:

- The `DrawBotBoot()` function is used to display the challenge with the values of the two random variables a and b.
- The `ValidBotBoot()` function is used to validate the input of the user (stored in the variable d) against the precomputed answer (stored in c).

As the validation code is served in the very form, it can be trivially reverse engineered to automatically solve it. A similar but a bit more complex example is the Jcap (Captcha Validation Javascript) [4], in which a limited number of images (181 in the Web site free code) are hashed and their hashes are served to the client page.

Most CAPTCHAs are generated and validated in the server side. For this purpose, the script that displays the form on the client side, makes a call to a generation script at the server, and another call to a validation script at well. If the validation code is

```html
<html>
  <head>
    <title>BotBoot</title>

    <script type="text/javascript">
    var a = Math.ceil(Math.random() * 10);
    var b = Math.ceil(Math.random() * 10);
    var c = a + b
    function DrawBotBoot()
    {
        document.write("What is "+ a + " + " + b +"? ");
        document.write("<input id='BotBootInput' type='text'
          maxlength='2' size='2'/>");
    }
    function ValidBotBoot(){
        var d = document.getElementById('BotBootInput').value;
        if (d == c) return true;
        return false;

    }
    </script>
  </head>
  <body>

  Are you human?<br />

  <script type="text/javascript">DrawBotBoot()</script>
  <input id="Button1" type="button" value="Check"
    onclick="alert(ValidBotBoot());"/>

  </body>
</html>
```

Fig. 24. A simple mathematical CAPTCHA validated on the client side.

sent to the client side (e.g., in cookies), then trying to unencode it is by far more feasible than trying to, for example, use OCR programs. Further, if a hash is used instead of a simple encoding, it is susceptible to a dictionary attack. For example, if the challenge is only 4 bytes long and consists of lowercase a–z, then an attacker can

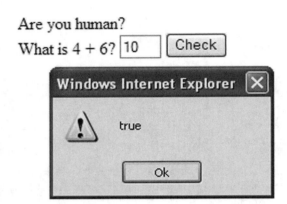

FIG. 25. The form and result of solving the simple mathematical CAPTCHA.

trivially build a list of hashes and their values, enabling the attacker to simply recognize the hash rather than having to OCR the image [137].

If challenges are replayed, another weakness arises. An attacker can have a database of the challenges already submitted, and reusing previously solved challenges as an easy way to automate the attack. If multiple answers are allowed for the same challenge, this database attack gets a multiplier.

It is recommended to record several data in the server side to discover anomalies that may reveal other weaknesses in the CAPTCHA implementation. For instance, Wilkins [137] recommends to log:

- Correct answer and submitted answer. These are important because it is possible to determine which characters legitimate users are having trouble with as well as identify when attackers are getting close to successfully breaking your CAPTCHA. Humans tend to consistently make small errors, while automated code will frequently make large ones.
- Time of puzzle generation and time of answer submission. These intervals should not be either too long or too short. If logs feature solution times of 10 ms, it is a fair bet that the system is broken.
- IP address requesting puzzle and IP address submitting answer. Consistent discrepancies may indicate sites redisplaying the challenges to users who unwittingly solve the puzzles on behalf of spammers.

5.2   Security Requirements on CAPTCHAs

Given the previous attacks described above, it makes sense to provide suggestions to make them and others ineffective. Apart from general and widely applicable considerations commented above (e.g., disallowing repeated answers, recording the source IP address of the answers, keeping a large database of challenges, etc.), specific types of CAPTCHAs have corresponding security requirements, most often aimed at protecting the AI component of the challenge.

These requirements, or advices, are frequently proposed by the very authors of the attacks. For instance, Yan and Salah El Ahmad [143] suggest a number of counter-measures to make OCR challenges resistant to their pixel-count attack, such as

- Making it hard to separate the text from the background—for example, using multiple colors for both foreground and background, including some fore-ground colors into the background and vice versa, etc.
- Making it hard to segment each image—for example, connecting characters with each other or adding more cracks in each character.
- Making it impossible to distinguish a character by counting its pixels—for example, making all characters have the same pixel count all the time.

Previous countermeasures can be reinforced by adding local and global random warp, generating distortions in the letters and in the full string displayed.

These and other measures can be generalized to those proposed by Kolupaev and Ogijenko [69] for making OCR CAPTCHAs more secure:

- Font tricks—include using artistic fonts, different font styles, upper and lower-case versions together, rotation, and distortion. This affects and damages the character recognition step.
- Adding noise and color models—including colors, dots, lines, circles, and rectangles, which can be hard to break. This makes difficult to separate the characters from the noise, for instance background from foreground.
- Letter overlap—one of the most powerful weapons available in CAPTCHA technology: if letters overlap and are still readable, this technique represents a very serious obstacle for recognizers.
- Number and type of letters—obviously, the more letters used, the less accurate a bot will be in its attempts. Also, there are letters hard to identify when noise is added, like a "C" versus a "G."

A major problem with previous proposals is that they affect not only bots but also humans. Again, it is difficult to keep a reasonable trade-off between human and bot recognition rates; a 100% secure CAPTCHA is not possible (as they may emerge new attacks that could break it), but it can be easy to make it useless because human recognition rates are too low.

Regarding audio CAPTCHAs, Soupionis and Gritzalis [118] have given a number of recommendations for making them more secure, organized in four categories:

1. Vocabulary attributes. They include the characters spoken (digits, letters, etc.)—the biggest the number of sounds, the harder the CAPTCHA; the variation of speakers (using an automated speech synthesizer, using one or several speakers, etc.)—discard speech synthesizers, and make use of as many speakers as possible, taking care that they do not repeat in the same challenge; the language dependence (English vs. other language speakers)—localize the CAPTCHA by using local speakers when possible.
2. Noise attributes. Either used as background noise, or as intermediate noise for making it difficult to isolate the sounds, it must be randomly and automatically generated.
3. Time attributes. The time of each sound, the time between sounds and the overall time of the challenge must be controlled to make them as random as possible. Otherwise, attacks can employ this information to improve their recognition rates.
4. Audio production attributes. The generation of the challenge must be automated and should guarantee that there are not frequent repetitions. Moreover, the audio file must be streamed instead of sent to the client side.

Some of the previous OCR and audio recommendations also apply to other types of challenges, like video- and question-based CAPTCHAs. For instance, the NuCaptcha [86] displays a video in which a three-letter code is shown. In consequence, all considerations regarding the vocabulary, either in OCR or in audio challenges, apply to it.

It is also desirable to test a CAPTCHA against standard/off-the-shelf toolkits for targeted purposes. A generic recommendation regarding OCR CAPTCHAs is testing their security against standard available OCR packages (e.g., OCRopus), possible with several preprocessing routines that apply random binarization filters available in standard image processing packages like ImageMagick [74]. This also applies to audio CAPTCHAs that should be tested, for example, with Sphinx [21].

As a final note, and given that there are potential attacks to the implementation of the CAPTCHA, it is a good idea to hire a penetration tester that may reveal implementation weaknesses. Instead of it, the CAPTCHA builders can run penetration tests on their own by using suitable tools like the Rational AppScan system mentioned above [61].

6. Alternatives to CAPTCHAs

In previous sections, we have presented a number of CAPTCHA technologies and their major pitfalls in terms of human efficiency and bot protection. Many CAPTCHAs nowadays pose usability problems that imply a limiting barrier for persons with disabilities. Moreover, CAPTCHA technologies are being routinely broken, and there are even relatively cheap commercial services in the hackers underground that provide CAPTCHA solving [18].

In consequence, protection against abuse of Web-based services intended for human beings can still be considered an open problem. Different technologies to achieve the same security goals are being proposed in certain applications, avoiding CAPTCHA usage. The proposed solutions can be organized into two groups:

1. Solutions based on Web technologies—exploiting the structure of HTML forms or URLs to prevent or discourage bots submitting them.
2. Solutions based on the analysis of the submitted content—only reasonable contents will be considered valid and, in consequence, automatically generated contents will be filtered out.

Regarding exploiting Web technologies, the work by Striletchi and Vaida [119,120] is focused on delivering the client side (the user browser) a new actioning way of sending back the filled form. Instead of using a classic submit button that can be easily recognized by a form processing system in a bot (e.g., a HTML form component like < input type = submit value = OK>), the form includes event handling functions that make use of JavaScript OnMouseOver and OnClick events. This way, only (human feasible) manual form handling is forced, as bots are supposed to be unable to handle the mouse pointer. Moreover, the form components are also randomized to avoid automated processing in the client side. However, this proposal is rather weak in the sense that there are automated cursor handling applications (e.g., Selenium) [88], intended for automated testing of Web applications, that may be used for breaking this type of security.

At the end, the previous proposal involves ensuring that a manual work is performed on the client side. Instead of doing this, and given that the key point is to ensure that using a bot is not worth, the client side can alternatively be forced to perform a computation that ideally should discourage hackers because the computational power is much higher than manually sending the filled form. This idea, previously mentioned as a "postage" approach (as CAPTCHAs can be regarded "human postage"), is exploited by Kaiser and Feng [66]. Most computational postage systems involve changes in the underlying communication protocol—for instance, Dwork et al. [40] have proposed a computational postage approach which is out from the current Simple Mail Transfer Protocol. Instead of changing the protocol, Kaiser and Feng proposal involves using modern Web technologies to deliver randomly modified links that can only be converted to the proper ones by executing attached translation functions. The translation involves the utilization of the client side resources, thus making it time- and power-consuming if being automated. The proposal is fully transparent regarding the HTTP. A potential pitfall of this proposal is that the Web is being accessed by many small devices that may not have the required computational power, so it is complemented with CAPTCHA delivery in the case of less powerful terminals.

On the other side, it is possible to analyze the contents submitted or sent to the protected application. Of course, this is highly specific to the actual application, as what is submitted depends on it. For instance, Oorschot1 and Stubblebine [125] propose to avoid dictionary attacks to login forms by ensuring that a person is in the loop. These authors have defined a login protocol that makes use of the history of failed logins and CAPTCHAs; keeping it simple, when a threshold in the count of failed logins is exceeded, the user is delivered a CAPTCHA. As this can be seen as another CAPTCHA application, it also suggests that the CAPTCHA may be replaced in this context by a pure history based protocol.

For the particular problem of comment spam in blogs, the commercial service Akismet [6] is offered to replace CAPTCHAs. This service is claimed to perform "hundreds of tests" on the submitted comment or track back, which can be guessed to include several anti-Web spam techniques like black lists, content analysis, etc. [8]. The service can be integrated to other kind of forms using the provided API, but if it is specialized (possibly trained) on comment spam, it should not be very effective on them. On the other side, the service provides a quarantine function that allows users to check blocked comments and track backs.

Another special case is automatic collection of resources, cheating an other abuses that are quite frequent in MMORPGs, that has been proposed to be stopped with CAPTCHAs (e.g., Refs. [46,141]. However, other alternatives exist that make use of Machine Learning on the human behavior at games. For instance, Kim et al. [67] have proposed to apply a number of Machine Learning algorithms on the nature of events produced by users, like key strokes, mouse clicks and movements, etc. Alternatively, the frequency of these events and also traffic analysis have been applied to bot detection by Chen et al. [27].

As a (bit funny) final alternative, it is clear that bots in particular environments can be detected by other humans. Of course, this is just the application of the Turing test in, for example, chat rooms, and as a manual method, it can not replace an automated test like a CAPTCHA as it is more costly and it violates the automated testing requirement in most environments. However, an interesting proposal made by Farfel and Conitzer [42], called Turing Trade, defines a collaborative/

competitive game in which users interrogate a potential bot and assess its humanity by betting their points on it. The authors demonstrate that the trading metaphor has a big predictive power, and that chat bots can be detected easily and quickly.

7. Conclusions and Future Trends

In this chapter, we have presented a survey of CAPTCHAs, a widespread security mechanism for protecting Web forms and other services from automated attacks, performed by hackers, spammers, etc., to abuse them. We have described their main characteristics, types, evaluation and security aspects, along with some alternatives to them.

From this chapter, two main conclusions arise:

- Some of the available CAPTCHAs, either in the research or in the commercial domains, are still hard to break. However, there are more and more broken CAPTCHAs everyday, so they should not be considered a fully secure method. Moreover, they pose particular usability and disability problems, and automated resolution rates that can be considered secure (e.g., 0.01%) are getting lower and lower as computational power increases and hackers make use of botnets.
- While millions of hours of human power are wasted, we can hardly find an example of an automated breaking method that has represented a major improvement in the AI state of the art. Unfortunately, this makes the von Ahn "win–win" equation invalid until the present date.

Captcha development continues on both the offensive (programs and systems that defeat CAPTCHAs) and defensive (improved CAPTCHAs) sides. Both sides are using more and more advanced techniques and attacks. This sort of "arms race" between researchers seeking more secure CAPTCHAs and the hackers, spoofers, and spammers trying to defeat the CAPTCHAs is likely to continue for some time.

REFERENCES

[1] Ads Captcha Ltd, Ads Captcha—Captcha Advertising, when ads meets captcha. Website: http://www.adscaptcha.com/, 2010.
[2] Alkacon Software GmbH, OpenCMS, the Open Source Content Management System/CMS. Website: http://www.opencms.org/, 2010.
[3] Amazon.com, Inc., Amazon Mechanical Turk. Website: https://www.mturk.com/, 2010.
[4] Archreality, Jcap (Captcha Validation Javascript). Website: http://www.archreality.com/jcap/, 2010.

[5] A. Elias, A. Spiros, Enhanced captchas: using animation to tell humans and computers apart, in: Proceedings of the 10th IFIP Open Conference on Communications and Multimedia Security (CMS'06), Springer, Berlin/Heidelberg, 2006, pp. 97–108, volume 4237/2006 of LNCS.

[6] Automattic, Inc., Akismet—Stop Comment Spam and Trackback Spam. Website: http://akismet. com/, 2010.

[7] B. Paul, F. Marc, G. Lior, L. Robert, L. Michael, S. Dominique, CAPTCHAs: The Good, the Bad, and the Ugly, in: Sicherheit 2010, 2010. Lecture Notes in Informatics. Gesellschaft fuer Informatik (GI).

[8] B.-Y. Ricardo, B. Paolo, H. Jose Maria Gomez, Adversarial Information Retrieval in the Web, UPGRADE (European Journal for the Informatics Professional) VIII (2007) 33–40.

[9] H. S. Baird. Document Image Defect Models and their Uses. in: Proceedings of the International Conference on Document Analysis and Recognition, pages 62–67, 1993.

[10] H.S. Baird, J.L. Bentley, Implicit captchas, in: Proceedings of SPIE/IS&T Conference on Document Recognition and Retrieval XII (DR&R2005), 2006, pp. 191–196.

[11] H.S. Baird, M.A. Moll, W. SuiYu, Scattertype: a legible but hard-to-segment captcha, in: Document Analysis and Recognition, 2005. Proceedings. Eighth International Conference on. vol. 2, 2005, pp. 935–939.

[12] H.S. Baird, M.A. Moll, S. Wang, A highly legible captcha that resists segmentation attacks, in: Proceedings of Second International Workshop on Human Interactive Proofs (HIP05), Springer, Berlin/Heidelberg, 2005, pp. 27–41, volume 3517/2005 of LNCS.

[13] H.S. Baird, T.P. Riopka, Scattertype: a reading captcha resistant to segmentation attack, in: IS&T/SPIE Document Recognition & Retrieval XII Conference, 2005, pp. 197–201.

[14] A. Basso, S. Sicco, Preventing massive automated access to web resources, Computers & Security 28 (3–4) (2009) 174–188.

[15] B. Richard, K. Stefan, Towards human interactive proofs in the text-domain, in: Proceedings of the 7th Information Security Conference, Springer Verlag, Berlin/Heidelberg, 2004, pp. 257–267.

[16] J.P. Bigham, A.C. Cavender, Evaluating existing audio captchas and an interface optimized for non-visual use, in: Proceedings of the 27th International Conference on Human Factors in Computing Systems, CHI '09, 2009, pp. 1829–1838. New York, NY, USA, ACM.

[17] D. Bradbury, Humans + porn = solved captcha, Network Security 2007 (11) (2007) 2.

[18] B. Elie, B. Steven, F. Celine, J.C. Mitchell, J. Dan, How good are humans at solving captchas? a large scale evaluation, in: Proceedings of the 2010 IEEE Symposium on Security and Privacy, SP '10, 2010, pp. 399–413. Washington, DC, USA, IEEE Computer Society.

[19] C. John, The Evolution of Malicious IRC Bots, in: Proceedings of the Virus Bulletin Conference 2005 (VB2005), 2005.

[20] captchas.net, captchas.net: Free CAPTCHA-Service. Website: http://captchas.net/, 2010.

[21] Carnegie Mellon University, CMU Sphinx—Speech Recognition Toolkit. Website: http:// cmusphinx.sourceforge.net/, 2010.

[22] Carnegie Mellon University, The Bongo CAPTCHA. Website: http://www.captcha.net/captchas/ bongo/, 2010.

[23] Carnegie Mellon University, The ESP-PIX CAPTCHA. Website: http://server251.theory.cs.cmu. edu/cgi-bin/esp-pix/esp-pix, 2010.

[24] A.A. Chandavale, A.M. Sapkal, R.M. Jalnekar, Algorithm to break visual captcha, in: Emerging Trends in Engineering and Technology (ICETET), 2009 2nd International Conference on, 2009, pp. 258–262.

[25] C. Kumar, L. Kevin, S. Patrice, C. Mary, Designing human friendly human interaction proofs (hips), in: CHI '05: Proceedings of the SIGCHI Conference on Human Factors in Computing Systems, 2005, pp. 711–720. New York, NY, USA, ACM.

[26] C. Kumar, P.Y. Simard, Using machine learning to break visual human interaction proofs (hips), in: L.K. Saul, W. Yair, B. Léon (Eds.), Advances in Neural Information Processing Systems 17, MIT Press, Cambridge, MA, 2005, pp. 265–272.

[27] K.-T. Chen, J.-W. Jiang, P. Huang, H.-H. Chu, C.-L. Lei, W.-C. Chen, Identifying mmorpg bots: a traffic analysis approach, EURASIP J. Adv. Signal Process 3 (2009) 1–3.

[28] M. Chew, H.S. Baird, Baffletext: a human interactive proof, in: 10th SPIE/IS&T Document Recognition and Retrieval Conference, 2003.

[29] M. Chew, J.D. Tygar, Image recognition CAPTCHAs, in: Proceedings of the 7th Information Security Conference (ISC 04), Springer, Berlin/Heidelberg, 2004, pp. 268–279. Lecture Notes in Computer Science.

[30] M. Chew, J.D. Tygar, Collaborative filtering captchas, in: Human Interactive Proofs: Second International Workshop (HIP 2005), Springer, 2005, pp. 66–81.

[31] C. Richard, G. Philippe, J. Markus, W. Lusha, W. XiaoFeng, Making captchas clickable, in: HotMobile '08: Proceedings of the 9th Workshop on Mobile Computing Systems and Applications, 2008, pp. 91–94. New York, NY, USA, ACM.

[32] A.L. Coates, H.S. Baird, R.J. Faternan, Pessimal print: a reverse turing test, in: Document Analysis and Recognition, 2001. Proceedings. Sixth International Conference on, 2001, pp. 1154–1158.

[33] C. Jing-Song, M. Jing-Ting, W. Xia, Z. Da, Z. Wu-Zhou, A captcha implementation based on 3d animation, in: Multimedia Information Networking and Security, 2009. MINES '09. International Conference on, vol. 2, 2009, pp. 179–182.

[34] C. Jing-Song, Z. Wu-Zhou, P. Yang, L. Yu, X. Bang, M. Jing-Ting, et al., A 3-layer dynamic captcha implementation, in: Education Technology and Computer Science (ETCS), 2010 Second International Workshop on, vol. 1, 2010, pp. 23–26.

[35] D. Dancho, Inside India's CAPTCHA solving economy, Website: http://www.zdnet.com/blog/security/inside-indias-captcha-solving-economy/1835, 2008.

[36] D. Greg Kochanski, L. Daniel, S. Chilin, A reverse turing test using speech, in: ICSLP, 2002, pp. 1357–1360.

[37] R. Datta, L. Jia, J.Z. Wang, Exploiting the human machine gap in image recognition for designing captchas, Information Forensics and Security, IEEE Transactions on 4 (3) (2009) 504–518.

[38] A. Desai, P. Patadia, Drag and drop: a better approach to captcha, in: India Conference (INDICON), 2009 Annual IEEE, 2009, pp. 1–4.

[39] Drupal Association, Drupal—Open Source CMS. Website: http://www.drupal.org/, 2010.

[40] C. Dwork, A. Goldberg, M. Naor, On Memory-Bound Functions for Fighting Spam, in: Proceedings of the 23rd Annual International Cryptology Conference (CRYPTO 2003), 2003.

[41] J. Elson, J.R. Douceur, J. Howell, J. Saul, Asirra: a captcha that exploits interest-aligned manual image categorization, in: Proceedings of 14th ACM Conference on Computer and Communications Security (CCS 2007), 2007, pp. 366–374.

[42] F. Joseph, C. Vincent, Turing Trade: a hybrid of a Turing test and a prediction market, in: Proceedings of The First Conference on Auctions, Market Mechanisms, and Their Applications (AMMA-09), 2009, pp. 61–73. Boston, MA, USA.

[43] R. Ferzli, R. Bazzi, L.J. Karam, A captcha based on the human visual systems masking characteristics, in: Multimedia and Expo, 2006 IEEE International Conference on, 2006, pp. 517–520.

[44] P.B. Godfrey, Text-based captcha algorithms, in: First Workshop on Human Interactive Proofs, 2002. http://www.adaddin.cs.cmu.edu/hips/events/abs/godfreyb_abstract.pdf. Unpublished Manuscript.

[45] P. Golle, Machine learning attacks against the asirra captcha, in: CCS '08: Proceedings of the 15th ACM Conference on Computer and Communications Security, 2008, pp. 535–542. New York, NY, USA, ACM.

[46] P. Golle, N. Ducheneaut, Preventing bots from playing online games, Comput. Entertain. 3 (3) (2005) 3.

[47] Google, Inc, reCAPTCHA: Stop Spam, Read Books. Website: http://www.google.com/recaptcha, 2010.

[48] G. Rich, K. Maryam, B. Shumeet, What's up captcha?: a captcha based on image orientation, in: WWW '09: Proceedings of the 18th International Conference on World Wide Web, 2009, pp. 841–850. New York, NY, USA, ACM.

[49] J. Grossman, T. Niedzialkowski, Hacking Intranet Websites from the Outside—Javascript Malware Just Got a Lot More Dangerous, in: Proceedings of Blackhat USA, Caesars Palace, Las Vegas, July 29-August 3, 2006. http://www.blackhat.com/presentations/bhusa-06/BH-US-06-Grossman.pdf Available.

[50] A. Gupta, J. Ashish, A. Raj, J. Abhimanyu, Sequenced tagged captcha: generation and its analysis, in: Advance Computing Conference, 2009. IACC 2009. IEEE International, 2009, pp. 1286–1291.

[51] C.J. Hernandez-Castro, A. Ribagorda, Pitfalls in CAPTCHA design and implementation: the Math CAPTCHA, a case study, Computers & Security 29 (1) (2010) 141–157.

[52] H.-C. Carlos Javier, R. Arturo, S. Yago, Side-channel attack on labeling captchas, The Computing Research Repository (CoRR) 2009.

[53] A. Heydon, M. Najork, Mercator: a scalable, extensible Web crawler, World Wide Web 2 (4) (1999) 219–229.

[54] A. Hindle, M.W. Godfrey, R.C. Holt, Reverse engineering captchas, in: Reverse Engineering, 2008. WCRE '08. 15th Working Conference on, 3 (3) 2008, pp. 59–68.

[55] H. Chien-Ju, W. Chen-Chi, C. Kuan-Ta, L. Chin-Luang, DevilTyper: A Game for Quantifying the Usability of CAPTCHA Tests, in: 7th ACM International Conference on Advances in Computer Entertainment Technology, Taipei, Taiwan, Nov. 2010.

[56] H. Jonathan, L. Jonathan, F. Jinjuan Heidi, D.A. John, Developing usable captchas for blind users, in: Assets '07: Proceedings of the 9th International ACM SIGACCESS Conference on Computers and Accessibility, 2007, pp. 245–246. New York, NY, USA, ACM.

[57] M.E. Hoque, D.J. Russomanno, M. Yeasin, 2d captchas from 3d models, in: SoutheastCon, 2006. Proceedings of the IEEE, 2006, pp. 165–170.

[58] M. Imsamai, S. Phimoltares, 3d captcha: a next generation of the captcha, in: Information Science and Applications (ICISA), 2010 International Conference on, 2010, pp. 1–8.

[59] I.F. Ince, Y.B. Salman, M.E. Yildirim, Y. Tae-Cheon, Execution time prediction for 3d interactive captcha by keystroke level model, in: Computer Sciences and Convergence Information Technology, 2009. ICCIT '09. Fourth International Conference on, 2009, pp. 1057–1061.

[60] I.F. Ince, Y. Ilker, Y.B. Salman, C. Hwan-Gue, Y. Tae-Cheon, Designing captcha algorithm: splitting and rotating the images against OCRs, in: Convergence and Hybrid Information Technology, 2008. ICCIT '08. Third International Conference on, vol. 2, 2008, pp. 596–601.

[61] International Business Machines Corp, IBM Rational AppScan. Website: http://www.ibm.com/developerworks/downloads/r/appscan/, 2010.

[62] International Business Machines Corp, IBM Web Content Management—Lotus. Website: http://www.ibm.com/software/lotus/products/webcontentmanagement/, 2010.

[63] Internet Archive, Internet Archive: Digital Library of Free Books, Movies, Music & Wayback Machine. Website: http://www.archive.org/, 2010.

[64] IUPR research group, OCRopus - open source OCR. Website: http://code.google.com/p/ocropus/, 2010.

[65] J. Abhimanyu, J. Ashish, A. Raj, T. Pahwa, Sequenced picture captcha: generation and its strength analysis, in: Internet Technology and Secured Transactions, 2009. ICITST 2009. International Conference for, 2009, pp. 1–8.

[66] E. Kaiser, W. Feng, mod kapow: protecting the web with transparent proof-of-work, in: INFOCOM Workshops 2008, IEEE, 2008, pp. 1–6.

[67] K. Hyungil, H. Sungwoo, K. Juntae, Detection of auto programs for mmorpgs, in: Z. Shichao, J. Ray (Eds.), AI 2005: Advances in Artificial Intelligence, volume 3809 of Lecture Notes in Computer Science, Springer, Berlin/Heidelberg, 2005, pp. 1281–1284.

[68] K. Kurt Alfred, Z. Richard, Balancing usability and security in a video captcha, in: SOUPS '09: Proceedings of the 5th Symposium on Usable Privacy and Security, 2009, pp. 1–11. New York, NY, USA, ACM.

[69] A. Kolupaev, J. Ogijenko, Captchas: humans vs. bots, Security Privacy, IEEE 6 (1) (2008) 68–70.

[70] L. Wen-Hung, A captcha mechanism by exchange image blocks, in: Pattern Recognition, 2006. ICPR 2006. 18th International Conference on, volume 1, 2006, pp. 1179–1183.

[71] W.H. Liao, C. Chang, Embedding information within dynamic visual patterns, in: Proceedings of the IEEE International Conference on Multimedia and Expo 2004 (ICME04), 2004, pp. 895–898.

[72] M.D. Lillibridge, M. Abadi, K. Bharata, A.Z. Broder, Method for selectively restricting access to computer systems, 2001. Technical report, U.S. Patent No. 6,195,698.

[73] L. Chi-Wei, C. Yu-Han, C. Liang-Gee, Bio-inspired unified model of visual segmentation system for captcha character recognition, in: Signal Processing Systems, 2008. SiPS 2008. IEEE Workshop on, 2008, pp. 158–163.

[74] ImageMagick Studio LLC, ImageMagick: Convert, Edit and Compose Images. Website: http://www.imagemagick.org/, 2010.

[75] H.G. Loebner, Home Page of the Loebner Prize, Website: http://www.loebner.net/Prizef/loebner-prize.html, 2010.

[76] O.B. Longe, A.B.C. Robert, U. Onwudebelu, Checking internet masquerading using multiple captcha challenge-response systems, in: Adaptive Science Technology, 2009. ICAST 2009. 2nd International Conference on, 2009, pp. 244–249.

[77] L. Daniel, Leveraging the captcha problem, in: Proc. of the Second International Workshop on Human Interactive Proofs, volume 3517/2005 of LNCS, Springer, Berlin/Heidelberg, 2005, pp. 97–110.

[78] P. Lupkowski, M. Urbanski, Semcaptcha: user-friendly alternative for ocr-based captcha systems, in: Computer Science and Information Technology, 2008. IMCSIT 2008. International Multiconference on, 2008, pp. 325–329.

[79] A. Markkola, J. Lindqvist, Accessible voice captchas for internet telephony, in: Proceedings of the Symposium on Accessible Privacy and Security (SOAPS'08), 2008. Pittsburgh, PA, USA.

[80] M. May, Inaccessibility of CAPTCHA: Alternatives to Visual Turing Tests on the Web, 2005. http://www.w3.org/TR/turingtest Technical report, W3C Working Group Note, Available at.

[81] A.J. Menezes, P.C. van Oorschot, S.A. Vanstone, Handbook of Applied Cryptography, CRC Press, Boca Raton, Florida, USA, 1997.

[82] D. Misra, K. Gaj, Face recognition captchas, in: Telecommunications, 2006. AICT-ICIW '06. International Conference on Internet and Web Applications and Services/Advanced International Conference on, 2006, p. 122.

[83] G. Mori, J. Malik, Recognizing objects in adversarial clutter: breaking a visual captcha, in: Computer Vision and Pattern Recognition, 2003. Proceedings. 2003 IEEE Computer Society Conference on, vol. 1, 2003, pp. I–134–I–141.

[84] G. Moy, N. Jones, C. Harkless, R. Potter, Distortion estimation techniques in solving visual captchas, in: Computer Vision and Pattern Recognition, 2004. CVPR 2004. Proceedings of the 2004 IEEE Computer Society Conference on, vol. 2, 2004, pp. II–23–II–28.

[85] M. Naor, Verification of a human in the loop or identification via the Turing test, 1996.

[86] NuCaptcha, Inc, NuCaptcha—The Most Secure Captcha. Website: http://www.nucaptcha.com/, 2010.

[87] O. Warner, The Cutest Human-Test: KittenAuth, Website: http://thepcspy.com/read/the_cutest_humantest_kittenauth/, 2010.

[88] OpenQA, Selenium web application testing system. Website: http://seleniumhq.org/, 2010.

[89] phpcaptcha.org, Securimage CAPTCHA—Free PHP Captcha Script. Website: http://www.phpcaptcha.org/, 2010.

[90] Plone Foundation, PloneCMS: Open Source Content Management. Website: http://plone.org/, 2010.

[91] A. Raj, J. Ashish, T. Pahwa, J. Abhimanyu, Analysis of tagging variants of sequenced tagged captcha (stc), in: Science and Technology for Humanity (TIC-STH), 2009 IEEE Toronto International Conference, 2009, pp. 427–432.

[92] T. Rob, Accesible Text CAPTCHA Logic Questions, Website: http://textcaptcha.com/, 2010.

[93] robotstxt.org, The Web Robots Pages. Website: http://www.robotstxt.org/, 2010.

[94] R. Yong, L. Zicheg, Artifacial: automated reverse turing test using facial features, in: MULTIMEDIA '03: Proceedings of the Eleventh ACM International Conference on Multimedia, 2003, pp. 295–298. New York, NY, USA, ACM.

[95] A. Rusu, R. Docimo, Securing the web using human perception and visual object interpretation, in: Information Visualisation, 2009 13th International Conference, 2009, pp. 613–618.

[96] R. Amalia, G. Venu, Handwritten captcha: using the difference in the abilities of humans and machines in reading handwritten words, 2004. Frontiers in Handwriting Recognition, International Workshop on (IWFHR'04), 0:226–231.

[97] R. Amalia, G. Venu, A human interactive proof algorithm using handwriting recognition, in: ICDAR '05: Proceedings of the Eighth International Conference on Document Analysis and Recognition, 2005, pp. 967–971. Washington, DC, USA, IEEE Computer Society.

[98] S. Graig, L. Jonathan, H. Harry, F. Jinjuan, Towards a universally usable human interaction proof: evaluation of task completion strategies, ACM Trans. Access. Comput. 2 (2010) 15:1–15:32.

[99] J.R. Searle, Minds, brains, and programs, Behav. Brain Sci. 3 (03) (1980) 417–424.

[100] S.C. Shapiro, Encyclopedia of Artificial Intelligence, second ed., John Wiley & Sons, Inc., New York, 1992.

[101] S.M. Shieber, Lessons from a restricted Turing test, Commun. ACM 37 (1994) 70–78.

[102] M. Shirali-Shahreza, Highlighting captcha, in: Human System Interactions, 2008 Conference on, 2008, pp. 247–250.

[103] M. Shirali-Shahreza, S. Shirali-Shahreza, Drawing captcha, in: Information Technology Interfaces, 2006. 28th International Conference on, 2006, pp. 475–480.

[104] M. Shirali-Shahreza, S. Shirali-Shahreza, Captcha for blind people, in: Signal Processing and Information Technology, 2007 IEEE International Symposium on, 2007, pp. 995–998.

[105] M. Shirali-Shahreza, S. Shirali-Shahreza, Collage captcha, in: Signal Processing and Its Applications, 2007. ISSPA 2007. 9th International Symposium on, 2007, pp. 1–4.

[106] M. Shirali-Shahreza, S. Shirali-Shahreza, Online collage captcha, in: Image Analysis for Multimedia Interactive Services, 2007. WIAMIS '07. Eighth International Workshop on, 2007, p. 58.

[107] M. Shirali-Shahreza, S. Shirali-Shahreza, Question-based captcha, in: Conference on Computational Intelligence and Multimedia Applications, 2007. International Conference on, vol. 4, 2007, pp. 54–58.

[108] M. Shirali-Shahreza, S. Shirali-Shahreza, Advanced collage captcha, in: Information Technology: New Generations, 2008. ITNG 2008. Fifth International Conference on, 2008, pp. 1234–1235.

[109] M. Shirali-Shahreza, S. Shirali-Shahreza, Motion captcha, in: Human System Interactions, 2008 Conference on, 2008, pp. 1042–1044.

[110] M.H. Shirali Shahreza, M. Shirali Shahreza, An anti-SMS-spam using CAPTCHA, in: Computing, Communication, Control, and Management, 2008. CCCM '08. ISECS International Colloquium on, vol.2, 2008, pp. 318–321.

[111] M.H. Shirali-Shahreza, M. Shirali-Shahreza, Localized captcha for illiterate people, in: Intelligent and Advanced Systems, 2007. ICIAS 2007. International Conference on, 2007, pp. 675–679.

[112] M.H. Shirali-Shahreza, M. Shirali-Shahreza, Multilingual captcha, in: Computational Cybernetics, 2007. ICCC 2007. IEEE International Conference on, 2007, pp. 135–139.

[113] S. Shirali-Shahreza, M. Shirali-Shahreza, Captcha for children, in: System of Systems Engineering, 2008. SoSE '08. IEEE International Conference on, 2008, pp. 1–6.

[114] S. Shirali-Shahreza, M. Shirali-Shahreza, A. Movaghar, Exam hip, in: Anti-counterfeiting, Security, Identification, 2007 IEEE International Workshop on, 2007, pp. 415–418.

[115] S.-S. Sajad, M. Ali, A New Anti-Spam Protocol Using CAPTCHA, in: Networking, Sensing and Control, 2007 IEEE International Conference on, 2007, pp. 234–238.

[116] P.Y. Simard, S. Richard, B. Josh, C. Julien, C. Iulian, Using character recognition and segmentation to tell computer from humans, in: ICDAR '03: Proceedings of the Seventh International Conference on Document Analysis and Recognition, 2003, p. 418. Washington, DC, USA, IEEE Computer Society.

[117] Solve Media, Inc, Solve Media. Website: http://www.solvemedia.com/, 2010.

[118] Y. Soupionis, D. Gritzalis, Audio captcha: existing solutions assessment and a new implementation for voip telephony, Computers & Security 29 (5) (2010) 603–618.

[119] C. Striletchi, M.F. Vaida, A distributed solution for restraining the web-bots access to on-line software applications, in: Computational Intelligence and Intelligent Informatics, 2009. ISCIII '09. 4th International Symposium on, 2009, pp. 69–73.

[120] C. Striletchi, M.F. Vaida, A web 3.0 solution for restraining the web-bots access to the on-line displayed content, in: Information Technology Interfaces, 2009. ITI '09. Proceedings of the ITI 2009 31st International Conference on, 2009, pp. 633–638.

[121] Symantec Corporation, MessageLabs Intelligence monthly report. 2010. Website:http://www.messagelabs.com/intelligence.aspx Technical report, Symantec Corporation, July 2010.

[122] T. Jennifer, S. Jiri, H. Sean, A. Luis Von, Breaking audio captchas, in: D. Koller, D. Schuurmans, Y. Bengio, L. Bottou (Eds.), Advances in Neural Information Processing Systems 21, 2009, pp. 1625–1632. Neural Information Processing Systems Foundation.

[123] A.O. Thomas, A. Rusu, V. Govindaraju, Synthetic handwritten captchas, Pattern Recogn. 42 (12) (2009) 3365–3373.

[124] A.M. Turing, Computing Machinery and Intelligence, Mind 59 (236) (1950) 433–460.

[125] P.C. Van Oorschot, S. Stubblebine, On countering online dictionary attacks with login histories and humans-in-the-loop, ACM Trans. Inf. Syst. Secur. 9 (3) (2006) 235–258.

[126] E.R. Vimina, An automated reverse Turing test using facial expressions, in: Human System Interactions, 2009. HSI '09. 2nd Conference on, 2009, pp. 314–317.

[127] E.R. Vimina, A.U. Areekal, Telling computers and humans apart automatically using activity recognition, in: Systems, Man and Cybernetics, 2009. SMC 2009. IEEE International Conference on, 2009, pp. 4906–4909.

[128] VirtuOz, Inc, Virtual and Self Service Agents. Website: http://www.virtuoz.com/, 2010.

[129] L. von Ahn, B. Manuel, N.J. Hopper, L. John, Captcha: using hard AI problems for security, in: Proceedings of Eurocrypt, vol. 2656, 2003, pp. 294–311.

[130] L. von Ahn, M. Blum, J. Langford, Telling humans and computers apart automatically—how lazy cryptographers do ai, Commun. ACM 47 (2004) 56–60.

[131] L. von Ahn, D. Laura, Labeling images with a computer game, in: CHI '04: Proceedings of the SIGCHI Conference on Human Factors in Computing Systems, 2004, pp. 319–326. New York, NY, USA, ACM.

[132] L. von Ahn, B. Maurer, C. McMillen, D. Abraham, M. Blum, reCAPTCHA: human-Based Character Recognition via Web Security Measures, Science 321 (5895) (2008) 1465–1468.

[133] W. Sui-Yu, H.S. Baird, J.L. Bentley, Captcha challenge tradeoffs: familiarity of strings versus degradation of image, in: Pattern Recognition, 2006. ICPR 2006. 18th International Conference on, vol. 3, 2006, pp. 164–167.

[134] WebSpamProtect.com, Free web form spam protection. CAPTCHA service. Online mail form builder. Website: http://webspamprotect.com/, 2010.

[135] W. Joseph, Eliza—a computer program for the study of natural language communication between man and machine, Commun. ACM 9 (1966) 36–45.

[136] WhiteHat Security, WhiteHat Security—Website Vulnerability Management. Website: http://www.whitehatsec.com/home/services/sentinelpe.html, 2010.

[137] W. Jonathan, Strong captcha Guidelines v1.2, 2009. Unpublished manuscript.

[138] WordPress.org, WordPress - WP Captcha-Free—WordPress Plugins. Website: http://wordpress.org/extend/plugins/wp-captcha-free/, 2010.

[139] X. Pablo, A. Santos, F. Marcial, C. Joaquim, A captcha in the text domain, in: M. Robert, T. Zahir, H. Pilar (Eds.), OTM Workshops (1), volume 4277 of Lecture Notes in Computer Science, Springer, Berlin/Heidelberg, 2006, pp. 605–615.

[140] T. Yamamoto, J.D. Tygar, M. Nishigaki, Captcha using strangeness in machine translation, in: Advanced Information Networking and Applications (AINA), 2010 24th IEEE International Conference on, 2010, pp. 430–437.

[141] J. Yan, Bot, cyborg and automated turing test, in: Fourteenth International Workshop on Security Protocols, 2006, pp. 190–197.

[142] J. Yan, A.S. El Ahmad, Breaking visual captchas with naive pattern recognition algorithms, in: Computer Security Applications Conference, 2007. ACSAC 2007. Twenty-Third Annual, 2007, pp. 279–291.

[143] J. Yan, A.S. El Ahmad, CAPTCHA security: a case study, IEEE Secur. Privacy 7 (4) (2009) 22–28.

[144] Y. Jeff, A. Ahmad Salah El, Usability of captchas or usability issues in captcha design, in: SOUPS '08: proceedings of the 4th Symposium on Usable Privacy and Security, 2008, pp. 44–52. New York, NY, USA, ACM.

[145] YUNiTI, YUNiTI Registration Page. Website: http://www.yuniti.com/register.php, 2010.

[146] Z. Wenjun, Zhang's captcha architecture based on intelligent interaction via ria, in: Computer Engineering and Technology (ICCET), 2010 2nd International Conference on, vol. 6, 2010, pp. V6–57–V6–62.

[147] B.B. Zhu, Y. Jeff, L. Qiujie, Y. Chao, L. Jia, X. Ning, et al., Attacks and design of image recognition captchas, in: Proceedings of the 17th ACM conference on Computer and Communications Security, CCS '10, 2010, pp. 187–200. New York, NY, USA, ACM.

ABOUT THE AUTHOR

José María Gómez Hidalgo holds a Ph.D. in Mathematics, and has been a lecturer and researcher at the Universidad Europea de Madrid for 10 years, where he has been the Head of the Department of Computer Science. Currently he is R&D and Training Director at the security firm Optenet. His main research interests include several Artificial Intelligence topics like Natural Language Processing and Machine Learning, with applications to Information Access, Adversarial Information Retrieval and Information Security including spam filtering and children protection in the Internet. He has taken part in around 15 research projects, leading some of them. José María has coauthored a number of research papers in the topics above. He is Program Committee member for several conferences and reviewer for a number of research journals. He has also reviewed research project proposals for the European Commission. Currently he serves as Chairman of the European Normalization Committee CEN/TC 365 "Internet Filtering."

Gonzalo Alvarez received his M.S. degree in Telecommunications Engineering from the University of the Basque Country (Spain) in 1995 and his Ph.D. degree in Computer Science from the Polytechnic University of Madrid (Spain) in 2000. He is a tenured scientist at the Spanish National Research Council (CSIC), at the Information Processing and Coding Department at the Applied Physics Institute. He is interested in cryptology and Internet security, fields in which he has authored over 400 articles in journals and conferences and many books. His scientific and dissemination experience is complemented with a deep practical knowledge about real world Internet security acquired through several projects both publicly and privately funded as security architecture designer, secure application developer, and security auditor.

Advances in Video-Based Biometrics

RAMA CHELLAPPA

Center for Automation Research, University of Maryland, College Park, Maryland, USA

PAVAN TURAGA

Center for Automation Research, University of Maryland, College Park, Maryland, USA

Abstract

Biometrics deals with the problem of uniquely identifying individuals based on physiological or behavioral attributes. Physiological biometrics involve measurement from body parts such as the fingerprint, face, iris, etc., whereas behavioral biometrics exploits cues such as gait, voice, expressions, etc. In this chapter, we discuss video-based biometrics involving faces and gait. We discuss spatiotemporal models appropriate for each task, followed by design of metrics for classification. We discuss how careful modeling of the variations of appearance and motion leads to improved biometric systems.

1. Introduction 184
2. Video-Based Face Recognition 186
    2.1. Parametric Model for Appearance and Dynamic Variations 187
    2.2. The Manifold Structure of Subspaces 189
    2.3. Video-Based Face Recognition Experiments 190
3. Video-Based Identification Using Gait 191
    3.1. Dynamic Time Warping 192
    3.2. Parametric Models for Shape Sequences 193
    3.3. Understanding the Space of Execution Variations 196
    3.4. Experiments on USF Gait Database 199

ADVANCES IN COMPUTERS, VOL. 83
ISSN: 0065-2458/DOI: 10.1016/B978-0-12-385510-7.00004-7

183

Copyright © 2011 Elsevier Inc.
All rights reserved.

4. Conclusions 200
   Acknowledgments 203
   References 201

1. Introduction

Biometrics involves the study of approaches and algorithms for uniquely recognizing humans based on physical or behavioral cues. Traditional approaches are based on fingerprint, face, or iris and can be classified as physiological biometrics, that is, they rely on physical attributes for recognition. Physiological biometrics is usually quite accurate when acquisition is done in controlled settings. However, this turns out to be a disadvantage when one is faced with uncooperative subjects and unconstrained acquisition conditions and environments, or when one is looking for suspects in a stealthy fashion. In such cases, one requires remote acquisition techniques that may not provide sufficiently clean physiological biometrics. As an alternative, "behavioral biometrics" have been gaining popularity, where the premise is that behavior is as useful a cue to recognize humans as their physical attributes. The advantage of this approach is that subject-cooperation is not necessary and it can proceed without interrupting or interfering with the subject's activity. Observing behavior usually implies longer-term observation of the subject. In the video-based surveillance setting, this takes the form of identifying humans based on video feeds. Advances in video analysis techniques now allow one to accurately detect and track humans and faces from medium to high-resolution videos. The availability of video brings about interesting questions about how to exploit the extra information.

A number of experimental studies have shown that motion information helps in recognizing objects by enhancing the recovery of information about shape [1] or by enhancing the observer's ability to find meaningful edges [2]. It provides more views [3] and also provides information about how features change over time [4]. In the case of faces, motion has special significance, as it encodes more information than simply the 3D structure of the face. This is in the form of behavioral cues such as idiosyncratic head movements and gestures which can potentially aid in recognition tasks. Video is a rich source of information in that it can lead to potentially better representations by offering more views of the face. Further, the role of facial motion for face perception has been well documented. Psychophysical studies [5] have found evidence that when both structure and dynamics information is available, humans tend to rely more on dynamics under non-optimal viewing conditions (such as low spatial resolution, harsh illumination conditions, etc.).

Gait refers to the style of walking of an individual. Studies in psychophysics indicate that humans have the capability of recognizing people from even impoverished displays of gait, indicating the presence of identity information in gait. It is interesting, therefore, to study the utility of gait as a biometric. In fact the nature of shape changes of the silhouette of a human provides significant information about the activity performed by the human, as well as reveals idiosyncratic movements of an individual. Consider the images shown in Fig. 1. It is not very difficult to perceive the fact that these represent the silhouette of a walking human.

Apart from providing information about the activity being performed, the manner of shape changes provides valuable insights regarding the identity of the object. Gait-based human ID is an area that has attracted significant attention due to its potential applications in remote biometrics. The discrimination between individuals is significantly improved if we take the manner of shape changes into account.

In this chapter, we discuss approaches that specifically model both the appearance and behavior of a subject either using faces or using gait. In the case of face, the model parameters capture coarse facial appearance and global dynamic information. In the case of gait, the model captures the shape of the human silhouette and the observed variability in walking styles by non-linear warps of the time-axis.

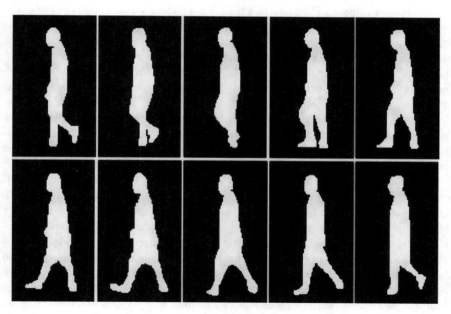

FIG. 1. Sequence of shapes as a person walks frontoparallely.

2. Video-Based Face Recognition

In video-based FR for biometrics, one is faced with the challenge of how to exploit the available extra information from video. This is usually done in one of the following ways: by using frame-based recognition algorithms and fusing the results, modeling the temporal correlations explicitly to recognize the human, or extracting joint appearance and behavioral features from the sequences. We briefly review each one here.

A straightforward approach to utilize temporal information for video-based face recognition is to fuse the results obtained by a 2D face recognition algorithm on each frame of the sequence. The video sequence can be seen as an unordered set of images to be used for both training and testing phases. During testing one can use the sequence as a set of probes, each of them providing a decision regarding the identity of the person. Appropriate fusion techniques can then be applied to provide the final identity. Perhaps the most frequently used fusion strategy in this case is majority voting [6,7]. Other techniques that utilize image-ensembles for object and face recognition [8–11] can be employed as well. For example, it was shown by Jacobs et al. that the illumination cone of a convex Lambertian surface can be approximated by a 9D linear subspace [12]. In Ref. [11], Zhou and Chellappa study the problem of measuring similarity between two ensembles by projecting the data into a Reproducing Kernel Hilbert Space (RKHS). The ensemble distance is then characterized as the probabilistic distance (Chernoff distance, Bhattacharyya distance, Kullback-Leibler (KL) divergence, etc.) in RKHS. Another common approach is to approximate the image-space of a single face/object under small variations as a linear subspace [9,13]. These approaches are purely data-driven approaches where no models are imposed on face appearance or dynamics. Thus, they work well when many views of the face are available in various poses. This leads us to the model-based approaches which try to generalize beyond the available visual information about the face.

Most face recognition approaches rely on a model of appearance for each individual subject. The simplest appearance model is a static image of the person. Such appearance models are rather limited in utility in video-based face recognition tasks where subjects may be imaged under varying viewpoints, illuminations, expressions, etc. Thus, instead of using a static image as an appearance model, a sufficiently long video which encompasses several variations in facial appearance can lend itself to building more robust appearance models. Several methods have been proposed for extracting more descriptive appearance models from videos. For example, a facial video is considered as a sequence of images sampled from an "appearance manifold" in Lee et al. [14]. In principle, the appearance manifold of a subject contains all possible appearances of the subject. In practice, the appearance manifold for each person is estimated from training data of videos. For ease of estimation, the appearance manifold is considered to be a collection of affine subspaces, where each subspace encodes a set of similar appearances of the subject. Temporal variations of appearances in a given video sequence are then modeled as transitions between the appearance subspaces. This method is robust to large appearance changes if sufficient 3D view variations and illumination variations are available in the training set. Further, the tracking problem can be integrated into this framework by searching for a bounding-box on the test image that minimizes the distance of the cropped region to the learnt appearance manifold.

In a related work, Arandjelovic and Cipolla [15] represent the appearance variations due to shape and illumination on human faces, using the assumption that the "shape-illumination manifold" of all possible illuminations and head poses is generic for human faces. This means that the shape-illumination manifold can be estimated using a set of subjects exclusive of the test set. They show that the effects of face shape and illumination can be learnt using probabilistic principal component analysis (PCA) from a small, unlabeled set of video sequences of faces in randomly varying lighting conditions. Given a novel sequence, the learnt model is used to decompose the face appearance manifold into albedo and shape-illumination manifolds, producing the classification decision using robust likelihood estimation.

In the next section, we describe a parametric model for appearance and dynamics to understand spatiotemporal variations in face sequences. We discuss the manifold structure of these models, which are then used to devise joint appearance and dynamic based recognition algorithms.

2.1 Parametric Model for Appearance and Dynamic Variations

A wide variety of spatiotemporal data have often been modeled as realizations of dynamical models. Examples include dynamic textures [16], human joint angle trajectories [17], and silhouettes [18]. A well-known dynamical model for such time-series data is the autoregressive and moving average (ARMA) model. Let $f(t)$ be a sequence of features extracted from a video indexed by time t. The ARMA model parametrizes the evolution of the features $f(t)$ using the following equations:

$$f(t) = Cz(t) + w(t), \quad w(t) \sim N(0, R), \tag{1}$$

$$z(t+1) = Az(t) + v(t), \quad v(t) \sim N(0, Q), \tag{2}$$

where, $z \in \mathbb{R}^d$ is the hidden state vector, $A \in \mathbb{R}^{d \times d}$ the transition matrix, and $C \in \mathbb{R}^{p \times d}$ the measurement matrix. $f \in \mathbb{R}^p$ represents the observed features while w and v are noise components modeled as normal with zero-mean and covariances $R \in \mathbb{R}^{p \times p}$ and $Q \in \mathbb{R}^{d \times d}$, respectively.

For high-dimensional time-series data (dynamic textures, etc.), the most common approach is to first learn a lower-dimensional embedding of the observations via PCA, and learn temporal dynamics in the lower-dimensional space. Closed form solutions for learning the model parameters (A, C) from the feature sequence $(f_{1:T})$ have been proposed by Doretto et al. and Overschee and Moor [16,19] and are widely used in the computer vision community. Let observations $f(1), f(2), \ldots, f(\tau)$ represent the features for the time indices $1, 2, \ldots, \tau$. Let $[f(1), f(2), \ldots, f(\tau)] = U \Sigma V^T$ be the singular value decomposition of the data. Then $\hat{C} = U$, $\hat{A} = \Sigma V^T D_1 V (V^T D_2 V)^{-1} \Sigma^{-1}$, where $D_1 = [0\ 0; I_{\tau-1}\ 0]$ and $D_2 = [I_{\tau-1}\ 0; 0\ 0]$.

The parameter C captures the observation-space or in other words represents the coarse facial appearance of the subject. The parameter A captures how the facial appearance changes over time. The model parameters (A, C) do not lie in a vector space. For comparison of models, the most commonly used distance metric is based on subspace angles between column-spaces of the observability matrices [20]. For the ARMA model of (Eq. (2)), starting from an initial condition $z(0)$, it can be shown that the *expected* observation sequence is given by

$$E \begin{bmatrix} f(0) \\ f(1) \\ f(2) \\ \vdots \\ \vdots \end{bmatrix} = \begin{bmatrix} C \\ CA \\ CA^2 \\ \vdots \\ \vdots \end{bmatrix} z(0) = O_\infty(M) z(0). \tag{3}$$

Thus, the expected observation sequence generated by a time-invariant model $M = (A, C)$ lies in the column space of the extended *observability* matrix given by

$$O_\infty^T = \left[C^T, (CA)^T, (CA^2)^T, \ldots, (CA^n)^T \right]. \tag{4}$$

In experimental implementations, we approximate the extended observability matrix by the finite observability matrix as is commonly done [21].

$$O_m^T = \left[C^T, (CA)^T, (CA^2)^T, \ldots, (CA^{m-1})^T \right]. \tag{5}$$

The size of this matrix is $mp \times d$. The column space of this matrix is a d-dimensional subspace of $\mathbb{R}^{mp}$, where d is the dimension of the state-space z in Eq. (2). d is typically of the order of 5–10.

Thus, given a database of videos, we estimate the model parameters as described above for each video. The finite observability matrix is computed as in Eq. (5). To represent the subspace spanned by the columns of this matrix, we store *an* orthonormal basis computed by Gram-Schmidt orthonormalization. Since, a subspace is a point on a *Grassmann* manifold [22,23], a linear dynamical system can be alternately identified as a point on the Grassmann manifold corresponding to the column space of the observability matrix. The goal now is to devise methods for classification and recognition using these model parameters. Given a set of videos for a given class, we would like to compute a parametric or nonparametric class-conditional density. Then, the maximum likelihood classification for each test instance can be performed using these class conditional distributions. To enable these, we need to understand the geometry of the Grassmann manifold. These methods were originally presented in Turaga et al. [23].

2.2   The Manifold Structure of Subspaces

The set of all d-dimensional linear subspaces of $\mathbb{R}^n$ is called the Grassmann manifold which will be denoted as $\mathcal{G}_{n,d}$. The set of all $n \times d$ orthonormal matrices is called the Stiefel manifold and shall be denoted as $\mathcal{S}_{n,d}$. As discussed in the applications above, we are interested in computing statistical models over the Grassmann manifold. Let $U_1\ U_2, \ldots, U_k$ be some points on $\mathcal{S}_{n,d}$ and we seek their sample mean, an average, for defining a probability model on $\mathcal{S}_{n,d}$. Recall that these U_is are tall, orthogonal matrices. It is easy to see that the Euclidean sample mean $\frac{1}{k}\sum_{i=1}^{k} U_i$ is not a valid operation, because the resultant mean does not have the property of orthonormality. This is because $\mathcal{S}_{n,d}$ is not a vector space. Similarly, many of the standard tools in estimation and modeling theory do not directly apply to such spaces but can be adapted by accounting for the underlying nonlinear geometry.

A subspace is stored as an orthonormal matrix which forms a basis for the subspace. However, since the choice of basis for a subspace is not unique, any notion of distance and statistics should be invariant to this choice. This requires us to interpret each point on the Grassmann manifold as an equivalence of points on the Stiefel manifold, where all orthonormal matrices that span the same subspace are considered equivalent.

A point U on $\mathcal{S}_{n,d}$ is represented as a tall-thin $n \times d$ orthonormal matrix. The corresponding equivalence class of $n \times d$ matrices $[U] = UR$, for $R \in GL(d)$ is called the Procrustes representation of the Stiefel manifold. Thus, to compare two points in $\mathcal{G}_{n,d}$, we simply compare the smallest squared distance between the corresponding equivalence classes on the Stiefel manifold according to the Procrustes representation. Given matrices U_1 and U_2 on $\mathcal{S}_{n,d}$, the smallest squared Euclidean distance between the corresponding equivalence classes is given by

$$d^2_{\text{Procrust}}([U_1],[U_2]) = \min_R \operatorname{tr}(U_1 - U_2 R)^T (U_1 - U_2 R), \qquad (6)$$

$$d^2_{\text{Procrust}}([U_1],[U_2]) = \min_R \operatorname{tr}(R^T R - 2U_1^T U_2 R + I_k). \qquad (7)$$

When R varies over the orthogonal group $O(d)$, the minimum is attained at $R = H_1 H_2^T = A(A^T A)^{-1/2}$, where $A = H_1 D H_2^T$ is the singular value decomposition of A. We refer the reader to Ref. [24] for proofs and alternate cases. Given several examples from a class $(U_1, U_2, \ldots, U_n)$ on the manifold, the class conditional density can be estimated using an appropriate kernel function. We first assume that an appropriate choice of a divergence on the manifold has been made such as the one above. For the Procrustes measure the density estimate is given by Chikuse et al. [24] as

$$\hat{f}(U;M) = \frac{1}{n} C(M) \sum_{i=1}^{n} K\left[M^{-1/2} \left(I_k - U_i^T U U^T U_i \right) M^{-1/2} \right], \qquad (8)$$

where $K(T)$ is the kernel function, M is a $d \times d$ positive definite matrix which plays the role of the kernel width or a smoothing parameter. $C(M)$ is a normalizing factor chosen so that the estimated density integrates to unity. The matrix valued kernel function $K(T)$ can be chosen in several ways. We have used $K(T) = \exp(-\operatorname{tr}(T))$ in all the experiments reported in this chapter. In this nonparametric method for density estimation, the choice of kernel width M becomes important. Thus, though this is a non-iterative procedure, the optimal choice of the kernel width can have a large impact on the final results. In general, there is no standard way to choose this parameter except for cross-validation. In the experiments reported here, we use $M = I$, the $d \times d$ identity matrix.

In addition to such nonparametric methods, there are principled methods to devise parametric densities on manifolds. Here we simply refer the reader to Ref. [22] for mathematical details. In brief, using the tangent structure of the manifold, it is possible to define the well-known parametric densities such as multivariate Gaussian, mixture-of-Gaussians, etc., on the tangent spaces and wrap them back to the manifold. Densities defined in such a manner are called "wrapped"-densities. In the experiments section, we use a wrapped-Gaussian to model class-condition densities on the Grassmann manifold. This is compared to the simpler nonparametric method described above.

2.3   Video-Based Face Recognition Experiments

We performed a recognition experiment on the NIST's Multiple Biometric Grand Challenge (MBGC) dataset. The MBGC Video Challenge dataset consists of a large number of subjects walking towards a camera in a variety of illumination conditions.

TABLE I

COMPARISON OF VIDEO-BASED FACE RECOGNITION APPROACHES USING (A) SUBSPACE ANGLES + ARC-LENGTH METRIC, (B) PROCRUSTES DISTANCE, (C) KERNEL DENSITY, (D) WRAPPED NORMAL DENSITY

Subset	Distinct subjects	Total sequences	Arc-length metric	Procrustes metric	Kernel density	Wrapped normal
S_2	143	395	38.48	43.79	39.74	63.79
S_3	55	219	48.85	53.88	50.22	74.88
S_4	54	216	48.61	53.70	50.46	75
Avg. (%)			45.31	50.45	46.80	71.22

Face regions are manually tracked and a sequence of cropped images is obtained. There were a total of 143 subjects with the number of videos per subject ranging from 1 to 5. In our experiments, we took subsets of the dataset which contained at least 2 sequences per person denoted as S_2, at least 3 sequences per person denoted as S_3, etc. Each of the face-images was first preprocessed to zero-mean and unity variance. In each of these subsets, we performed a leave-one-out testing. The results of the leave one out testing are shown in Table I. Also reported are the total number of distinct subjects and the total number of video sequences in each of the subsets. In the comparisons, we show results using the "arc-length" metric between subspaces [25]. This metric computes the subspace angles between two subspaces and takes the Frobenius norm of the angles as a distance measure [25]. We also show comparisons with the Procrustes measure, the kernel density estimate with $M = I$ and a parametric wrapped Gaussian density on the manifold. The wrapped Gaussian is estimated on the tangent-plane centered at the mean-point of the dataset. The mean, more formally defined as the Karcher mean, is defined as the point that minimizes the sum of squared geodesic distances to all other points. The tangent-plane being a vector space allows the use of multivariate statistics to define class-conditional densities. We refer the reader to Ref. [22] for mathematical details.

As can be seen, statistical methods outperform nearest-neighbor based approaches. As one would expect, the results improve when more examples per class are available. Since the optimal kernel-width is not known in advance, this might explain the relatively poor performance of the kernel density method.

3. Video-Based Identification Using Gait

As mentioned earlier, gait refers to the style of walking of an individual. To use gait as a biometric, the choice of feature and the choice of model governing a gait sequence are important. The features must be reasonably robust to operating conditions and should yield good discriminability across individuals. The human silhouette in general is a popular feature as it captures the motion of most of the body parts. It also supports night vision capability as it can be derived from IR imagery also. Shape has been used by several researchers for gait recognition. Niyogi and Adelson [26] obtained spatiotemporal solids by aligning consecutive images and use a weighted Euclidean distance for recognition. Sarkar et al. [27] provide a baseline algorithm for gait recognition using silhouette correlation. Han and Bhanu [28] use the gait energy image while Wang et al. use Procrustes shape analysis for recognition [29]. Foster et al. [30] use area based features. Bobick and Johnson [31] use activity specific static and stride parameters to perform recognition. Collins et al. build a silhouette based nearest neighbor classifier [32] to do recognition. Several researchers [33,34] have used Hidden Markov Models (HMM) and their variants such as pHMMs [35] for the task of gait based identification. Another shape based method for identifying individuals from noisy silhouettes is provided in Niyogi and Adelson [36].

Once a feature has been chosen, the next question to address is how does one compare a gait sequence to another one. These sequences may be of differing length (number of frames) and therefore in order to compare these sequences we need to perform time normalization (scaling). A linear time scaling would be inappropriate because in most scenarios this time scaling would be inherently nonlinear. Dynamic time warping (DTW) which has been successfully used by the speech recognition [37] community is an ideal candidate for performing this nonlinear time normalization. However, certain modifications to the original DTW are also necessary in order to account for the non-Euclidean structure of the shape space. One can also explore parametric models of the type discussed previously, and we shall compare the performance of such models later in experiments.

3.1 Dynamic Time Warping

Dynamic time warping is a method for computing a nonlinear time normalization between a template vector sequence and a test vector sequence. These two sequences could be of differing lengths. It was experimentally shown [38] that the intrapersonal variations in gait of a single individual can be better captured by DTW rather than by linear warping. The DTW algorithm which is based on dynamic programming computes the best nonlinear time normalization of the test sequence in order to match the template sequence, by performing a search over the space of all allowed time normalizations. The space of all time normalizations allowed is cleverly constructed using certain temporal consistency constraints. We list the temporal consistency constraints that we have used in our implementation of DTW below.

- *End point constraints*: The beginning and the end of each sequence is rigidly fixed. For example, if the template sequence is of length N and the test sequence is of length M, then only time normalizations that map the first frame of the template to the first frame of the test sequence and also map the Nth frame of the template sequence to the Mth frame of the test sequence are allowed.
- The warping function (mapping function between the test sequence time to the template sequence time) should be monotonically increasing. In other words the sequence of "events" in both the template and the test sequences should be the same.
- The warping function should be continuous.

Dynamic programming is used to efficiently compute the best warping function and the global warping error.

We choose the "shape" of the human silhouette as the feature. We resort to Kendall's definition of shape [39] to represent the human silhouette in each video frame. Given a video sequence, we first perform background subtraction to extract the silhouette of the human. We then uniformly sample points on the outer contour of the silhouette to obtain the preshape vector. The procedure for obtaining shapes from the video sequence is illustrated in Fig. 2. Note that each frame of the video sequence maps to a point on the hyperspherical shape manifold. The spherical nature of the shape-space must be taken into account in the implementation of the DTW algorithm. This implies that during DTW computation, the local distance measure used must take into account the non-Euclidean nature of the shape-space. Therefore, it is meaningful to use the Procrustes shape distance [39]. It is important to note that the Procrustes distance is not a metric since it is not commutative. Moreover, the nature of the definition of constraints makes the DTW algorithm noncommutative even when we use a distance metric for the local feature error. If $A(t)$ and $B(t)$ are two shape sequences then we define the distance between these two sequences $D(A(t), B(t))$ as

$$D(A(t), B(t)) = DTW(A(t), B(t)) + DTW(B(t), A(t)), \tag{9}$$

where $DTW(A(t), B(t)) = \frac{1}{T}\sum_{t=1}^{T} d(A(f(t)), B(g(t)))$ (f and g being the optimal warping functions). Such a distance between shape sequences is commutative. The isolation property, that is, $D(A(t), B(t)) = 0$ iff $A(t) = B(t)$, is enforced by penalizing all nondiagonal transitions in the local error metric.

3.2   Parametric Models for Shape Sequences

As in the case of video-based face recognition, another useful approach is to use parametric models of shape change to describe gait. In this case, when shape is used as the feature, we need to define these models on the tangent spaces of the

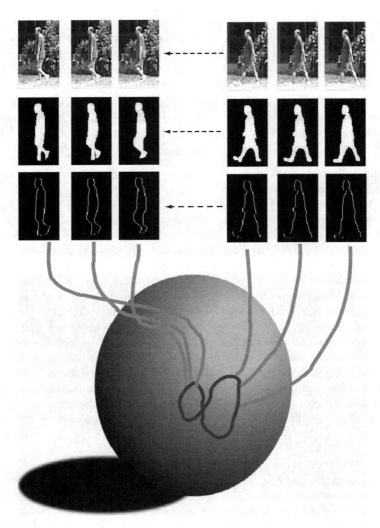

FIG. 2. Illustration of the sequence of shapes obtained during a walking cycle. Each frame in the video is processed to obtain a preshape vector. These vectors lie on a complex hyperspherical manifold. Image courtesy [18].

shape-manifold. This is because the shape-manifold is not a vector space. We describe both autoregressive (AR) and autoregressive and moving average (ARMA) models on tangent space projections of the shape manifold.

3.2.1 State-Space Models on Tangent Space

The autoregressive (AR) model is a simple time-series model that has been used very successfully for prediction and modeling especially in speech. The probabilistic interpretation of the AR model is valid only when the space is Euclidean. Therefore, we build an AR model on the tangent space projections of the shape sequence. Once the AR model is learned we can use this either for synthesis of a new shape sequence or for comparing shape sequences by computing distances between the model parameters.

The time series of the tangent space projections of the preshape vector of each shape is modeled as an AR process. Let, $s_j, j = 1, 2, \ldots, M$ be the M such sequences of shapes. Let us denote the tangent space projection of the sequence of shape s_j (with mean of s_j as the pole) by α_j. Now, the AR model on the tangent space projections is given by

$$\underline{\alpha}_j(t) = A_j \underline{\alpha}_j(t-1) + w(t), \tag{10}$$

where, w is a zero-mean white Gaussian noise process and A_j is the transition matrix corresponding to the jth sequence. For convenience and simplicity, A_j is assumed to be a diagonal matrix.

For all the sequences in the gallery, the transition matrices are obtained and stored. The transition matrices can be estimated using the standard Yule-Walker equations [40]. Given a probe sequence, the transition matrix for the probe sequence is computed. The distances between the corresponding transition matrices are added to obtain a measure of the distance between the models. If A and B (for $j = 1, 2, \ldots, N$) represent the transition matrices for the two sequences, then the distance between the models is defined as $D(A, B)$

$$D(A, B) = \left\| A_j - B_j \right\|_{\mathrm{F}}, \tag{11}$$

where $\| \ \|_{\mathrm{F}}$ denotes the Frobenius norm. The model in the gallery that is closest to the model of the given probe is chosen as the correct identity.

The ARMA model as discussed previously in Section 2.1 can also be used for modeling gait. However, as in the case of the AR model discussed above, we need to define it in the tangent space of the manifold. Let us assume that the time-series of tangent projections of shapes (about its mean as the pole) is given by $\alpha(t)$, $t = 1, 2,$ $\ldots, \tau$. Then, the ARMA model is defined as

$$\alpha(t) = Cx(t) + w(t), \quad w(t) \sim N(0, R), \tag{12}$$

$$x(t+1) = Ax(t) + v(t), \quad v(t) \sim N(0, Q). \tag{13}$$

The model estimation procedures and distance computation between models is done as described in Section 2.1.

3.2.2 Results on the USF Database

The USF database [27] consists of 71 people in the gallery. Several covariates, such as camera position, shoe type, surface, and time, were varied in a controlled manner to design a set of challenge experiments [27]. The results are evaluated using cumulative match score[1] (CMS) curves and the identification rate. The results for the seven experiments on the USF database are shown in Fig. 3. These results were originally reported in Veeraraghavan et al. [18].

3.3 Understanding the Space of Execution Variations

Results on gait-based person identification shown in Tanawongsuwan and Bobick [41] indicate that it is very important to take into account the temporal variations in the person's gait. Various external conditions (such as surface, shoe) induce systematic time-warping variations within the gait signatures of each individual. The function space of temporal warpings for each individual amounts to learning the class of person specific warping functions. By learning the function space of these variations, we are able to account for the effects of such external conditions. In the following, we discuss a method that represents the observed gait sequences of an individual as time-warps of a nominal or average gait sequence. Methods to estimate the nominal sequence, and the time-warps associated to an individual will be described. These methods were originally reported in Veeraraghavan et al. [42].

For now, let us assume that for each frame of the video, an appropriate feature has been extracted and that the video data has now been converted into a feature sequence given by $f^1, f^2, \ldots,$ for frames 1, 2, $\ldots,$ respectively. We will use F to denote the feature space associated with the chosen feature. Let γ be a diffeomorphism (a diffeomorphism is a smooth, invertible function with a smooth inverse) from [0, 1] to itself with $\gamma(0) = 0$ and $\gamma(1) = 1$. Also, let Γ be the set of all such functions.

---

[1] Plot of percentage of recognition versus rank.

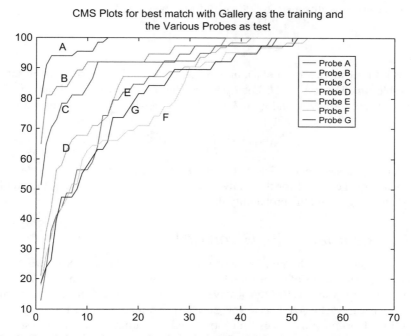

Fɪɢ. 3. Cumulative match scores using dynamic time warping on shape space. These results were first reported in Veeraraghavan et al. [18].

We will use elements of Γ to denote time warping functions. Our model for the observed gait of an individual consists of an average gait sequence given by $g:[0, 1] \to \mathcal{F}$, which is a parameterized trajectory on the feature space, and the set of time-warped realizations of this gait given by

$$r(t) = g(\gamma(t)), \quad \gamma \in \Gamma. \tag{14}$$

In our model, the variability associated with γ in each class will be modeled using a distribution P_γ on Γ. For the convenience of analysis and computation, we prefer to work with $\psi = +\sqrt{\dot\gamma}$ instead of γ directly. There is a bijection between γ and ψ and the probability models on ψ directly relate to equivalent models on γ. Thus, we will introduce probability distributions P_ψ on the set of all ψs, for each activity class.

The parameters of this model are $g(t)$, the nominal gait sequence, and P_ψ, the probability distribution on square-root representations of time warping functions. Here, we restrict our analysis to cases where the nominal activity trajectory $g(t)$ is deterministic but unknown. We will consider parametric forms of densities for P_ψ and reduce the problem of learning P_ψ to one of learning the parameters of the distribution P_ψ.

Let the space of all square-root density forms be given by

$$\Psi = \left\{ \psi : [0, 1] \to \mathbb{R} | \psi \geq 0, \int_0^1 \psi^2(t)dt = 1 \right\}. \tag{15}$$

This is the positive orthant of a unit hypersphere in the Hilbert space of all square-integrable functions on $[0, 1]$. Let $T_\psi(\Psi)$ be the tangent space to Ψ at any given point ψ. Then, for any v_1 and v_2 in $T_\psi(\Psi)$, the Fisher-Rao metric is given by

$$\langle v_1, v_2 \rangle = \int_0^1 v_1(t)v_2(t)dt. \tag{16}$$

Given N gait sequences of an individual $r_1, r_2, r_3, \ldots, r_N$, we need to learn the parameters of the model for this individual. This amounts to learning the nominal gait sequence $g(t)$ and the probability distribution P_ψ.

3.3.1   Estimating P_ψ Given $g(t)$

Let us assume that the nominal gait sequence $g(t)$ is known. Now we need to estimate the parameters of the warping distribution which is given by P_ψ. In order to learn P_ψ, we first warp each of the observed realizations of gait to the known nominal gait sequence given by $g(t)$. This warping can be performed using the DTW algorithm. The DTW algorithm provides us with corresponding warping functions $\gamma_i(t)$ such that $\int_0^1 \|r_i(t) - g(\gamma_i(t))\|^2 dt$ is minimized. Then, we can compute ψ_is using $\psi_i = \sqrt{\dot{\gamma}_i}$.

Now, we have several samples $\psi_1, \psi_2, \ldots$ to estimate the distribution P_ψ. Since Ψ is a sphere, its geometry is well known. It is a Riemannian manifold whose expressions for geodesics, exponential maps, and inverse exponential maps on Ψ are known. Consequently, the algorithms for computing sample statistics, defining probability density functions, and generating inferences also become straightforward. Mathematical details of these procedures can be found in Turaga et al. [22].

Thus, given the nominal gait sequence $g(t)$, we can estimate the parameters of the warping distribution P_ψ, namely its Karcher mean $\bar{\psi}_K$ and its covariance stored indirectly using m singular values $\lambda_1, \lambda_2, \ldots, \lambda_m$ and corresponding singular vectors $u_1, u_2, \ldots, u_m$.

3.3.2   Estimating $g(t)$ Assuming Known Warping Functions

For the given gait sequences $r_1, r_2, \ldots$ of an individual, assume that the corresponding warping functions $\gamma_1, \gamma_2, \ldots$ are also given. Then, we can estimate the nominal or average gait sequence $g(t)$ using

$$\bar{g}(t) = \frac{1}{N} \sum_{i=1}^{N} r_i\left(\gamma_i^{-1}(t)\right).$$

(17)

3.3.3 Iteratively Estimating g(t) and P_ψ

In a realistic setting, we would neither know the average gait sequence $g(t)$ nor would we know the distribution over time-warps P_ψ. Given N gait sequences r_1, r_2, r_3, ..., r_N of an individual, we would like to learn the parameters of the model for this activity. We do this by iteratively estimating P_ψ and refining our estimate of the nominal gait sequence $\bar{g}(t)$ using the steps described in the previous two sections. We first initialize the nominal gait sequence to one of the realizations say $g_{\text{init}}(t) = r_1(t)$. Then we estimate P_ψ using the method described in Section 3.3.1. We then refine the estimate of the nominal gait sequence using the method described in Section 3.3.2. These two steps are iterated till convergence. In practice, we find that the iterations converge very quickly (within 4 or 5 iterations).

3.4 Experiments on USF Gait Database

In order to compare the performance of our algorithm with the current state of the art algorithms, we performed a gait-based person identification experiment on the publicly available USF gait database [27]. The USF database consists of 71 people in the Gallery. Various covariates like camera position, shoe type, surface, and time were varied in a controlled manner to design a set of challenge experiments [27]. We performed a round-robin recognition experiment in which one of the challenge sets was used as test while the other seven were used as training examples. The process was repeated for each of the seven challenge sets on which results have been reported. Table II shows the identification rates of our algorithm with a uniform distribution on the space of warps (P_{Unif}), our algorithm with a wrapped Gaussian distribution on the tangent space of warps with shape as a feature and with binary image feature (P_{Gauss} and P_{GaussIm}). For comparison, the table also shows the baseline algorithm [27], simple DTW on shape features [18], and the image-based HMM [33] algorithm on the USF dataset for the 7 probes A–G. As most of these other algorithms could not account for the systematic variations in time-warping for each individual, the recognition experiment they performed was not round robin but rather used only one sample per individual for learning. Therefore, to ensure a fair comparison, we also implemented a round-robin experiment using the linear warping ($P_L W$).

TABLE II
COMPARISON OF IDENTIFICATION RATES ON THE USF DATASET

Probe	Baseline	DTW shape	HMM shape	HMM image	pHMM [43]	P_{LW}	P_{Unif}	P_{Gauss}	$P_{GaussIm}$
Avg.	42	42	41	50	65	51.5	59	59	64
A	79	81	80	96	85	68	70	78	82
B	66	74	72	86	89	51	68	68	78
C	56	52	56	74	72	51	81	82	76
D	29	29	22	32	57	53	40	50	48
E	24	20	20	28	66	46	64	51	54
F	30	19	20	17	46	50	37	42	56
G	10	19	19	21	41	42	53	40	55

Note that the experimental results reported in this table contain varying amounts of training data. While columns 2–6 (Baseline–pHMM) used only the gallery sequences for training, the results reported in columns 7–10 ($P_{LW} - P_{GaussIm}$) used all the probes except the test probe during training.

The average performance of our algorithms P_{Unif} and P_{Gauss} is better than all the other algorithms that use the same feature (DTW/HMM (Shape) [18] and Linear warping P_{LW}) and is also better than the baseline [27] and HMM [33] algorithms that use the image as a feature. The improvement in performance while using binary image as a feature is shown in the last column ($P_{GaussIm}$). The experimental results presented here clearly show that using multiple training samples per class and learning the distribution of their time warps makes significant improvement to gait recognition results. While most algorithms based on learning from a single sample led to overfitting and therefore performed much better when the gallery was similar to the probe (probe A–C), they also performed very poorly when the gallery and the probes were significantly different. But, since our algorithm has good generalization ability the performance of our algorithm did not suffer from overfitting and therefore did not drop as much when moving from probes A–C to probes D–G.

4. Conclusions

In this chapter we discussed spatiotemporal models for describing face and gait variations in video-based biometrics. We showed that one can derive person specific behavioral cues by understanding the modeling the variations within the same individual. The mathematical tools needed for this task were described and we derived efficient algorithms for recognition.

ACKNOWLEDGMENTS

Drs Kevin Zhou, Ashok Veeraraghavan, Anuj Srivastava, Amit Kale, Aravind Sundaresan, A.N. Rajagopalan, Amit Roy-Chowdhury, Narayanan Ramanathan, and Gaurav Aggarwal contributed to the development of algorithms discussed in this chapter. This work was funded in part by the Office of Naval Research (ONR) MURI grant N00014-08-1-0638.

REFERENCES

[1] S. Ullman, The Interpretation of Visual Motion, MIT Press, Cambridge, MA, 1979.
[2] N. Rubin, N. Albert, Real-world scenes can be easily recognized from their edge-detected renditions: just add motion!, J. Vis. 1 (3) (2001) 37.
[3] G. Pike, R. Kemp, N. Towell, K. Phillips, Recognizing moving faces: the relative contribution of motion and perspective view information, Vis. Cogn. 4 (4) (1997) 409–438.
[4] J. Stone, Object recognition: view-specificity and motion-specificity, Vis. Res. 39 (24) (1999) 4032–4044.
[5] A.J. O'Toole, D. Roark, H. Abdi, Recognizing moving faces: a psychological and neural synthesis, Trends Cogn. Sci. 6 (2002) 261–266.
[6] X. Liu, T. Chen, S.M. Thornton, Eigenspace updating for non-stationary process and its application to face recognition, Pattern Recognit. 36 (2003) 1945–1959.
[7] G. Shakhnarovich, J.W. Fisher, T. Darrell, Face recognition from long-term observations, in: Proceedings of the European Conference on Computer Vision, vol. 3, 2002, pp. 851–865.
[8] T.K. Kim, J. Kittler, R. Cipolla, Discriminative learning and recognition of image set classes using canonical correlations, IEEE Trans. Pattern Anal. Mach. Intell. 29 (6) (2007) 1005–1018.
[9] J. Hamm, D.D. Lee, Grassmann discriminant analysis: a unifying view on subspace-based learning, in: International Conference on Machine Learning, Proceedings of the 25th International Conference on Machine Learning, Helsinki, Finland, 2008, pp. 376–383.
[10] O. Arandjelovic, G. Shakhnarovich, J. Fisher, R. Cipolla, T. Darrell, Face recognition with image sets using manifold density divergence, in: Proceedings of IEEE Conference on Computer Vision and Pattern Recognition, IEEE Computer Society, San Diego, USA, 2005, pp. 581–588.
[11] S.K. Zhou, R. Chellappa, From sample similarity to ensemble similarity: probabilistic distance measures in reproducing kernel hilbert space, IEEE Trans. Pattern Anal. Mach. Intell. 28 (6) (2006) 917–929.
[12] R. Basri, D. Jacobs, Lambertian reflectance and linear subspaces, in: Proceedings of IEEE International Conference on Computer Vision, vol. 2, 2001, pp. 383–390.
[13] W. Fan, D.-Y. Yeung, Locally linear models on face appearance manifolds with application to dual-subspace based classification, in: Proceedings of IEEE Conference on Computer Vision and Pattern Recognition, IEEE Computer Society, New York, NY, USA, 2006.
[14] K.C. Lee, J. Ho, M.H. Yang, D. Kriegman, Video-based face recognition using probabilistic appearance manifolds, in: Proceedings of IEEE Conference on Computer Vision and Pattern Recognition, vol. 1, 2003, pp. 313–320. Madison, WI, USA.
[15] O. Arandjelovic, R. Cipolla, Face recognition from video using the generic shape-illumination manifold, in: Proceedings of European Conference on Computer Vision, 2006, pp. 27–40.
[16] G. Doretto, A. Chiuso, Y.N. Wu, S. Soatto, Dynamic textures, Int. J. Comput. Vision 51 (2) (2003) 91–109.
[17] A. Bissacco, A. Chiuso, Y. Ma, S. Soatto, Recognition of human gaits, in: Proceedings of IEEE Conference on Computer Vision and Pattern Recognition, vol. 2, 2001, pp. 52–57.

[18] A. Veeraraghavan, A. Roy-Chowdhury, R. Chellappa, Matching shape sequences in video with an application to human movement analysis, IEEE Trans. Pattern Anal. Mach. Intell. 27 (12) (2005) 1896–1909.

[19] P.V. Overschee, B.D. Moor, Subspace algorithms for the stochastic identification problem, Automatica 29 (3) (1993) 649–660.

[20] K.D. Cock, B.D. Moor, Subspace angles between ARMA models, Syst. Control Lett. 46 (2002) 265–270.

[21] P. Saisan, G. Doretto, Y.N. Wu, S. Soatto, Dynamic texture recognition, in: Proceedings of IEEE Conference on Computer Vision and Pattern Recognition, vol. 2, 2001, pp. 58–63.

[22] P. Turaga, A. Veeraraghavan, A. Srivastava, R. Chellappa, Statistical analysis on manifolds and its applications to video analysis, in: D. Schonfeld, C. Shan, D. Tao, L. Wang (Eds.), Video Search and Mining, Studies in Computational Intelligence, Springer-Verlag, 2010. Ch. 5.

[23] P. Turaga, A. Veeraraghavan, R. Chellappa, Statistical analysis on stiefel and grassmann manifolds with applications in computer vision, in: Proceedings of IEEE Conference on Computer Vision and, Pattern Recognition, 2008, pp. 1–8.

[24] Y. Chikuse, Statistics on Special Manifolds, Springer, New York, 2003. Lecture Notes in Statistics.

[25] A. Edelman, T.A. Arias, S.T. Smith, The geometry of algorithms with orthogonality constraints, SIAM J. Matrix Anal. Appl. 20 (2) (1999) 303–353.

[26] S. Niyogi, E. Adelson, Analyzing and Recognizing Walking Figures in xyt, 1994 Tech. Rep. 223. MIT Media Lab Vision and Modeling Group.

[27] S. Sarkar, P.J. Phillips, Z. Liu, I.R. Vega, P. Grother, K.W. Bowyer, The HumanID gait challenge problem: data sets, performance, and analysis, IEEE Trans. Pattern Anal. Mach. Intell. 27 (2) (2005) 162–177.

[28] J. Han, B. Bhanu, Individual recognition using gait energy image, 2003 Workshop on Multimodal User Authentication (MMUA, 2003) (2003) 181–188.

[29] L. Wang, H. Ning, W. Hu, T. Tan, Gait recognition based on Procrustes shape analysis, Image Processing, 2002. Proceedings, 2002 International Conference on Image Processing, vol. 3, 2002, pp. III-433- III-436.

[30] J. Foster, M. Nixon, A. Prugel-Bennett, Automatic gait recognition using area-based metrics, Pattern Recognit. Lett. 24 (2003) 2489–2497.

[31] A.F. Bobick, J.W. Davis, The recognition of human movement using temporal templates, IEEE Trans. Pattern Anal. Mach. Intell. 23 (3) (2001) 257–267.

[32] R. Collins, R. Gross, J. Shi, Silhoutte based human identification using body shape and gait, in: IEEE International Conference on Automatic Face and Gesture Recognition, 2002, pp. 351–356.

[33] A. Kale, A. Sundaresan, A.N. Rajagopalan, N.P. Cuntoor, A.K. Roy-Chowdhury, V. Kruger, et al., Identification of humans using gait, IEEE Trans. Image Process. 13 (9) (2004) 1163–1173.

[34] L. Lee, G. Dalley, K. Tieu, Learning pedestrian models for silhoutte refinement, in: Proceedings of IEEE International Conference on Computer Vision, 2003.

[35] Z. Liu, S. Sarkar, Improved gait recognition by gait dynamics normalization, IEEE Trans. Pattern Anal. Mach. Intell. 28 (6) (2006) 863–876.

[36] D. Tolliver, R.T. Collins, Gait shape estimation for identification, in: Audio-and Video-Based Biometrie Person Authentication, 2003, pp. 734–742.

[37] L. Rabiner, B. Juang, Fundamentals of Speech Recognition, Prentice Hall, Upper Saddle River, NJ, USA, 1993.

[38] A. Forner-Cordero, H. Koopman, F. Van der Helm, Describing gait as a sequence of states, J. Biomech. 39 (5) (2006) 948–957.

[39] D.G. Kendall, Shape manifolds, procrustean metrics and complex projective spaces, Bull. Lond. Math. Soc. 16 (1984) 81–121.
[40] J. Proakis, D. Manolakis, Digital Signal Processing: Principles, Algorithms and Applications, third ed., Prentice Hall, New Jersey, 1995.
[41] R. Tanawongsuwan, A.F. Bobick, Performance analysis of time-distance gait parameters under different speeds, in: Proceeding AVBPA'03 Proceedings of the 4th international conference on Audio- and video-based biometric person authentication, 2003, pp. 715–724.
[42] A. Veeraraghavan, A. Srivastava, A.K. Roy Chowdhury, R. Chellappa, Rate-invariant recognition of humans and their activities, IEEE Trans. Image Process. 18 (6) (2009) 1326–1339.
[43] Z. Liu, S. Sarkar, Improved gait recognition by gait dynamics normalization, IEEE Trans. Pattern Anal. Mach. Intell. 28 (6) (2006) 863–876.

ABOUT THE AUTHOR

Prof. Rama Chellappa is a Minta Martin Professor of Engineering, Professor of Electrical and Computer Engineering, and a Permanent member of the University of Maryland Institute for Advanced Computer Studies (UMIACS) at University of Maryland, College Park. He also directs the Center for Automation Research. Prof. Chellappa has published numerous book chapters, peer-reviewed journal, and conference papers in image and video processing, analysis, and recognition. He has received several research, teaching, and service awards. He is a Fellow of IEEE, IAPR, and OSA. He is serving as the President of IEEE Biometrics Council. His research interests are image processing, image understanding, and pattern recognition. His e-mail address is rama@umiacs.umd.edu.

Dr. Pavan Turaga received his B.Tech. in Electronics and Communication Engineering from the Indian Institute of Technology, Guwahati in 2004, and M.S. and Ph.D. degrees in Electrical and Computer Engineering from the University of Maryland, College Park in 2007 and 2009, respectively. He is a research associate in the Center for Automation Research, at the University of Maryland Institute for Advanced Computer Studies (UMIACS). His research interests are in computer vision, pattern recognition, machine learning, and their applications. He can be reached at pturaga@umiacs.umd.edu.

Action Research Can Swing the Balance in Experimental Software Engineering

PAULO SÉRGIO MEDEIROS DOS SANTOS

System Engineering and Computer Science Department, COPPE/Federal University of Rio de Janeiro, Rio de Janeiro, Brazil

GUILHERME HORTA TRAVASSOS

System Engineering and Computer Science Department, COPPE/Federal University of Rio de Janeiro, Rio de Janeiro, Brazil

Abstract

In general, professionals still ignore scientific evidence in place of expert opinions in most of their decision making. For this reason, it is still common to see the adoption of new software technologies in the field without any scientific basis or well-grounded criteria, but on the opinions of experts. Experimental Software Engineering is of paramount importance to provide the foundations to understand the limits and applicability of software technologies. The need to better observe and understand the practice of Software Engineering leads us to look for alternative experimental approaches to support our studies. Different research strategies can be used to explore different Software Engineering practices. Action Research can be seen as one alternative to intensify the conducting of important experimental studies with results of great value while investigating the Software Engineering practices in depth. In this chapter, a discussion on the use of Action Research in Software Engineering is presented. As indicated by a technical literature survey, along the years a growing tendency for addressing different research topics in Software Engineering through Action Research studies has been seen. This behavior can indicate the great potential of its applicability in our scientific field. Despite their clear benefits and diversity of application, the initial findings also revealed that the

ADVANCES IN COMPUTERS, VOL. 83
ISSN: 0065-2458/DOI: 10.1016/B978-0-12-385510-7.00005-9

Copyright © 2011 Elsevier Inc.
All rights reserved.

rigor and control of such studies should improve in Software Engineering. Aiming at better explaining the application of Action Research, an experimental study (*in vivo*) on the investigation of the subjective decisions of software developers, concerned with the refactoring of source code to improve source code quality in a distributed software development context is depicted. A Software Engineering theory regarding refactoring and some guidance on how to accomplish an Action Research study in Software Engineering supplement the discussions in this chapter.

1. Introduction 206
2. Action Research Overview 210
   2.1. Background 211
   2.2. Action Research Process 214
3. The Use of Action Research in Software
   Engineering: A Preliminary Survey? 219
   3.1. Method 219
   3.2. Results 220
4. Using Action Research in Software Engineering: An *In Vivo* Study 225
   4.1. Diagnosis 226
   4.2. Planning 229
   4.3. Actions 234
   4.4. Evaluation and Analysis 235
   4.5. Reflections and Learning 243
5. Applying Action Research to Software Engineering 254
   5.1. Practices and Discussion 256
   5.2. Recommendations 261
6. Final Considerations 270
   Acknowledgments 270
   References 270

1. Introduction

Software Engineering is a multidisciplinary discipline involving different social and technological features. To understand how software engineers maintain complex software systems, it is necessary to investigate not only the tools and processes they use but also the cognitive and social processes surrounding them. It requires the study of human activities. We need to understand how software engineers individually develop software as well as how teams and organizations coordinate their efforts [1].

One possible approach to support this understanding is experimentation. Experimental Software Engineering is of paramount importance to provide the foundations to understand the limits and applicability of software technologies. It intends to make the practice of Software Engineering predictable and economically feasible. Indeed, the importance of experimentation has grown significantly over the recent years as many technical literature surveys and researchers have pointed out, such as Sjøberg et al. [2], Basili and Elbaum [3], Höfer and Tichy [4], and Kampenes et al. [5].

However, despite all the perceived importance, experimentation still does not seem to have achieved broad use and expansion in Software Engineering as other science fields demonstrate today, for example, Medicine [6]. For instance, some years ago Tichy [7] had pointed out that there was no solid evidence in comparing basic technologies for the practice of Software Engineering such as the paradigms of functional and object-oriented development, present in almost all industrial software projects. Both certainly have advantages and disadvantages. And, in an attempt to show such technologies to the Software Engineering community, demonstrations and heuristics were usually developed to support their selection and use. However, demonstrations rarely produce solid evidence. Despite all the effort invested to reveal evidence about different software technologies other than development paradigms, the use of these kinds of evaluation can still be seen in the field. Different factors can be attributed to this limited application of experimentation in Software Engineering. For example, the complexity, cost, and risks concerned with different types of experiments apparently represented obstacles to its adoption [8].

The understanding of Software Engineering researchers on the importance of experimentation had promoted the first and relevant experiences with the experimental method in Software Engineering. According to Basili et al. [9], those experiments were strongly influenced by areas such as Physics and Medicine which, due to their level of maturity, focused on controlled studies. This type of study can be difficult to control in real software projects as the large number of unknown context variables may present a high degree of risk to these experiments [10]. Additionally, experimental studies can be time consuming and generate large volume of information making the management of scientific knowledge difficult [11].

Later, the lessons learned with controlled studies were described in books dedicated exclusively to the topic [8,12]. Based on this experience, researchers started to investigate how to enlarge the experimentation opportunities by introducing new methods and research strategies such as case studies, ethnography, surveys, and interview techniques [1,13–15] in the field.

A motivation for the search for new research approaches relates to the fact that although controlled studies and measurement allow the observation of relationships among variables by means of statistical tests, their limitations may restrict what one can see and, therefore, investigate [16]. Similarly, years later, Kitchenham [17] stated that the excessive emphasis on using controlled studies in Software Engineering "may place ourselves examining phenomena that are a result of abstracting the technology away from its usage context and not the characteristics of the technology itself." In other words, the premature insistence on accuracy can inhibit the progress and lead scientists to formulate problems in ways that can be measured but have limited relevance in relation to the characteristics of the problem [18]. For this reason, researchers run the risk of considering the professionals from industry responsible for misusing their proposed software technologies when the actual problem is theirs, in failing to understand the complexity of the context under which the technologies will be used [17].

The need to better observe and understand the practice of Software Engineering leads us to look for alternative experimental approaches. Consequently, this takes us to one of the core Software Engineering research concerns: the relevance of scientific results. Relevance relates to the usefulness of the results in an industrial context (e.g., providing results that enable the development of guidelines) as well as in the academic context (e.g., allowing a better understanding of a phenomenon through the construction of theories) [19]. Other researchers have also emphasized this need, such as Kitchenham et al. [20] and Glass [108]. The industry itself shows the importance of increasing the relevance of studies in Software Engineering. Recent works [21,22] suggest that professionals ignore scientific evidence in place of expert opinion in most of their decision making. For this reason, it is still common that new software technologies are adopted without any scientific basis or well-grounded criteria, and the opinions of experts may be limited as their experience is contained in a limited set of options.

Therefore, different research strategies should be used to explore the different features in Software Engineering practice. The methodology in Action Research can be seen as an alternative to intensify the execution of relevant studies and the acquisition of great value results [23] while allowing for in-depth investigation of the practices in Software Engineering.

Action Research has its origins associated with the early interventionist practices carried out by Kurt Lewin in the 1940s in the course of social–technical experiments. The initial stimulus for the rise and design of the main Action Research objectives and aspirations came from a generalized difficulty at that time in translating the results of social research into practical actions [24].

The history of Action Research is usually split into at least two stages [25]. The first stage relates to Kurt Lewin's initial practices, and the other one is associated with the resurgence of interest in educational research on Action Research in the early 1970s, after its initial rejection due to the predominance of a positivist stance in the Social Sciences. Some reasons for this renewed interest in Action Research include, for example, the claim that the professionalization of teachers should be improved by also giving them a researcher role to allow assessing curricular guidelines in the classroom and improving teaching practices [24]. Thus, seen in this way, Action Research was transformed from a method through which professionals applied the scientific theories of Social Sciences in practice to a method that allowed practitioners to assess the adequacy of their own tacit theories in their practice. Nowadays, Action Research is also used in other scientific areas such as management, nursing, and information systems [26] to support the role of researching in their daily activities.

This brief description of the history of Action Research shows how the methodology has evolved through the many changes caused by new interpretations and uses researchers from different science fields gave it [27]. A clear example of this continuous transformation process is represented by the work of Baskerville and Wood-Harper [28]. Researchers were able to identify a large diversity of Action Research processes, represented by 10 different "formats" used in the area of information systems. Fortunately, apart from all of these proposals, a comprehensive Action Research process (based on the 1978 Susman and Evered [29] model) can be identified, which can support the accomplishment of Action Research studies in Software Engineering [30].

As it will be described in this chapter, Action Research is starting to support studies in Software Engineering. Its characteristics suggest its application can benefit research in the field, as it simultaneously allows the performing of research and action. The action is usually associated with some transformation in a community, organization or project, while the research is characterized by a wide understanding of a transformation phenomenon by the researcher (research community), person (client), or both. Avison et al. [31] emphasize that Action Research regards "more what practitioners do than what they say they do." According to this claim, Sjöberg et al. [19] have pointed the Action Research methodology as "the kind of study where the most realistic scenario is found" as it involves a real industry context to investigate the results of concrete actions.

The social challenges dealt with by researchers in Software Engineering investigations make Action Research a useful research methodology due to its characteristics and possibility of obtaining relevant results. We found out that there is an increasing tendency on using Action Research in Software Engineering to address different research topics indicating a great potential for its applicability in the area. The initial findings also revealed that the rigor and control of Action Research studies should be improved in Software Engineering-related studies. This can stem from borrowing a methodology from other scientific domain (Social Sciences) where studies are usually described using a different way of communicating and exchanging thoughts. Thus, even if there are few studies using the methodology of Action Research in Software Engineering, a discussion of the particularities of the methodology in the area seems necessary, further considering the increasing interest in its use.

Aiming at addressing these issues, we conducted two Action Research studies. Besides the expected benefits to the software project, the aim is to observe how Action Research can be applied in Software Engineering. The first study investigated a check-list-based inspection technique to improve the comprehensibility of use case models in a real software project. This study was first planned to strictly follow Action Research procedures. However, our previous experiment on accomplishing controlled studies concerned with software inspections influenced us to rely excessively on quantitative data, although the study was indeed an Action Research-based study. Therefore, we decided to better understand Action Research to improve our investigation capabilities. So, in Section 2, the reader can find descriptions of the main concepts of Action Research, as well as its limits and advantages, comparing it to other methodologies and showing its process and core principles. After that, to supplement this overview, Section 3 aims at illustrating the results of a technical literature survey conducted to evaluate the current degree of use of Action Research in Software Engineering.

Having become better acquainted with the methodology, the second study spontaneously emerged from a problematic situation related to source code quality in a distributed software development context which the authors participated in at that time. The second study examined the subjective decision concerned with source code refactoring. Due to its richer scenario and adherence to the Action Research methodology, including the use of qualitative data techniques (i.e., grounded theory), this will be tackled in Section 4. However, the working experiences in both studies will underlie our suggestions, recommendations, and practices on how to apply and when to choose Action Research as a research methodology in Software Engineering (in Section 5). Finally, in Section 6, some conclusions are given, including additional remarks intending to strengthen this intended chapter argument: Action Research can swing the balance to support the revealing of evidence in Experimental Software Engineering.

2. Action Research Overview

Based on the understanding of how Action Research is positioned within scientific research paradigms this section details many aspects of the methodology and describes a canonical process identified in the technical literature. To understand the objectives, limitations and benefits of research strategies, the main criteria distinguishing them are going to be addressed in this section. For the sake of simplicity, there is no intention to go into excessive detail in any of them.

2.1 Background

The distinction between research strategies can be made by exploring the paradigm concept. A paradigm can be seen as a set of basic truths (whose veracity we cannot ascertain) dealing with primary principles (axioms and doctrines). This set represents a worldview defining the nature of the "world," the place of each individual, and a set of possible relationships with the world and its parts [32]. For Hathaway [33], scientific paradigms can essentially act as a lens through which researchers can observe and understand the problems in their areas and produce scientific contributions to them. The scientific paradigms impose what researchers consider as data, what their role in scientific research is, what to consider knowledge, and how reality is seen and accessed. In short, scientists bring about their daily assumptions based on the knowledge, reality, and research strategies they hold. Scientific paradigms are usually marked by ontology, epistemology concepts, and methodology [32]. Epistemology relates to the nature of human knowledge and how it is understood and communicated, ontology deals with the basic issues of the nature of the world, regardless of who tries to observe it, and methodology addresses how (which methods and approaches) individuals acquire knowledge on the world.

The four predominant scientific paradigms found in the technical literature [1,32,34] can be summarized as follows:

- *Positivism* states that all knowledge should be based on logical inference from a set of observable facts. Positivists are reductionists because they study the events by breaking them into simpler components. This corresponds to their belief that scientific knowledge can be built incrementally from verifiable observations and the inferences based on them. In other words, data and analysis are neutral and do not change due to the fact that they are being observed. However, a positivist view is usually inappropriate to address social phenomena when they involve humans and their experiences, as it ignores the ability to reflect on the problems and to act on them in an inter-dependent approach. The positivist paradigm is closely related to the controlled study strategy; however, surveys and case studies can also be conducted under this paradigm.
- *Constructivism*, also known as interpretivism, rejects the idea of separating scientific knowledge from its human context. Constructions are not more or less absolutely "true" but simply more or less well formed and/or sophisticated, better informing on the complexity of the object studied. Constructivists focus

less on theory verification and more on understanding how different people grasp the world and how they attribute meaning to their actions. Theories may arise in this process but always linked to the studied context producing the so-called local theory. Constructivism is typically associated with ethnography but can often be related to exploratory case studies, Action Research (Refs. [35] *apud* [25]), and surveys.

- *Critical theory* considers scientific knowledge from its ability to release people from schools of thought. Critical theorists argue that research is a political act as knowledge gives power to different groups in society or strengthens existing authority power structures. In this sense, they choose what to research based on who will help and prefer the participatory approaches or supporting roles. Therefore, it is assumed that the investigator and investigated object are interactively linked, with the values of the researcher inevitably influencing the investigation. In Software Engineering, this paradigm can be associated, for instance, to the software process improvement and agile methods communities. Moreover, critical theorists often make use of case studies to draw attention to something that needs to be modified. However, it is Action Research that best reflects this paradigm (Refs. [36] *apud* [25]).

- *Pragmatism* recognizes that all knowledge is incomplete and estimated at certain level, and its value depends on the acquiring method. For pragmatists, knowledge is judged by how useful it can be to solve practical problems. Therefore, there is a degree of relativism: what is useful for one person may not be for another one, and thus truth is relative to the observer. To overcome this criticism, pragmatists emphasize the importance of consensus as the external "guardian" of objectivity; this can be seen for instance in the case of tradition/practice (are the results consistent with current knowledge?) and community (publishers, judges, and professionals). In short, the pragmatist adopts the engineering approach to research and emphasize practical rather than abstract knowledge, using any appropriate method to obtain it. One method often used, especially when there is no *a priori* known solution, is Action Research, as it allows the combination of different research strategies and data collection techniques (Refs. [37] *apud* [25]).

These scientific paradigms can be classified into two main approaches to obtain and construct knowledge: quantitative and qualitative. Positivism is related to the quantitative approach, while the other paradigms to the qualitative one [34]. A scientific paradigm can use both approaches, but always focuses more on one of them depending on its main orientation.

The quantitative approach aims at measuring and analyzing the causal relationships between variables representing the observed object characteristics. It operates with data in numerical form, collected from a representative sample, and usually analyzed using statistical methods. This way, the main goal is to identify the independent and dependent variables, reducing problem complexity so that the initial hypotheses can be confirmed or refuted [12]. The main disadvantages of this approach concern the fact that its objectivist and reductionist nature limits a detailed (descriptive) understanding of the real world properties and characteristics so that the observation of part of reality cannot be accomplished without losing the phenomenon importance in the whole [38].

The qualitative approach, however, is best described by evaluating how it differs from the quantitative one [39]: (1) it approximates the investigated perspective through interviews and observation, (2) it tends to emphasize detailed descriptions while the quantitative approach is less concerned with this kind of detail, (3) qualitative data are represented not only by numbers but by text and images too. For Seaman [40], the main advantage of using a qualitative approach is that it requires the researcher to dive into the complexity of the problem instead of abstracting it. Thus, the qualitative approach is often used to answer "how/why" a causality phenomenon revealed by quantitative approaches occurred. However, the drawback that generated knowledge can be considered more "vague" and "fluid," especially in a technical community such as that of Software Engineering [40]. Further, this makes results more difficult to aggregate or simplify.

To understand how the qualitative and quantitative approaches relate to the aforementioned scientific paradigms, the graph in Fig. 1 illustrates the intensity with which the four scientific paradigms make use of these approaches. It is interesting to observe, considering all the paradigms where Action Research appears as an option, its wide use spectrum, ranging from an observer role by the researcher

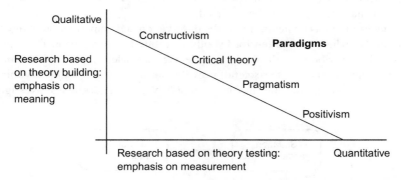

Fig. 1. Scientific paradigms and the qualitative and quantitative approaches—evolved from Healy and Perry [34].

in constructivism to a facilitator position in critical theory and reaching a more active problem solving stance in pragmatism [27]. For this reason, it is not always possible to classify each Action Research study into one paradigm, even if the researcher adopts one position as a foundation. But what is best defined in Action Research as a paradigm is a nonpositivist stance, that is, a nonartificial separation between the observer and that which is observed.

2.2 Action Research Process

Action Research can be defined as "a kind of social research with experimental basis that is conceived and conducted in close association with an action or a collective problem resolution where researchers and participants are involved in a cooperative way" [41]. In terms of process, the essence behind this definition can be thought into two stages (Fig. 2). The first stage involves researchers and participants who collaboratively analyze a problem situation. Based on this examination, they formulate theories meant to explain the circumstances faced. These theories are in fact conjectures and speculative practical knowledge, which are translated to a research topic later on. The second stage involves what we can call collaborative practical experiments (attempts). In this stage, changes are introduced and their effects studied. These two stages are iterated until the problem can be solved.

Argyris et al. [18] makes an analogy between experimentation and a process similar to the one shown in Fig. 2 saying that the practical knowledge embedded in the action (represented by the identification of causal factors that can be manipulated to get the desired consequences within a set of circumstances) is the hypothesis being tested. If the intended consequences occur, then the hypothesis is confirmed. Otherwise it is rejected (or the alternative hypotheses based on the supposed environmental conditions can be accepted).

Even when there is no neutrality on the observation and manipulation of the study environment, which is required for hypothesis refutation, any scientific methodology should contribute to the body of scientific knowledge in a consistent and rigorous way. Moreover, the scientific evaluation of any proposition within the body of scientific knowledge has to be replicable. As a result, an investigation

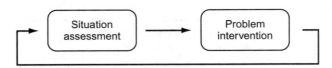

Fig. 2. Action research two-stage simplified process—adapted from Baskerville [42].

process similar to that shown in Fig. 2 is rarely adopted directly in practice as it does not define any kind of guidance regarding these issues.

According to Checkland and Holwell [43], any research methodology can be linked to the following elements: a cohesive set of ideas forming a conceptual framework F that is used in a methodology M to investigate an area of concern A. In Software Engineering, we could suppose the following research grounded on the positivist stance: use of controlled studies (methodology M) to investigate whether software maintainability (area of concern A) can be improved by object orientation (conceptual framework F; see top of Fig. 3).

However, Action Research changes the role of F, M, and even A, as the researcher becomes involved in the transformations occurring in a given situation [43]. This way, the researcher interested in a research theme can declare F and M and then go into a real-world situation related to the area of concern A in which that theme is relevant. As a result, Action Research not only represents M as in the Natural Sciences but also requires a research protocol merged into M, *which* is embedded with the practical and scientific conceptualizations from F allowing the research process to be recoverable by anyone interested in submitting the research to critical analysis (see the bottom of Fig. 3). Nevertheless, even with this, Action Research does not obtain the repeatability property present in natural sciences, but it is sufficient to clarify the processes and models that allowed the researcher to make the interpretations and derive the conclusions. The importance of making the criteria explicit before conducting the research is also emphasized by Avison et al. [31] who claim that without it the evaluation of the results tends to be compromised, and eventually what is being described may be action (but not research) or research (but not action).

The process shown in Fig. 3 provides important indications of issues that should be addressed to provide rigor to Action Research but it still does not have a detailed guide explaining how the research should be conducted. For this purpose, other researchers have expanded the basic framework that guides the process. The most common process is from Susman and Evered [29]. According to Davison et al. [30], it has achieved the status of "canonical" process, consisting of five stages (Fig. 4):

(1) *Diagnostic*: consists of exploring the research field, stakeholders, and their expectations holistically. In this stage, there is also the research theme definition that is represented by the designation of the practical problem and knowledge area to be addressed.

(2) *Planning*: stage where actions are defined to the faced circumstances. These definitions are guided by hypotheses portraying the researchers' formulated assumptions about possible solutions and results. These hypotheses, however, should follow the scientific theoretical formulation.

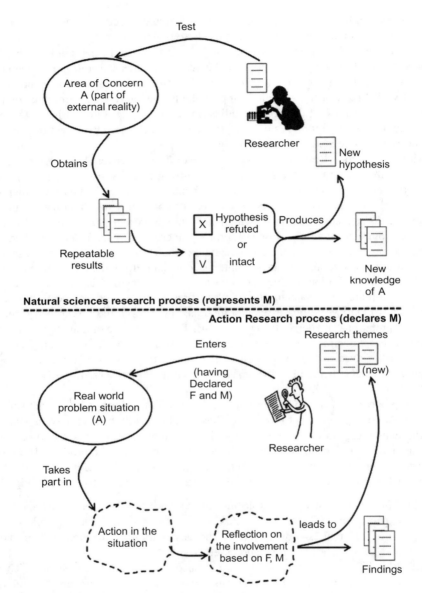

Fɪɢ. 3. Action Research and Natural Sciences—process comparison—adapted from Checkland and Holwell [43].

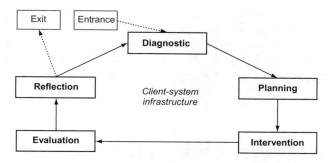

FIG. 4. Action Research canonical process—based on Davison et al. [30].

(3) *Intervention*: corresponds to the planned actions implementation. An essential element in this stage is the seminar technique that can be used to exam, discuss, and make decisions about the investigation process [41].
(4) *Evaluation*: stage where the intervention effects are analyzed considering the theoretical background used as basis to the actions definition.
(5) *Reflection*: involves the dissemination of acquired knowledge among participants and other organization departments. The learning experience is facilitated by the previous collaboration among participants and researchers in the technical topics.

Apart from these stages, the research environment requires a contract/agreement to legitimize the actions and possible benefits for both parties (researchers and organization), which builds up the so-called client-system infrastructure. There are two additional steps that are not directly part of the cycle but relate to the start and end of the Action Research process. For Avison et al. [44], the start of an Action Research study requires attention as there should exist a perceived need for real improvements by the client, which has to demand scientific support. Otherwise, there is a risk of one starting studies focused on irrelevant themes (where there is no perspective to the researcher for generating knowledge) or not starting studies as the so-called *iceberg* themes (where the client does not discern the need for improvements and therefore does not seek help from a researcher). The other additional step regards the criteria to finish the study. This should occur whenever both parties involved are satisfied with the outcome. That is why a contract/agreement is so important, to clearly state interests such as this. While this condition is not achieved, the Action Research process allows iterations to enable the achievement of results incrementally. This iterative process is especially advantageous when the initial diagnosis cannot be entirely performed.

Moreover, the cycle defined in Fig. 4, although not explicitly represented, allows some iteration and adaptation between the stages. For instance, the researcher can return to the diagnosis stage after an initial attempt to plan the study has not been completed because of a lack of better problem description, or if the researcher can update the study plan during the course of action taking some unexpected events into consideration.

2.2.1   Other Action Research Characteristics

The process described in the previous section already anticipated some of the key characteristics of Action Research such as a cyclical process model, the need for an agreement/contract between the client and the researcher, and learning through reflection. Additionally, Davison et al. [30] define two essential Action Research characteristics that the authors call "principles of canonical Action Research":

- *Theory principle*: researchers should ground themselves upon theories as a way to guide and focus their activities. Theories not only help conducting the research and taking actions to solve a problem but also support on reporting study results and positioning them in the existing accomplished research in the field. In most cases, theories are presented this way: in a situation S with evident environmental conditions F, G, and H, results X, Y, and Z are expected from actions A, B, and C.
- *Change through the action principle*: defines the essence of Action Research which is the indivisibility between research and action. The lack of action in a problem situation suggests the absence of a meaningful problem. Actions have to be planned in order to address the observed problems allowing the researcher to justify each action or reparation of part or the whole of the problem diagnosed.

All these characteristics make Action Research singular among the research methodologies. Action Research differentiates itself from routine practice because it is proactive and strategically driven by theories and research techniques. At the same time, it distinguishes itself from "normal" scientific research because of its flexibility in recognizing the importance of collaboration between researchers and subjects, and the value of using the best available evidence even when not having a good baseline to make precise judgments on the outcomes [45].

3. The Use of Action Research in Software Engineering: A Preliminary Survey?

To investigate the use of Action Research in Software Engineering, a technical literature survey has been conducted. We selected nine major Software Engineering journals and three conference proceedings in the period of 1993 to June 2010. The results up to June 2009 were presented in Ref. [46]. In this section, we provide the updated results up to June 2010. As it will be presented later, these new results reinforce the increasing interest in the Action Research methodology by the Software Engineering community.

There are other technical literature surveys in Software Engineering that investigated particular categories of empirical studies including controlled experiments [2] and quasi-experiments [5], but as far as these authors are aware there is no one specifically concerned with Action Research. We identified 22 papers in the journals and conferences—six found in the last update (July 2009 to June 2010). To update the results, we ran the same search strings and used the same information extraction form as described in [46]. Although Action Research studies represent a very small fraction of the studies being conducted in Software Engineering, they are concerned with different Software Engineering contexts and thus are sufficient for exemplify to researchers the potentials of Action Research. However, the results of the survey have shown a better definition of what can be considered an Action Research study in Software Engineering is needed. For instance, several studies that self reported to be Action Research were in fact case studies (and vice versa). The overloading in the classification of empirical studies was also previously observed by Sjøberg et al. [19].

3.1 Method

To conduct this survey, we followed some of the criteria and steps of the approach employed in other technical literature reviews [2,47]. The journal and conferences chosen are the same ones as Sjøberg et al. [2], which are considered relevant to Software Engineering research. The journals are the ACM Transactions on Software Engineering Methodology (TOSEM), Empirical Software Engineering (EMSE), IEEE Computer, IEEE Software, IEEE Transactions on Software Engineering (TSE), Information and Software Technology (IST), Journal of Systems and Software (JSS), Software Maintenance and Evolution (SME), and Software: Practice and Experience (SP&E). The conferences are the International Conference on Software Engineering (ICSE), the IEEE International Symposium on Empirical

Software Engineering (ISESE), and the IEEE International Symposium on Software Metrics (METRICS). The International Symposium on Empirical Software Engineering and Measurement (ESEM) was included in this survey as it merged the METRICS and ISESE conferences used in Sjøberg et al. [2] beginning in 2007.

The terms used for the search were gathered from Baskerville and Wood-Harper [28]: *Action Research, Action Learning, Action Science, reflective practice, critical systems theory, systems thinking, and participative research.* Using these terms, we found 189 papers from which 22 were selected. From the initial 189 papers, 151 were eliminated by title and abstract, and the remaining 31 were entirely read. The main applied criterion when selecting the papers was to evaluate whether it really represented an Action Research study. To do this, we drove our decision based on the set of criteria for acceptable Action Research studies given by Lau [47] (mentioned in the previous section): a real need for change, theory-based iterative problem solving, genuine collaboration with participants, and honesty in theorizing research from reflection; amended by the Action Research principles defined by Davison et al. [30]: researcher–client agreement, cyclical process model, theory use, change through action, and learning through reflection. However, driven by the presupposition that the finding of an Action Research study in Software Engineering that met all these criteria and principles would be difficult, we defined Action Research adherence levels to classify the studies. It aims at being more open when selecting the papers. The idea to have the adherence levels came from one of the selected papers where the authors explicitly stated that they conducted the research study inspired by the Action Research methodology [48]. All the information extracted from the papers is summarized in Table I.

We tried to be rigorous by selecting only *SE research* papers, as some journals and conferences also contain information systems items. SE applies Computer Science fundamentals to the development of software systems. Information systems are concerned with the business community needs in terms of computing, and especially information. Thus, both SE and information systems fields have certain elements in common—computing concepts, systems development, and information technology—but they also have clearly distinguishable goals [50].

3.2 Results

In this section, we present three major results. First, the distribution of the publications along the years, journals and conferences are shown. Then we have two sections to characterize the domains and contexts within which Action Research studies were conducted and that describe how they were done.

Publication distribution is shown in Table II (only journals and conferences from where papers were selected are listed). Adherence levels defined earlier in Table I

TABLE I
INFORMATION EXTRACTED FROM THE PAPERS

Information	Description	Based on
Problem	The research problem, usually related to the AR diagnosis	Lau [47]
Action	Action implemented	Lau [47]
Reflection	Reflections from the actions implemented and problem solution	Lau [47]
IEEE Taxonomy	Used to classify the research topics	IEEE Keyword Taxonomy [49]
Adherence	*Inspired*: when the focus is on the researchers learning from a real problem resolution exploring SE research without controlling the study by the AR principles; *Based*: when the AR methodology is modified or combined with other empirical methods; *Genuine*: When the full essence of action research methodology is present	–
Type	*Action Research*: focusing on change and reflection; *Action Science*: trying to solve conflicts between espoused and applied theories; *Participatory Action Research*: emphasizing participant collaboration; *Action Learning*: for programmed instruction and experiential learning	Avison et al. [31]
Length	Length of the study	Sjøberg et al. [2]
Data collection	Qualitative or quantitative, including the techniques used for data collection	–
AR control structures	Initialization *Researcher*: field experiment; *Practitioner*: classic action research genesis; *Collaboration*: evolves from existing interaction Authority *Practitioner*: consultative action warrant; *Staged*: migration of power to the client; *Identity*: practitioner and researcher are the same Formalization *Formal*: specific written contract; *Informal*: broad, perhaps verbal, agreements; *Evolved*: informal or formal shift into opposite form	Avison et al. [44]
AR cycles	Number of AR cycles conducted	Davison et al. [30]

TABLE II
DISTRIBUTION OF THE SELECTED PAPERS

Journals and conferences	1993–1998			1999–2004			2005–2010		
	(I)	(B)	(G)	(I)	(B)	(G)	(I)	(B)	(G)
ESE				1			1		
ICSE					2				2
IEEE SW				1			2		
IST					1	1			5
SME								1	
SP&E	1					1	1		
TSE								1	1
Totals	1			2	1	4	3	3	8
		1			7			14	

are now abbreviated in Table II as Inspired (*I*), Based (*B*), and Genuine (*G*). From the distribution, it is possible to see that the number of reports on Action Research studies presents a smooth increase along the years, with more studies being reported in the past 2 years. Notice that in the last period (2005 to June 2010) of data collection some 2010 conferences and journals had not yet published their proceedings (e.g., ESEM), thus providing a partial view of this period.

The number of studies inspired by Action Research is relatively high, about 30%. This means that there is a need to improve rigor in Action Research studies as to whether we want Action Research investigations to form a solid ground for further research and industrial applications in SE. This situation is even worse if we consider the studies that mentioned Action Research but were eliminated as they could not even be classified in the lowest (i.e., inspired) adherence level.

3.2.1 Research Topics and Contexts

It is interesting to see that Action Research is being applied to a wide spectrum of Software Engineering research domains (Table III), ranging from the more social side (e.g., Management and Software Engineering Process) to the more technical end (e.g., Software Construction and Programming Environments). The topic with the wider number of studies is Software Engineering Process, more specifically Process Implementation and Change. This is also the topic where most of the

TABLE III
RESEARCH TOPICS ACCORDING TO THE IEEE TAXONOMY

IEEE Taxonomy	# Articles
Distribution, maintenance, and enhancement	2
Documentation	Lindvall and Sandahl [51]
Maintenance management	Polo et al. [52]
Management	3
Project control and modeling	Canfora et al. [53]
Time estimation	Staron and Meding [54]
Risk management	McCaffery et al. [55]
Programming environments/construction tools	1
Environments for multiple-processor systems	Vigder et al. [56]
Requirements/specifications	3
Elicitation methods	Maiden and Robertson [57]
	Napier et al. [58]
Process	Kauppinen et al. [59]
Reusable software	1
Reuse models	Bosch [60]
Software and system safety	1
Software and system safety	Gutierrez et al. [61]
Software architectures	2
Domain-specific architectures	Bengtsson and Bosch [62]
Patterns	Mattsson et al. [63]
Software construction	2
Data design and management	Fernández-Medina and Piattini [64]
Programming paradigms	Lycett [65]
Software engineering process	6
Process implementation and change	Fitzgerald and O'Kane [66], Kautz et al. [67], Salo and Abrahamsson [68], Nielsen and Tjørnehøj [69], and Pino et al. [70]
Software process models	Abrahamsson and Koskela [48]
Miscellaneous	1
Software libraries	Staron et al. [71]

inspired adherence level articles were concentrated mainly because their authors interleaved the software improvement process with the Action Research process leaving implicit when they were assuming the researcher or the consulting roles. Other topics include architecture knowledge management, agile methods, component-based development, scientific workflows, software inspection, and security.

As regards the diagnosis/action/reflection extracted information, we could classify it into three major formats: (1) evaluation of technology introduction through lessons learned (presenting similarities with case studies), (2) technology conception and/or tailoring with intense collaboration and changing through intervention focus (the AR most genuine format where problem solution is initially unknown), and (3) SE activities facilitation and observation (having a consulting component).

In general, the more technical initiatives were closely related to formats (1) and (2). For example, one of the papers reported a maintenance methodology created in the context of an organization, while in another case, the formalization of software architecture design rules in the context of model-driven development was introduced. However, the more social research efforts were more related to the format (3) as it was the case of the software process improvement papers.

3.2.2   Execution Details

Many papers did not describe the data collection techniques, study length, and number of Action Research cycles. Therefore, the extraction of information on execution details was problematic. Moreover, almost all papers did not explicitly define the Action Research type and control structures. The Action Research control structures are an important component of an Action Research study execution as it reveals the process followed, and why decisions were taken. The definition of the Action Research type, in its turn, shows why some Action Research characteristics were emphasized. Although this information was not explicit, we could in some cases implicitly deduce them from the overall research actions and context description. Figure 5 shows the number of papers as per Action Research type and control structures. In examining Fig. 5, we can see that most of the reported studies described in the papers are of the Action Research type, and are started by practitioners having authority over the research execution (identity authority) that is carried out without any formalization. This appears to be an interesting find as it possibly means that researchers are conducting studies considering a small number of organizational constraints. Nevertheless, it is worth reiterating that a large percentage of the papers do not mention their control structures.

All papers made intensive use of qualitative data, confirming this intrinsic characteristic of Action Research in Software Engineering. Four studies used quantitative data, indicating that quantitative research is also a possibility in Action Research.

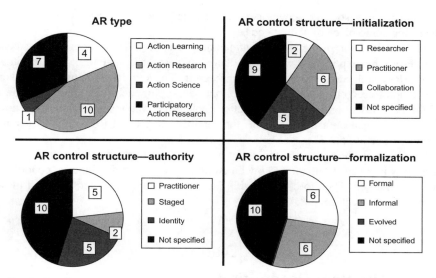

FIG. 5. Classification of selected papers as per Action Research types and control structures defined in Table I.

Observation was by far the most mentioned data collection technique, followed closely by interviews. For quantitative data, metrics were reported to be used in all papers.

Finally, the length of the studies ranged from 2 months to 5 years (mean time was 21 months and 16 for the standard deviation). This result shows that the use of Action Research is very flexible regarding the study duration and is most influenced by the research topic, software technology, and activities involved. Five studies did not specify their length. For the number of Action Research cycles, only three papers explicitly mentioned to be one cycle. But, from the linear description in the other papers, we believe the same behavior can be expected for most of the other cases.

4. Using Action Research in Software Engineering: An *In Vivo* Study

The research theme addressed in this study concerns source code refactoring. Two very distinct aspects of this theme are investigated. The initial objective when starting this study was to use the software refactoring process to externalize knowledge about architectural styles and source code conventions in the software project. However, due to the features of Action Research, the researchers were motivated to understand how software developers decide the appropriate refactoring moment regarding some piece of source code.

The organization of the study documentation has been derived during its execution. From this experience, we would like to suggest a template to be used in other Action Research studies in Software Engineering. The template structure is based on the Action Research stages consisting of one section for each stage, including some additional subsections intending to better explain the whole study. Details on how the template can be used to support the reporting of Action Research studies are shown in Section 5.2.3.

Even though the results of the study were relevant to the software project, this section is intended to illustrate how an Action Research study could be conducted and documented. Therefore, we would like to remind the readers to focus on these aspects in this section.

4.1 Diagnosis

4.1.1 Problem Description

Architectural styles and coding conventions represent essential elements in the construction stage of software development, associated with important quality characteristics such as readability and maintainability. In addition, these elements have strong social and managerial implications as they can support the project team organization [72].

The definition and documentation of architectural styles and coding conventions should be *a priori* worked on in a regular basis. However, in teams with a limited number of members, these issues can be worked on by means of direct communication. However, when new members join the team, including remote ones, direct communication turns out to be not the appropriate medium for this kind of knowledge dissemination, especially considering when communication can compromise the productivity of the developers and affect software quality. Additionally, there are two issues that should be considered into this context: (1) new developers learning the process overloads communication and (2) remote teams introduce difficulties to the communication among all the members of the team.

To reduce the impact on the communication of knowledge among team members (being previously done through direct dissemination among the local ones), knowledge should be externalized and explicitly described. One immediate way to proceed in knowledge externalization could be to use the more experienced software project developers to explicit it. However, due to their larger experience, there is a possibility that more experienced developers would not be able to understand the real needs of the less experienced members in terms of information, as these basic needs are not part of the more experienced developers daily activities.

Presented with these risks, this study investigated mechanisms to allow knowledge externalization related to architectural styles and coding conventions, considering the needs of new project team members, mainly the remote ones.

4.1.2   Project Context

The software project within which the research was conducted aims at the developing of a new Web-based information system to support the activities concerned with the management of R&D engineering projects in the context of a nonprofit Science and Technology Foundation (STF) at the Federal University of Rio de Janeiro. It represents a medium-to-large software project including seven modules (over 200 use cases) and covering different organization departments such as human resources, accounting, and project management. The software was modularized and developed following an incremental life cycle. Among the factors that justified this decision, we can mention the stakeholder interest (1) on partial deliveries of the product and (2) on the gradual replacement of the current system by the new one. The STF follows a reference software development process model based on MPS.BR from the G up to the C level [73]. MPS.BR is a nationwide program for software process improvement in Brazilian organizations. The main goal of this initiative is to develop and disseminate a Brazilian software process model (named MPS Model) aimed at establishing a feasible path for organizations to achieve benefits from implementing software process improvement at reasonable costs, especially in small- and mid-size enterprises. The performance of companies using the MPS-BR has been followed via periodical assessments, and results are positive [74].

The STF new information system was developed using Java technology. The designed software architecture is based on the layered model-view-controller (MVC) architectural style where the View layer was implemented using JavaServer Faces (JSF—a Web framework that uses graphic interface components to create Web interfaces) and the Model and Controller layers using plain Java. At the time of the study (November 2008), the team was distributed and consisted of three software designers and two software developers at the STF site (denominated by team L) plus six developers physically located in another city 200 km away from Rio de Janeiro (team R). The average experience of the team L with software development was of about 7 years (varying between 3 and 15 years), while the team R had about 2.5 years (varying between 1.5 and 4 years). Moreover, the team L had three professionals responsible for specification and quality assurance activities.

Each module construction was implemented in iterations made by a set of conceptually related use cases. In each iteration, the software design stage consisted of the designers defining business classes to form the Model layer. After the design was released, the developers at the remote site were responsible to implement both the View and Controller layers. The communication between the teams used Internet apparatuses such as email, instant messaging systems, and video conference. It is also worth mentioning that all software project issues such as defects, adjustments, and tasks were registered and monitored using the TRAC system (issue tracking system) [75].

The detailed documentation on the architectural style and coding conventions used was not an outcome of the project development process. Most of these definitions were brought from the Sun official documentation [76] and industry recommendations [77]. However, some adaptations and modifications were made by the development team. One of them, for example, regards the creation of an own mechanism to perform the validation of input data forms, ignoring the ones provided by the JSF technology.

In March 2008, time when a new software project module development was starting, Team R was added to the project. At that time, this represented an increase from 8 to 14 professionals. These new Team R members received onsite face-to-face training for 2 days. During the training sessions, the technology used in the project was presented, and issues regarding the construction procedures were discussed. The following topics were addressed:

- The Java and JSF technologies.
- The MVC architectural style, including discussions on object-oriented paradigm concepts, such as encapsulation and reuse through inheritance.
- Source code naming conventions and organization. This was presented to reimplement a previous use case from an earlier software project module.
- Configuration management activities.
- The development process overview, including the specification and testing activities.

In spite of these initial training and monitoring activities having been conducted, the more experienced members from team L some identified some issues related to the quality of the source code as implemented at the end of the first iteration of the members of team R. Even though this behavior is not desired, it is common to observe it in other projects due to, among other reasons, the lack of familiarity with the project (problem domain) even if the technologies used are well known [78]. These issues regarded the failure to follow source code organization according to tacit coding conventions and architectural styles expected by the more experienced members.

4.1.3   Research Theme

The research theme concerned with the previously presented scenario can be defined as follows: strategies to detect nonconformances in source code caused by lack of knowledge of the software project coding conventions and architectural styles. The intention is to use refactoring techniques to identify coding nonconformances when compared with the tacit knowledge held by the experienced developers. This way, we worked on source code refactoring aiming at improving its quality as usually perceived by the more experienced developers in the software project.

According to Mens and Tourwe [79], the main idea in refactoring is to redistribute or rewrite classes, attributes, and methods through classes' hierarchy, to facilitate further adaptation and extension. In other words, the goal in refactoring is to improve the software's internal structure, keeping its external behavior. Thus, based on the nonconformances detected in the less experienced developers' implemented code, we expected that it could be possible to define what knowledge on source code conventions should become explicit. To support this expectation, the fact that inspections/reviews are a useful tool for organizational learning is being explored, as good development patterns can be observed during the reading for refactoring.

4.2   Planning

In this section, the planning stage is described. It begins with a technical literature survey where some works on the research theme can be examined. Based on that, the intervention focus can be set and the hypotheses associated to the outcomes can be defined. Moreover, the instruments, tools, and techniques that are expected to be used in the research are presented.

4.2.1   Literature Survey

Given the research theme, the search for published papers in the technical literature focused on inspection techniques that could offer some guidance on how the source code should be read and could also assist in revealing nonconformances. We sought techniques requiring as little training effort as possible. Just the explanation on their application should be enough to allow their application. Additionally, we looked for technical articles introducing mechanisms that could reveal the underlying reasons for the captured nonconformances. The literature survey was conducted on an *ad hoc* basis, and papers were selected by convenience.

Two studies were selected in this survey: Dunsmore et al. [80] and Mäntylä [81]. They set the ground to design the procedure for source code reading (see form in Table IV). Dunsmore et al. [80] describe a use case-based inspection technique that allows object-oriented source code reading by exploring its dynamic model perspective. The steps of the technique encompass (1) *the selection of one use case*, (2) *the derivation of scenarios from it (e.g., "save invoice," "cancel invoice")*, and (3) *reading the class methods responsible for scenario execution*.

In order to categorize the refactoring suggestions produced by the source code inspection, we used the concepts from a Mäntylä and Lassenius [82] study which is subsequent to the Mäntylä [81] study and directly related to it. Mäntylä and Lassenius [82] describe an experimental study aimed at understanding why and when developers perceive the need for source code refactoring. It is a qualitative study where subjects were instructed to register why they felt the source code should

TABLE IV
FORM CONTENT USED IN THE STUDY

Procedure steps
1. Select one use case from the software
2. Extract use scenarios from the use case (e.g., "save invoice," "cancel invoice")
3. Read through the class methods responsible for scenario execution. Check if the correct methods are being invoked and if the scenario state is being kept and manipulated in a consistent way by the system
4. For each class method, register the refactoring opportunities according to your previous knowledge of the project (e.g., excessive nesting, naming, visual source code organization, among others)

Form fields
1. Use case
2. Scenario description
3. Class name
4. Method name
5. Would you apply refactoring to this method? (answer from 1 to 5: 1, No; 2, Unlikely; 3, Likely; 4, Yes, but only at another moment in the project; 5, Yes, right now)
6. Explain your decision to the above question. If refactoring is needed explain why, what, and how the method should be improved. If the method is OK explain what quality attributes are being met, including agreed project patterns. If your answer is 'Likely' provide your reasoning too. If appropriate, mention the source code lines involved in your explanation

---

undergo refactoring. The authors analyzed these records, extracting a taxonomy of defects (poor algorithm, poor internal organization, minor structure issues, duplicated code, too many temporary variables, poor readability, poor method name, wrong indentation, poor comments, poor parameter layout, long method, or extracted method). We decided to explore the same taxonomy during our source code refactoring process. To do that, we included the following step into the procedure described in Table IV: (4) *registering refactoring decisions for each method according to the previous knowledge of the developers*. Moreover, Mäntylä [81] suggests a set of source code metrics that could be used to evaluate some properties of the source code under refactoring. These metrics were also used in our study aiming at comparing the results of the studies and will be described in the next section.

4.2.2 Action Focus

4.2.2.1 Objectives. We defined the goals of the study using the Goal-Question-Metric (GQM) approach as proposed by Basili et al. [83] as follows:

analyze the using of source code refactoring *for the purpose of* characterizing *with respect to* externalization of knowledge associated with the architectural styles and coding conventions *from the point of view* of the software engineers *in the context of the development of* Web information systems by distributed teams.

Additionally, a secondary goal was included to compare the results of this study with Mäntylä [81]:

analyze source code measurable characteristics *for the purpose of* characterizing (can it explain the refactoring decision subjective evaluation?) *with respect to* the predictability of the measurements *from the point of view* of the software engineers *in the context of the development of* Web information systems by distributed teams.

4.2.2.2 Research Questions. The objectives will be achieved when answers (results) have been given to the following questions (in reverse order of objectives):

- Q.1. What source code aspects or characteristics does a developer use when identifying refactoring as necessary? This question aims at understanding the primary motivation to experienced developers identify a refactoring opportunity.
- Q.2. Is source code refactoring useful to externalize knowledge on architectural styles and coding conventions used in a software project, particularly those a

developer needs when getting involved in new projects? The idea of this question is to assess whether the refactoring opportunities identified in question 1 can be used as an input in documenting the architectural styles and coding conventions used in the project.

4.2.2.3 Expected Outcomes (Data Collection). Question Q.1 has the following operational questions associated:

- Q.1.1. What is the refactoring effect over the source code metrics?
- Q.1.2. What are the source code characteristics that affect developer decisions?
- Q.1.3. What types of refactoring are exclusively identified by the experienced developers?
- Q.1.4. Is it possible to classify the identified refactoring opportunities to reflect expected source code quality characteristics?
- Q.1.5. What is the perception of the developers on the refactoring effect over source code quality?

The source code metrics suggested in Mäntylä [81] (lines of code, number of parameters, cyclomatic complexity, invoked methods, fan-in, and fan-out) will be used to support answers to questions Q1.1 and Q1.2. According to Mäntylä [81], these metrics were selected based on their acceptance described in the technical literature, aiming at characterizing the methods from different perspectives. A brief description for each metric is given below:

- *Lines of code*: number of lines in source code (including comments).
- *Number of parameters*: number of parameters of a method.
- *Cyclomatic complexity*: #edges − #vertices + #connected components in a control flow graph.
- *Invoked methods*: number of methods invoked inside a method.
- *Fan-in*: number of input variables used in a method, including its parameters and global variables.
- *Fan-out*: number of output variables updated in a method, including the return command and global variables.

Returning to the operational questions, we planned a categorization activity with the developers based on the Mäntylä and Lassenius [82] taxonomy of defects to answer question Q.1.4. Finally, questions Q.1.3 and Q.1.5 will be answered in interviews with the developers.

Question Q.2 is associated to the following operational questions:

- Q.2.1. Should the description of the refactoring opportunities as identified by the developers contain details on what motivated their identification?
- Q.2.2. Should the source code refactoring be performed by those who wrote the source code in order to facilitate their grasping the tacit knowledge involved in the coding conventions?
- Q.2.3. How can tacit knowledge be acquired and made explicit?

Question Q.2.1 will be captured by the form presented in Table IV. In its turn, question Q.2.2 just requires project management activities to be answered. Last but not least, question Q.2.3 will be discussed between the project members from both teams (L and R).

4.2.3 Hypotheses (Suppositions)

- There is some tacit knowledge concerned with the project organization conforming with an architectural style, and with coding conventions.
- The use of the Dunsmore et al. [80] inspection technique of the source code refactoring will allow knowledge externalization related to the architectural styles and coding conventions used in the software project.

4.2.4 Operational Definitions

4.2.4.1 Techniques. Semistructured interviews will be the main qualitative data collection approach during the interventions. Additionally, characterization forms will also be filled in by the participants. Quantitative data will be directly extracted from the source code and analyzed using descriptive and predictive statistics.

4.2.4.2 Instruments. Table IV shows the information contained in the discrepancy (nonconformance or refactoring suggestion) form that will be used by the developers to describe the source code refactoring opportunities. Apart from the fields that should be filled by the developers, the form has the description of the procedure steps that should be observed to facilitate source code reading and understanding. According to Dunsmore et al. [80], source code comprehension can be simplified as it forces the reading of one use case in its turn. Steps 1, 2, and 3 were directly brought from Dunsmore et al. [80], while fields 5 and 6 were brought from Mäntylä and Lassenius [82]. The other fields and steps were formulated specifically for the context of this study.

TABLE V
SEMISTRUCTURED INTERVIEW 1

Refactoring-related topics
   (i)   Were the questions and procedure suggested useful to focus the refactoring process on the agreed purpose?
   (ii) How would you rate each given explanation for the refactoring opportunities using the Mäntylä and Lassenius [82] taxonomy of defects? (Q.1.4)
   (iii) What is the refactoring effect on source code quality? (Q.1.5)
   (iv) What kind of refactoring do you think could only be identified by the experienced developers? (Q.1.3)
   (v)   Did you miss any characteristic to be captured on the given form? Were the blank fields enough for the exceptions?

TABLE VI
SEMISTRUCTURED INTERVIEW 2

Knowledge externalization topics
   (vi)   How did the identified refactoring opportunities facilitate the learning of coding conventions and architectural styles as used in the project?
   (vii) Decision on how to formalize the externalized knowledge (Q.2.3)
   (viii) In your opinion, was the refactoring useful as a means to externalizing knowledge? Do you still feel that some knowledge was not externalized?

Two interviews were planned aiming at discussing the topics shown in Tables V and VI.

4.2.4.3 *Tools.*

For the extraction of source code metrics and the quantitative data analysis, the tools "Understand—Source Code Analysis & Metrics" (http://www.scitools.com/) and SPSS (http://www.spss.com/) tools, respectively, were used.

4.3 Actions

Initially, development team R was notified on some issues regarding quality as seen in the source code. Most of them were due to communication failures and the learning process of working in a distributed way. For this reason, source code refactoring should be started trying to show the team how the source code should be structured.

Two more experienced developers from team L (a designer/developer and a developer) were selected to perform the source code review and identify the refactoring opportunities. Each one of them was in charge of reviewing different use cases.

The procedure steps and form fields (Table IV) were presented to the developers who also received instructions on how to fill them in. The instructions basically included the review focus, which gave overall instructions on how to search for source code nonconformances according to what developers perceived as coding conventions or architectural styles tacitly used in the project. The definition of nonconformance was kept generic in an attempt to maintain the subjectivity in refactoring decisions and to capture richer descriptions of the opportunities. Some examples were discussed using the prior knowledge of developers on refactoring, including concepts on the object-oriented paradigm (inheritance, readability, maintainability, among others). Following the instructions, the refactoring process was started, and after its completion, the information filled in the forms was sent to the developers who originally built the use cases.

Based on the refactoring opportunities identified and registered in the forms by team L members, team R was instructed to apply refactoring to the source code. It was also instructed that the original source code versions should be recorded (using the version control system) together with the time spent with each method that received refactoring. As planned, those responsible for the construction of the use cases applied refactoring to their own source code, but could disagree on the suggested refactoring opportunities.

Lastly, we started the planned semistructured interviews (Tables V and VI). Interviews 1 and 2 were made with the developers. The interviews were first recorded, and next could be transcribed. Besides, after the interview, team L developers were asked to rate their refactoring opportunities with the researcher using the Mäntylä and Lassenius [82] taxonomy for defect categories.

4.4 Evaluation and Analysis

In this section, two different types of data will be analyzed. One is the source code metrics extracted before and after refactoring, in an attempt to answer questions Q.1.1, Q.1.2, and Q.1.4. The other is concerned with the interviews transcript, used to discuss questions Q.1.3, Q.1.5, and Q.2.3.

4.4.1 Analyzing Source Code Metrics

As previously discussed, each developer described what motivated the identification of each suggested refactoring opportunity. Based on this description, the defect taxonomy was applied and evolved. The categories of defects (see Section 4.2.1) as well as a summary of the refactoring effects on the source code metrics considering each defect category are shown in Table VII. Two new defect categories have emerged in the context of this study—"low cohesion" and "unused code" (underlined in Table VII). The developers reviewed 47 methods. In 37 of them, there was at least one refactoring opportunity. The average size of the methods was 32 lines of code (with large variation, $\sigma = 34$).

To observe the effect on the metrics, it is interesting to split the refactoring suggestions into two categories: defects and improvements. Both types are separated in Table VII by an empty line. In each row (Table VII), the values were calculated by subtracting the metric value before and after the refactoring and summed up by category. Thus, negative values represent a decrease in the metric value after the refactoring. Even when the developers were not asked, they found additional defects during the review. Many of these defects, based on their descriptions, were related to incomplete features or, in other words, omission defects. As a result, we can see through the metrics that the correction of defects increased both the source code size and complexity. However, analyzing the improvement category for refactoring opportunities we can see (Table VII, total line) that the result was opposite to the

TABLE VII
METRICS VARIATION BEFORE AND AFTER SOURCE CODE REFACTORING

Category	Refactoring opportunities	Cyclomatic complexity	Fan-in	Fan-out	Lines of code	Remote methods invoked
Defect	6	5	5	7	60	7
Poor algorithm	7 (17.9%)	−3	−1	−3	−14	1
Poor internal organization	7 (17.9%)	−1	−11	−5	−1	2
Minor structure issues	7 (17.9%)	−4	−1	−5	−9	0
Low cohesion	6 (15.4%)	−1	1	6	− 4	6
Duplicated code	3 (7.7%)	−8	−3	−23	− 39	−21
Too many temporary variables	2 (5.1%)	0	0	1	−2	0
Unused code	1 (2.5%)	0	0	0	0	0
Poor readability	1 (2.5%)	0	0	0	1	0
Poor method name	1 (2.5%)	0	0	0	0	0
Wrong indentation	1 (2.5%)	0	0	−1	18	0
Poor comments	1 (2.5%)	0	0	0	7	0
Poor parameter layout	1 (2.5%)	0	0	0	2	0
Long method or extract method	1 (2.5%)	−21	−3	−57	−157	−57
Total (except defect category)	39 (100%)	−38	−18	−87	−198	−69

former. In this case, applying refactoring meant a reduction in source code size, complexity, and coupling (considering the fan-in, fan-out, and remote methods invoked (RMI) metrics).

In order to improve our capability of observation and data analysis, the refactoring effect over the metrics was normalized, and its variation described through percentages. Percentage values were calculated thus: each metric variation value was divided by the metric value before refactoring. For instance, for a 4-line reduction in a method with 20 lines, we would have a -20% variation. After this normalization, the data were analyzed using *boxplots*. Only the four most common categories were analyzed. For each *category*, the potential outliers were kept in order to enhance the analysis considering that there were not many data points to be included.

The information shown in Fig. 6 corresponds to the *poor algorithm* category. It is possible to observe the most affected metrics: cyclomatic complexity and lines of code. This behavior can suggest that the perception of developers of what a poor algorithm represents is associated with an incorrect or unnecessary use of control statements, which is coherent with the general understanding of an algorithm that should be improved. Clearly evidencing this perception one of the developers used the following statement when describing the refactoring suggestion: "Only the first 'if' is necessary, because if the search filters do not include the SSN, the 'else' of the second 'if' would appropriately create the list."

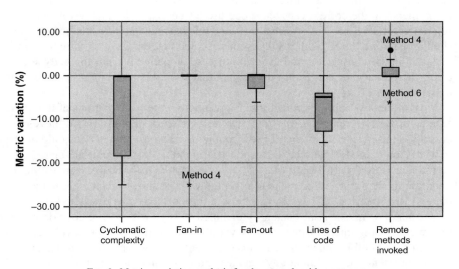

Fig. 6. Metrics variation analysis for the poor algorithm category.

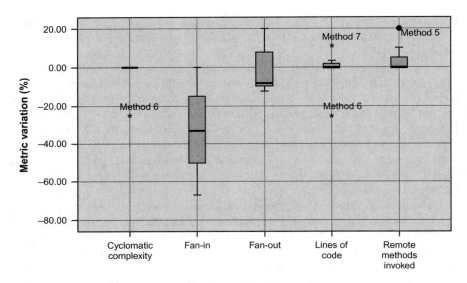

FIG. 7. Metrics variation analysis for the poor internal organization category.

Figure 7 shows that the most affected metric in the *poor internal organization* category is fan-in. Indeed, more than half suggestions in this category involved recommending the correct variable scope use, as described by one developer: "the reference variable 'searchForm' has its scope relevance only to this method and thus should be defined in it." Other suggestions included recommending variables initi-alization in the constructor and avoiding the use of static text into the body source code (there is one special file in the project that should be used in case static texts exist).

Most of the low cohesion refactoring suggestions were for violations of the MVC architectural style regarding the *low cohesion* category. The following developer description illustrates this scenario: "the totalizing installment method should not be in the 'form' class. It should be the responsibility of the 'InstallmentList' class." The mentioned "form" class is part of the View layer, which is basically responsible for maintaining the values filled in the forms. Figure 8 also shows an increase in the fan-out and RMI metrics. Nearly, no variation in lines of code was registered.

The *minor structure issues* category included worries with source code organiza-tion such as assignment of unnecessary variables as pointed by one developer: "an assignment to null is unnecessary in this case" or "it is not appropriate to instantiate the 'Installment' class without any state set and then consecutively invoke its 'sets'

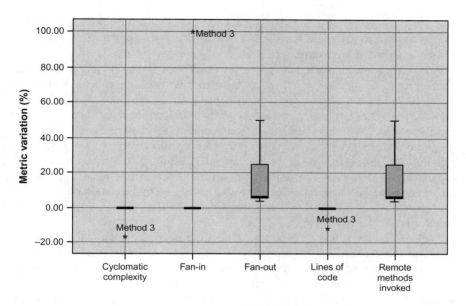

F<small>IG</small>. 8. Metrics variation analysis for the low cohesion category

method. It is better to write a constructor that can receive all the parameters needed."
Due to its more generic nature, the *minor structure issues* category virtually had no
significant metric variation pattern and presented a large number of outlier data
points. For this reason, the *boxplot* analysis has been omitted.

4.4.2 Explaining the Refactoring Decisions

The metrics variation analysis presented in the previous section examined the
effect over the source code metrics *after* source code refactoring. In this section, the
source code structural characteristics *before* source code refactoring will be
explored in an attempt to explain what metrics can have influenced the decision of
the developers when suggesting a refactoring opportunity. This way, regression
analysis was used to investigate how these characteristics could have affected the
developers' decision. The categorical regression method was used in this analysis as
it presents several advantages over traditional methods such as the ability to create
combined regression models, where different independent variable types can coexist
and the dependent variable can be represented in any scale (nominal, ordinal, or
ratio). Additionally, the categorical regression has better performance in a data set

with few data points, several variables, and many different values for each variable. Due to these features, the categorical regression has been applied in this analysis. The accepted error level (alpha) is 5%.

For each category analyzed in the previous section, a regression model is created. The source code metrics were used as independent variables, and the refactoring decisions for each method were used as dependent ones (using a nominal "Yes," "No" scale). The methods that did not receive any refactoring suggestion were considered as "No" (10 methods in total) and those that received refactoring suggestions were considered as "Yes" (the total depends on the category, although common quantities are six or seven methods). Besides, the methods classified exclusively as defects were used as "No" in the dependent variable to create the regression models. The refactoring focus did not regard the detection of defects. In case defects were not present, these methods could not have any impact on the refactoring suggestions.

Table VIII shows the regression model for the poor algorithm category, which seems able to explain 88.8% (adjusted R^2) of the refactoring suggestions. According to the results, the most important predictor is lines of code, followed by cyclomatic complexity (we are considering the absolute value of standardized beta, as there are some nominal scale variables; besides, the absolute value of the correlation coefficient defines the proportional variation of the dependent variable, not considering the influence of predictors' variables). Even when suggesting some fan-in metric influence the model seems to be consistent with Fig. 6, which shows that the same metrics were the most affected ones after refactoring.

The model shown in Table IX involves 63.6% of the refactoring suggestions. The most important predictor is RMI. Despite the model indicating the RMI metric as the most important regarding the developers' suggestions, the most affected metric after refactoring (see Fig. 7) was fan-in. To investigate what could be influencing this

TABLE VIII
REGRESSION MODEL FOR THE *POOR ALGORITHM* CATEGORY

Adjusted R^2	0.888	*p*-value	0.018
Model predictors			

Predictors	Standardized beta	*p*-value	Correlation coefficient
Cyclomatic complexity	− 5.909	0.037	− 0.847
Fan-in	− 4.239	0.026	− 0.828
Fan-out	4.324	0.078	0.904
Lines of code	7.576	0.022	0.855
Remote methods invoked	− 4.154	0.058	0.910

difference, the first step was to check whether the noninfluence of the fan-in predictor in the Table IX model could indicate some similarity regarding the metrics values for those methods refactoring was applied to or not. One issue identified regarded the way one of the developers identified the problems in the methods. For instance, methods that were making use of large scope variables were not properly identified. This seems to represent the origin of the difference between the model in Table IX and the behavior seen in Fig. 7. Even so, the model was able to capture the influence of the remote methods invocation metric as also identified in Fig. 7, although with greater intensity.

The most important metrics for developers' suggestions regarding the low cohesion category were RMI and fan-out (Table X). This model can answer 67.6% of the refactoring needs for this category, and it is aligned with the behavior seen in Fig. 8.

It was not possible to create a statistically significant model for the minor structure issues category. In fact, this should be expected as this category produced the highest number of outliers, as previously discussed. In this case, this result is also consistent with the observed behavior, and no type of indication can be asserted.

TABLE IX
REGRESSION MODEL FOR THE *POOR INTERNAL ORGANIZATION* CATEGORY

Adjusted R^2	0.636	p-value	0.047
	Model predictors		
Predictors	Standardized beta	p-value	Correlation coefficient
Cyclomatic complexity	−0.998	0.783	−0.641
Fan-in	0.190	0.831	0.171
Fan-out	3.160	0.091	0.603
Lines of code	2.666	0.337	0.727
Remote methods invoked	−5.115	0.012	−0.752

TABLE X
REGRESSION MODEL FOR THE *LOW COHESION* CATEGORY

Adjusted R^2	0.676	p-value	0.021
	Model predictors		
Predictors	Standardized beta	p-value	Correlation coefficient
Cyclomatic complexity	0.581	0.916	0.421
Fan-in	−0.213	0.941	−0.191
Fan-out	−4.401	0.033	−0.538
Lines of code	−1.417	0.605	−0.729
Remote methods invoked	5.215	0.020	0.596

To complement the data analysis, it is possible to observe through the metrics analysis before refactoring (regression models) that developer refactoring decisions are consistent with the effects in these metrics after refactoring. Therefore, as the source code metrics represent the structural characteristics of the source code, it is possible to observe that the same characteristics influencing developers' decisions were somehow directly affected after the accomplishing of the refactoring.

4.4.3 Perception on Code Quality and Learning—Qualitative Analysis

This section describes the qualitative analysis of the data collected from the developers throughout the semistructured interviews (Section 4.2.4.2). Considering the goals of the study, it has been found that interview questions (iii), (iv), (vi), (vii), and (vii) (Tables V and VI) should be the most significant ones as they relate directly to the results expected (questions Q.1 and Q.2).

The analysis will be supported by the use of grounded theory [84], with some adaptations from Baskerville and Pries-Heje [85]. According to Baskerville and Pries-Heje [85], Action Research usually modifies the grounded theory element roles as it brings preset categories, possibly including a central category, which can be obtained from the research theme definition (Section 4.1.3) and from the initial literature review (Section 4.2.1). This way, the characteristic of grounded emergence of one theory is not genuinely reached as expected by the canonical grounded theory principles [84]. Therefore, the so-called grounded Action Research [85] selects the grounded theory components according to the study objectives, focusing on the open and axial coding. Figure 9 shows the general canonical coding process overview. Its application in this study has been done until the axial coding stage (represented by the categories in Fig. 9), based on interview transcriptions.

The main open coding objective is to reveal the essential concepts embedded in the data (in this case, represented by the statements made by the developers). So, the observations in the viewpoints of the participants are decomposed and organized into events or ideas by receiving meaningful labels (codes) [85]. An additional open coding goal is categorizing the concepts, synthesizing them, and supporting comprehension of the phenomena studied.

After performing the open coding process, we were able to get the results shown on Table XI. Each category was related to the research questions as defined in Section 4.2.2.2 as a way to represent their answers. The categories with IDs beginning with "I" correspond to the ones extracted from the research theme. The association between categories and questions can be understood as the axial coding from the grounded theory. The relationships between the categories are related to the

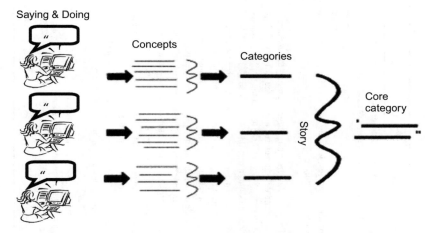

Fig. 9. Coding process overview—adapted from Baskerville and Pries-Heje [85].

corresponding questions. At the end, the "argument" column represents the link between the category and the concepts/codes discovered in adjacent data.

From the perspective of construct validity, it is important to mention that the research questions (Section 4.2.2.2) allowed the definition of practical questions (Section 4.2.2.3) and some of them associated to the semistructured interviews (Tables V and VI). This way, the trace from the research questions to the transcriptions can be observed, over which the grounded theory-based analysis has been produced. This analysis approach intends to objectively demonstrate how the results were obtained.

Despite the simplicity of Table XI some comments are still necessary. Categories from Q.2 were able to support the learning stage in this study because they represented the basis to elaborate the documentation that is going to be used by the developers to learn on what previously was being considered tacit code patterns. Besides, the qualitative analysis and consequently all categories allowed to explore the different significance levels, which were built by the different actions conducted to serve as input to build local theories (Section 4.5.2.1) [86]. The learning process and reflections on the results will be detailed in the next section.

4.5   Reflections and Learning

This section intends to explore the results of the study as project learning. This way, these results will be explored aiming at their organization and reflection on the knowledge acquired from the actions.

TABLE XI

QUALITATIVE ANALYSIS CATEGORIES (GROUNDED THEORY)

ID	Question	Category	Argument
I1	–	The source code refactoring process is analogous to source code inspection and easily applied under the perspective of the system dynamic execution according to the use cases models	Developers when experienced using use cases artifacts can explore them to read OO code more efficiently [80]
I2	–	The refactoring process brings as benefit the learning regarding the defect patterns that can be documented through the results analysis	Different studies suggest learning as one of the positive results of applying refactoring
C2	Q.1	Tacit coding patterns are more present in the software architecture and source code structure (problem solution), representing essential knowledge for understanding the source code	According to developers, knowledge regarding the architectural style and design patterns used in the software project allows to know *a priori* where to find the implementation of functionalities into a distributed OO code
C3	Q.1	The more experienced developers are aware (and know) on the tacit patterns used in the software project and, therefore, can identify when they are being neglected	The developers that applied refactoring in their own source code reinforced they were able to explicitly perceive (with the support of refactoring suggestions) a more uniform source code organization they did not consider before
C4	Q.2	The learning concentrated on making explicit tacit reasons regarding the source code organization and internalization of coding patterns used in the software project	A direct result from refactoring: the descriptions of refactoring suggestions presented the reasons as to why source code should be organized in a specific way and the participants could see defect patterns (in this case, through refactoring)
C5	Q.2	Knowledge regarding the architecture style and design patterns used in the project can be explained in the shape of directives that will guide developers in the use of a single development standard	The participants understood that the directives would be the most adequate way to guide (objectively, specifically, and focused) novice developers in the software project
C6	Q.2	All lessons learned shall be documented as categorized to facilitate their search and the reading of the directives	The directives set can grow along the time. Categorization will help to keep the document focused in its proposal depending on the context (i.e., directives related to naming conventions regarding domain classes)

4.5.1   Learning

After the semistructured interviews and data analysis, it was defined how the tacit knowledge concerned with the architectural style and coding patterns could be externalized. This externalization represents one of the main learning elements into the context of this study as it allowed the remote development team and future developers to familiarize themselves with the working patterns used in the software project.

Knowledge externalization was accomplished by elaborating directives from the identified problems throughout refactoring. The directives goal is to inform on how to structure the source code and project, where each one of them deals with a particular issue. Besides the directives, the participants decided by a set of information that should be integrated to each directive aiming at allowing them to be used in practice. The defined set of information is as follows:

- *Directive*: generic description (applicable to different contexts) for a rule regarding the source code organization and definition of a coding pattern.
- *Motivation/example*: Explanations or examples on how the directive should be applied.
- *Arguments*: the reasons for the directive to be used.
- *Type*: directive category (related to the refactoring categorization but without applying a "negative perspective," that is: poor readability was adjusted to be just readability).
- *Impact level*: subjective evaluation regarding the influence on code quality if the directive is not applied. Three possible values can be used: 1, low; 2, medium; or 3, high.
- *Affected classes*: types of classes where the directives can be more useful. For example, domain or utilities "Controller" classes.

An initial group of directives was defined by the researchers and from that moment evolved with the contributions from all the developers involved with refactoring in the software project. Several improvements were suggested. For instance, developers suggested new types, examples, modifications in the descriptions of directives, among others. From the 45 detected refactoring needs (including refactoring opportunities + defects), 43 were used to define 23 directives. One directive can be related to one or more refactoring needs as some directives entail more than one refactoring need.

After the definition and evolution of the initial group, the directives were made available to the development team through a Wiki system already used in the software project, the TRAC system [75]. The TRAC (by using a plug-in) allows the association of categories ("tags"), which can be indexed and searched. The Wiki represents a useful technology in this context as it allows the continuous improvement of the directives by the project team. As only a part of the source code was reviewed for refactoring, it is possible that new directives will pop up when additional parts of the project are reviewed. For the sake of simplicity, only some examples are being presented here, including a description in Table XII and a concrete directive instance in the TRAC system on Fig. 10.

Just after the agreement on the initial group of directives, all the developers recently integrated into the development team were asked to read the software project directives. One other expected benefit of this knowledge use is maintenance. It is expected that future maintenance will be accomplished by a totally different team, and the directives represent useful knowledge for future interventions. The evaluation of this documentation usability is out of the scope of this study and represents an interesting work opportunity for future investigations.

4.5.2   Reflections

As previously mentioned, the main basis for the conducting of this study were the works by Mäntylä [81] and Mäntylä and Lassenius [82], which demonstrated how the study could be planned and organized to capture and analyze the quantitative (source code metrics) and qualitative (refactoring description suggestions) data, respectively. The intention is to compare or to comparatively interpret the results, even considering this study does not represent a concrete replication of previous Mäntylä's studies. A first comment regards the categorization used to identify the main refactoring factors. Considering this and previous studies, most of the categories are coinciding. Only two new categories were identified (considering the universe of 22 categories identified by Mäntylä and Lassenius [82]). This result reinforces the validity of the conceived categorization indicating these categories can appropriately represent the refactoring decisions. However, it also indicates the need for additional studies aiming at the verification of possible new categories. Besides, 11 categories from the original study were not identified in this work, which can indicate that the expertise of the researchers may have influenced the results.

The regression models prepared in both studies differ in some aspects and deserve to be detailed. The regression model based on the source code metrics described in Mäntylä [81] was able to explain only 30% of the refactoring decisions in the original study. Using the same approach, it was not possible to create any statistically significant model in this study. However, for one group of participants in Mäntylä's study [81], a list of preset, different types of design shortcomings concerned with encapsulation, data abstraction, modularity, and hierarchy (called

TABLE XII
DIRECTIVES EXAMPLES

Directive	Motivation/example	Arguments	Type	Impact level	Affected classes

Static methods should be statically accessed, without instantiating the class containing the method	`Not correct:`
	`Classe c = new Nome Classe();`
	`c.metodoInvocado();`
	`Correct:`
	`NomeClasse.metodoInvocado();`
		There does not exist a need of creating a class instance to invoke a static method. Besides, memory space would be unnecessarily used	Algorithmic structure	2	All

Security verifications (facilities access) shall verify if the grants of the identified user allow access to one specific functionality	Access verifications were checking only the user role (and not the functionalities associated to the role). There are standard system roles capturing the permissions required for system actors, and specified in the use cases model. This model defines which actors can have access to the functionalities. The similarity between grants and actor role in project context allowed this misconception	The user management module allows the maintenance of roles and grants by associating functionalities to the roles. This way, different roles can be created and have access to one same functionality. Therefore, access verification should be done considering the grants associated to the role and not just considering the roles	Design structuring	3	Controller/domain
Always possible (and needed) Boolean expressions shall be used as a method result	`return` `!(curso.isStatusEncerrado());`	In this case, the reduction of lines of code (in case of if/else constructors are being used) improves readability	Readability	2	All

Always make use of the transaction management service when the persistence of the whole entity is needed or when the persistent class is responsible for persisting other classes	`GerenteTransacaoBD gtBD = new`
	`GerenteTransacaoBD(new ITransaction[]`
	`{proposta, projeto});`
	`gtBD.iniciarTransacao();`
	`try {`
	`proposta.save();`
	`projeto.save();`
	`} catch (Exception e) {`
	`gtBD.recuperarTransacao();`
	`throw(e);`
	`}`
	`gtBD.finalizarTransacao();`
		If there is no controlling and transaction restoring in the case of failure, inconsistent data can be incorrectly saved	Design structuring	3	Controller

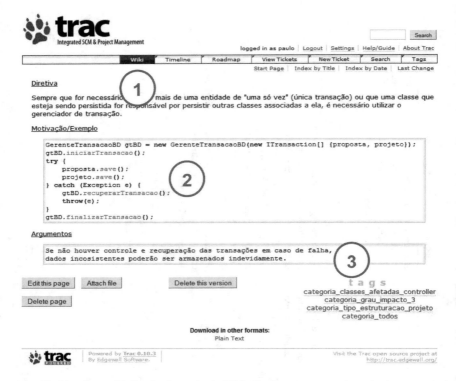

Fig. 10. Directive registering in the project's Wiki. The figure corresponds to the last example in Table XII: 1, directive; 2, motivation/example; 3, arguments.

"code smells" by Fowler et al. [87]) in object-oriented code (e.g., long method) was presented, where they were asked to look for the "code smells" in the source code. Aggregating the models by "code smells" allowed getting better performance and explaining 70% of the refactoring decisions for two or three "code smells." Using a similar approach in our study, after the categorization of the refactoring decisions, a regression model was created for some of the categories, with observable performance improvement and explaining from 63.6% until 88.8% in three from four categories.

Even so, there is some mismatch with Mäntylä's results [81]. In our study, source code metrics have been successfully used as source code refactoring decision predictors in one regression model. In Mäntylä [81], the model was just statistically significant when considering the presence or absence of "code smells" (not to decide on code refactoring). One possible reason for this difference can be associated with the experience of the developers in the project context, in our study. There was an expectation that practical knowledge could be useful to identify defects related to deviations in coding patterns and architectural styles. This way, there was consistency in the types of source code deviations identified, which possibly produced significantly better regression models for refactoring decisions.

There is some research exploring metrics to develop software technologies to detect refactoring opportunities in source code [79]; however, these technologies usually produce a lot of false-positive suggestions, requiring supplementary human evaluation in most of the cases [88]. Therefore, it is expected that the results presented in this work can support the creation of more effective tools. In fact, the use of regression models to reduce the number of false positives on code metrics-based analysis has demonstrated itself useful in near investigation fields, such as defects detection. Ruthruff et al. [89] show how defects automatically reported by CASE tools (statically analyzing the source code by using source code metrics) can be filtered through regression models. These models can identify those reported issues having more chance to represent real defects. These regression models are usually based on manually filtered historical data.

This result can be used to motivate, for instance, the building of specific case tools to support the decision making regarding refactoring as these tools could allow self-calibration with real data from the software projects they are being used in. These data will include some historical subjective evaluation, according to the way the regression models have been created in our work. This way, the suggestion of Fowler et al. [87] on keeping human evaluation in the detection of refactoring opportunities could be supported, even if indirectly.

Other work used to support our study [80] defined a systematic procedure to read the different methods in the classes refactoring should be applied in. Considering both studies the developers reported that an important characteristic of this procedure is concerned with the possibility of thinking about the methods considering their execution contexts. An additional and important feature regards the fact the technique explores use cases models as the basis for its application avoiding the need for training as use case models represent a well-known artifact commonly used in the software project.

However, despite their importance and influence, we could not relate all results to the aforementioned works of Dunsmore et al. [80], Mäntylä [81], and Mäntylä and Lassenius [82]. Two additional features have been explored in our study: (1) the use of refactoring as a means to explicit knowledge and document architectural styles and coding patterns for the software project; (2) to compare the source code metrics-based regression models with the observed metrics effects after refactoring.

The first feature represents the learning dimension of our study. Therefore, we believe it can represent important evidence regarding the possibility of inspections (reading), and can also support the externalization and documentation of tacit knowledge on architectural styles and coding standards. The refactoring process allowed the development team to think about its previous experience and, while describing the refactoring needs, to state the reasons why refactoring was considered necessary. Besides this indication, different quantitative and qualitative analysis moments were able to demonstrate the concrete existence of tacit knowledge that could impact the quality of the software being produced. For instance, the quantitative analysis after considering the existence of tacit knowledge has highlighted the same metrics that could be influenced by the developers' decisions regarding refactoring. It can indicate that developers were conscious and consistent in their decisions based on their (tacit) knowledge. It can be seen by observing the impact caused in the same set of source code metrics. Regarding the qualitative analysis, apart from allowing the identification on how the lessons learned should be organized and formatted, it revealed the way tacit knowledge can emerge and be molded into the software architecture and source code structure as a collaborative and cooperative development work result.

4.5.2.1 *Theory Construction.* Aiming to systematically organize and structure the series of events and knowledge concerned with this study, we decided to ambitiously represent them as a theory. The use of theories in Software Engineering is still uncommon, but due to the richness of the observations from action interpretations the building of such theory could facilitate the communication of ideas and generated knowledge [86]. Apart from that, the preparation of the theories represents an interesting strategy to facilitate its future aggregation through secondary studies [6], as it can clearly explain the applicability and limitations of the investigated software technology. According to Sjøberg et al. [86], there are three different levels of sophistication or complexity regarding the theories:

- *Level 1*: small stable and concrete relationships based on direct observation;
- *Level 2*: mid-range theories with some degree of abstraction but still heavily connected to the observations;
- *Level 3*: general theories looking to explain phenomena in the context of Software Engineering.

These levels establish markers in the generation of theories but can also represent complete theories by themselves. According to Sjøberg et al. [86], the development of theories in Software Engineering should be initially focused on levels 1 and 2. The theory elaborated in this work can be considered a Level 1 theory.

Sjøberg et al. [86] suggest the description of theories should be split into four parts: constructs (the basic elements), propositions (how the constructs relate), explanations (why the proposition was specified), and scope (what the universe of discourse in which the theory can be applicable is). This way, the construction of theories should involve five steps: (1) definition of constructs, (2) definition of propositions, (3) providing explanations to justify the theory, (4) defining the scope of the theory, and (5) testing the theory through experimental studies. Sjøberg et al. also state that the use of a grounded theory can facilitate the identification of the main concepts (constructs) and their relationships (propositions and explanations). As a consequence, the constructs that will be presented have been based mainly on the grounded theory analysis conducted in our study.

Figure 11 shows the graphical theory schema (Table XIII presents the theory elements in detail). The notational semantics has been defined by Sjøberg et al. [86] and is explained below. A construct is represented as a class or a class attribute. A class is represented by a box with its name written at the top, such as, for instance,

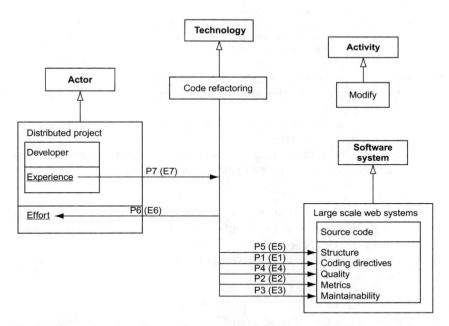

FIG. 11. Theory diagram on the use of source code refactoring to explicit coding conventions in a medium-to-large scale Web software project.

TABLE XIII
DESCRIPTION OF THEORY ELEMENTS

Constructs

C1 *Code refactoring* (based on the reading technique of use cases by Dunsmore et al. [80] and registering the refactoring suggestions according to the work of Mäntylä and Lassenius [82]

C2 *Source code structure* (structural properties perceptible in the source code, e.g., readability, algorithm structure)

C3 *Source code quality* (number of defects per lines of code)

C4 *Source code metrics* (lines of code, number of parameters, cyclomatic complexity, number of invoked remote methods, "fan-in," "fan-out")

C5 *Coding directives* (coding standards and architectural styles)

C6 *Maintenance facility* (regarding the effort needed to maintain the source code)

C7 *Developer experience* (developer involvement time in the project where the source code will be reviewed for refactoring)

C8 *Effort* (total man-hours/hours allocated to project activities)

Propositions

P1 Source code refactoring positively influences coding directives

P2 Source code refactoring positively influences source code metrics (value reduction)

P3 Source code refactoring positively influences source code maintenance (facilitates)

P4 Source code refactoring positively influences source code quality

P5 Source code refactoring positively influences source code structure

P6 Source code refactoring negatively influences software project activities effort (increase)

P7 The effects of code refactoring are reduced when the developer does not have previous experience with the software project context

Explanations

E1 The coding directive can be constructed or evolve.

☐ The descriptions of refactoring suggestions explain the way the source code was structured

☐ The directives are directly derived from the refactoring suggestions

E2 Source code metrics values reduce

☐ The measures usually display a reduction after refactoring, mainly because the main goal of refactoring focus on improving source code features such as readability and performance

E3 Source code maintenance is facilitated

☐ The coding directives allow *a priori* understanding on how the source code is organized and, therefore, facilitate its understanding when some maintenance activity is needed

☐ The source code structure becomes more homogeneous which can ease future maintenance

E4 Source code quality improves

☐ Developers identify source code defects (even when it does not represent main refactoring focus, source code inspection is being applied)

E5   The source code structure improves
- ☐ The source code structure becomes more homogeneous throughout the entire software project, according to the previous knowledge of the developers
- ☐ The size and complexity of the source code are reduced

E6   The project effort increases
- ☐ Need to allocate resources (people, man/hour) to accomplish the activities related to source code refactoring

E7   The developers experience in the project allows
- ☐ Capturing and reasoning on the coding standards used in the project
- ☐ Identifying deviations in coding standards during refactoring
- ☐ Identifying defects related to requirements and domain knowledge
- ☐ Executing refactoring activities in less time

Scope

This theory is supposed to be applicable to software projects with distributed teams (same native language and time zone) creating and modifying medium/large scale Web Information Systems on Java based development platforms and using incremental development supported by VV&T activities

---

"Distributed Project." A class can have a subclass (using the same generalization notation as in UML) or a component class (drawn as a box inside another box such as, for instance, "Source Code"). Usually, if the construct represents a particular variable value, then the construct is modeled as a subclass or a component class. However, if the focus concerns the values variations, then the construct is a variable modeled as a class attribute, such as "Effort." An attribute is described as text in the class box bottom (below the horizontal line). All the constructs are underlined in Fig. 11.

A relationship is modeled as an Arrow; an Arrow from A to B means that A affects B, where A is a class or an attribute and B is an attribute. Considering a relationship, B can also be a relationship in itself, also represented by an Arrow. In this case, A is called a moderator, as in the case of "Experience" in Fig. 11. It means A affects the direction and/or intensity of the B relationship effect, so the moderators can be defined as propositions (see proposition P7 in Table XIII).

The inheritance bases for all the classes are called archetypes (actor, technology, activity, and software system). According to Sjøberg et al. [86], the typical scenario in Software Engineering can be represented as an actor that applies a technology to support some activities in one software system (planned or existing). Some examples of an activity archetype class are creating, modifying, and analyzing (details given in Ref. [86]).

5. Applying Action Research to Software Engineering

If properly planned and executed, the Action Research methodology with its dual objective of improving organizational problems and generating scientific knowledge leads to a "win–win" scenario for both professionals (organization) and researchers.

The primary goal of Action Research is represented by its self-changing process that is not only observed by the researchers but also influenced by them. This makes Action Research especially appropriate to investigate not homogenous through time phenomena [43] that are not reproducible. Usually, these phenomena are social events such as most of the Software Engineering activities. Hence, in order for Action Research to be well conducted and provide relevant results, it imposes the researcher an additional set of knowledge items and abilities [90]. First, it is necessary that the researcher holds a deep knowledge of the organization's processes and organizational culture. Second, the researcher should be able to interpret and understand the field under observation; plan and conduct the interventions; collect, analyze, and construct the intervention data; formulate concepts and theories, and prepare theoretical explanations; and establish collaboration with people and the organization, including the dealing with ethical issues.

Most of this knowledge and abilities required by Action Research are constantly demanded during the execution of the research because the proposed solution that is being implemented depends directly on the decisions of the researcher. These decisions are crucial not only to allow generating genuine scientific knowledge but also to conciliate this with the organization's business needs. They are even more decisive if one considers that in Action Research, the intervention occurs in a real environment where *in vivo* study results can directly affect the organization. Add to this the fact that, contrary to controlled studies, the observed object is not promptly available but is elaborated and manipulated during the research with the participants. This way, even though careful planning has to be considered in Action Research studies its reach is limited by the improvisations made by the researchers in their daily activities.

However, although heavily challenged by different demands faced in its activities, a researcher initiating with Action Research is usually only supported by generic descriptions and diagrams (as shown in Section 2, which are commonly found in the technical literature) that can lead to a vision far from what Action Research actually represents [91]. Indeed, several researchers argue that Action Research is more closed to a notion of strategy rather than a methodology or technique [92]. Some researchers even question whether Action Research could not be considered a research paradigm [47]. In consequence, Action Research is usually defined and presented as general recommendations for, as an example, simultaneously performing action and research, collaborative research, and learning by reflection. These different perspectives for Action Research leave open important issues in terms of knowledge and abilities necessary to its practice in specifics disciplines such as Software Engineering.

Thus, it is not a coincidence that several disciplines have already addressed this theme, including Nursing [93,94], Political Research [92], Management [95], Operations and Production Management [96], Logistics [39], Marketing [97,98], and Communications and Media Research [99]. Generally, these studies can be categorized into two types. The ones that discuss the potential benefits' Action Research can introduce to their disciplines [39,92,93,98,99]. This is what we have aimed at in Sections 2 and 3. And those that propose Action Research adaptations and guidelines according to the particularities of their areas [94–97]. This is what we intend to focus on in this section.

In the areas above that have employed Action Research, we can clearly see particular focuses on the use of Action Research. For instance, Meyer [94] has a special interest in the ethical issues concerned with the consent of the participants in a context marked by a large number of different specialists and intense turnover of the professionals as in the case of several nursing wards; Ballantyne [97] points out the importance of a collaborative spirit establishment via Action Research as a foundation for the formulation and dissemination of marketing strategies among the organization staff; and Hearn and Foth [99] highlight the ability of Action Research in revealing tacit knowledge embedded in an organization, which wants to expose its identity in new communication media forms.

Therefore, based on the way Action Research has been applied to these areas, we gathered a set of practical issues that deserve to be discussed in order to guide and foster Action Research studies in Software Engineering. All of these issues will be addressed in the following sections:

(1) What are the essential abilities software engineers should have to apply Action Research?
(2) What are the relevant Action Research aspects in the research process management?
(3) How can the organizational culture influence reflection and collaboration?
(4) What are the possible ethical conflicts generated in conducting an Action Research study?
(5) How can new (scientific) knowledge be generated?
(6) What are the benefits of Action Research for the construction of theories?

(7) How can the learning be extracted from the interventions?

(8) What are the main formats Action Research can have in Software Engineering?

5.1   Practices and Discussion

5.1.1   Learning and Difficulties in Using the Action Research Methodology

Starting an Action Research study in Software Engineering is no trivial task. One first hurdle to be overcome by the researcher is the lack of guidelines on how to use Action Research in Software Engineering. The absence of technical papers on this theme can lead the researcher to an uncomfortable situation where one should not only understand the Action Research methodology but also find a way to apply it in the field.

After understanding the main benefits and limitations of the methodology in Action Research, the researcher should then evaluate whether it is really appropriate to one's research purposes. At this point, it is important to be certain that the principles of Action Research can be met: changing through action and learning by reflection. Still, in certain cases, it can be difficult to perceive the difference between an Action Research study and a Case Study. This difficulty is even more noticeable when there is more emphasis on observation than on action at certain moments. Nevertheless, if there is an intention to change the organizational culture and a concern with the wide consciousness of its employees on the situation faced and the solutions adopted, then Action Research can be considered as a feasible option for an investigation methodology.

However, in many cases, the assessing of the suitability of Action Research for research purposes cannot be done before a precise situation diagnosis is made or even before the planning stage. This occurs because only in the diagnosis stage, the researcher has the chance to examine in detail the problem being addressed and take an informed decision on whether Action Research fits the problem investigation. Similarly, only during the planning stage, can the researcher create solutions and assess if Action Research is appropriate for its conclusion. For instance, over the refactoring study meetings described in the previous section where one of the authors played both professional and researcher roles, the experienced developers in the project saw quality issues in the source code produced by the remote team, which had recently been integrated in the project. In moments like this, the researcher should have a refined sensibility to perceive a research opportunity. From the scientific point of view, this sensibility is associated to the awareness of the state of the art of the theme under investigation as well as an understanding of the scientific methodology, especially that concerning the reflexive and critical thinking (e.g., formulation of hypotheses and their potential answers to guide how the intervention will be driven). From the point of view of the practitioner, it is associated with a refined technical knowledge on the problem being addressed to allow the researcher to adopt a pragmatic stance based on one's experience. Thus, considering these preconditions to start an Action Research study and the lack of guidelines for its application in Software Engineering, the low number of Action Research studies can be justified, as described in Section 3; especially when considering that software engineers usually do not have the habit of being reflexive of their actions [100].

Consequently, it is up to the diagnosis and planning stages to enable researchers to develop their initial feeling on the real need to scientifically investigate a problem. These stages enable the identification of primary causes and circumstances faced by an organization and to propose the design of a possible solution. In the refactoring study, the diagnosis allowed hypothesizing the existence of tacit knowledge based on the analysis on how the teams were structured and its implications to the remote communication among its members that possibly led to the problems that are detected (poor source code quality). However, only during the planning stage (more specifically in the technical literature survey), it was possible to check that the theme had not been much explored yet. Indeed, no study has specifically addressed the circumstances faced, but the researcher (by using technical knowledge and based on the studies reasonably related to the problem) was able to choose the source code refactoring as a feasible way to solve the problem. It is important to note that until the planning, the research theme had not been completely defined (i.e., using source code refactoring as a mean to externalize tacit knowledge associated with the architectural style and coding conventions). Consequently, the diagnosis stage needed to be revised, regarding especially the definition of the research theme. This characterizes an important Action Research process property regarding the possibility of iteration between stages.

Another important aspect that deserves attention during planning is data collection. The previous definition of what data should be collected shields the researcher from unexpected events allowing one to focus on the monitoring of actions and the participating in interventions. Obviously, unplanned events will happen but the Action Research methodology can accommodate this kind of deviation. Nevertheless, it is still necessary to register these events to allow the researcher to justify them. It gives greater rigor to the relevance of both the research and the results. As an example of this kind of deviation in the refactoring study, we initially planned that each developer would review all the source code related to all listed use cases but later decided that the best strategy would be to split the work between the two developers in order to save project resources. This separation was only possible because the categorization of refactoring needs allowed data aggregation regardless of the reviewer. Hence, it is important to note that this decision was taken only after ascertaining it would not impact data analysis.

Still concerned with data collection, it is also necessary to observe how to proceed with the collection. Automated forms (e.g., voice recording) provide the researcher with additional time to conduct the interventions. Even if at a first glance, this appears to be a trivial issue, in the refactoring study this was not initially planned and caused the interviews with the developers to take longer than necessary and planned. In studies with a large number of participants, this issue can be even more critical.

As a final remark regarding learning, it was interesting to observe how Action Research can accommodate the use of different types of data (quantitative and qualitative) and data analysis techniques. This reinforces the methodology flexibility in achieving its main goals: diagnosed problem solution, organizational learning, and scientific knowledge generation.

5.1.2   Managing Research Interventions: Collaboration + Tacit Knowledge + Reflection = New Knowledge Opportunity

Due to its characteristics, Action Research is dependent on the collaborative participation of the involved people to allow the evidencing of tacit knowledge on the know-how of the performed interventions. Thus, with the analysis of/reflection on these actions, one can identify relevant phenomena that show the interrelationships (seldom of cause–effect) between the solution and problem.

Different factors can affect the intensity of collaboration in an Action Research study. Being a research with, and for, the professionals in the investigated organization, the management of the research actions requires special attention with the selection of the participants, who should be engaged to take part in the research, to allow them to genuinely collaborate to achieve the global goals. It would also be convenient if a good professional relationship existed among them, to allow creating a less constrained environment for the emergence of new ideas, facilitating spontaneous communication and the dissemination of knowledge throughout the organization. Evidently, these conditions cannot always be met. To overcome the risks, it is important for the researcher to have diplomatic abilities in getting support from upper management to implement the intended actions. According to Ballantyne [97], it is also important that the researcher shows commitment toward the set goals, acting on the same condition level of other participants in an attempt to create an atmosphere of trust and giving confidence to them in challenging the established organizational culture with their actions. In other words, the behavior of the researcher is important to indicate that one is on the same "side" of the participants and that one should not be intimidated by upper management. In the refactoring study, this was naturally achieved as the researchers already were organization employees.

All the participants enter an Action Research study as apprentices even if they are specialists in their working areas. Nevertheless, a great variety of knowledge and skills are crucial and can include not only their direct experiences but also their indirect ones (e.g., industry consensus or advisory companies). This type of knowledge is frequently named tacit knowledge and represents the know-how professionals bring in to perform their tasks. Rus and Lindvall [100] argue that the software development process is a design process where all involved have a great number of decisions to make and, in order to develop complex software systems, they need to communicate among themselves so that the individual (tacit) knowledge can be disseminated and used in the project, and by the organization as a whole. This way, communication plays an important role in the research as it is the conducting medium that enables collaboration among the participants.

During the studies we conducted, all of these elements, that is, collaboration, tacit knowledge, and dialog, were widely explored. The refactoring study, for instance, started with hypothesizing the existence of tacit knowledge on coding conventions (i.e., practical knowledge) that could be made explicit through the process of source code refactoring. Therefore, the first thing done in that study was trying to make the software developers indirectly reflect on their practices while they identified and registered the coding conventions established by them in an unplanned way. In order to facilitate this process, we tried to avoid an unfriendly disposition between the local and remote teams by informing the remote team that quality assurance was always a major concern in the project and the responsibility for the problem faced was not exclusively theirs but instead of both teams, in learning how to work remotely. The researcher should always be aware of these types of organizational and interpersonal issues. Due to this configuration and the overall study organization, the problem was naturally faced as a normal project activity, having the dialog between the developers flow spontaneously. The dialog background consisted of the recorded refactoring opportunities. From these descriptions, the teams could interact exploring their own points of view and, supported by the researcher, decided how they could demonstrate tacit knowledge, and what coding conventions were more relevant. All these decisions were also documented and later disseminated to the rest of the team. To summarize this process, and putting the importance of collaboration and dialog in a few words, Schein [101] argues that dialog is the form of "thinking together to construct shared meanings."

From all the manipulation of tacit knowledge used by the developers and the disclosure of their behaviors during the execution of the activities, the reflection (characterized by learning in Action Research studies) represents an immediate outcome from the interventions. Clearly, in many cases, additional effort will be needed to format the outcome before it can be disseminated to the organization. It was the case in the refactoring study when we decided to use the TRAC system (Wiki-based system). However, the most important is that the organization becomes aware of how the circumstances were faced and the problem solved in a way that it can be avoided in the future. Further, it is up to the researcher to inform the participants on the results from the academic point of view and how it relates to their learning. These academic results aim at demonstrating that interventions to achieve effects represent new scientific knowledge, by comparing them with other studies published in the technical literature, always exploring collaboration and the rich meaning layers of tacit knowledge that Action Research can exploit.

Based on the research process under discussion, it is possible to realize how the collaboration, tacit knowledge, and reflection are essential elements for the practice of Action Research, in enabling the building of new knowledge. Indeed, Rus and Lindvall [100] note that knowledge in an organization can be created/rise from learning, problem resolution, innovation, or creativity. Thus, Action Research can be thought of as a means to allow the process of knowledge creation by not only working in the organizational context but also trying to manage it under a scientific perspective. Theory building can be useful to the latter objective as we intended to demonstrate with the refactoring study.

5.1.3 Ethical Issues

Being a collaborative research in a real context, the ethical issues involved in an Action Research study become even more important. From the researcher's point of view, it can be difficult to pursue their concurrent scientific goals, especially considering the requirements to publish in journals and conferences. This way, this can be an ethical issue that researchers should not put the problem solution in an unfavorable position in relation to their academic interests as the initial agreement between the parties (researchers and organization) should always aim at addressing a real problem. Researchers should try as much as possible to fit the research tasks as normal project activities and what is not possible to be addressed should be registered to later analysis. This reinforces our prior discussion on the importance of using automated mechanisms to collect data that can allow researchers concentrate on the solution of the problem. As a consequence, even though the Action Research study is conducted in "real time," most of the analysis is usually retrospectively executed. In our studies, we used several automatic or even "implicit" data collection instruments such as voice recording, source code metrics, and inspection software tools (the use case inspection study was not described in this chapter).

A second issue regarding ethics concerns the participants' agreement in taking part of the research. As it is conducted in the organization, they work for and as it deals with a real problem, those involved feel compelled to participate as several research activities overlap their professional responsibilities. To alleviate this feeling, it should also be offered to these professionals that their individual data will not be published even though they will be participating one way or another. Hence, the freedom in consenting cannot be always achieved, and once the project has been initiated, it becomes even more difficult to the professionals to feel comfortable in making their decisions as they are already involved in the process. Therefore, it is important to reinforce that the researcher should try to act on the same condition level of other participants so that they can get the impression they are being supported in their activities.

Apart from these issues, the researcher should not put common ethical issues away from any research effort, such as honesty, the privacy of the participants, among others.

5.2   Recommendations

5.2.1   Engineering Software and Building Theories

As discussed in the beginning of this chapter, even today, the adoption of *ad hoc* solutions throughout software development is still common because of the pressure produced by the time to market or lack of knowledge. Unfortunately, this goes against the Software Engineering definition given by Boehm [102]: "the practical application of scientific knowledge in the design and construction of computer programs and the associated documentation required to develop, operate, and maintain them." Yet, Action Research can bring this initial expectancy on Software Engineering into reality as it is designed to use and apply scientific knowledge in real contexts even where there is pressure for quick results, due to its dual research and action goals.

Action Research accepts that scientific results, even in their preliminary stages, can be used in practice for an immediate feedback on their value. Additionally, the Action Research methodology allows an *ad hoc* solution to be collaboratively developed, even when no scientific results are directly related to the problem faced. But, contrary to the common practices in Software Engineering, special

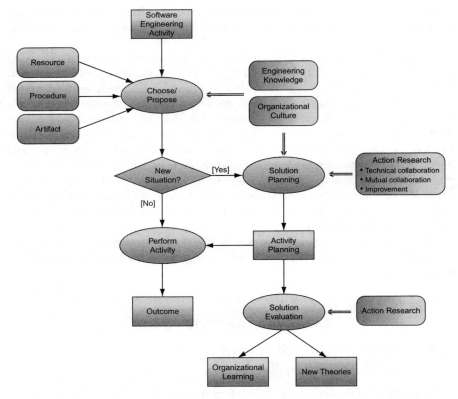

FIG. 12. Construction of new theories through Action Research in Software Engineering.

attention is given to reflecting on, and learning from, the results achieved. Figure 12 illustrates this process.

According to Falbo et al. [103], a software process can be characterized by the activities planned to be executed and the resources, procedures, and artifacts whose use is planned. In each activity, the resources, procedures, and artifact should be defined to produce the desired product, supported by an engineering reasoning and influenced by the organizational culture (Table XIV).

However, at some point in the software process, the knowledge on Software Engineering can be insufficient in a given situation (e.g., it may not be possible to know what procedure to adopt in one specific software design activity). In this case, the Action Research methodology can be used to address the problem in a pragmatic

TABLE XIV
KEY TERMS IN THE PRACTICE DIMENSIONS OF SOFTWARE ENGINEERING, ADAPTED FROM
HIGGS ET AL. [104]

Evidence-based practice can be thought as justifying the engineering decisions on the best available evidence

Engineering reasoning is the decision-making process associated with the application of different techniques and scientific principles to define a software technology that is properly designed and economically viable so that it allows its final conception

Engineering decision making is a sequence of judgments made by engineers when interacting with the environment considering a set of restrictions (resources, material resistance, schedule, among others)

Engineering judgment consists of balancing available evidence with knowledge on the context and domain

Propositional knowledge is derived from research and theory

Expertise knowledge has its origins associated with a rigorous assessment and processing of the professional experience

Personal knowledge results from the personal life experience

---

way without excluding scientific rigor. As shown in Fig. 12, the first step is to plan how the activity will be conducted by searching, as an example, for a procedure that is provided by the scientific community, or choosing to develop it within the organization itself. Then, the activity is regularly performed while, at the same time, its execution will be evaluated so to subsidize organizational learning and the building of new theories. The three Action Research formats we identified in our technical literature survey as shown in Section 3 were named technical collaboration, mutual collaboration, and improvement, based on the nomenclature provided by Holter and Schwartz-Barcott [93]. The first one focuses on testing a technology in a real context; in the second one, researcher and participants jointly identify the problems, their causes, and possible interventions; and the last one aims at facilitating Software Engineering activities. We can rate our refactoring study under the second format. But most important is to notice how the role of the researcher changes between the formats, acting as observer in the first, participant in the second, and facilitator in the third.

Nevertheless, to identify when a new problem is being faced or, in other words, detecting a genuine research opportunity may not be an easy task. Given the constant flow of events and context variables found in a real environment, these opportunities can be hidden or can be incorrectly identified. As a basic rule, the research theme at hand should not have a trivial solution or, to put it in another way, it should be something that is not available in the industry as a common solution to the problem. As an example, in the refactoring study, the documentation on the tacit coding conventions and architectural styles used in the project could not be automatically performed by a tool because knowledge was tacit. Moreover, systematic procedures to produce this documentation were not found either.

The organizational culture can also be an inhibiting factor in identifying new research opportunities or even become a barrier to resisting change. Normally, it is related to the beliefs of individuals, as well as the actions and practices of the organization (Fig. 13) [98]. In one of the studies we conducted regarding the inspection of the description for use cases [105], several discrepancies pointed out by the checklist used were initially rejected because the participants argued that the use cases were being specified in that way since the beginning of the project and thus they were not seeing any problem in what had been indicated as discrepancies. Hence, more than hampering the identification of new research opportunities, the organizational culture can be the source of the problem that is faced as it becomes the basis for incorrect affirmations.

The researchers should deal with this context by using tacit knowledge and exploring relationships to their advantage, to tackle the challenges and promote new actions and interventions in the organization without putting aside their history, whilst attempting not to cause disagreement. The role of the researchers is thus to conduct the interventions as naturally as possible, trying not to cause major disruptions. If they can fulfil this role, they will be able to manipulate the worldview of the participants toward the proposed interventions goals and reproduce the phenomena identically to the usual daily practice of the organization, contributing to an improved relevance in the results, for the organization and for the research. In order to make this happen as naturally as possible, researchers should also consider

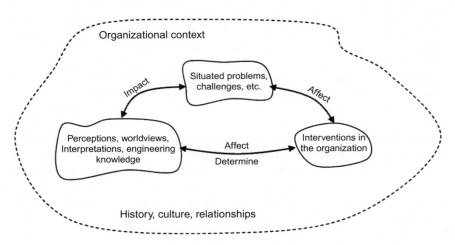

Fig. 13. Organizational context in Software Engineering—adapted from McKay and Marshall [91].

the Software Engineering practice dimensions previously mentioned. To support the research in this issue, we suggest the mapping between the dimensions and Action Research provided in Table XV.

Figure 14 illustrates how this research process fits into an organizational context. As previously discussed, after data collection, the researcher can organize it for further analysis and then conduct the analyses using a technique that can produce knowledge, serving as input for organizational learning and to produce scientific knowledge, possibly in the shape of a theory. The dash lines in Fig. 14 show the main source of constructs, propositions, and explanations that form a theory. During the manipulation and organization of the data collected, the researcher can recognize the central concepts and objects used and affected by the research that will become the immediate candidates for constructors. Since most part of the collected data in an Action Research study is qualitative, data analysis cannot allow the accurate establishment of cause–effect relationships, but at least it can support the definition of propositions among the constructs of the theory. However, the explanations of the theory have their origins associated with the observations made by the researcher along the interventions, interpreted by one's theoretical and personal values (i.e., personal, expertise-based, and propositional knowledge).

Due to the way in which theories are built in Action Research, they tend to be of level 1 (minor working relationships that are concrete and directly based on observations) or level 2 (theories of the middle range involving some abstractions but that are still closely linked to observations). The theory built on the refactoring study can be classified on level 1. Theory building in Software Engineering represents a recent research endeavor for several researchers who are trying to offer some sort of guidelines to this end (e.g., Ref. [86]). Thus, from what we discussed in this section, it seems that Action Research is suitable for constructing and evaluating Software Engineering theories, but special attention should be given to research rigor so that relevant results can be produced.

TABLE XV
MAPPING ACTION RESEARCH AND SOFTWARE ENGINEERING PRACTICE DIMENSIONS

Action Research	Software Engineering practice key terms
Diagnosis	Personal knowledge and expertise
Planning	Evidence-based practice, engineering reasoning, propositional and personal knowledge
Intervention	Engineering reasoning, personal, expertise, and propositional knowledge
Evaluation	Propositional knowledge
Reflection	Personal, expertise, and propositional knowledge

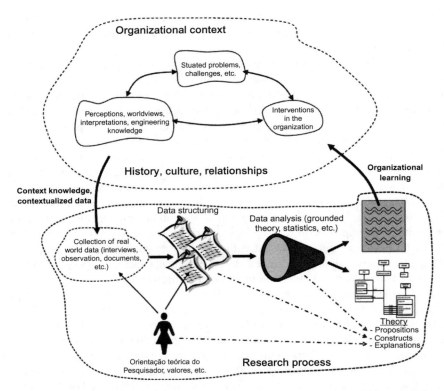

Fig. 14. Action Research process in theory building—evolved from McKay and Marshall [91].

5.2.2 Research Rigor and the Results Relevance

The relevance of Action Research results to Software Engineering practice is clear. However, no results are indeed relevant if the means by which they were obtained are not legitimate. To demonstrate result legitimacy, it is necessary that a minimum level of rigor is present when conducting the research, which can show that the effects described in the explanations (of the theories) were obtained as an effect of the proposed solution.

Recommendations and strategies to give rigor to Action Research have been widely discussed in the technical literature [30,44]. There are at least two fundamental aspects that can characterize the rigor of a study. One is the control level applied when conducting the study, aimed at minimizing researcher bias and the influence of other variables over the outcomes. The previously mentioned papers address this issue. The second is how theoretical knowledge is kept explicit during the research actions [85]. To address this latter issue, in the absence of approaches in the technical literature, we worked on the Action Research planning and analysis stages using the GQM approach [83].

The GQM approach is based on the supposition that, in order to effectively measure, goals should be established so that they can guide the preparation of questions to direct the definition of measurements for a particular context. The GQM is set by two processes [106]: a top-down refinement from the objectives to questions and then in measurements and a bottom-up analysis from the data collected to evaluate them as regards the goals established.

We have used the GQM approach in all Action Research studies that we conducted. We slightly modified the GQM nomenclature to better fit the defined report study format and the Action Research characteristics. So, initially, the research goals are set at the conceptual level, considering the object of study, the point of view adopted and the context of the study. Then, the research questions are defined on the practical level where the object of study is characterized according to a quality aspect that is chose for investigation. Lastly, the operational questions determine what data should be collected, keeping the track of the research questions and goals. The "operational questions" expression is used in place of metrics due to the Action Research capability of using quantitative and qualitative data.

We were able to find in our Action Research studies that, when using GQM, the planning stage becomes more focused because data interpretation is dealt with in advance. Further, it is possible to track the outcomes to the initial goals defined for the study, conferring it an improved rigor. For instance, in the refactoring study, GQM was useful in mapping the *grounded theory* categories and research questions, supporting the building of the theory.

Hence, in the same way, the GQM approach can link the metrics to the research questions and goals in quantitative studies, it can be used in Action Research studies to keep track of the manipulated tacit knowledge and explicit its use when explaining the observed phenomena. Based on this experience, we suggest the combined use of the Action Research and GQM approach as shown in the refactoring study. It will be described in the next section.

5.2.3 An Action Research Template Study Report

Despite the vast material found in the technical literature on Action Research, we could not find any template to report general Action Research studies, including Software Engineering. Hence, in this section, we propose a template to report Action

TABLE XVI
ACTION RESEARCH REPORT TEMPLATE

---

(1) Diagnosis
    (a) Problem description
    (b) Project context
    (c) Research theme
(2) Planning
    (a) Literature Survey
        (i) Initial study (optional)
    (b) Action focus
        (i) Objectives
        (ii) Research questions
        (iii) Expected outcomes
    (c) Hypotheses
    (d) Operational definitions
        (i) Techniques
        (ii) Tools
        (iii) Instruments
        (iv) Study design (optional)
(3) Actions
(4) Evaluation and analysis
(5) Reflections and learning
    (a) Learning
    (b) Reflections

Research studies (Table XVI), derived from our experiences in conducting different Action Research studies in Software Engineering. Although simple, the template is heavily connected with the Action Research process (Section 2.2), presenting one section for each correspondingly process stage. In the sequence, each section is going to be explained.

5.2.3.1 *Diagnosis.*

The description of the diagnosis stage was split into three sections: problem description, project context, and research theme. Problem description describes the problem faced so that its importance can be remarked. This description should then be contextualized, showing where it is happening, in order to complete diagnosis description. Finally, the research theme section summarizes the problem that will be addressed, linking to the following sections.

5.2.3.2 Planning. This section is one of the most detailed sections as it
supports research execution. Based on the diagnosis previously made, the first step
intends to describe the technical literature survey that will ground the planning.
It should indicate the important aspects of the studies that will be used through the
interventions. If the current results of these studies are still being developed or are
premature, it is possible to execute an initial (small-scale) controlled study to better
evaluate the software technology and thus minimize the risks of applying it in the
real scenario. This initial study should also be described in the planning section.
Next, the "action focus" section defines the research goals through the use of the
GQM approach. From the establishing of the research goals, some hypotheses are
determined, showing some expectations on the behaviors of the environment during
the interventions. Lastly, the operational definitions should be considered, such as
the tools that will be used, analysis techniques, and any other resources necessary to
research execution. Optionally, the researcher can also plan how the participants will
be organized during the activities, which is common for controlled studies.

5.2.3.3 Actions. This section put the interventions in a chronological
way, describing how the activities were performed during the research. One basic
rule: the more details the better it will be. Special attention should be given to the
description of administrative or organizational issues such as the impossibility to
execute a planned activity because of an intervention by upper management or the
lack of resources.

5.2.3.4 Evaluation and Analysis. The goal of this section is to
describe the data analysis process and its findings. It is important, when describing
the data analysis to try and keep an explicit link between the results obtained from
the collected data and the initial objectives. This will preserve the traceability of the
outcomes to the diagnosed problem and will assist in giving rigor to the research, as
previously discussed.

5.2.3.5 Reflections and Learning. The last section has a two-
fold goal, as Action Research does. First, it is necessary to explore the results
achieved against the state of the art found in technical literature. During this
examination, the studies used in the "technical literature survey" section should be
emphasized to compare, if possible, the outcomes of the studies.

In a second part, the description of the learning process should not mention only
the "physical" material generated in the context of, and for, the organization, but
should also try to depict the learning experience of the participants and how it
influenced the organizational culture.

6. Final Considerations

In this chapter, we described our experience in applying the Action Research methodology in Software Engineering. We extracted a set of recommendations and practices we think can be useful to other researchers interested in using Action Research to investigate real-world Software Engineering issues where some new software technology is being adopted, or that should be tailored to a specific environment, or even be built from scratch, supported by state-of-the-art corresponding knowledge.

The Action Research methodology is regarded "as the most realistic research setting found because the setting of the study is the same as the scenario the results will be applied in for a given organization, apart from the presence of the researcher (s)" [19]. Further, we could see that its features are quite suited to dealing with the social component in Software Engineering practice. All of this is strengthened by the growing interest of the Software Engineering community in the Action Research methodology as we could find out in a technical literature survey on the use of Action Research in the field. However, it should also be noted that the use of Action Research is not always followed by rigor.

Thus, the Action Research methodology is an appealing alternative to contribute to the domain of Software Engineering research, offering the possibility to conduct studies in new situations. This can lead to an additional number of results with increased relevance as Action Research ensures direct access to the know-how of the practitioners which, in many surveys and controlled studies, for example, is not attainable. As stated by Polanyi [107]: "we know more than we can say."

ACKNOWLEDGMENTS

The authors would like to thank the CNPq, CAPES, and FAPERJ agencies for their support to the ESE Group at COPPE research projects. This research is inserted into the context of the eSEE—Experimental Software Engineering Environment. These results could not have been attained without the collaboration of the SIGIC Development Team and the COPPETEC Foundation.

REFERENCES

[1] S. Easterbrook, J. Singer, M.-A. Storey, D. Damian, Selecting empirical methods for software engineering research, in: F. Shull, J. Singer, D.I.K. Sjøberg (Eds.), Advanced Topics in Empirical Software Engineering, Springer-Verlag, London, United Kingdom, 2008, 312–336.
[2] D.I.K. Sjøberg, J.E. Hannay, O. Hansen, V.B. Kampenes, A. Karahasanović, N.-K. Liborg, et al., A survey of controlled experiments in software engineering, IEEE Trans. Software Eng. 31 (9) (2005) 733–753.

[3] V. Basili, S. Elbaum, Empirically driven SE research: state of the art and required maturity, in: Invited Talk, ICSE 2006, Shanghai, 2006.

[4] A. Höfer, W.F. Tichy, Status of Empirical Research in Software Engineering, in: V. Basili, D. Rombach, K. Schneider, B. Kitchenham, D. Pfahl, R. Selby (Eds.), Experimental Software Engineering Issues: Assessment and Future Directions, Springer-Verlag, Germany, Dagstuhl Castle, 2007 LNCS 4336.

[5] B. Kampenes, T. Dybå, J.E. Hannay, D.I.K. Sjøberg, A systematic review of quasi-experiments in software engineering, Inform. Software Technol. 51 (1) (2009) 71–82.

[6] S.M. Charters, D. Budgen, M. Turner, B. Kitchenham, P. Brereton, S.G. Linkman, Objectivity in research: challenges from the evidence-based paradigm, Australian Software Engineering Conference, 2009, pp. 73–80.

[7] W.F. Tichy, Should computer scientists experiment more? IEEE Comput. (1998) 32–40.

[8] N. Juristo, A.M. Moreno, Basics of Software Engineering Experimentation, Kluwer Academic Publisher, USA, 2001.

[9] V.R. Basili, R.W. Selby, D.H. Hutchens, Experimentation in software engineering, IEEE Trans. Software Eng. 12 (1986) 733–743.

[10] V. Basili, The role of experimentation: past, current, and future, Proceedings of the 18th International Conference on Software, Engineering, 1996, pp. 442–450.

[11] F. Shull, J. Carver, G.H. Travassos, An empirical methodology for introducing software processes, 8th European Software Engineering Symposium and 9th ACM SIGSOFT Symposium on the Foundations of Software Engineering (FSE-9) and 8th European Software Engineering Conference (ESEC), Vienna, Austria, September, 2001.

[12] C. Wöhlin, P. Runeson, M. Höst, M.C. Ohlsson, B. Regnell, A. Wesslén, Experimentation in Software Engineering: An Introduction, Kluwer Academic Publishers, Massachusetts, USA, 2000.

[13] R. Harrison, N. Badoo, E. Barry, S. Biffl, A. Parra, B. Winter, et al., Directions and methodologies for empirical software engineering research, Empirical Software Eng. 4 (4) (1999) 405–410.

[14] C. Wöhlin, M. Höst, K. Henningsson, Empirical Research Methods in Software Engineering, in: A.I. Wang, R. Conradi (Eds.), Lecture Notes in Computer Science: Empirical Methods and Studies in Software Engineering: Experiences from ESERNET, Springer-Verlag, Germany, LNCS 2765, 2003.

[15] M.V. Zelkowitz, Techniques for Empirical validation, in: V. Basili, D. Rombach, K. Schneider, B. Kitchenham, D. Pfahl, R. Selby (Eds.), Experimental Software Engineering Issues: Assessment and Future Directions, Springer-Verlag, Germany, Dagstuhl Castle, 2007 LNCS 4336.

[16] S.H. Pfleeger, Albert Einstein and empirical software engineering, IEEE Comput. 32 (10) (1999) 32–37.

[17] B. Kitchenham, Empirical Paradigm – The Role of Experiments, in: V. Basili, D. Rombach, K. Schneider, B. Kitchenham, D. Pfahl, R. Selby (Eds.), Experimental Software Engineering Issues: Assessment and Future Directions, Springer-Verlag, Germany, Dagstuhl Castle, 2007 LNCS 4336.

[18] C. Argyris, R. Putnam, D.M. Smith, Action Science, in: Jossey-Bass Social and Behavioural Science Series, first ed., San Francisco, USA, 1985.

[19] D.I.K. Sjøberg, T. Dybå, M. Jørgensen, The future of empirical methods in software engineering research, FOSE '07: Future of Software Engineering, Washington, DC, USA, 2007, pp. 358–378.

[20] B.A. Kitchenham, T. Dybå, M. Jørgensen, Evidence-based software engineering, in: ICSE 2004, IEEE Computer Society Press, Edinburgh, United Kingdom, 2004, pp. 273–281.

[21] B. Kitchenham, D. Budgen, P. Brereton, M. Turner, S. Charters, S. Linkman, Large-scale software engineering questions—expert opinion or empirical evidence? IET Software 1 (5) (2007) 161–171.

[22] A. Rainer, D. Jagielska, T. Hall, Software Practice versus evidence-based software engineering research, Proceedings of the Workshop on Realising Evidence-Based Software, Engineering, ICSE-2005, 2005.

[23] R. Baskerville, A.T. Wood-Harper, A critical perspective on Action Research as a method for information systems research, J. Inform. Technol. 11 (1996) 235–246.

[24] W. Carr, Philosophy, Methodology and Action Research, J. Philos. Educ. Special Issue Philos. Methodol. Educ. Res. 1 40.2 (2006) 421–437.

[25] P. Reason, H. Bradbury, Introduction: inquiry and participation in search of a world worthy of human aspiration, in: P. Reason, H. Bradbury (Eds.), Handbook of Action Research: Participative Inquiry and Practice, Sage, Thousand Oaks, CA, 2001, pp. 1–14.

[26] B. Dick, Action research literature: themes and trends, Action Res. 2 (2004) 425–444.

[27] A. Burns, Action research: an evolving paradigm? Lang. Teach. 38 (2) (2005) 57–74.

[28] R. Baskerville, A.T. Wood-Harper, Diversity in information systems action research methods, Eur. J. Inform. Syst. 2 (7) (1998) 90–107.

[29] G.L. Susman, R.D. Evered, An assessment of the scientific merits of Action Research, Adm. Sci. Q. 23 (1978) 582–603.

[30] R.M. Davison, M.G. Martinsons, N. Kock, Principles of canonical action research, Inform. Syst. J. 14 (1) (2004) 65–86.

[31] D.E. Avison, F. Lau, M.D. Myers, P.A. Nielsen, Action Research, Commun. ACM 42 (1) (1999) 94–97.

[32] E.G. Guba, Y.S. Lincoln, Competing paradigms in qualitative research, in: N.K. Denzin, Y. S. Lincoln (Eds.), Handbook of Qualitative Research, Sage, Thousand Oaks, CA, 1994, pp. 105–117.

[33] R.S. Hathaway, Assumptions underlying quantitative and qualitative research: implications for institutional research, Res. Higher Educ. 36 (5) (1995) 535–562.

[34] M. Healy, C. Perry, Comprehensive criteria to judge validity and reliability of qualitative research within the realism paradigm, Qual. Market Res. Int. J. 3 (3) (2000) 118–126.

[35] J.D. Ludema, D.L. Cooperrider, F.J. Barret, Appreciative Inquiry: the power of the unconditional positive question, in: P. Reason, H. Bradbury (Eds.), Handbook of Action Research: Participative Inquiry and Practice, Sage, Thousand Oaks, CA, 2001, pp. 1–14.

[36] W. Carr, S. Kemmis, Becoming Critical: Education, Knowledge and Action Research, Falmer Press, Basingstoke, 1986.

[37] D.J. Greenwood, M. Levin, Introduction to Action Research: Social Research for Social Change, Sage Publications, Thousand Oaks, CA, 1998.

[38] S.E. Krauss, Research paradigms and meaning making: a primer, Qual. Rep. 10 (4) (2005) 758–770.

[39] D. Näslund, Logistics needs qualitative research—especially Action Research, Int. J. Phys. Distrib. Logis. Manage. 32 (5) (2002) 321–328.

[40] B.C. Seaman, Qualitative methods in empirical studies of software engineering, IEEE Trans. Software Eng. 25 (4) (1999) 557–572.

[41] M. Thiollent, Action Research Methodology, 15th ed., Cortês Editora, São Paulo, Brazil, 2007 (in Portuguese).

[42] R. Baskerville, Educing theory from practice, in: N. Kock (Ed.), Information Systems Action Research: An Applied View of Emerging Concepts and Methods, Springer, New York, 2007.

[43] P. Checkland, S. Holwell, Action Research: Its Nature and Validity, Syst. Pract. Action Res. 11 (1) (1998) 9–21.

[44] D.E. Avison, R. Baskerville, M. Myers, Controlling action research projects, Inform. Technol. People 14 (2001) 28–45.

[45] D. Tripp, Action Research: a methodological introduction, Educação e Pesquisa (31:3) (2005) 443–466.

[46] P.S.M. Santos, G.H. Travassos, Action Research use in Software Engineering: an Initial Survey, 3rd International Symposium on Empirical Software Engineering and Measurement, Orlando, USA, 2009, pp. 414–417.

[47] F. Lau, A review on the use of action research in information systems studies, in: A. Lee, J. Liebenau, J. DeGross (Eds.), Information Systems and Qualitative Research, Chapman & Hall, London, United Kingdom, 1997, pp. 31–68.

[48] P. Abrahamsson, J. Koskela, Extreme programming: a survey of empirical data from a controlled case study, Proceedings of International Symposium on Empirical Software Engineering, 2004, pp. 73–82.

[49] IEEE Keyword Taxonomy. (2002). http://www2.computer.org/portal/web/publications/acmsoftware, 2010.

[50] V. Ramesh, R.L. Glass, I. Vessey, Research in computer science: an empirical study, J. Syst. Sw. (2004) 165–176.

[51] M. Lindvall, K. Sandahl, Practical implications of traceability, J. SP&E 26 (10) (1996) 1161–1180.

[52] M. Polo, M. Piattini, F. Ruiz, Using a qualitative research method for building a software maintenance methodology, Software Pract. Exp. 32 (13) (2002) 1239–1260.

[53] G. Canfora, F. Garcia, M. Piattini, F. Ruiz, C.A. Visaggio, Applying a framework for the improvement of the software process maturity in a software company, J. Software Pract. Exp. 36 (3) (2006) 283–304.

[54] M. Staron, W. Meding, Predicting weekly defect inflow in large software projects based on project planning and test status, Inform. Software Technol. 2008.

[55] F. McCaffery, J. Burton, I. Richardson, Improving software risk management in a medical device company, 31st International Conference on Software Engineering, 2009, pp. 152–162.

[56] M. Vigder, N.G. Vinson, J. Singer, D. Stewart, K. Mews, Supporting scientists' everyday work: automating scientific workflows, IEEE Software 25 (2008) 52–58.

[57] N. Maiden, S. Robertson, Developing use cases and scenarios in the requirements process, Proc. ICSE 2005 (2005) 561–570.

[58] N.P. Napier, L. Mathiassen, R.D. Johnson, Combining perceptions and prescriptions in requirements engineering process assessment: an industrial case study, IEEE Trans. Software Eng. 35 (5) (2009) 593–606.

[59] M. Kauppinen, M. Vartiainen, J. Kontio, S. Kujala, R. Sulonen, Implementing requirements engineering processes throughout organizations: success factors and challenges, Inform. Software Technol. 46 (2004) 937–953.

[60] J. Bosch, Toward Compositional Software Product Lines, IEEE Software 27 (3) (2010) 29–34.

[61] C. Gutierrez, D.G. Rosado, E. Fernandez-Medina, The practical application of a process for eliciting and designing security in web service systems, Inform. Software Technol. 51 (12) (2009) 1712–1738.

[62] P. Bengtsson, J. Bosch, Haemo dialysis software architecture design experiences, Proceedings of the 21st ICSE, 1999, pp. 516–525.

[63] A. Mattsson, B. Lundell, B. Lings, B. Fitzgerald, Linking model-driven development and software architecture: a case study software engineering, IEEE Trans. Software Eng. 35 (2009) 83–93.

[64] E. Fernández-Medina, M. Piattini, Designing secure databases, Inform. Software Technol. 47 (7) (2005) 463–477.

[65] M. Lycett, Understanding 'Variation' in component-based development: case findings from practice, Inform. Software Technol. 43 (3) (2001) 203–213.

[66] B. Fitzgerald, T. O'Kane, A Longitudinal study of software process improvement, IEEE Software 16 (3) (1999) 37–45.

[67] K. Kautz, H.W. Hansen, K. Thaysen, Applying and adjusting a software process improvement model in practice: the use of the IDEAL model in a small software enterprise, Proc. 22nd Int'l Conf. Software Eng, IEEE CS Press, Limerick, Ireland, 2000, pp. 626–633.

[68] O. Salo, P. Abrahamsson, Integrating Agile Software Development and Software Process Improvement: A Longitudinal Case Study, ISESE, Australia, Noosa Heads, 2005.

[69] P.A. Nielsen, G. Tjørnehøj, Social networks in software process improvement, J. Software Maintenance Evol. Res. Pract. 22 (1) (2010) 33–51.

[70] F.J. Pino, C. Pardo, F. Garcia, M. Piattini, Assessment methodology for software process improvement in small organizations, Inform. Software Technol. 52 (10) (2010) 1044–1061.

[71] M. Staron, W. Meding, C. Nilsson, A framework for developing measurement systems and its industrial evaluation, Inform. Software Technol. 51 (4) (2009) 721–737.

[72] R. Kazman, L. Bass, Making architecture reviews work in the real world, IEEE Software 19 (1) (2002) 62–73.

[73] SOFTEX, MPS.BR: Brazilian Software Process Improvement', General Guide Version 1.2, Campinas, SP, SOFTEX, 2007.

[74] G.H. Travassos, M. Kalinowski, iMPS 2009: characterization and performance variation of software organizations that adopted the MPS model, in: Association for Promotion of the Excellence the Brazilian Software—SOFTEX 2009, 978-85-99334-18-8. http://www.softex.br/mpsbr/_livros/arquivos/Softex%20iMPS%202009%20Ingles_vFinal_12jan10.pdf. (2009) Accessed August 2010.

[75] TRAC, TRAC: Integrated Software Configuration and Project Management http://trac.edgewall.org/, 2003. Accessed July 2010.

[76] Sun, Code Conventions for the Java Programming Language, Sun Microsystems, 1999. http://java.sun.com/docs/codeconv/. Accessed July 2010.

[77] J. Crupi, D. Alur, D. Malks, Core J2EE Patterns: Best Practices and Design Strategies, Prentice Hall PTR, Santa Clara, California, USA, 2001.

[78] K.H. Bennet, V.T. Rajlich, Software maintenance and evolution: a roadmap, in: The Future of Software Engineering, ACM Press, 2000, pp. 73–87.

[79] T. Mens, T. Tourwe, A survey of software refactoring, IEEE Trans. Software Eng. 30 (2) (2004) 126–139.

[80] A. Dunsmore, M. Roper, M. Wood, Practical code inspection techniques for object-oriented systems: an experimental comparison, IEEE Software 20 (4) (2003) 21–29.

[81] M.V. Mäntylä, An experiment on subjective evolvability evaluation of object-oriented software: explaining factors and interrater agreement, International Symposium on Empirical Software Engineering, 2005, pp. 277–286.

[82] M.V. Mäntylä, C. Lassenius, Drivers for software refactoring decisions, Proceedings of the 2006 ACM/IEEE International Symposium on Empirical Software Engineering (ISESE'06), New York, NY, USA, 2006, pp. 297–306.

[83] V.R. Basili, G. Caldiera, H.D. Rombach, The goal question metric approach, in: The Encyclopaedia of Software Engineering, vol. 2, John Wiley & Sons. Inc., New York, NY, USA, 1994, pp. 528–532.

[84] A. Strauss, J. Corbin, Basics of Qualitative Research: Grounded Theory Procedures and Techniques, Sage, Newbury Park, CA, 1990.

[85] R. Baskerville, J. Pries-Heje, Grounded action research: a method for understanding IT in practice, Account. Manage. Inform. Technol. 9 (1999) 1–23.

[86] D.I.K. Sjøberg, T. Dybå, B.C.D. Anda, J.E. Hannay, Building theories in software engineering, in: F. Shull, J. Singer, D.I.K. Sjøberg (Eds.), Advanced Topics in Empirical Software Engineering, Springer-Verlag, 2008.

[87] M. Fowler, K. Beck, J. Brant, W. Opdyke, D. Roberts, Refactoring: Improving the Design of Existing Code, first ed., Addison Wesley, New Jersey, USA, 1999.

[88] C. Parnin, C. Görg, A catalogue of lightweight visualizations to support code smell inspection, Proceedings of the ACM Symposium on Software Visualization, 2008, pp. 77–86.

[89] J.R. Ruthruff, J. Penix, J.D. Morgenthaler, S. Elbaum, G. Rothermel, Predicting accurate and actionable static analysis warnings: an experimental approach, Proceedings of the 30th International Conference on Software Engineering, 2008, pp. 341–350.

[90] R.L. Baskerville, Investigating information systems with action research, Communications of the Association for Information Systems, volume 2, 1999.

[91] J. McKay, P. Marshall, Driven by two masters, serving both, in: N. Kock (Ed.), Information Systems Action Research: An Applied View of Emerging Concepts and Methods, Springer, New York, 2007.

[92] C.G. Heatwole, L.F. Keller, G.L. Wamsley, Action research and public policy analysis: sharpening the political perspectives of public policy research, Political Res. Q. 29 (1976) 597–609.

[93] I.M. Holter, D. Schwartz-Barcott, Action research: what is it? How has it been used and how can it be used in nursing? J. Adv. Nurs. 18 (2) (1993) 298–304.

[94] J.E. Meyer, New paradigm research in practice: the trials and tribulations of action research, J. Adv. Nurs. 18 (7) (1993) 1066–1072.

[95] S. Ottosson, Participation action research: a key to improved knowledge of management, Int. J. Technol. Innov. Entrepreneurship Technol. Manage. 23 (2) (2003) 87–94.

[96] R. Westbrooke, Action Research: a new paradigm for research in production and operations management, Int. J. Operations Prod. Manage. 15 (12) (1995) 6–20.

[97] D. Ballantyne, Action Research reviewed: a market-oriented approach, Eur. J. Market. 38 (3/4) (2004) 321–337.

[98] S. Kates, J. Robertson, Adapting action research to marketing, Eur. J. Market. 38 (3/4) (2004) 418–432.

[99] G. Hearn, M. Foth, Action research in the design of new media and ICT systems, in: K. Kwansah-Aidoo (Ed.), Topical Issues in Communications and Media Research, Nova Science, New York, NY, 2005.

[100] I. Rus, M. Lindvall, Knowledge management in software engineering, IEEE Software (19:3) (2002) 26–38.

[101] E.H. Schein, The process of dialogue: creating effective communication, Syst. Thinker 5 (5) (1994) 1–4.

[102] B.W. Boehm, Software engineering, IEEE Trans. Comput. (1976) 1.226–1.241.

[103] R.A. Falbo, C.S. Menezes, A.R.C. Rocha, A systematic approach for building ontologies, Proceedings of the IBERAMIA'98, Lisbon, Portugal, 1998.

[104] J. Higgs, A. Burns, M. Jones, Integrating clinical reasoning and evidence-based practice, AACN Clin. Issues 12 (2001) 482–490.

[105] P.S.M. Santos, G.H. Travassos, Quality inspection in use case descriptions: an experimental evaluations in a real project, IX Brazilian Symposium of Software Quality, Belém, Brazil (in Portuguese), 2010, pp. 261–275.

[106] F. Latum, R. Solingen, B. Hoisl, M. Oivo, H.D. Rombach, G. Ruhe, Adopting GQM-based measurement in an industrial environment, IEEE Software 15 (1) (1998) 78–86.

[107] M. Polanyi, The Tacit Dimension, Routledge and Keoan Paul, London, 1966.

[108] R.L. Glass, Making research more relevant while not diminishing its rigor, IEEE Software 26 (2) (2009) 96–96.

About the Author

Paulo Sérgio Medeiros dos Santos is a doctorate student at COPPE—Federal University of Rio de Janeiro—Brazil where he received his master's degree in 2009. His current research interests include Experimental Software Engineering, research methodologies and theory building, cognitive science, and artificial intelligence, applied to software engineering. He has industrial experience in software development as a developer and architect, and currently works at a major Brazilian oil company. Most of the information regarding his research projects and working activities can be found at http://ese.cos.ufrj.br/ese. He can be contacted at pasemes@cos.ufrj.br.

Guilherme Horta Travassos is a professor of software engineering with the Systems Engineering and Computer Science Department at COPPE/Federal University of Rio de Janeiro—Brazil. He is also a 1D CNPq—Brazilian Research Council researcher. He received his doctorate degree from COPPE/UFRJ in 1994 and spent 2 years with the Experimental Software Engineering Group at the University of Maryland—College Park, in a postdoctoral position (1998/2000). He leads the Experimental Software Engineering Group at COPPE/UFRJ. His current research interests include experimental software engineering, e-science and nonconventional Web applications, software quality, and VV&T concerned with object-oriented software. He is a member of ISERN, ACM and SBC (Brazilian Computer Society). He can be contacted at ght@cos.ufrj.br.

Functional and Nonfunctional Design Verification for Embedded Software Systems

ARNAB RAY

Fraunhofer Center for Experimental Software Engineering, Maryland, USA

CHRISTOPHER ACKERMANN

Department of Computer Science, University of Maryland, Maryland, USA

RANCE CLEAVELAND

Department of Computer Science, University of Maryland, Maryland, USA

CHARLES SHELTON

Robert Bosch North America, Research and Technology Center, Pennsylvania, USA

CHRIS MARTIN

Robert Bosch North America, Research and Technology Center, Pennsylvania, USA

ADVANCES IN COMPUTERS, VOL. 83
ISSN: 0065-2458/DOI: 10.1016/B978-0-12-385510-7.00006-0

277

Copyright © 2011 Elsevier Inc.
All rights reserved.

Abstract

In model-based design verification, software models are checked against functional and nonfunctional requirements. Many of the mathematically well-founded theories developed for functional verification suffer from limitations (poor integration with industrial modeling tools and inability to scale to larger, more complicated systems) that restrict their practical adoption. Nonfunctional verification approaches, because of their inherent subjectivity ("what does it mean for a system to be modifiable?"), remain largely *ad hoc* and manual. There is also another overarching problem in that functional and nonfunctional verification take place on widely different representations of the system making it difficult to ensure that these representations are consistent with each other. This chapter highlights the latest research done into (1) a practical, formal, coverage-based functional verification approach called instrumentation-based verification, (2) quality attribute reasoning, a semiautomated, nonfunctional verification theory, and (3) an integrated functional and nonfunctional verification approach for model-based development.

1. Introduction 279
2. Background 281
   2.1. Model-Based Development 281
   2.2. Functional Verification 282
   2.3. Nonfunctional Verification 283
3. Instrumentation-based Verification 284
   3.1. The IBV Approach 285
   3.2. A Reference Architecture for Monitor Models 289
   3.3. Closing Remarks on IBV 294
4. Quality Attribute-Based Reasoning 296
5. Integrated Functional and Nonfunctional Verification 300
   5.1. Extracting Structural Information from Functional models 301
   5.2. Extracting Quantitative Information from Functional Models 301
   5.3. Modifiability Metric 302
   5.4. Connectivity Metric 307
   5.5. Integrated Functional–Nonfunctional Verification 309
6. Tool Support 313
   6.1. Creating Scenarios 315
   6.2. Visualization 317
7. Conclusion 318
   References 318

1. Introduction

Model-based engineering [1] with a particular focus on executable visual speci-
fications [2] has emerged as a best practice in embedded applications (aerospace,
automotive, medical) where a high degree of confidence [3] needs to be placed in the
software. Since modeling notations like Simulink [4] and ASCET [5] are provided
with a precise notion of what it means to execute, designs rendered in them may be
simulated just like C or Java code. This property of executability enables engineers'
construction methods and tools to check whether their models meet expectations of
proper behavior as captured by the requirements.

The ability to perform verification in the design phase itself allows engineers to
catch bugs early in the development lifecycle where they are cheaper and easier to
fix [6]. Because of this benefit, there is currently an enormous interest in model-
based design verification techniques, particularly, into those that support formal
reasoning [7].

In general, design verification consists of two kinds of activities. On one hand,
there is *functional verification* [8] where the design is checked against requirements
that specify how the software must and must not behave (functional requirements).
On the other hand, there is *nonfunctional verification* [9] where requirements that
describe expectations on the impact the software will have on the system it is part of
and the organization that is responsible for it are confirmed against the design.

Model-based design verification has several challenges:

1. The functional verification domain has been an active area of investigation for
   the past 30 years. While inspections [10] and code review [11] still remain
   popular manual verification strategies, the focus of existing research is on
   automated and semiautomated math-based analysis techniques like model
   checking [12,13] and theorem proving [14–16].

   However, these methods are not without their shortcomings. Model-checking
   suffers from severe scalability issues [17,18], which often make it infeasible
   for applying on complicated concurrent software systems [19]. Theorem
   proving requires a lot of expert user guidance, introducing a large amount of
   overhead to product development time [20].

   Another problem is that most of the tools and techniques [21–24] developed
   for formal verification have been created in a research environment where,
   in order to make the analysis feasible, the input notations have been kept
   rudimentary [25]. However, in the industrial space, tools that are popularly
   used like Simulink and ASCET support a wide variety of modeling constructs in order to simplify the activity of modeling. Because of this

incompatibility in their fundamental approaches, techniques developed in the research community are poorly integrated with commercial modeling tools. As a result, engineers can often do little more than to invoke the native simulation features of their design tools and make *ad hoc* assessment about the veracity of their designs.

2. Nonfunctional requirements, because they involve properties like resource usage (does the software make appropriate use of scarce bandwidth?), and modifiability (does the structure of the software appropriately support future modifications?) cannot be seen to be simply defining set of valid/invalid traces.
   Consequently, nonfunctional requirements typically cannot be formally checked against the system in the way that functional requirements are but instead are reasoned about in a more ad hoc informal way through structured discussions and brainstorming [26–28]. This kind of analysis is often criticized as lacking in rigor.

3. Functional verification is done on models (specifically set of traces) while nonfunctional verification is performed by analyzing the architecture (i.e., what the components of the system are and how they are connected). These two representations of the system, the functional and the nonfunctional models, are not the same, representing alternate views of the system specification. Sometimes, these views are so different from each other than it becomes difficult to make an argument that these two alternate representations are consistent with each other, that is, they represent the same system.

The motivation of this chapter is to show how each of these challenges can be addressed in a practical, industrial context. More specifically, our chapter has the following three themes:

1. *Instrumentation-based verification* (IBV) [29], an automated, formal testing-based approach to the design verification of functional requirements. In IBV, functional requirements are formalized as *monitors*, or small models in the same modeling notation in which designs are given. Intuitively, the purpose of these monitors is to observe the behavior of a controller design model and raise a flag whenever the controller's behavior deviates from the associated requirement. Engineers may then check the correctness of a design model by connecting the monitors to the design and running automatically generated tests on the resulting *instrumented* model to see if any monitors ever raise flags.

2. *Quality attribute-based reasoning* (QAR) [30], a semiautomated process for verifying nonfunctional requirements. In QAR, the software architecture of a system is described in terms of responsibilities (a unit of functionality) and their dependencies. This software architecture together with a nonfunctional requirement (expressed as a quality attribute scenario) is provided as inputs to

a reasoning framework (RF), which then decides if the architecture satisfies that requirement. If it does not, then the framework provides suggestions or tactics to the engineer so that the architecture could be modified in order to satisfy the particular nonfunctional requirement.

3. An integrated approach for verifying functional and nonfunctional requirements. In this approach, functional models in notations such as Simulink are used to drive both functional and nonfunctional verification by automatically extracting nonfunctional design models from functional ones. This automated extraction of artifacts used for nonfunctional analysis will ensure that the different system views remain consistent throughout.

The rest of the chapter is organized as follows. Section 2 provides a background in model-based development (MBD), and functional and nonfunctional verification. Section 3 discusses IBV, while Section 4 discusses QAR. Section 5 talks about our integrated approach for functional and nonfunctional verification, while Section 6 concludes with future work.

2. Background

This section reviews (1) Model-based development, (2) functional verification, and (3) nonfunctional verification.

2.1 Model-Based Development

MBD is a software development paradigm that uses mathematical abstractions called *models* to represent design-time artifacts. Models can be of two kinds—static (e.g., those that show class or object hierarchy and relations between them) or dynamic (e.g., state-machines and data-flow diagrams). While static modeling has been standard practice for decades now, as part of object-oriented design, dynamic modeling is a relatively novel approach which is gaining popularity particularly in the embedded systems community.

In dynamic modeling, engineers capture system and software design information using graphical and hierarchical notations that have execution semantics, that is, they have a precise notion of what it means to "run." In that respect, executable models are like normal programming languages like C+/Java in that they may be simulated debugged and tested in similar ways.

However, they also have certain advantages over programming languages. By virtue of being visual representations of design, they generally can be created much more rapidly than code. Additionally, being constructed at a higher level of abstraction models are free from low-level implementation details and thus are easily understandable and reusable.

Because of the above advantages, modeling notations like Simulink/Stateflow and ASCET are being extensively used in the embedded industry to encode software and system design. Automated code-generators are used to convert models, that is, higher level representations to code, that is, lower level representations in the same manner that code is converted by a compiler to even lower level representations like assembly language.

For this chapter, we use Simulink as the modeling notion on which the approaches detailed are illustrated. In Simulink, a model consists of a number of blocks that exchange data via signals. These blocks are hierarchical; a block, in turn, may consist of other blocks and interconnections between them. Blocks that contain other blocks are typically referred to as *subsystems*. In Fig. 1, a Simulink diagram is shown of an abstracted automotive body-control application function. The top subsystem (X) handles all high-level inputs and provides all outputs of the diagram. X processes the input signals and controls the subsystems Y, and Z accordingly. Both Y and Z report on their results by feeding back signals to X.

2.2   Functional Verification

A *functional requirement* is a statement of what the system must or must not do, usually expressed in the form: if a given condition holds, then the system should respond appropriately. *Functional verification* consists of checking whether the software satisfies the functional requirements.

In projects that follow MBD, code is automatically generated from models and then flashed onto the hardware. Tests are then run on the hardware–software combination (known as hardware-in-the-loop testing) and if the tests pass, the system is considered to have been successfully verified.

Hardware-in-the-loop testing is an expensive and time-consuming process not only because physical test beds and environments are difficult to maintain but also because errors that are discovered postcode generation are tougher to rectify (in terms of time and cost) than if they had been caught in the modeling phase itself. The principal criticism of existing practices in functional verification of models is that the executable property of modeling notations is not properly leveraged. Since models can be run like code, a significant part of functional verification can potentially be pushed upstream in the development cycle.

A variety of techniques have been developed to provide automated and semiautomated methods for model verification that take advantage of the execution semantics of modeling notations. These include (1) guided simulation [31] where scenarios deduced from the use cases are "run" on the model and the outputs produced studied to

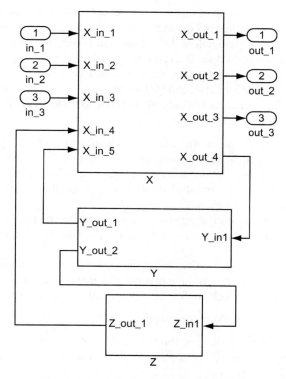

FIG. 1. Example functional model in Simulink.

see if they are what was expected (2) model-checking, an automated technique which given a model and a property expressed in a logical language determines if the model satisfies the property and if it does not supplies the user with a counter example (3) deductive reasoning wherein theorems are sought to be proven on software models.

2.3 Nonfunctional Verification

A *nonfunctional requirement* specifies criteria that can be used to evaluate the operation of a system. It defines a restriction on the way the system is (e.g., any change to module M should not take more than three person-days) with respect to a certain *quality attributes* (e.g., modifiability, availability, security). Unlike functional requirements, nonfunctional requirements are properties of the whole system (sometimes referred to as emergent properties), "visible" neither at the level of traces nor at the level of subcomponents. Hence, standard approaches for functional verification, which rely critically on compositionality (analyzing a system by analyzing its parts), cannot be used for nonfunctional verification. As a result, reasoning about nonfunctional attributes has traditionally been done in an ad hoc and subjective fashion.

Among the more organized and structured frameworks for understanding design implications of nonfunctional requirements that are used in industrial software development is the Architecture Tradeoff Analysis Method (ATAM) [32–34].

An ATAM process takes as its input:

(1) Attribute-specific questions related to stimuli (e.g., What happens when 10 users are logged in at the same time?), responses (e.g., What will be the connection latency if ten users are logged in?), and decisions (e.g., What back-up services are invoked under heavy load) that enable elicitation of nonfunctional requirements.

(2) Prioritized scenario or short statements describing interactions between stakeholders and systems are formulated and prioritized based on achievability and risk.

(3) Architectural approaches that are manual, largely *ad hoc* methods for reasoning about architectural design alternatives whose goal is to see how different choices affect the way in which nonfunctional requirements are satisfied.

The outputs of the ATAM process are:

1. *Risks*: This relates to the probability of failure of the project based on the parts of the design that have not been finalized or decisions taken whose implications are not understood.

2. *Sensitivity points*: This identifies the nonfunctional qualities of the design that are critically affected by tuning design parameters, for example, using a time-division multiplexed communication protocol would increase safety in comparison to using contention-based communication.

3. *Tradeoff points*: This identifies the design attributes which affect one or more nonfunctional qualities of the design in such a way that all of them cannot be positively impacted at the same time. For instance, increasing the key size may lead to greater security but may reduce system throughput and usability.

3. Instrumentation-based Verification

IBV is a technique for functional verification of models. In IBV, functional requirements are formalized as *monitors*, or small models in the same modeling notation in which designs are given. As the name suggests, the purpose of these monitors is to monitor the behavior of a controller design model and raise a flag whenever behavior deviating from the associated requirement is detected. Once requirements are captured as monitors, the IBV verification process involves connecting the monitors into the design model and then determining if the resulting *instrumented* model to can ever cause a monitor to raise its flag. This determination can be performed in several different ways: model checking, simulation of the model, etc. The method discussed in this section uses coverage-based testing [35]. The tool used to illustrate IBV is the Reactis® tool [36] from Reactive Systems Incorporated.

3.1   The IBV Approach

The IBV method described here involves the following steps.

1. Formalization of requirements as monitor models.
2. Instrumentation of design model with monitors.
3. Coverage-based testing of instrumented design model.

The IBV methodology will be illustrated using an example of a cruise-control application in an automobile (this example was obtained from Reactis distribution). One typical requirement for such a system is that the cruise control should not try to control vehicle speed when the vehicle is traveling too slowly. If this threshold speed is 30 mph, for example, the requirement would be:

"If vehicle speed is less than 30 mph, then the cruise control shall remain inactive."

Figure 2 shows a formalization of this requirement as a monitor model in Simulink. This monitor tracks the *speed* and *active* (true if the cruise control is actively controlling vehicle speed, and false otherwise) values in the main cruise-control model in order to check that whenever *speed* < 30, then *active* is false. The model first determines if the undesired behavior has been observed by conjoining (AND block) the result of checking whether *speed* < 30 and the *active* input value. If the AND block outputs true, a violation has been detected; if it outputs false, then the current status is satisfactory with respect to the requirement. In order to make the monitor model to output true if everything is fine and false otherwise, the output of the AND block is therefore negated (NOT block). So long as no violation has been detected, the model keeps its *ok* output at true. When a violation is found, it writes false to ok, indicating that a violation has been uncovered.

Once functional requirements have been encoded as monitor models, the next step in the IBV procedure is to embed them in the main design model. Figure 3 shows how the monitor model for the cruise-control requirement may be attached to a larger Simulink model for the cruise control. The diagonal lines show how the inputs

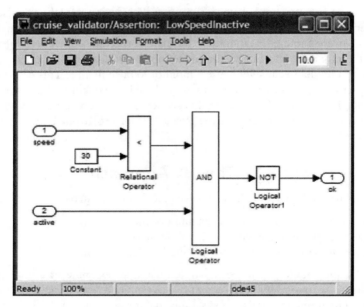

FIG. 2. A sample monitor model.

of the monitor model are connected into the main controller model. Conceptually, the instrumented model consisting of the controller and monitor models is one larger model and may be maintained as such. Practically speaking, however, it is good practice to maintain the application and instrumentation separately. Tools like Reactis are able to maintain instrumentation and the main model in separate files.

Figure 4 shows the results panel of applying Reactis test generation to the instrumented model from Fig. 3. The test cases computed by Reactis consist of sequences of input vectors; each vector contains one value for each input port in the model. The model in Fig. 3 contains eight inputs ("onOff," "accelResume," etc.), so each input vector in a test sequence would contain eight values. To run such a test on a model, one provides the input vectors, in order, to the model, one after the other, starting with the model in its initial configuration. After each individual input vector is processed, the model produces an output vector as a result (the model in Fig. 3 has three outputs, so the output vectors would contain three values each). The result of applying a test, then, is a sequence of output vectors. Reactis uses a combination of Monte-Carlo simulation heuristics and constraint solving to compute sets of test sequences that, when run on the model, aim to provide 100% coverage of the various structural coverage criteria (e.g., branch coverage) that Reactis tracks. As it

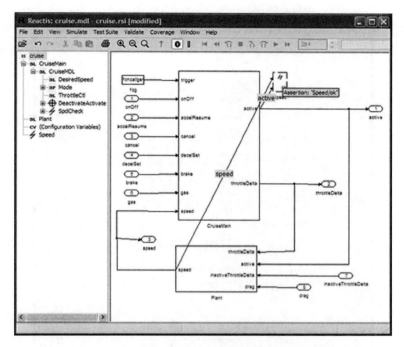

Fig. 3. A design model instrumented with the monitor model from Fig. 2.

computes these sequences of input vectors, it also captures the resulting output vectors produced by the model. Consequently, the test suites produced by the tool consist of sequences of input-vector/output-vector pairs.

Note that Reactis also reports the number of monitor models ("assertions," in Reactis terminology) that have been violated while it is constructing tests. In Fig. 4, the single monitor model has reported a violation during the testing process.

Once a design model has been instrumented with monitor models, the final step in the IBV methodology is to test the instrumented model to search for requirements violations. An obvious question that arises is which, and how many, tests to run. The IBV described here relies on model-based versions of coverage criteria, such as statement coverage, decision coverage, modified condition/decision coverage, etc., to determine when enough testing has been performed. Tools like Reactis provided automated support for constructing test suites that achieve 100% of standard coverage criteria.

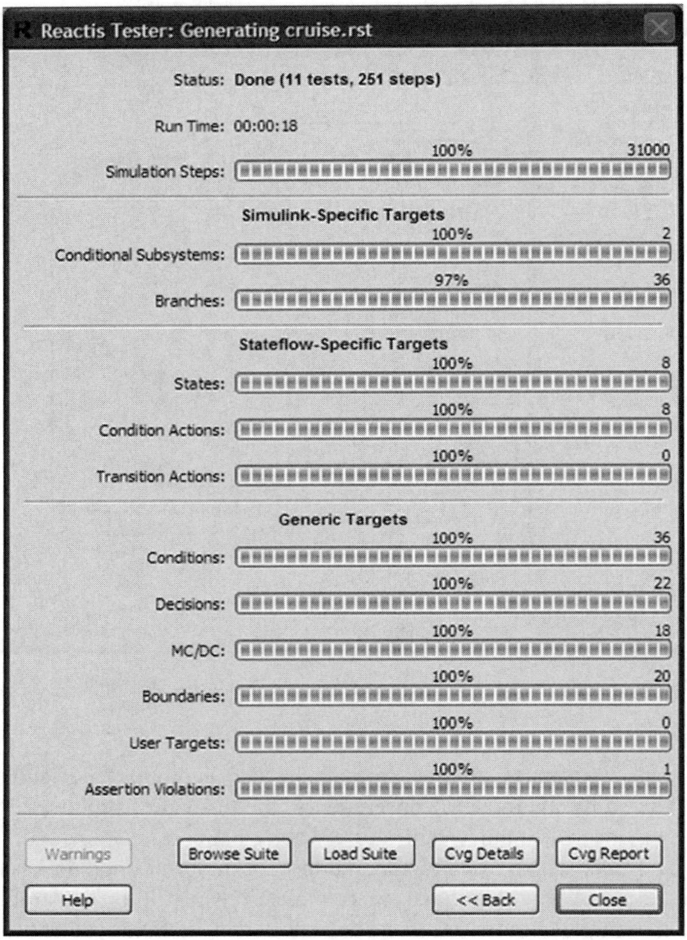

FIG. 4. Coverage data for testing instrumented model in Fig. 3. Note assertion violation indicated in last line.

Given that a violation has occurred, the next step in an IBV-based process would be to identify the test causing the violation in order to use it to debug the controller model. Figure 5 gives a snapshot of Reactis after having run the instrumented model on the tests constructed by the tool. One may see in this case that in Step 146 of Test 11, the monitor was violated.

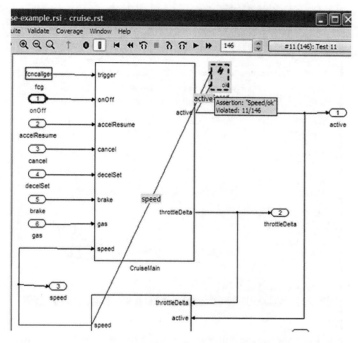

FIG. 5. Graphical indication showing violation of requirement. The pop-up indicates that Step 146 of Test 11 induced the error.

The screenshot in Fig. 6 shows the actual test data created by Reactis for Test 11. Step 146, indeed, shows a discrepancy: the speed is approximately 26 mph, and the active is true (1.0). A developer may then use this information to diagnose the problem in the model. In this case, an improperly set constant within the controller model is the source of the error.

3.2   A Reference Architecture for Monitor Models

The practical feasibility of IBV rests in large part on the efficiency with which monitor models can be constructed from requirements. This section describes a *reference architecture* for monitor models that can be used to standardize the form of such models. By using the reference architecture as a template, system engineers can start their formalization efforts with a common outline that directs their thinking to how to encode the main modules within the architecture. The architecture is rather

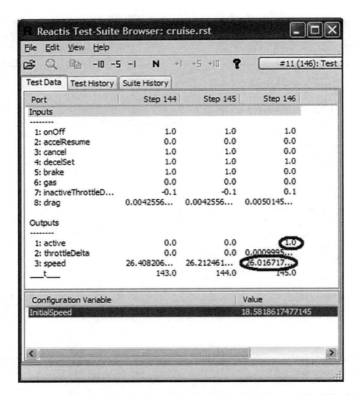

Fig. 6. Test showing violation of requirement. Note that in Step 146, the speed is < 30, while the value of "active" is 1.0 (true).

simple, but it has proved remarkably useful as a mechanism for organizing the requirements formalization process.

Figure 7 contains our reference architecture for monitor models and consists of three submodels.

- A *condition* submodel describing when the requirement is triggered.
- A *validation*, or "expected value," submodel that computes the expected values of outputs based on the requirement.
- A *comparison* model that compares these expected outputs with the actual outputs coming from the design model.

A system engineer using this architecture to formalize a requirement would adjust the input interface to collect the relevant data from the design model and specify the

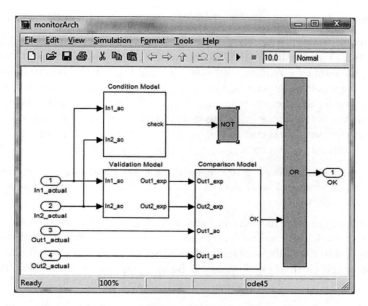

FIG. 7. The monitor-model reference architecture. White rectangles represent subsystems that must be provided by the system engineer.

logic for each of the three submodels. The resulting completed model would then be available for use in the rest of the IBV process specified above.

Operationally, the validation model takes in two kinds of data from the design model: the inputs that are relevant for the requirement, and the requirement-related outputs produced by the design model in response to the requirement-relevant inputs. It first uses these values to determine if the requirement has been triggered, then uses the validation submodel to determine the expected output values, based on the requirement, and compares these expected outputs with the actual values from the design model using the comparison submodel. If the expected and the actual outputs do not agree, and the output of the condition model is "true" (meaning the output of the NOT block is "false," and the output of the OR block is hence the same as the output of the validation comparison submodel), the monitor sets its output (here called OK) to false, representing the fact that the requirement has been violated.

The form for this architecture is derived from the fact that requirements are often in conditional form. As an example, consider the (anonymized) requirement below taken from a production automotive requirements document.

In case of a timeout while awaiting a control signal S, the feature shall be deactivated.

This requirement only specifies behavior when a timeout of the control signal S has occurred. We refer to this condition as the *trigger* for the requirement. A monitor model formalizing the requirement would include logic in the condition submodel for checking whether the timeout has occurred. The remaining submodels would be used to compute the desired status of the feature (*deactivated*) and to compare this result with the actual status, which would be read from the design model.

To illustrate these ideas concretely, we use the reference architecture to develop a monitor model for another requirement of a cruise control, which is given as follows.

While the cruise control is active, if the desired and actual speeds of the vehicle differ by more than 1 mile per hour, then the cruise control shall correct this difference within 3 s.

The first step in using the reference architecture is to identify the data needed from the design model. Three values are referred to in the requirement: the active status of the cruise control, and the actual and desired speeds. This results in the high-level model structure given in Fig. 8; note that input *active* is a Boolean that is true if the

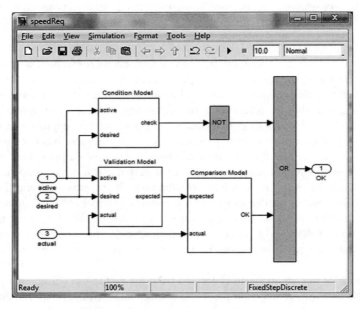

Fig. 8. Top-level architecture for cruise-control monitor model.

cruise control is active and false otherwise. All three values may be thought of as inputs in the design model, while *actual* can also be seen as an output.

The next step in the development of this model is to design the condition submodel. In this case, the requirement is triggered if the cruise control is active (note that the desired speed does not factor into this condition). This leads to the subsystem depicted in Fig. 9. Note that the value of the *active* input is passed straight through to the *check* output; if *active* is "true" then the submodel will output "true" on *check*.

Defining the validation submodel is also straightforward. If the cruise control is active, then the desired value denotes the expected vehicle speed; otherwise, the actual value does. A Simulink switch block can be used to implement this logic, as depicted in Fig. 10: based on the value of the control signal (the middle input into the block), either the upper input is passed through (if the control is "true") or the lower one is (if the control is "false").

The final task is to devise the comparison submodel. In many cases, this model is very simple, as it only requires comparisons of the expected and actual values for equality. In the case of this requirement, the comparison is rather more complicated because it requires determining whether *desired* and *actual* differ by more than a certain amount over a given time interval in which the cruise control is active.

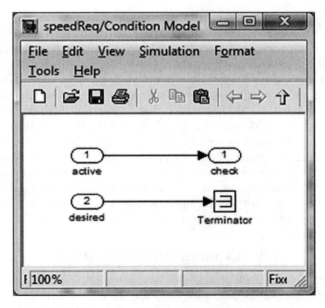

FIG. 9. Condition submodel for cruise-control monitor model.

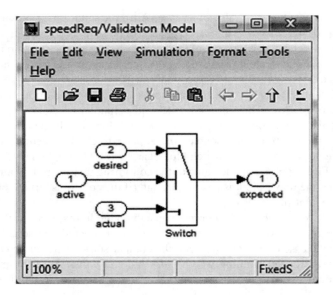

FIG. 10. Validation submodel for cruise-control monitor model.

The strategy adopted here is to define a timer that "runs" when the difference in these values is too large and the cruise control is active and is "reset to 0" otherwise. If the value of this timer ever exceeds 3, then a violation has been detected, and the output of the comparison model should be "false."

Figure 11 gives the corresponding Simulink for this submodel. In Simulink, timers can be implemented in different fashions; this implementation uses a reset-table discrete integrator. The logic ensures that the integrator is reset (to 0) whenever the difference between *desired* and *actual* either shifts from exceeding 1 to being less than 1 or vice versa. The signal being integrated is "0" when the difference is less than 1 (i.e., the value of the integrator's output does not change as time progresses). If the difference is greater than 1, then the signal being integrated is the constant "1," meaning that the value of the integrator's output reflects the time since it was last reset. While these operations may appear complex, it is standard practice when modeling real-time systems in Simulink.

3.3 Closing Remarks on IBV

We close this section with a discussion about some of the theoretical and practical aspects of IBV. One obvious question regarding the method is this: Which kinds of functional requirements can be captured as monitor models? The specifics of the

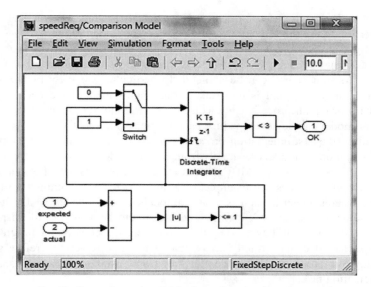

Fig. 11. Comparison submodel for the cruise-control monitor model.

answer will depend on the modeling notation, but generally speaking, monitor models capture so-called *safety properties*, in the taxonomy of functional properties defined by Lamport [37]. Safety properties generally assert that "something bad does not happen"; in the case of a monitor model, the occurrence of a bad event is signaled by the setting of the monitor's output flag to false. Lamport also defines a class of properties that he calls *liveness* assertions: these state that "something good eventually happens." Monitor models cannot be used to encode general liveness properties, although they can capture so-called *bounded*-liveness properties ("something good happens within a given time"). Safety and liveness can be formally characterized by a group of logics that have support for "past" and "future" constructs called temporal logic [38]. For real-time systems, bounded-liveness properties are generally preferred when describing what behavior a system must exhibit.

Another issue involves the use of the design-modeling language to formalize requirements. In IBV, requirements are captured as monitor models, which must be coded in the same notation as the design modeling is done. In traditional requirements approaches, the requirements and notations are different, and this is often viewed as desirable because of the danger of "design creep": requirements may become so detailed that they bleed over into design. According to this point of view, IBV opens the door for requirements that may become too detailed, as they involve the same tools as those used for design. However, there are good practical reasons for preferring to use the same notation: the same model-management tools (editors, versioning, simulators, style checkers, etc.) may be used to manage monitor models as well as design models. We also believe that with good requirements-elicitation practices, "design creep" can be avoided. In particular, we view monitor-model formulation as a step that is undertaken after requirements have been captured, rather than during this process. Once a discrete list of requirements has been defined, a monitor model can be developed for each single requirement.

Regarding the instrumentation process, our experience is that tool support for maintaining monitor models separately from design models is essential, for a variety of reasons. First, in modern MBD processes, design models are often inputs into later development stages; for example, code may be generated automatically from them. Extraneous material such as monitor models must not be allowed to interfere with these activities. Second, monitor models should be available for inspection, reuse, and adaptation; if they are only to be found embedded within a design model, these processes become virtually impossible. Tools like Reactis therefore support the storing of monitor models in files separate from design models and manage the instrumentation task.

A final issue involves the use of coverage-based testing as the method for searching for violations. Traditional practice would involve running simulations of design models, with manual inspections of the results then employed to determine if any errors exist. Apart from the time consuming and expensive reliance of human inspection, such an approach is problematic when there are possible rare events that may not arise in the simulations that are performed. However, model-checking techniques inspect all possible execution scenarios; however, in practice such methods are combinatorially expensive, and this limits their effective applicability to relatively small design models. Our experience is that coverage-based testing offers a reasonable compromise between pure simulation and model checking: the fact that tests are constructed that cover the model logic completely helps ensure that rare events will be present in the test data, while the fact that the method is testing based helps it avoid the computational complexity associated with model checking.

4. Quality Attribute-Based Reasoning

In ATAM, architectures are reasoned about using largely manual and *ad hoc* techniques. QAR [39] refers to a methodology, implemented in tools like ArchE [40] and RAPT [41,42] that seek to automate, to a substantial degree, the task of reasoning about architectures with respect to quality attributes.

The analysis performed as part of QARs is implemented in the ArchE/RAPT approach by RFs. A RF can be defined to be an expert system that evaluates the software architecture with respect to a particular quality attribute. Each RF can process requirements for its quality, generate an initial architecture design based on the requirements, evaluate how well a user-defined architecture satisfies the quality requirement and then propose design suggestions (tactics) to improve the architecture, and bring it closer to satisfying its quality requirements.

A RF has two kinds of inputs

1. *The quality attribute model*: The quality attribute model is a mathematical abstraction of the software design. It contains both structural and numerical information. The structural information consists of the architecture arranged in the form of responsibilities (a responsibility is a unit of functionality) and relationships (a relationship exists between two responsibilities if one depends on the other). The numerical information consists of measures (e.g., execution times, cost to implement a change) that are used to annotate the structural elements.

As an example, let us consider the modifiability quality attribute. The quality attribute model is given as an *impact graph*. The nodes of the impact graph are the responsibilities, and the edges are the relationships.

In the modifiability model two types of quantitative information are used.

- *Cost of change (COC)*: Each responsibility has an associated cost of modification (say d). Any change request that directly affects this responsibility is assumed to incur a cost of d person-days.
- *Probability of change propagation (PCP)*: Because of the presence of relationships between responsibilities, a responsibility B may contribute indirectly to the total cost of modification of responsibility A if B is connected via a relationship to A. The cost of propagation of a change from A to B is calculated by multiplying the PCP (p) from A to B with the direct cost to modify B.

The COC information is used to label the corresponding node in the impact graph, while the PCP data label the relevant edge. In this way, an impact graph incorporates both structural and quantitative information.

In Fig. 12, we have an impact graph where each node is labeled with a responsibility (X, Y, and Z), the directed edges represent dependencies (in this case the dependencies are bidirectional), and the COC and PCP numbers weight the nodes and the edges.

2. *Quality attribute scenarios*: Quality attribute scenarios define the software quality requirements in a concise format. Each scenario includes a response measure that specifies a quantitative constraint that can be evaluated based on

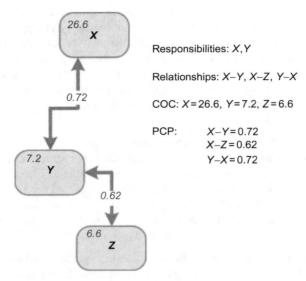

Responsibilities: *X, Y*

Relationships: *X–Y*, *X–Z*, *Y–X*

COC: *X* = 26.6, *Y* = 7.2, *Z* = 6.6

PCP: *X–Y* = 0.72
              X–Z = 0.62
              Y–X = 0.72

FIG. 12. Example impact graph.

the results of an RF model. A scenario is defined by six parts: stimulus, source of stimulus, environment, artifact, response, and response measure. The response measure is the critical part of the scenario because it provides a quantitative constraint with which to evaluate whether the scenario is satisfied. Each RF takes the set of scenarios for its quality attribute and uses their response measures as constraints to evaluate whether the model derived from the architecture satisfies its requirements.

For example, let us consider the scenario specified in Table I. This scenario specifies a change to the input interface for responsibility *X*. It is expected that this scenario primarily affects responsibility *X* but also affects the responsibilities *Y* and *Z*. *X* will need to send additional signals to *Y* and *Z* based on the new input signal and both must be able to handle the modified signals. Thus the change is expected to propagate from the responsibility *X* to the two other responsibilities *Y* and *Z*.

RFs: Each RF consists of the following components:

- Scenario and Responsibility Parameter Definition
- Initial Design Creation
- Model Interpretation and Evaluation
- Suggest Design Tactics
- Apply Design Tactics

TABLE I
AN EXAMPLE MODIFIABILITY SCENARIO

Modifiability scenario: A new input shall be added to the X subsystem that carries a Boolean value. The new input signal represents an additional condition under which the subsystems Y and Z shall be activated	
Source of stimulus	Requirements team
Stimulus	Addition of an input Boolean signal to affect subsystems Y and Z
Environment	Normal operation
Artifact	Subsystem X
Response	Make change
Response measure	Within 7 days

We describe these modules using the modifiability RF as an example.

In the *Scenario and Responsibility Parameter Definition* module, the scenario type for the RF's quality is defined. Each scenario specified for this quality must conform to the format as defined by the RF. When considering modifiability each scenario's response measure determines how many time units it should take to implement a change.

In addition to the scenario type definition, each RF defines a set of parameters that must be provided as input for each functional responsibility. These parameters are required as inputs for the execution of the analysis model. The modifiability RF requires that each responsibility specifies a COC and every dependency between responsibilities be annotated with a PCP.

The *Initial Design Creation* module contains rules for generating an initial architecture design. This is required when a project starts only with a requirements specification and there is no existing architecture design to evaluate.

In case of modifiability, the rules are that the initial architecture be an impact graph where every node represents a task, every edge represents a data dependency, every node has a weight equal to the COC associated with the responsibility it corresponds to, and every edge has a weight equal to the PCP between the two responsibilities it connects.

The *Model Interpretation and Evaluation* module contains the rules to interpret a model internal to the RF from the architecture design. In this phase, the model is evaluated and the results are used to judge whether the architecture satisfies its scenarios. For example, given an impact graph with assigned COC and PCP, an evaluation function can be defined that estimates the cost of changing one or more responsibilities. The evaluation function calculates for each responsibility the probability that changing a specific responsibility would propagate to it. The average cost for this change can then be calculated by computing the sum of all the COCs times the calculated probability.

If the architecture does not satisfy some of the scenarios for a given quality, the RF will execute the *Suggest Design Tactics* module. In this module, there are rules to select possible design changes to the architecture and evaluate whether they improve the model in the RF. The RF will select the most promising tactics that show the greatest improvement in terms of satisfying the scenarios for that quality, and send them to the Seeker for arbitration with possible tactics from other RFs. The Seeker module is independent from all of the ArchE RFs and will decide which tactics taken from all of the RFs to present to the user. The Seeker makes this decision by prioritizing the tactic suggestions received from the RFs according to their net improvement of the architecture design toward satisfying all requirements scenarios. The user will then select a tactic to apply to change the architecture design.

In the modifiability RF, design tactic suggestions include adding an intermediary responsibility to reduce dependencies between functional responsibilities, merging semantically related functional responsibilities into a single software module, and applying information hiding with a functional interface responsibility. The modifiability RF will try these tactics out for each task that does not satisfy its scenario, reevaluate the modifiability model impact graph, and select the tactics that produce the greatest overall modifiability improvement for the architecture modules and the modifiability scenarios specified.

Finally, the *Apply Design Tactics* module contains the rules that receive the user's input for selecting a tactic, and will alter the architecture design according to the user's response. For example, if the user selects an add intermediary tactic for a responsibility, the modifiability RF has the rules that make ArchE update the responsibility impact graph, and update the COC and PCP values in the architecture design.

5. Integrated Functional and Nonfunctional Verification

QAR approaches as detailed in the last section fit uneasily with existing MBD workflows, as the models required for functional and quality attribute analysis are in different notations and must be constructed and managed separately as a result.

This section defines a mapping from functional models given in Simulink to impact graphs that ArchE can analyze using modifiability as an example. Specifically, the structural and quantitative information required to annotate the nonfunctional models (impact graph in this case) is derived automatically from the functional models. This forms a basis for the unification of the verification activities for functional and nonfunctional design attributes. The way this is accomplished is by enabling two hitherto disconnected activities to be integrated into a tightly coupled one that works on a single model. Designers would now construct a single functional model and subject it to both functional and nonfunctional verification using the mechanisms outlined in this section.

As noted in Section 4, impact graphs contain two sorts of information: structural and numerical. The rest of this section describes how each of these types of information is computed from functional models.

5.1   Extracting Structural Information from Functional models

An impact graph, one may recall, consists of nodes representing responsibilities and edges reflecting relationships. The first step in extracting an impact graph from a Simulink model is to what structural elements within the Simulink model itself these correspond to.

The intuition underlying this mapping is to conceive of the top-level subsystems of a given Simulink model as system components. In the nonfunctional domain, the analogs to these components are the responsibilities that, through data dependencies, together discharge the overall purpose of the system. Based on this intuition, the top-level subsystems in the functional model are mapped to responsibilities in the nonfunctional model.

Similarly, the connections between subsystems in the functional model have relationships as their analogs in the nonfunctional domain. Formalizing, if subsystem A is mapped to responsibility R and subsystem B to responsibility S, then a relationship exists between R and S if and only if there exists a connection between A and B in the functional model. Note that the directionality of the connection is not taken into account: if A reads inputs from B or writes outputs to B, there is a connection between R and S. The reason for this has to do with the bidirectionality of modifiability: if one modifies the data type of a variable, for example, then both the statements that write to that variable as well as the ones that read from that variable may require modification.

The conceptual mapping of the structural elements of the nonfunctional model to functional model is summarized in Table II.

5.2   Extracting Quantitative Information from Functional Models

The quantitative information required to populate impact graphs is obtained from two metrics computed on the functional model.

TABLE II
MAPPING BETWEEN NONFUNCTIONAL AND FUNCTIONAL STRUCTURAL ELEMENTS

Nonfunctional structural elements	Corresponding functional elements
Responsibilities	Subsystems
Relationships	Connections

TABLE III
MAPPING BETWEEN NONFUNCTIONAL AND FUNCTIONAL STRUCTURAL ELEMENTS

Impact graph quantities	Corresponding functional model measures
Cost to change a responsibility (COC)	Modifiability metric
Probability of change propagation (PCP)	Connectivity metric

- *Modifiability metric*: Captures how expensive in terms of man-days it is to modify a given subsystem.
- *Connectivity metric*: Measures the degree of connectedness between two subsystems.

It should be noted that though modifiability metric (MM) and connectivity metric are similar in nature to structural metrics like coupling and cohesion (traditionally defined on code), they are distinguished from them by the fact that these new metrics are defined purely in terms of the modeling constructs used in the automotive software domain (namely Simulink models).

Table III summarizes the relationship between these metrics and the associated quantities used to annotate impact graphs.

5.3   Modifiability Metric

As described in the previous section, each responsibility has an associated COC number that captures the estimated number of man-days needed to perform any kind of modification to it. The MM provides a means of calculating these COC numbers from functional models.

No definition of such a metric is known to exist in the research literature; the closest approach is that followed by Vitkin et al. [43], who derived structural metrics from Simulink models for the purpose of estimating autocoding effort. In the following, their approach is first summarized, and then the adaptations needed to reflect an appropriate notion of modifiability are detailed.

Vitkin et al.'s calculation of the autocoding effort for a functional model has as its basis the complexity values for the blocks and the interblock connections in the model.

A functional model consists of different types of blocks, each of which has a set of parameters. When autocoding a functional model, each parameter must be set by the user and this setting requires manual effort. The effort is accounted for by assigning a complexity value to each block (BSON), which is defined to be equal to the number of parameters the block has. Based on the individual complexity values for each block, the total block complexity, BC, of a given model is the sum of all individual block complexities.

$$BC = \sum_{k=1}^{N} BSON_k$$

where BC is the total block complexity of functional model, N is the number of blocks in functional model, and $BSON_k$ is the individual BC of block k.

Regarding connections, two types are distinguished in Vitkin's work: those that carry binary values, and those that carry nonbinary ones. While autocoding binary connections are trivial, the same task for nonbinary connections requires greater effort, as it is necessary to ensure that the variables in the generated code are precise enough and can hold large enough values. The complexity for binary connections is thus ignored (MCN $=0$), and all nonbinary connections have a complexity value of 1 ($MCN = 1$). The total connection complexity, CC, is then the sum of all individual line complexities.

$$CC = \sum_{l=1}^{L} MCN_l$$

where CC is the total CC of functional model, L is the number of connections in functional model, and MCN_l is the individual CC of connection l.

The total autocode complexity of the functional model now becomes a weighted sum of the total BC and the total CC.

$$MC = K1 * BC + K2 * CC$$

where MC is the total model complexity, $K1$ is the weight for total BC, and $K2$ is the weight for total CC.

The values of the tuning coefficients $K1$ and $K2$ depend upon the type of auto-generated code along with other organizational characteristics, namely the experience of engineers, tooling environment, etc. By adjusting the coefficients, one can take into account these factors into the final calculation. Vitkin et al. state that $K1$ and $K2$ should be determined empirically.

Several modifications to the original formulation of Vitkin numbers are necessary in order to adapt it to the domain of modifiability. On one hand, the complexity values for blocks and connections that express the effort for autocoding a model do not necessarily reflect the effort for modifying it. Further, the values for the coefficients $K1$ and $K2$, the weights for blocks and lines, need to be appropriately defined for the modifiability domain. The basic principle for defining the MM, however, remains the same: the modifiability measure for a subsystem is calculated by accumulating the complexities of all blocks and lines that are contained in it.

5.3.1   Block Complexity

When a new basic block is added to a functional model, several tasks have to be performed. First, the engineer must decide which basic block, among the choices provided by Simulink, is to be added. This requires an understanding the semantics of the block, that is, what it does. Second, the engineer needs to determine where to insert the block. Third, the engineer must locate the basic block in the library, drag it into the model, and connect all its input and output ports. Last, the functional model must be tested after the block is added.

Based on the above observations, a scheme that assigns complexity values to each block was developed.

A list was created with the 30 basic blocks that were used in our study. Each block was then evaluated with respect to the difficulty and effort for creating that block and rated on a scale from 1 to 10, with 1 being the least complex and 10 being the most complex (the term "BCN" is used to refer to this number). For instance, the "inport" block was considered to be of low complexity and was assigned a BCN of 1. The "switch-case" block requires a number of Boolean expressions and was assigned a BCN of 5 (Table IV).

5.3.2   Connection Complexity

The modifiability CC, CCN, for every connection was set to 1. Since when creating a new connection, its data type plays no role in the effort needed to create it, no distinction is made between binary and nonbinary connections (in contrast to the Vitkin approach), and an equal complexity value is assigned to both of them.

These BCN and CCN values are typically determined by engineers who were already familiar with the design of functional models, and they might not reflect the situation in different contexts or domains. For example, the numbers will be higher

TABLE IV
LIST OF SAMPLE BLOCKS AND THE MODIFICATION
COMPLEXITIES THAT WERE ASSIGNED TO THEM

Block	BCN
Subsystem	1
Outport	1
Costant	3
Inport	1
Merge	2
Memory	3
Switch-case	5
Action port	3
If	5

for novice modelers than for experts. To adapt to a different environment, one can modify this scheme according to particular needs and preferences.

5.3.3   Coefficients

Using the coefficients $K1$ and $K2$ provided in Vitkin resulted in an effort estimation that was much higher than the experimental data collected in the course of building the 74 models alluded to above. Accordingly, adjustments were made: 0.02 for $K1$ and 0.001 for $K2$ produced the results that coincided most closely with recorded effort.

5.3.4   Modifiability Metric Formula

In a last step, the formula for computing the total complexity of a subsystem is given. The modifiability of a subsystem is calculated by applying the formula for the total complexity to the blocks and connections that are contained in the respective subsystem. The MM for a subsystem is as follows:

$$MM = K1 * BMC + K2 * CMC$$

BMC stands for the total block-modification complexity, and CMC stands for the total connection-modification complexity. The BMC is the sum of the individual modification complexities of the blocks contained in the subsystem. Likewise, the total CMC is the sum of the modification complexities of the connections contained in the subsystem.

$$BMC = \sum BCN_k$$

$$CMC = \sum CCN_l$$

Here, k ranges over the blocks in the subsystem, while l ranges over the connections.

The example in Fig. 13 shows a high-level subsystem having three inputs and one output signal.

Figure 14 shows the blocks and connections that are contained in that high-level subsystem. Each block is annotated with its modification complexity (BCN) value. The modifiability value of the high-level subsystem is computed based on the complexity of the subsystems and connections it contains.

The total BC is determined by multiplying the count of each subsystem with its complexity value and then summing over these values.

$$BMC = 2*1 + 1*3 + 1*3 + 2*2 + 1*4 + 1*1 = 17$$

Since each connection has a complexity value of 1, the CC is the sum over all connections.

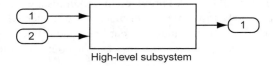

FIG. 13. High-level subsystem of a functional model.

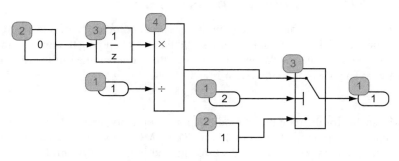

FIG. 14. The subsystems inside the high-level subsystem annotated with their respective complexity values.

$$CMC = 7$$

The modifiability of the high-level subsystem is then computed by adding up the weighted block and CC.

$$\begin{aligned} MM &= 0.02 * 17 + 0.001 * 7 \\ &= 0.34 + 0.007 \\ &= 0.347 \end{aligned}$$

Modeling the high-level subsystem is thus estimated to require 0.347 man-days.

5.4   Connectivity Metric

The connectivity metric assigns PCP numbers (i.e., edge weights of the impact graph) derived from design models in Simulink. The metric is based on the following intuition: the more the number of connections between two Simulink subsystems, and the deeper they are, the greater the chance that modifying one will lead to the modification of another, that is, the greater will be the probability that change propagates between their corresponding responsibilities.

The connectivity metric is defined in terms of signal propagation. A change that affects one subsystem percolates to its neighbors that are connected to it via signals. For instance, a change to a subsystem (called hereafter the *source*) might cause a change to the range of values, the precision, etc. of a signal that it outputs. The signal then travels to a neighboring subsystem (the *target*), which may also require modification as a result. The reverse is also true. A modification to a target subsystem might cause modifications to the data type of signal, which in turn might require changing the source subsystem to adapt to the modified data type.

If the target subsystem is atomic (i.e., is a single block), it is said to be fully impacted by the signal, that is, the connectivity between source and target is 1 (100%). When the target subsystem contains multiple blocks, it needs to be determined to what extent these are affected by the signal in order to estimate the total impact to the target subsystem. The illustration in Fig. 10 shows such a setup. Subsystem a is the source subsystem, and it is connected to the target subsystem b, which contains blocks c, d, e, f, g, h, and i. The signal that is output by the source subsystem a travels to blocks contained in b, in this case c. Since the signal is an input to c, it also affects its output signal, which is input to d and e. The signal propagates in the same way to f. However, the signal never reaches the g, h, and i.

This is used to define the degree of impact that can propagate though a connection, that is, its connectivity. First, it is assumed that all blocks that are affected by the connection have been identified. (They can be determined by tracing the signals in an affected subsystem using, for example, a transitive-closure algorithm.) In the example in Fig. 15, the affected blocks are c, d, e, and f.

Previously a complexity value for subsystems was defined. Now the *affected complexity* (AC) is defined to be the sum of the complexities of all affected blocks.

$$AC = \sum_{\text{affected blocks}} BCN_i$$

The AC in the example is the sum of the complexities of the blocks a–f, that is, 14. The AC expresses how much complexity in a subsystem is affected by a single signal.

The next step computes connectivity as the percentage of total complexity that is affected by the connection. The total complexity is simply the sum of the complexity values of all the blocks it contains. For instance, the total complexity of subsystem b is 21.

$$CN = \frac{AC}{\text{Total subsystem complexity}}$$

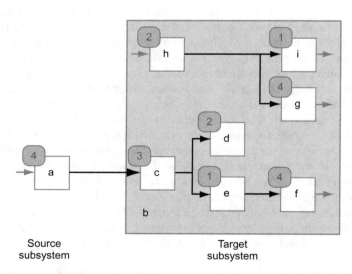

Source   Target
subsystem   subsystem

FIG. 15. Conceptual view of functional model in which the external connection emanates from subsystem a and impacts parts of the target subsystem b.

In summary, to compute the connectivity of a connection, we first determine all blocks in the target subsystem that are affected by it, compute the AC, and then divide it by the total subsystem complexity.

In the example, we have determined the affected subsystems to be a–f. The AC is 14 and the total complexity is 21. The connectivity of the relationship in direction from a to b, therefore, $20/28 = 0.67 = 67\%$.

A simple extension to the approach enables it to handle multiple connections between subsystems. The affected subsystems are determined by identifying all subsystems that are affected by a signal from any of the external connections that originate in the source subsystem and end in the target subsystem. Computing the AC and the connectivity is then done in the same fashion as described earlier for single connections.

5.5 Integrated Functional–Nonfunctional Verification

This section illustrates the concepts defined in the previous sections with the example functional model introduced previously. Figure 16 shows the top-level view of the model. Each step of extracting the structural and quantitative information from the functional model and the way the impact graph is updated in each step is illustrated in the following discussion. The steps in sequence are:

1. Extracting responsibilities from the functional model.

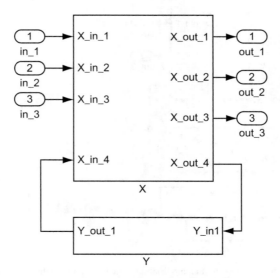

FIG. 16. The high-level view of the example model.

2. Calculating COC from the MM.
3. Extracting relationships from the functional model.
4. Calculating PCP from the connectivity metric.

Each step is discussed in turn below.

5.5.1 Extracting Responsibilities

The functional model of the example has three top-level subsystems: X, Y, and Z. Each of these subsystems is represented in the modifiability model as responsibilities. Figure 17 shows all the responsibilities for the example system that are extracted from the functional model.

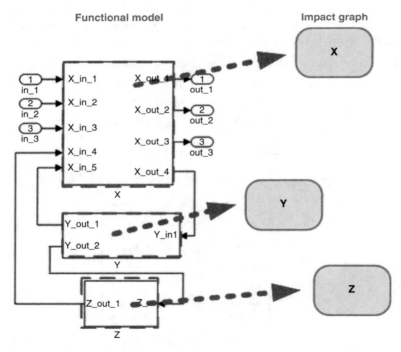

FIG. 17. The responsibilities of the modifiability model on the right are created based on the subsystems in the functional model on the left.

5.5.2   Computing the COC

Figure 18 shows the MM values for each responsibility in the example model. It is to be noted that the cost of modifying the functionality represented by the responsibility X is significantly higher than both Y and Z. More precisely, a modification to responsibility X is estimated to take 26.6 man-days, while modifications to Y and Z take 7.2 and 6.6 man-days, respectively.

5.5.3   Extracting Relationships

Relationships in the impact graph express data dependencies among responsibilities. A relationship has a source responsibility and a target responsibility, that is, a relationship is directed; however, in the case of modifiability, every relationship also

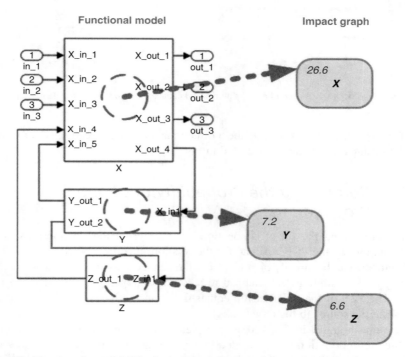

Fig. 18. Mapping of responsibilities in the impact graph to subsystems in the functional model. The modification (MM) values for each responsibility are also shown.

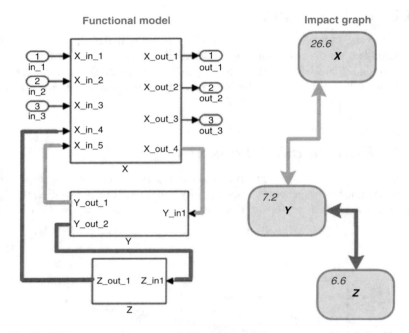

Fɪɢ. 19. Blocks are mapped to responsibilities and connections are mapped to relationships.

has its inverse included, reflecting the bidirectionality of modification. The mapping of relationships to signals is illustrated in Fig. 19.

5.5.4 Computing the Probability of Change Propagation

After computing the set of connections that represent the relationships in the functional model, the PCP attribute for the relationships must be computed. These PCP numbers can be directly obtained from the connectivity metric. The source and the target responsibilities are mapped to a source and a target subsystem, respectively. The PCP of that relationship equals the connectivity metric for all connections from the source to the target subsystem.

The impact graph in Fig. 20 is complete, as it contains the structural and quantitative information that is needed to evaluate quality attribute scenarios. This section has illustrated how the information for building the impact graph can be extracted from functional models.

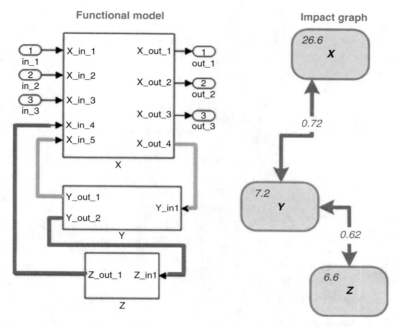

F$_{IG}$. 20. Computation of the probability of change propagation values from connectivity values of connections in the functional model.

6. Tool Support

We developed a tool that supports the process described in Section 5, namely the initial responsibility mapping and the computation of relationships, COC, and PCP, for automating the extraction of nonfunctional information from functional models.

The tool is implemented in Java as a plug-in for the Eclipse development environment from IBM. It consists of an importer for functional models in the Simulink notation, a graphical representation of the impact graph, and a user interface to show details about the mapping between functional model and impact graph. Further, the tool provides an interface to ArchE, which can be used to evaluate quality attribute scenario. Figure 21 shows the architecture of the setup. The user uses only the graphical user interface of the tool to provide his/her input and observes the output. The tool extracts all necessary information automatically from the functional model and communicates with ArchE to evaluate the scenarios against the impact graphs derived from the functional model.

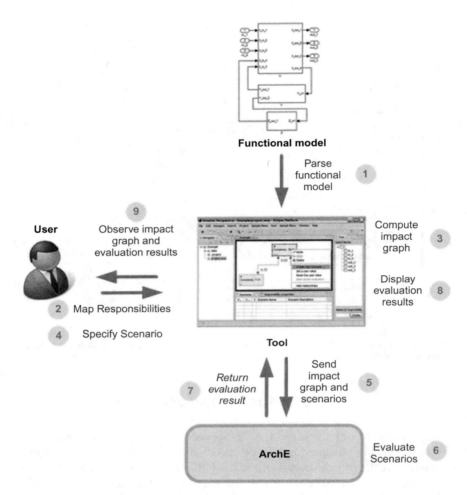

Fig. 21. Architecture and information flow for evaluating modifiability scenarios.

The user begins by specifying the functional model on which nonfunctional properties are to be verified. She does this by choosing a Simulink model file. The tool then parses the block/subsystem hierarchy of the functional model and shows it in a tree structure. On the highest level of the tree structure are also the high-level blocks and subsystems of the functional model.

The user then selects the subsystems that should be represented as responsibilities in the impact graph. By default, the name of the responsibility is chosen to be the name of the subsystem that is mapped to it, but can be modified. Upon creating the responsibility, the tool automatically establishes a mapping between all blocks and connections that are contained in the chosen subsystems. Also, the tool computes the COC for the new responsibility via the MM measure defined earlier, using a settings file that stores all block complexities. Customizing the COC computation to suit a different domain is only a matter of changing the settings file.

If there are at least two responsibilities in the impact graph, the tool determines the relationships and the probabilities of change propagation thereof. Specifically, it determines all relevant signals in the functional model and maps them to the appropriate relationship. Using a graph traversal algorithm, it then computes all blocks that are affected by the relationship and then calculates the PCP using the connectivity metric. The relationships are represented as arrows in the impact graph and are annotated with the PCP values (Fig. 22).

6.1   Creating Scenarios

After the modifiability model has been built, the user can provide the nonfunctional requirements that are to be checked on the models. These nonfunctional requirements are written in the form of quality attribute scenarios. The responsibilities on which the

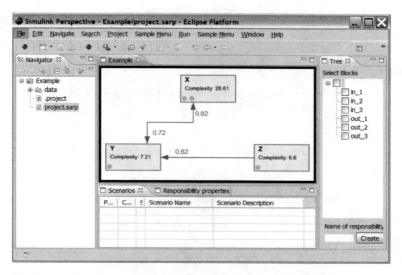

FIG. 22. The user interface of the tool. The center shows the final impact graph of the example functional model.

attributed scenario is to be evaluated are input to the tool. A window then opens up in which other scenario information can be specified (Fig. 23).

The actual verification of the modifiability scenarios is conducted by ArchE. The user starts the verification process by clicking a button. The tool sends the impact graph and scenarios to the ArchE back-end and awaits a response. Upon finishing the evaluation, ArchE sends the results back, and the tool visualizes any violations in the user interface. It also displays an estimate for the modifiability of the current scenario, that is, the number of man-days needed to implement the scenario. An icon indicates whether the quality attribute scenario holds. In the example, the scenario is violated since the change cannot be implemented within 7 days as specified (Fig. 24).

If ArchE has determined that a scenario is violated, the user has several options for resolving the problem. Two of them are lowering the complexity value of the affected responsibility and lowering the PCP. Of course, in order to achieve either one, refactoring is necessary, which can potentially be time consuming. The tool allows the user to

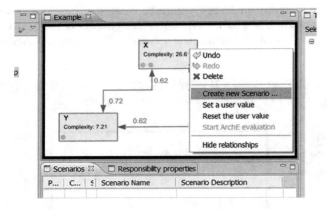

Fig. 23. The user selects one or more responsibilities and creates a scenario.

CurrentValue	Satisfied	Scenario Name	scenario Description
36.304320...	●	Example Scenario	A new input shall be adde...

Fig. 24. Visualization of the evaluation results in the tool.

simulate the refactoring by allowing the user to provide a custom value for both the responsibility complexities and the PCPs. The impact graph and the scenarios can then be evaluated with the custom values. This is a quick solution for finding a setup that satisfies the quality attribute requirements without actually implementing the change.

6.2 Visualization

Depending on the size of the functional model, the impact graph might become quite large, and the diagram might be very crowded with responsibilities and relationships. A few graphical features address this issue. First, to allow the engineer to focus on certain parts of the model, the user has the option to hide all relationships. He or she can then click on one of the responsibilities to show all of its incoming and outgoing relationships. Second, colored dots indicate the number of relationships of each responsibility and their PCP. Each relationship that is connected to the responsibility is represented as a dot. The dots function as traffic lights that indicate if the PCP of the respective relationship is low (green), medium (orange), or high (red). This highlights responsibilities that are affected to a large extent by other responsibilities and can support the user in quickly identifying the areas of the model that might cause problems when evaluating a modifiability scenario.

Figure 25 shows the final impact graph that was created based on mapping the subsystems X, Y, and Z to a responsibility. The relationships and all quantitative characteristics were computed automatically.

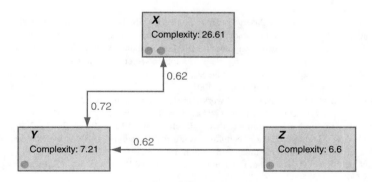

Fig. 25. Impact graph of the example functional model as produced by the tool.

7. Conclusion

This chapter has provided an overview of the latest research done in the automotive software industry on functional and nonfunctional verification and their integration. Ideas detailed in this chapter like IBV have found novel applications in other domains such as medical device software verification.

We have presented our work at industry conferences and one of the insights we obtained was how pervasive the problem of integrated functional and nonfunctional verification was for developers in different corporations and how difficult it was to reconcile artifacts produced during functional design with nonfunctional quality-driven design plans. There were also comments made as to how managers seem to allocate few resources for nonfunctional attribute-driven design verification, essentially expecting the satisfaction of nonfunctional requirements to follow naturally from good functional design practices, whereas it was observed in practically that it was often not the case. Concerns were expressed as to the paucity of industry-standard tools for nonfunctional analysis and to the *ad hoc* subjectiveness and overall expenses incurred by the adoption of methods like ATAM. Given this context, there was considerable interest shown in the approaches adopted in our study.

Future work in this direction will involve further fine-tuning of the calibrations in the extraction process, and continued development of a combined functional/nonfunctional design-time verification workflow. Experimenting with the tool on ongoing modeling efforts will also provide insight into the utility of nonfunctional design verification.

REFERENCES

[1] A. Wayne Wymore, Model-Based Systems Engineering. ISBN 978–0849380129, 1993.
[2] D. Harel, E. Gery, Executable object modeling with statecharts, Proceedings of the 18th international Conference on Software Engineering (Berlin, Germany, March 25–29, 1996), International Conference on Software Engineering, IEEE Computer Society, Washington, DC, pp. 246–257.
[3] High Confidence Software and System Needs, Interagency Working Group in Information Technology Research and Development Report, 2001.
[4] Mathworks Simulik. http://www.mathworks.com/ products/simulink/, 2011.
[5] ASCET. http://www.etas.com/en/products/ ascet_software_products.php, 2011.
[6] Bran Selic, The pragmatics of model-driven development, IEEE Software 20 (5) (2003) 19–25.
[7] D. Kalish, R. Montague, Logic: Techniques of Formal Reasoning. ISBN 978–0195155044, 1980.
[8] A. Meyer, Principles of Functional Verification. ISBN 978–0750676175, 2003.
[9] J. Mylopoulous, E. Yu, B. Nixon, L. Chung, Non-Functional Requirements in Software Engineering. ISBN 978–0792386667, 1999.
[10] T. Gilb, D. Graham, Software Inspection. ISBN: 978–0201631814, 1994.

[11] Y. Ken Wong, Modern Software Review—Techniques and Technologies. ISBN: 978–1599040134, 2006.
[12] E. Clarke. O. Grumberg, D. Pereld, Model Checking. ISBN: 978–0262032704, 1999.
[13] C. Baier, J. Katoen, K. Larsen, Principles of Model Checking. ISBN: 978–0262026499, 2008.
[14] Y. Bertot, P. Casteran, Interactive Theorem Proving. ISBN: 978–3540208549, 2004.
[15] J. Schumann, Automated Theorem Proving in Software Engineering. ISBN: 978–3540679899, 2001.
[16] C. Chang, R. Lee. Symbolic Logic and Mechanical Theorem Proving. ISBN: 978–0121703509, 1973.
[17] J.R. Burch, E.M. Clarke, K.L. McMillan, D.L. Dill, J. Hwang, Symbolic model checking: 10E20 states and beyond. LICS, in: 1990.
[18] E.M. Clarke, O. Grumberg, D.E. Long, Model checking and abstraction, in: Proceedings of the Nineteenth Annual ACM Symposium on Principles of Programming Languages, January 1992, (1992).
[19] E. Clarke, O. Grumberg, D. Long, Verification tools for finite-state concurrent systems, in: A Decade of Concurrency—Reflections and Perspectives, Lecture Notes in Computer Science, vol. 803, 1994.
[20] J. Halpern, M. Vardi, Model checking vs. theorem proving: a manifesto, in: John Mccarthy, V. Lifschitz (Eds.), Artificial Intelligence and Mathematical Theory of Computation, Academic Press Professional, San Diego, CA, 1991, pp. 151–176.
[21] Shankar Owre, J. Rushby, PVS: a prototype verification system, in: CADE 11 Conference Proceedings, 1992.
[22] L. Moura, S. Owre, H. Ruess, J. Rushby, N. Shankar, M. Sorea, et al., SAL 2, Proceedings of Computer Aided Verification CAV, LNCS 3114, Springer Verlag, pp. 496–500, 2004.
[23] J.-C. Gregoire, G.J. Holzmann, D. Peled (Eds.), The Spin Verification System American Mathematical Society, DIMACS Series, vol. 32, 19970-8218-0680-7 203.
[24] R. Iosif, R. Sisto, dSPIN: a dynamic extension of SPIN, in: Proceedings of the 6th SPIN Workshop, LNCS 1680, 1999, pp. 261–276.
[25] J. Woodcock, P.G. Larsen, J. Bicarregui, J. Fitzgerald, Formal methods: practice and experience, ACM Comput. Surv. 41 (4) (2009) 1–36.
[26] Q. Nguyen, Non-functional requirements analysis modeling for software product lines, in: International Workshop on, 2009 ICSE Workshop on Modeling in Software Engineering, 2009, pp. 56–61.
[27] L. Chung, B.A. Nixon, E. Yu, J. Mylopoulos, Non-functional requirements in software engineering, in: V. Basili, M. Zelkowitz (Eds.), International Series in Software Engineering, vol. 5, Springer, 1999, p. 476.
[28] M. Glinz, On non-functional requirements, in: 15th IEEE International Requirements Engineering Conference (RE 2007), (2007), pp. 21–26.
[29] C. Ackermann, A. Ray, R. Cleaveland, J. Heit, C. Shelton, C. Martin, Model-Based Design Verification: A Monitor Based Approach, in: A Monitor Based Approach. Society of Automotive Engineers (SAE) World Congress 2008, Detroit, USA, 2008.
[30] A. Diaz-Pace, H. Kim, L. Bass, P. Bianco, F. Bachmann, Integrating quality-attribute reasoning frameworks in the ArchE design assistant, in: S. Becker, F. Plasil, R. Reussner (Eds.), Proceedings of the 4th international Conference on Quality of Software-Architectures: Models and Architectures, Karlsruhe, Germany, October 14–17, 2008, Lecture Notes in Computer Science, vol. 5281, Springer-Verlag, Berlin, Heidelberg, 2008, pp. 171–188.

[31] A. Bakshi, MILAN: a model based integrated simulation framework for design of embedded systems, in: ACM SIGPLAN 2001 Workshop on Languages, Compilers, and Tools for Embedded Systems, 2001.

[32] Felix Bachmann, Len Bass, Mark Klein, Preliminary Design of ArchE: A Software Architecture Design Assistant (CMU/SEI-2003-TR-021), 2003.

[33] Rick Kazman, Mark Klein, Mario Barbacci, Howard Lipson, Thomas Longstaff, S. Jeromy Carrière, Architecture tradeoff analysis method, in: Proceedings of ICECCS, Monterey, CA, August 1998, 1998.

[34] R. Kazman, L. Bass, M. Klein, T. Lattanze, L. Northrop, A basis for evaluating software architecture analysis methods, Software Qual. J. 13 (2005) 329–335.

[35] J. Takahashi, Y. Kakuda, Extended model-based testing toward high code coverage rate, in: J. Kontio, R. Conradi (Eds.), Proceedings of the 7th international Conference on Software Quality (June 09–13, 2002), Lecture Notes in Computer Science, vol. 2349, Springer-Verlag, London, 2002, pp. 310–320.

[36] Reactive Systems Inc. http://reactive-systems.com, 2011.

[37] S. Owicki, L. Lamport, Proving liveness properties of concurrent programs, ACM Trans. Prog. Lang. Syst. 4 (3) (1982) 455–495.

[38] D. Gabbay, I. Hodkinson, M. Reynolds, M. Finger, Temporal Logic: Mathematical Foundations and Computational Aspects, Clarendon Press, 2000, ISBN 978-0198537694.

[39] S. Kim, D. Kim, L. Lu, S. Park, Quality-driven architecture development using architectural tactics, J. Syst. Software 82 (8) (2009) 1211–1231.

[40] L. Bass, J. Ivers, M. Klein, P. Merson, K. Wallnau, Encapsulating quality attribute knowledge, in: Proceedings of the 5th Working IEEE/IFIP Conference on Software, Architecture, November 06–10, 2005, 2005.

[41] C. Shelton, C. Martin, Using models to improve the availability of automotive software architectures, ICSE Workshops SEAS '07, IEEE, 20–26 May 2007 (2007) 9–19.

[42] Felix Bachmann, Len Bass, Mark Klein, Charles Shelton, Designing software architectures to achieve quality attribute requirements, in: IEEE Proceedings on Software, August 2005, (2005), pp. 153–165.

[43] Lev Vitkin, Susan Dong, Rick Searcey, B.C. Manjunath, Effort estimation in model-based software development, in: Society for Automotive Engineers World Congress 2006, 2006.

ABOUT THE AUTHOR

Arnab Ray is a research scientist at Fraunhofer Center for Experimental Software Engineering located in College Park, MD, USA. He received a bachelor of engineering in computer science and engineering from Jadavpur University and a Ph.D. in computer science from State University of New York in Stonybrook in 2004. His research interests include application of model-based development techniques to the engineering of high-confidence software and their application to automotive and medical domains, formal methods, and computer security. He also holds an adjunct assistant professor position at the University of Maryland at College Park and has been a National Science Foundation funded Scholar-in-Residence at the Food and Drug Administration.

Christopher Ackermann is a research scientist at the Fraunhofer USA—Center for Experimental Software Engineering in College Park, MD, USA. Christopher received a Bachelor's Degree from the University of Applied Sciences in Mannheim, Germany and a master's degree as well as a Ph.D. from the University of Maryland. In the past, he has been involved in a variety of projects concerning software architecture analysis, model-based verification, visualization, and empirical studies. Working closely with practitioners, Christopher has experience in transferring knowledge and technologies from academia to industry. His current research focuses mainly on the architecture analysis especially of distributed systems from a behavioral perspective with the goal to address maintainability and reliability concerns.

Rance Cleaveland is professor of computer science at the University of Maryland at College Park, where he is also executive and scientific director of the Fraunhofer USA Center for Experimental and Software Engineering. Before joining Maryland in 2005, he held professorships at the State University of New York at Stony Brook and at North Carolina State University. He also cofounded Reactive Systems, Inc., in 1999 to commercialize tools for model-based testing of embedded software. In 1992, he received Young Investigator Awards from the National Science Foundation and from the Office of Naval Research. He has published over 100 papers in the areas of software verification and validation, formal methods, model checking, software specification formalisms, and verification tools. Cleaveland received B.S. degrees in mathematics and computer science from Duke University and M.S. and Ph.D. degrees from Cornell University.

Charles Shelton is a senior research engineer at the Robert Bosch Research and Technology Center located in Pittsburgh, PA, USA. He received a bachelor of science in computer engineering from the University of Maryland Baltimore County in 1998, and a master's degree and a Ph.D. in computer engineering from Carnegie Mellon University in 2000 and 2003, respectively. He has been a researcher at Bosch focusing on the topics of software engineering and software architecture since he received his Ph.D. in 2003. His current work focuses on improving software designs and architectures by developing software tools that can automatically analyze and optimize software models to remove unused or unnecessary calculations and information.

Christopher Martin is currently a senior manager at Robert Bosch Corporate Research in Stuttgart, Germany. After graduating from the Carngie Mellon University Department of Electrical and Computer Engineering with a bachelor's degree in 2000 and a master's degree in 2001, Chris was one of the initial members of the Robert Bosch Research and Technology Center (RTC) in Pittsburgh, PA, USA, which was Bosch's first foray into advanced research and development in the USA. Over the past 10 years, he has been active in the area of networked embedded systems in the automotive and building technology domains. Since 2005, he has lead research groups (first in the USA and currently in Germany) that focus on the impact of standardized information technology on traditional embedded systems. He also serves as an FP7 Expert in Information and Communication Technology (ICT) and in this role acts as an expert reviewer for the CESAR project ("Cost efficient methods and processes for safety-relevant embedded systems").

Author Index

Note: The letters '*f*' and '*t*' following the locators refer to figures and tables respectively.

A

Abadi, M., 131
Abdi, H., 184
Abhimanyu, J., 134, 138, 155, 159
Abraham, D., 126, 149
Abrahamsson, P., 220, 223*t*
Ackermann, C., 280
Adelson, E., 191–192
Ahmad Salah El, A., 151
Albert, N., 184
Ali, M., 126
Alur, D., 228
Amalia, R., 135, 155
Anda, B.C.D., 243, 250, 251–253, 265
Anderson, R., 84
Arandjelovic, O., 186, 187
Areekal, A.U., 139
Argyris, C., 208, 214
Arias, T.A., 191*t*
Arnold, M., 53–55
Arturo, R., 166
Artz, D., 61–62, 84
Ashish, J., 134, 138, 155, 159
Avcıbaş, I., 87, 88
Avison, D.E., 209, 215, 217, 221*t*

B

Bachmann, F., 280, 284, 296
Badoo, N., 207
Baier, C., 279
Bailey, K., 63, 84, 85, 86–87

Baird, H.S., 114, 131–132, 135, 137, 152
Bakshi, A., 282–283
Ballantyne, D., 255, 258–259
Bang, X., 142
Barbacci, M., 284
Barni, M., 55
Barret, F.J., 211
Barry, E., 207
Bartolini, F., 55
Basili, V.R., 207, 231, 266–267
Baskerville, R.L., 208, 209, 214*f*, 217, 220, 221*t*, 242, 243*f*, 254, 266–267
Basri, R., 186
Bass, L., 226, 280, 284, 296
Basso, A., 121–123, 140, 158
Bauer, F.L., 52, 53–55, 54*f*, 56–58
Bazzi, R., 133–134
Beck, K., 246–248, 249
Bengtsson, P., 223*t*
Bennet, K.H., 228
Bentley, J.L., 135, 137, 152
Bertot, Y., 279
Bhanu, B., 191–192
Bharata, K., 131
Bianco, P., 280
Bicarregui, J., 279
Biffl, S., 207
Bigham, J.P., 153
Bissacco, A., 187
Blum, M., 117, 125, 126, 131, 149
Bobick, A.F., 191–192, 196

Boehm, B.W., 261
Bosch, J., 223*t*
Bowyer, K.W., 191–192, 196, 199, 200
Bradbury, D., 165
Bradbury, H., 208–209, 211, 212
Brant, J., 246–248, 249
Brereton, P., 207, 208, 250
Broder, A.Z., 131
Budgen, D., 207, 208, 250
Burch, J.R., 279
Burns, A., 209, 213*f*, 263*t*
Burton, J., 223*t*

C

Caldiera, G., 231, 266–267
Callinan, J., 100–101
Canfora, G., 223*t*
Carlos Javier, H.-C., 166
Carrière, S.J., 284
Carr, W., 208–209, 212
Carver, J., 207
Casner, S., 83
Casteran, P., 279
Cavender, A.C., 153
Celine, F., 149–150, 171
Chandavale, A.A., 162
Chandramouli, R.A., 85, 86
Chang, C., 135, 279
Chang, E., 93
Chao, Y., 163
Charters, S.M., 207, 208, 250
Checkland, P., 215, 216*f*, 254
Chellappa, R., 186, 187, 189, 190, 191*t*, 194*f*,
    196, 197*f*, 198, 199, 200
Chen-Chi, W., 151
Chen, K.-T., 172
Chen, T., 186
Chen, W.-C., 172
Chew, M., 132, 138, 143, 156, 158
Chien-Ju, H., 151
Chikuse, Y., 190
Chilin, S., 144

Chin-Luang, L., 151
Chiuso, A., 187, 188
Chi-Wei, L., 162
Chu, H.-H., 172
Chung, L., 279, 280
Cipolla, R., 186, 187
Clarke, E.M., 279
Claypoole, R.L., 86, 87, 88
Cleaveland, R., 280
Clinton, H., 58–61, 59*f*, 60*f*
Coates, A.L., 114, 131–132
Cock, K.D., 188
Collins, R.T., 191–192
Cooperrider, D.L., 211
Corbin, J., 242
Crupi, J., 228
Cuntoor, N.P., 191–192, 199, 200
Curran, K., 63, 84, 85, 86–87

D

Dalley, G., 191–192
Damian, D., 206–207, 211–212
Dancho, D., 165
Daniel, L., 119, 144, 160
Dan, J., 149–150, 171
Darrell, T., 186
Datta, R., 139
Davis, J.W., 191–192
Davis, M., 55
Davison, R.M., 209, 215–217, 217*f*, 218,
    220, 221*t*, 266–267
Da, Z., 142–143
Delp, E.J., 55
Desai, A., 140
Diaz-Pace, A., 280
Dick, B., 208–209
Dill, D.L., 279
Dittmann, J., 82
Docimo, R., 140
Dominique, S., 149
Dong, S., 302

Doretto, G., 187, 188
Douceur, J.R., 127, 136
Ducheneaut, N., 172
Dunsmore, A., 230, 233, 244t, 249, 252t
Du, R., 75, 87, 88
Duren, M., 55
Duric, Z., 53, 82, 84
Dwork, C., 171–172
Dybå, T., 207, 208, 209, 219, 243, 250, 251–253, 265, 270

E

Easterbrook, S., 206–207, 211–212
Edelman, A., 191t
Eggers, J.J., 99
El Ahmad, A.S., 162, 169
Elbaum, S., 207, 249
Elias, A., 143
Elie, B., 149–150, 171
El-Khalil hydan, R., 73
El-Khalil, R., 73
Elson, J., 127, 136
Enfinger, F., 101
Evered, R.D., 209, 215–217

F

Falbo, R.A., 262
Fan, W., 186
Farid, H., 87, 88
Faternan, R.J., 114, 131–132
Feng, W., 171–172
Fernández-Medina, E., 223t
Ferzli, R., 133–134
Finger, M., 294–295
Fisher, J.W., 186
Fitzgerald, B., 223t
Fitzgerald, J., 279
Forner-Cordero, A., 192–193
Foster, J., 191–192
Foth, M., 255
Fowler, M., 246–248, 249

Frederick, R., 83
Fridrich, J., 75, 85, 86, 87–88
Fries, B., 64–65, 66t
Fries, M., 64–65, 66t

G

Gabbay, D., 294–295
Gaj, K., 139
Garcia, F., 223t
Gery, E., 279
Gilb, T., 279
Glass, R.L., 208, 220
Glinz, M., 280
Godfrey, M.W., 162, 163
Godfrey, P.B., 145
Goldberg, A., 171–172
Goljan, M., 85, 86, 87–88
Golle, P., 136, 163, 172
Görg, C., 249
Govindaraju, V., 135
Graham, D., 279
Graig, S., 152
Greenwood, D.J., 212
Greg Kochanski, D., 144
Gregoire, J.-C., 279
Gritzalis, D., 144, 170
Grossman, J., 123
Gross, R., 191–192
Grother, P., 191–192, 196, 199, 200
Grover, A., 17
Grumberg, D., 279
Grumberg, O., 279
Guba, E.G., 211
Gunsch, G.H., 86, 87, 88
Gupta, A., 134, 159
Gutierrez, C., 223t

H

Hall, T., 208
Halpern, J., 279
Hamm, J., 186
Han, J., 191–192

Hannay, J.E., 207, 219–220, 221*t*, 243, 250,
    251–253, 265
Hansen, H.W., 223*t*
Hansen, O., 207, 219–220, 221*t*
Harel, D., 279
Harkless, C., 131, 162, 163
Harrison, R., 207
Harry, H., 152
Hathaway, R.S., 211
Hayati, P., 93
Healy, M., 212, 213*f*
Hearn, G., 255
Heatwole, C.G., 254–255
Heit, J., 280
Henningsson, K., 207
Hernandez-Castro, C.J., 117,
    163–164
Heydon, A., 123, 166
Higgs, J., 263*t*
Hindle, A., 162, 163
Hodkinson, I., 294–295
Höfer, A., 207
Hogea, D., 85, 86, 87–88
Hoisl, B., 267
Ho, J., 186–187
Holter, I.M., 255, 262–263
Holt, R.C., 162, 163
Holwell, S., 215, 216*f*, 254
Holzmann, G.J., 279
Honeyman, P., 64, 86, 87, 88,
    100–101
Hopper, N.J., 113, 116
Hoque, M.E., 140
Hosmer, C., 53, 55, 101, 102
Höst, M., 207
Howell, J., 127, 136
Huang, P., 172
Hutchens, D.H., 207
Hu, W., 191–192
Hwang, J., 279
Hwan-Gue, C., 132
Hyde, C., 53, 101, 102
Hyungil, K., 172

I

Ilker, Y., 132
Imsamai, M., 140
Ince, I.F., 132, 141
Inch, S., 74
Iosif, R., 279
Iulian, C., 120, 132
Ivers, J., 296

J

Jackson, J.T., 86, 87, 88
Jacobs, D., 186
Jacobson, V., 83
Jagielska, D., 208
Jajodia, S.G., 53, 63, 64, 69, 71, 82, 84,
    86–87
Jalnekar, R.M., 162
Jeff, Y., 151, 163
Jennifer, T., 163
Jia, L., 139, 163
Jiang, J.-W., 172
Jing-Song, C., 142–143
Jing-Ting, M., 142–143
Jinjuan, F., 152
Jinjuan Heidi, F., 154
Jiri, S., 163
Joaquim, C., 144–145
John, C., 124
John, D.A., 154
John, L., 113, 116
Johnson, N.F., 53, 63, 64, 69, 71, 82, 84,
    86–87
Johnson, R.D., 223*t*
Jonathan, H., 154
Jonathan, L., 152, 154
Jonathan, W., 149, 158, 162, 166–168
Jones, M., 263*t*
Jones, N., 131, 162, 163
Jørgensen, M., 208, 209, 219, 270
Jose Maria Gomez, H., 125, 172
Joseph, F., 172–173
Joseph, W., 112

Josh, B., 120, 132
Juang, B., 192
Julien, C., 120, 132
Juntae, K., 172
Juristo, N., 207

K

Kahn, D., 53, 61, 86
Kaiser, E., 171–172
Kakuda, Y., 284–285
Kale, A., 191–192, 199, 200
Kalinowski, M., 227
Kalish, D., 279
Kampenes, V.B., 207, 219–220, 221t
Karahasanović, A., 207, 219–220, 221t
Karam, L.J., 133–134
Kates, S., 255, 264
Katoen, J., 279
Kauppinen, M., 223t
Kautz, K., 223t
Kazman, R., 226, 284
Keller, L.F., 254–255
Kelly, J., 100–101
Kemick, D., 100–101
Kemmis, S., 212
Kemp, R., 184
Kendall, D.G., 193
Keromytis, A.D., 73
Kessler, G.C., 69, 71, 74
Kevin, L., 146–147, 152
Kim, D., 296
Kim, H., 280
Kim, S., 296
Kim, T.K., 186
Kitchenham, B.A., 207, 208, 250
Kittler, J., 186
Klein, M., 284, 296
Kock, N., 209, 215–217, 217f, 218, 220, 221t, 266–267
Kolata, G., 100–101
Kolupaev, A., 169
Kontio, J., 223t

Koopman, H., 192–193
Koskela, J., 220, 223t
Krätzer, C., 82
Krauss, S.E., 212–213
Kriegman, D., 186–187
Kruger, V., 191–192, 199, 200
Kuan-Ta, C., 151
Kühne, T., 82
Kuhn, M.G., 84
Kujala, S., 223t
Kumar, C., 132, 146–147, 152, 162
Kurt Alfred, K., 143, 152
Kutter, M., 99
Kwok, S.H., 55

L

Lamont, G.B., 86, 87, 88
Lamport, L., 294–295
Lang, A., 82
Langford, J., 117, 125, 131
Larsen, K., 279
Larsen, P.G., 279
Lattanze, T., 284
Latum, F., 267
Lau, F., 209, 215, 220, 221t, 244t, 254–255
Laura, D., 127, 137, 143, 156
Lee, D.D., 186
Lee, K.C., 186–187
Lee, L., 191–192
Lee, R., 279
Lei, C.-L., 172
Levin, M., 212
Lewis, S., 82
Liang-Gee, C., 162
Liao, W.H., 135
Liborg, N.-K., 207, 219–220, 221t
Lillibridge, M.D., 131
Lincoln, Y.S., 211
Lindqvist, J., 144
Lindvall, M., 223t, 256–257, 259, 260
Lings, B., 223t
Linkman, S.G., 207, 208, 250

Lior, G., 149
Lipson, H., 284
Liu, X., 186
Liu, Z., 191–192, 196, 199, 200, 200*t*
Loebner, H.G., 112
Long, D.E., 279
Longe, O.B., 120, 127–128
Longstaff, T., 284
Ludema, J.D., 211
Luis Von, A., 163
Lu, L., 296
Lundell, B., 223*t*
Lupkowski, P., 146
Lusha, W., 152, 154
Lycett, M., 223*t*
Lyu, S., 88

M

Maiden, N., 223*t*
Malik, J., 131, 160–161, 161*f*
Malks, D., 228
Manjunath, B.C., 302
Manolakis, D., 195
Manoo, F., 100–101
Mäntylä, M.V., 230–231, 232, 233, 234, 235,
   246–248, 249, 252*t*, 253
Manuel, B., 113, 116
Marc, F., 149
Marcial, F., 144–145
Markkola, A., 144
Markus, J., 152, 154
Marshall, P., 254–255, 264*f*, 266*f*
Martin, C., 280, 296
Martin, J.R.H., 99
Martinsons, M.G., 209, 215–217, 217*f*, 218,
   220, 221*t*, 266–267
Maryam, K., 140
Mary, C., 146–147, 152
Mathiassen, L., 223*t*
Mattsson, A., 223*t*
Maurer, B., 126, 149
Ma, Y., 187

May, M., 152–153
Mazurczyk, W., 83
McCaffery, F., 223*t*
McCullagh, D., 88, 101
McDonald, A.D., 84
McKay, J., 254–255, 264*f*, 266*f*
McMillan, K.L., 279
McMillen, C., 126, 149
Meding, W., 223*t*
Memon, N., 87, 88
Menezes, A.J., 118
Menezes, C.S., 262
Mens, T., 229, 249
Merson, P., 296
Mews, K., 223*t*
Meyer, A., 279
Meyer, J.E., 255
Michael, L., 149
Misra, D., 139
Mitchell, J.C., 149–150, 171
Moll, M.A., 132
Montague, R., 279
Montgomery, D., 100–101
Moor, B.D., 188
Moreno, A.M., 207
Morgenthaler, J.D., 249
Mori, G., 131, 160–161, 161*f*
Moura, L., 279
Movaghar, A., 145
Moy, G., 131, 162, 163
Murdoch, S.J., 82
Myers, M.D., 209, 215, 217, 221*t*, 244*t*
Mylopoulus, J., 279, 280

N

Najork, M., 123, 166
Naor, M., 112, 171–172
Napier, N.P., 223*t*
Näslund, D., 213, 255
Needham, R., 84
Nelson, B., 101
Newman, R.C., 81–82

Nguyen, Q., 280
Niedzialkowski, T., 123
Nielsen, P.A., 209, 215, 221*t*, 223*t*, 244*t*
Nilsson, C., 223*t*
Ning, H., 191–192
Ning, X., 163
Nishigaki, M., 146
Nixon, B.A., 279, 280
Nixon, M., 191–192
Niyogi, S., 191–192
Northrop, L., 284

O

Ogijenko, J., 169
Ohlsson, M.C., 207
Oivo, M., 267
O'Kane, T., 223*t*
Onwudebelu, U., 120, 127–128
Opdyke, W., 246–248, 249
O'Toole, A.J., 184
Ottosson, S., 255
Overschee, P.V., 188
Owicki, S., 294–295
Owre, S., 279
Özer, H., 87, 88

P

Pablo, X., 144–145
Pahwa, T., 134, 138, 155, 159
Paolo, B., 125, 172
Pardo, C., 223*t*
Park, S., 296
Parnin, C., 249
Parra, A., 207
Patadia, P., 140
Patrice, S., 146–147, 152
Paul, B., 149
Peled, D., 279
Penix, J., 249
Pereira, S., 99
Pereld, D., 279
Perry, C., 212, 213*f*

Petitcolas, F.A.P., 99–100
Pfleeger, S.H., 208
Philippe, G., 152, 154
Phillips, A., 101
Phillips, K., 184
Phillips, P.J., 191–192, 196, 199, 200
Phimoltares, S., 140
Piattini, M., 223*t*
Pike, G., 184
Pino, F.J., 223*t*
Podilchuk, C.I., 55
Polanyi, M., 270
Polo, M., 223*t*
Potdar, V., 93
Potter, R., 131, 162, 163
Pries-Heje, J., 242, 243*f*, 266–267
Proakis, J., 195
Provos, N., 64, 86, 87, 88, 100–101
Prugel-Bennett, A., 191–192
Pun, T., 99
Putnam, R., 208, 214

Q

Qiujie, L., 163

R

Rabiner, L., 192
Rainer, A., 208
Raj, A., 134, 138, 155, 159
Rajagopalan, A.N., 191–192, 199, 200
Rajlich, V.T., 228
Ramesh, V., 220
Ray, A., 280
Reason, P., 208–209, 211, 212
Regnell, B., 207
Reynolds, M., 294–295
Rey, R.F., 64–65
Ribagorda, A., 117, 163–164
Ricardo, B.-Y., 125, 145, 172
Richard, C., 152, 154
Richard, S., 120, 132
Richardson, I., 223*t*

Richard, Z., 143, 152
Rich, G., 140
Riopka, T.P., 132
Roark, D., 184
Robert, A.B.C., 120, 127–128
Robert, L., 149
Roberts, D., 246–248, 249
Robertson, J., 255, 264
Robertson, S., 223t
Rob, T., 146, 157
Rocha, A.R.C., 262
Rombach, H.D., 231, 266–267
Roper, M., 230, 233, 244t, 249, 252t
Rosado, D.G., 223t
Rothermel, G., 249
Rowland, C.H., 82
Roy-Chowdhury, A.K., 187, 191–192, 194f,
    196, 197f, 199, 200
Rubin, N., 184
Ruess, H., 279
Ruhe, G., 267
Ruiz, F., 223t
Runeson, P., 207
Rushby, J., 279
Rus, I., 256–257, 259, 260
Russomanno, D.J., 140
Rusu, A., 135, 140
Ruthruff, J.R., 249

S

Saisan, P., 188
Sajad, S.-S., 126
Salman, Y.B., 132, 141
Salo, O., 223t
Sandahl, K., 223t
Sankur, B., 87, 88
Santos, A., 144–145
Santos, P.S.M., 219, 264
Sapkal, A.M., 162
Sarkar, S., 191–192, 196, 199, 200, 200t
Saul, J., 127, 136
Schein, E.H., 259

Schmucker, M., 53–55
Schulzrinne, H., 83
Schumann, J., 279
Schwartz-Barcott, D., 255, 262–263
Seaman, B.C., 213
Sean, H., 163
Searcey, R., 302
Searle, J.R., 112
Selby, R.W., 207
Selic, B., 279
Seward, J., 101
Shactman, N., 100–101
Shakhnarovich, G., 186
Shamir, A., 84
Shankar, N., 279
Shapiro, S.C., 116–117
Shelton, C., 280, 296
Shieber, S.M., 112
Shi, J., 191–192
Shirali-Shahreza, M.H., 126, 137, 139,
    140, 142–143, 145, 154
Shirali-Shahreza, S., 137, 139, 142–143,
    145, 154
Shull, F., 207
Shumeet, B., 140
Sicco, S., 121–123, 140, 158
Simard, P.Y., 120, 132, 162
Simmons, G.J., 85
Singer, J., 206–207, 211–212, 223t
Sisto, R., 279
Sjøberg, D.I.K., 207, 208, 209, 219–220,
    221t, 243, 250, 251–253, 265, 270
Smith, D.M., 208, 214
Smith, S.T., 191t
Soatto, S., 187, 188
Solingen, R., 267
Sorea, M., 279
Soukal, D., 85, 86, 87–88
Soupionis, Y., 144, 170
Spiros, A., 143
Srivastava, A., 189, 190, 191t, 196, 198
Staron, M., 223t
Stefan, K., 145

Steuart, C., 101
Steven, B., 149–150, 171
Stewart, D., 223*t*
Stone, J., 184
Storey, M.-A., 206–207, 211–212
Strauss, A., 242
Striletchi, C., 171
Stubblebine, S., 172
Sui-Yu, W., 132, 135, 152
Su, J.K., 99
Sulonen, R., 223*t*
Sundaresan, A., 191–192, 199, 200
Sungwoo, H., 172
Susman, G.L., 209, 215–217
Szczypiorski, K., 83

T

Tae-Cheon, Y., 132, 141
Takahashi, J., 284–285
Tanawongsuwan, R., 196
Tan, T., 191–192
Thaysen, K., 223*t*
Thiollent, M., 214, 217
Thomas, A.O., 135
Thornton, S.M., 186
Tichy, W.F., 207
Tieu, K., 191–192
Tjørnehøj, G., 223*t*
Tolliver, D., 191–192
Tourwe, T., 229, 249
Towell, N., 184
Travassos, G.H., 207, 219, 227, 264
Tripp, D., 218
Turaga, P., 189, 190, 191*t*, 198
Turing, A.M., 111–112
Turner, M., 207, 208, 250
Tygar, J.D., 138, 143, 146, 156, 158

U

Ullman, S., 184
Urbanski, M., 146

V

Vaida, M.F., 171
Van der Helm, F., 192–193
van Oorschot, P.C., 118, 172
Vanstone, S.A., 118
Vardi, M., 279
Vartiainen, M., 223*t*
Veeraraghavan, A., 187, 189, 190, 191*t*,
    194*f*, 196, 197*f*, 198, 199, 200
Vega, I.R., 191–192, 196, 199, 200
Venu, G., 135, 155
Vessey, I., 220
Vigder, M., 223*t*
Vimina, E.R., 139
Vincent, C., 172–173
Vinson, N.G., 223*t*
Visaggio, C.A., 223*t*
Vitkin, L., 302
Voloshynovskiy, S., 99
von Ahn, L., 113, 116, 117, 125, 126, 127,
    131, 137, 143, 149, 156

W

Wallnau, K., 296
Wamsley, G.L., 254–255
Wang, J.Z., 139
Wang, L., 191–192
Wang, S., 132
Warner, O., 127
Wayner, P., 53, 69, 71, 85, 87
Welch, T.A., 77
Wen-Hung, L., 140
Wenjun, Z., 139
Wesslén, A., 207
Westbrooke, R., 255
Winter, B., 207
Wöhlin, C., 207
Wolthusen, S.D., 53–55
Wong, Y.K., 279
Woodcock, J., 279
Wood-Harper, A.T., 208, 209, 220

Wood, M., 230, 233, 244*t*, 249, 252*t*
Wu, Y.N., 187, 188
Wu-Zhou, Z., 142–143
Wymore, A.W., 279

X

XiaoFeng, W., 152, 154
Xia, W., 142–143

Y

Yago, S., 166
Yamamoto, T., 146
Yang, M.H., 186–187
Yang, P., 142

Yan, J., 116, 126, 162, 165, 169, 172
Yeasin, M., 140
Yeung, D.-Y., 186
Yildirim, M.E., 141
Yong, R., 140
Yu, E., 279, 280
Yu-Han, C., 162
Yu, L., 142

Z

Zelkowitz, M.V., 207
Zhu, B.B., 163
Zicheg, L., 140

Subject Index

A

Action Research, software engineering.
  See also Software engineering
  adherence levels, 220–222, 221*t*, 222*t*
  application
    decisions, researcher, 254
    ethical issues, 254–255, 260–261
    learning and difficulties, 256–258
    management, interventions, 258–260
    rigor and results relevance, 266–267
    self-changing process, 254
    template study report, 267–269
    theories, building, 261–265
    ''win-win'' scenario, 254
  canonical process, 217*f*
  characteristics, 218
  client-system infrastructure, 217
  contract/agreement, 217
  definition, 214
  execution
    control structures, 224
    extraction, information, 224
    length, studies, 225
    papers, classification, 225*f*
    qualitative and quantitative data,
      224–225
  hypothesis refutation, 214–215
  in vivo study
    actions, 234–235
    diagnosis, 226–229
    evaluation and analysis, 235–243
    planning, 229–234
    reflections and learning, 243–253

    source code refactoring, 225–226
    template structure, 226
  iteration and adaptation, stages, 218
  literature survey, 219
  method
    journal and conferences, 219–220
    research papers, 220
    terms, search, 220
  Natural Sciences-process comparison,
    216*f*
  publication distribution, 220–222
  researcher, transformations, 215
  research methodology, elements, 215
  research topics and contexts
    classification formats, 224
    IEEE taxonomy, 223*t*
  stages, 215–217
  two-stage simplified process, 214*f*
AI. *See* Artificial intelligence
Anti-phishing measures, 37–41
Anti-phishing working group (APWG),
  14–15
Anti-spoofing measures, 41–42
Artificial intelligence (AI). *See also* Attacks,
  CAPTCHA
  attacks, 158, 160–164
  Loebner Prize, 112
  problem, 116
  puzzle, 118
ATM transactions, 35
Attacks, CAPTCHA
  AI
    cognitive CAPTCHA, 163–164

Attacks, CAPTCHA (Continued)
    description, 160
    EZ-Gimpy challenge, break, 160–161,
      161*f*
    IMAGINATION CAPTCHA, 163, 164*f*
    individual characters, 162–163
    open source packages, 164
    reCAPTCHA, 162
    segmentation, 162
    shape recognition techniques, 161–162
    blind guessing
      classification, 158
      dictionary, 158–159
      image collage CAPTCHA, 159
      Pictionary attack, 159
    relay
      cost-effectiveness, 165–166
      human "recognizer", 165
      machines as human, 164–165
      MMORPGs cheating, 165
    side-channel, 166–168
Autoregressive and moving average
    (ARMA) model, 187, 188, 195–196
Autoregressive (AR) model, 195

B

Bitmap (BMP) image, 64

C

CAPTCHA. *See* Completely automated
    public Turing test to tell computers and
    humans apart
CardSleuth
    credential management and control, 32*f*
    description, 31
    ID scan, 32, 33*f*
COC. *See* Cost of change
Completely automated public Turing test to
    tell computers and humans apart
    (CAPTCHA)
    AI, 110
    alternatives

Akismet, 172
    failed logins, 172
    handling functions, 171
    "postage" approach, 171–172
    solutions, groups, 171
    Turing Trade, 172–173
applications and robots
    abusers, 126
    Asirra CAPTCHA, 129*f*
    collateral, 126–127
    goals, 122–123
    human and machine users, 122
    KittenAuth CAPTCHA, 128*f*
    legitimate purposes, 123–124
    malicious activities, 124–126
    security service, 126
    Web robots, 121–122
attacks
    AI, 160–164
    blind guessing, 158–159
    relay, 164–166
    side-channel, 166–168
audio, 143–144
cognitive, 144–146
description
    AI problems, 116–117
    computational problems, 117
    goal, 116
    random values, 117
evaluation
    accessibility problems, 152–154
    advertisement-based CAPTCHA, 156
    audio CAPTCHAs, 155
    automated and economical challenge,
      154
    challenges, 154–155
    databases, 155–156
    efficiency, 147–152
    practicality, 156
    requirement groups, 147
    trade-off, 146–147
false positive/machine recognition, 157
human recognition rate, 157

image
  2D, 135–140
  3D, 140–141
  video, 142–143
implementation and deployment
  generation, test instance, 120
  reCAPTCHA, 120–121
  steps, Generalized Classical CAPTCHA
    algorithm, 120
  Web form, protection, 119–120
multiple challenge-response system
    (M-CR CAPTCHA), 127–128
OCR
  AltaVista, 131
  arcs, 132, 133f
  BaffleText, 132, 133f
  challenges, 130
  choices, 130–131
  GIMPY, 131, 132f
  handwritten text, 135, 136f
  masking, 133–134, 134f
  PessimalPrint, 131–132
  sequenced tagged CAPTCHA, 134,
    135f
properties
  automated system, 119
  Internet environments, 117
  security purposes, 117–119
protection scheme, 158
security requirements
  audio, 170
  counter-measures, OCR, 169
  human and bot recognition rates,
    169–170
  local and global random warp, 169
  NuCaptcha, 170
  penetration tester, 170
Semantic Networks, 111
Turing test and origin
  advertising, 115, 115f
  AltaVista search engine, 113–114
  bots, chat rooms, 114
  differences, Naor's proposal, 113

EZ-GIMPY, 114, 114f
"imitation game", 111–112
Naor's humanity test, 112
popularization, 115
problems, collection, 112–113
reCAPTCHA, 115f
reverse, 111–112
vision and natural language processing,
    113
Weizenbaum's Eliza, 112
World Wide Web-related industry,
    114–115
verification requests, 157
visual and nonvisual, 127, 130f
Convert communication channel
stego and protocols
  cryptography methods, 81
  description, 80
  organization security policies,
    81–82
  TCP, 82
  WLANs, 82
streaming channels
  jamming attack, 82
  VoIP, 82
  WetStone Technology, 82–83
VoIP-based steganography
  data loss and corruption issue, 83–84
  error correction, 83
  RTP, 83
  ubiquitous proliferation, 84
Cost of change (COC)
  architecture design, 300
  computation, 311
  definition, 297
  evaluation function, 299
  impact graph, 297
  modifiability metric, 302–307

D

Department of motor vehicle (DMV), 13
Digital carrier files

Digital carrier files (Continued)
  color palette modification
    anomalies, 78
    binary values, 79*f*
    24-bit RGB array, 77–78
    close color pairs, 78, 79
    file size and color buddies, 77
    Gif-It-Up, 75–76
    Lempel–Ziv–Welch (LZW)
      compression, 77
    sorted, 79*f*
    steganography, 76–77, 77*f*
    stego carrier image, 78*f*
    Washington mall carrier file, 76, 76*f*
  convert communication channel
    stego and protocols, 80–82
    streaming channels, 82–83
    VoIP-based steganography, 83–84
  data appending, 73–75
  encoding algorithm modification, 71
  format modification
    description, 79–80
    Snow, 80, 81*f*
  grammar selection
    phrases and clauses, 71
    spammimic.com, 72, 73
    stego, 71–72
  image and audio, 67
  LSB overwriting
    ASCII and IA5, 68
    description, 68
    GIF image file, 69*f*
    RGB color, 68
    S-Tools, 69
    WAV carrier file signal level
      comparison, 70*f*
Digital technology basics, steganography
  audio
    analog signals, 65
    analog-to-digital conversion, 64
    bit rate, uncompressed music, 65–66
    digital formats, 66*t*

    encoding description, 64
    PCM, 64–65, 65*f*
  images and color
    24-bit true, 64
    intensity levels RGB, 63, 63*f*
    JPEG, 64
    palettes and 8-bit, 64
    red–green–blue (RGB) color cube,
      62–63, 62*f*
  payload compression
    randomized, 66–67, 68*f*
    size reduction, 66
    S-tools, 67*f*
Digital watermarking, 55
Dynamic time warping (DTW)
  programming, 193
  temporal and test vector sequences,
    192–193
  walking cycle shape sequence,
    193, 194*f*

E

Embedded software systems
  challenges, model-based design
    verification, 279–280
  design phase, 279
  functional verification
    definition, 282
    hardware-in-the-loop testing, 282
    model structure, 283*f*
    techniques, 282–283
  IBV. *See* Instrumentation-based
    verification
  integrated functional and nonfunctional
    verification
    COC computation, 311
    connectivity metric, 307–309
    extracting responsibilities, 310
    modifiability metric, 302–307
    probability change propagation, 312
    quantitative information extraction,
      301–302

relationship extraction, 311–312
structural information extraction, 301
MBD. *See* Model-based development
model-based engineering, 279
nonfunctional verification
definition, 283–284
inputs and outputs, ATAM process, 284
QAR. *See* Quality attribute-based
reasoning
tool support
scenarios creation, 315–317
visualization, 317
Encryption *vs.* trust
"details" tab invalid digital certificates,
17, 19*f*
lock icon, 16–17
revoked certificates, 17, 20*f*
valid *vs.* invalid digital certificates,
17, 18*f*
Executive Order 9397, 12–13
Extended validation (EV) certificates, 25,
27*f*

F

Face recognition (FR), video-based
appearance model, 186–187
2D face recognition, 186
experiments, 190–191
parametric model, 187–189
"shape-illumination manifold", 187
subspaces manifold structure
Grassmann and Stiefel, 189
Procrustes measure, density estimate,
190
smallest square Euclidean distance,
189–190
"wrapped"-densities, 190
Federal privacy Act of 1974, 12–13
Functional and nonfunctional verification,
embedded software systems
block complexity, 304
COC computation, 311

connection complexity, 304–305
connectivity metric
affected complexity (AC), 308
signal propagation, 307
Simulink subsystems, 307
transitive-closure algorithm, 307–308
extracting responsibilities, 310
modifiability metric
autocoding effort, 302
binary and nonbinary connection, 303
block complexity (BC), 303
modifiability metric formula
BCN value, 306
definition, 305
probability change propagation, 312
quantitative information extraction, 301
relationship extraction, 311–312
sequence, 309–310
structural information extraction
designers, 300–301
QAR approach, 300

G

Gif-It-Up, 75–76
Gram-Schmidt orthonormalization, 189
Graphics interchange format (GIF), 64
Grassmann manifold, 189

H

Heartland Payment Systems, 6, 8
Hidden Markov models (HMM), 191–192
9/11 Hijackers, 3–4
Hypertext transfer protocol (HTTP)
description, 15–16
neutral Web site, Firefox v 3.6.3, 46*f*
trusted, visual indicators
authenticated certificate, 19, 27*f*
Firefox v 3.6.3, 21*f*
Google Chrome v 5, 22*f*
Microsoft Internet Explorer v 8, 22*f*
Safari v 5, 21*f*

Hypertext transfer protocol (HTTP)
(Continued)
untrusted, visual indicators
Firefox v 3.6.3, 23f
Google Chrome v 5, 24f
Microsoft Internet Explorer v 8, 24f
Safari v 5, 23f

I

IBV. *See* Instrumentation-based verification
Iceberg themes, Action Research, 217
Identity theft
crimes, 2, 3f
dangers, 3–4
fungible credentials
counterfeit, 13–14
description, 13
inadequate credential management
procedures
CardSleuth. *See* CardSleuth
''look and feel'' authentication, 31
modus operandi
dump underground prices, 29–30
fungible credentials, 26–27
Golden Dump, 28–29
Internet compounds accessibility,
27–28
Malaysia-based dumpsite forum, 30, 30f
Russia-based dumpsite selling dumps,
29f
New York Times Square incident, 4
phishing
description, 14
growth, 14–15
Secure Online Transactions, 15–25
SMiShing and *Vishing*, 14
problems
fraudulent financial transactions, 11
reasons, USA, 11–12
SSN. *See* Social Security Number
statistical data
compromised record, 7f, 8t, 9f, 10f

Heartland Payment Systems, 6, 8
ITTFROC, 6–8
organization types, 10f, 11t
thieves defeating strategies
description, 32–33
ID theft, precautions, 33–46
remediation, 47
victims, 4–5, 5f
ID theft, precautions
offline transactions
ATM, 35
document and information handling,
33–34
financial accounts and records, 34–35
online transactions
anti-phishing measures, 37–41
anti-spoofing measures, 41–42
defense, 35–36
financial transactions, 43
Firefox privacy and security add-ons,
36f
PayPal site, 37f
precautions, 44–46
trust indicators, 42
visual indicators, phishing web site. *See*
Visual indicators
visual warning, ZoneAlarm, 35f
remediation, 47
In vivo study, Action Research
action focus
data collection, 232–233
objectives, 231
research questions, 231–232
analysis, source code metrics
defect taxonomy, 235–237
low cohesion category, 238, 239f
metrics variation, 236t
minor structure issues category,
238–239
percentage values, 237
poor algorithm category, 237, 237f
poor internal organization category,
238, 238f

code quality and learning
 open coding process, 242–243
 qualitative analysis categories, 244*t*
 semistructured interviews, 242, 243
form fields, 235
hypotheses/suppositions, 233
interviews, 235
learning
 directives, 247*t*
 knowledge externalization, 245
 refactoring needs, 245
 TRAC system, 245–246
literature survey
 form content, 230*t*
 inspection techniques, 229, 230
 Mäntylä and Lassenius study,
  230–231
operational definitions
 instruments, 233–234
 techniques, 233
 tools, 234
problem description
 architectural styles and coding
  conventions, 226
 knowledge, 226–227
 need, project team member, 227
project context
 module construction, 228
 module development, 228
 MPS.BR, 227
 STF information system, 227
refactoring decisions
 independent variables, 240
 low cohesion category, 241, 241*t*
 poor algorithm category, 240, 240*t*
 regression method, 239–240
 RMI, 240–241, 241*t*
 source code metrics, 242
reflections
 "code smells", 246–249
 false-positive suggestions, 249
 refactoring factors, 246
 refactoring process, 250

theory construction, 250–253
research theme, 229
source code refactoring
 communication failures, 234–235
 research theme, 225–226
template structure, 226
Instrumentation-based verification (IBV)
 method
 actual test data, testing instrumental
  model, 289, 290*f*
 architecture, monitor models
  comparison, submodel, 293–294,
   295*f*
  condition design, 293, 293*f*
  data identification, 292–293
  definition, 289–290
  reset-table discrete integrator, 294
  submodels, 290
  top-level, 292*f*
  validation model, 291, 293, 294*f*
 coverage data, testing instrumental model,
  288*f*
 cruise-control application, 285
 description, 284–285
 "design creep", 295–296
 embedded with Simulink model,
  285–286, 288*f*
 extraneous material, 296
 input-vector/output-vector pairs,
  286–287
 monitor model, 285, 286*f*, 290, 291*f*
 Reactis test generation, 286–287, 288*f*
 safety and liveness, 294–295
 steps, 285
 violation, 288, 289*f*

J

Joint photographic experts group (JPEG)
 image, 64
JPEG image steganalysis
 encoding, 89, 89*f*
 header analysis, 89, 90*f*
 hue rendering, 89–91, 91*f*

JPEG image steganalysis (Continued)
JPEG Hide and Seek (JPHS) stego
software, 89, 90f
quantized DCT
analysis, 91–92, 93f
histogram, 91, 92f
JP Hide-and-Seek (JPHS), 71

K

KittenAuth CAPTCHA, 128f

L

Least-significant bit (LSB) overwriting,
68–70
Lempel-Ziv-Welch (LZW) compression,
77
Low-tech stego methods
concealment ciphers, 58–61
image/text block hiding, 61–62
semagrams, 56–58

M

Model-based development (MBD)
advantages over programming languages,
281–282
dynamic modeling, 281
Simulink/Stateflow and ASCET, 282
static modeling, 281
Multiple biometric grand challenge
(MBGC), 190–191

N

Niels Provos' stegdetect, 96–97
NuCaptcha challenge, 142f

O

Offline transactions
ATM, 35
document and information handling,
33–34

financial accounts and records,
34–35
Online transactions precautions
anti-phishing measures
sites verification, 41f
visual indicators, web sites. *See* Visual
indicators
visual warning, ZoneAlarm, 40f
anti-spoofing measures
Iconix www.iconix.com, 42, 43f
SpoofStick, 42f, 41–42
defense
Firefox privacy and security add-ons,
36, 36f
tools, 35–36
visual warning, ZoneAlarm, 35f
financial transactions, 43
Firefox privacy and security add-ons,
36f
PayPal site, 37f
precautions, 44–46
trust indicators
description, 42
visual, WOT, 44f
WOT, action, 45f
visual indicators, phishing web site. *See*
Visual indicators
visual warning, ZoneAlarm, 35f

P

PCP. *See* Probability of change propagation
PessimalPrint, 114, 131–132
Phishing
description, 14
number and sophistication phenomenal
growth
APWG, 14–15
Global and crimeware map, 15, 15f
secure online transactions
domain validation *vs.* EV certificates,
25
encryption *vs.* trust, 16–17
HTTP, 15–16

"lock", 16
"lock" icon visual indicator, 25
visual indicators, 17–25
SMiShing and *Vishing*, 14
Principal component analysis (PCA), 187
Probability of change propagation (PCP)
connectivity metric, 307, 315
definition, 297
impact graph, 299
mapping, 302*t*
modifiability RF, 299
Pulse code modulation (PCM), 64–65, 65*f*

Q

QAR. *See* Quality attribute-based reasoning
Quality attribute-based reasoning (QAR)
apply design tactics module, 300
ArchE and RAPT, 296
components, RF, 298
cost of change (COC), 297
impact graph, 297, 298*f*
initial design creation module, 299
model interpretation and evaluation
module, 299
probability of change propagation (PCP),
297
quality attribute scenarios, 297, 298
reasoning framework (RF), 297
scenario and responsibility parameter
definition module, 299
suggest design tactics module, 300
Quantization error, 64–65

R

Real-time transport protocol (RTP), 83
Reasoning framework (RF)
components, 298
modules, 299
QAR, 280
Reproducing Kernel Hilbert space (RKHS),
186
RF. *See* Reasoning framework

S

SARC's Steganography Application
Fingerprint Database (SAFDB),
94
SARC Steganography Analyzer Signature
Scanner (StegAlyzerSS), 98, 99*f*
Secure socket layer (SSL), 16, 16*f*, 25
"Security Breach Notification Laws",
12–13
Shape sequence parametric models
AR and ARMA, 193–195
tangent space state-space models,
195–196
USF database, 196
Social Security Act of 1935, 12–13
Social Security Number (SSN)
description, 12–13
President's Identity Theft Task Force
Report, 13
Software engineering
Action Research
approaches, 212
constructivism, 211
critical theory, 212
description, 208
in vivo study, 225–253
intensity, paradigms, 213–214, 213*f*
paradigm, 211–212
positivism, 211
pragmatism, 212
process, 214–218
qualitative approach, 213
quantitative approach, 212–213
scientific research paradigms,
210–211
use, 219–225
check-list-based inspection technique,
210
continuous transformation process,
209
description, 206–207
experimentation, 207

Software engineering (Continued)
  premature insistence, accuracy, 208
  relevance, scientific results, 208
  social challenges, 209–210
  source code quality, 210
SpoofStick, 41–42, 41–42
Spread spectrum steganography methods, 85
Steganography
  binary, image and audio files, 55
  classification, 53–55, 54*f*
  covered/concealment and ciphers, 55
  description, 52
  detection
    JPEG images, 235–239
    prisoner's problem, 234–235
    steganalysis, 235–243
  and digital carrier files
    color palette modification, 75–79
    convert communication channel, 80–84
    data appending, 73–75
    encoding algorithm modification, 71
    format modification, 79–80
    grammar selection, 71–73
    LSB overwriting, 68–70
  digital technology basics
    audio, 64–66
    images and color, 62–64
    payload compression and, 66–67
  vs. digital watermarking, 55
  Jargon codes, 54
  linguistic, 54
  low-tech stego methods
    concealment ciphers, 58–61
    image/text block hiding, 61–62
    semagrams, 56–58
  open codes, 54
  semagrams, 54
  stego, 53
  technical, 53
  time-sensitive, 55–56
  tools, detection
    Gargoyle software, 94, 94*f*
    SARC, 94

StegAlyzerAS, 95*f*
stego carrier file detection, 96–100
stego detection programs, 93–94
Stego Hunter output, 95*f*
S-Tools, 96
Steganography Analysis and Research
  Center (SARC), 94
Stego carrier file detection
  DCT coefficient analysis, 98*f*
  2 Mosaic attacks, 99–100, 100*f*
  Niels Provos' stegdetect, 96–97
  prisoner's problem, 99
  StegAlyzerSS, 98, 99*f*
  Stegbreak, 98–99
  Stego Watch, 97–98, 97*f*
  WetStone Technologies' Stego Suite, 97
  xsteg output, 96*f*

T

Time-sensitive steganography, 55–56
Transmission control protocol/internet
  protocol (TCP/IP), 67
Transport layer security (TLS), 15–16
Trust indicators, 42

U

USF gait database experiments
  algorithm performance, 200
  identification rates, 199, 200*t*
U.S. Treasury's Terrorist Financing Tracking
  Program (TFTP), 4

V

Video-based biometrics
  FR
    appearance and variations, parametric
      model, 187–189
    experiments, 190–191
    subspaces manifold structure, 189–190
  gait, 185, 185*f*
  identification, gait

DTW, 192–193
execution variation space, 196–199
features and models, 191–192
HMM, 191–192
scaling, 192
sequences comparison, 192
shape sequence parametric models,
    193–196
USF database experiments, 199–200
motion information, 184
physiological, 184
Visual indicators
Firefox, site identification, 45*t*
Firefox v 3.6.3
    invalid certificate warning, HTTPS
        connection, 19–25
    lock icon, 17–19
    phishing web sites, 38*f*
invalid certificate warning, untrusted
    HTTPS
    Firefox v 3.6.3, 23*f*
    Google Chrome v 5, 24*f*
    Microsoft Internet Explorer v 8, 24*f*
    Safari v 5, 23*f*

"lock" icon, favicon spoof
    missing, status bar, 27*f*
    SSL, 25
    undermines, 26*f*
neutral Web site, HTTP, 46*f*
trusted HTTPS connection
    authenticated certificate, 19
    Firefox v 3.6.3, 21*f*
    Google Chrome v 5, 22*f*
    Microsoft Internet Explorer v 8, 22*f*
    Safari v 5, 21*f*
web site, phishing
    Apple Safari v 5, 39*f*
    Firefox v 3.6.3, 38*f*
    Google Chrome v 5, 40*f*
    Internet Explorer v 8, 39*f*
    warning, ZoneAlarm, 40*f*
VMware Browser Appliance, 45, 46*f*
VoIP-based steganography, 83–84

W

Web crawler, 123
Wireless local area networks (WLANs), 82

Contents of Volumes in This Series

Volume 60

Licensing and Certification of Software Professionals
  DONALD J. BAGERT
Cognitive Hacking
  GEORGE CYBENKO, ANNARITA GIANI, AND PAUL THOMPSON
The Digital Detective: An Introduction to Digital Forensics
  WARREN HARRISON
Survivability: Synergizing Security and Reliability
  CRISPIN COWAN
Smart Cards
  KATHERINE M. SHELFER, CHRIS CORUM, J. DREW PROCACCINO, AND JOSEPH DIDIER
Shotgun Sequence Assembly
  MIHAI POP
Advances in Large Vocabulary Continuous Speech Recognition
  GEOFFREY ZWEIG AND MICHAEL PICHENY

Volume 61

Evaluating Software Architectures
  ROSEANNE TESORIERO TVEDT, PATRICIA COSTA, AND MIKAEL LINDVALL
Efficient Architectural Design of High Performance Microprocessors
  LIEVEN EECKHOUT AND KOEN DE BOSSCHERE
Security Issues and Solutions in Distributed Heterogeneous Mobile Database Systems
  A. R. HURSON, J. PLOSKONKA, Y. JIAO, AND H. HARIDAS
Disruptive Technologies and Their Affect on Global Telecommunications
  STAN MCCLELLAN, STEPHEN LOW, AND WAI-TIAN TAN
Ions, Atoms, and Bits: An Architectural Approach to Quantum Computing
  DEAN COPSEY, MARK OSKIN, AND FREDERIC T. CHONG

Volume 62

An Introduction to Agile Methods
  DAVID COHEN, MIKAEL LINDVALL, AND PATRICIA COSTA
The Timeboxing Process Model for Iterative Software Development
  PANKAJ JALOTE, AVEEJEET PALIT, AND PRIYA KURIEN
A Survey of Empirical Results on Program Slicing
  DAVID BINKLEY AND MARK HARMAN
Challenges in Design and Software Infrastructure for Ubiquitous Computing Applications
  GURUDUTH BANAVAR AND ABRAHAM BERNSTEIN

Introduction to MBASE (Model-Based (System) Architecting and Software Engineering)
  DAVID KLAPPHOLZ AND DANIEL PORT
Software Quality Estimation with Case-Based Reasoning
  TAGHI M. KHOSHGOFTAAR AND NAEEM SELIYA
Data Management Technology for Decision Support Systems
  SURAJIT CHAUDHURI, UMESHWAR DAYAL, AND VENKATESH GANTI

Volume 63

Techniques to Improve Performance Beyond Pipelining: Superpipelining, Superscalar, and VLIW
  JEAN-LUC GAUDIOT, JUNG-YUP KANG, AND WON WOO RO
Networks on Chip (NoC): Interconnects of Next Generation Systems on Chip
  THEOCHARIS THEOCHARIDES, GREGORY M. LINK, NARAYANAN VIJAYKRISHNAN, AND MARY JANE IRWIN
Characterizing Resource Allocation Heuristics for Heterogeneous Computing Systems
  SHOUKAT ALI, TRACY D. BRAUN, HOWARD JAY SIEGEL, ANTHONY A. MACIEJEWSKI, NOAH BECK,
    LADISLAU BÖLÖNI, MUTHUCUMARU MAHESWARAN, ALBERT I. REUTHER, JAMES P. ROBERTSON,
    MITCHELL D. THEYS, AND BIN YAO
Power Analysis and Optimization Techniques for Energy Efficient Computer Systems
  WISSAM CHEDID, CHANSU YU, AND BEN LEE
Flexible and Adaptive Services in Pervasive Computing
  BYUNG Y. SUNG, MOHAN KUMAR, AND BEHROOZ SHIRAZI
Search and Retrieval of Compressed Text
  AMAR MUKHERJEE, NAN ZHANG, TAO TAO, RAVI VIJAYA SATYA, AND WEIFENG SUN

Volume 64

Automatic Evaluation of Web Search Services
  ABDUR CHOWDHURY
Web Services
  SANG SHIN
A Protocol Layer Survey of Network Security
  JOHN V. HARRISON AND HAL BERGHEL
E-Service: The Revenue Expansion Path to E-Commerce Profitability
  ROLAND T. RUST, P. K. KANNAN, AND ANUPAMA D. RAMACHANDRAN
Pervasive Computing: A Vision to Realize
  DEBASHIS SAHA
Open Source Software Development: *Structural Tension in the American Experiment*
  COSKUN BAYRAK AND CHAD DAVIS
Disability and Technology: Building Barriers or Creating Opportunities?
  PETER GREGOR, DAVID SLOAN, AND ALAN F. NEWELL

Volume 65

The State of Artificial Intelligence
  ADRIAN A. HOPGOOD
Software Model Checking with SPIN
  GERARD J. HOLZMANN

Early Cognitive Computer Vision
    JAN-MARK GEUSEBROEK
Verification and Validation and Artificial Intelligence
    TIM MENZIES AND CHARLES PECHEUR
Indexing, Learning and Content-Based Retrieval for Special Purpose Image Databases
    MARK J. HUISKES AND ERIC J. PAUWELS
Defect Analysis: Basic Techniques for Management and Learning
    DAVID N. CARD
Function Points
    CHRISTOPHER J. LOKAN
The Role of Mathematics in Computer Science and Software Engineering Education
    PETER B. HENDERSON

Volume 66

Calculating Software Process Improvement's Return on Investment
    RINI VAN SOLINGEN AND DAVID F. RICO
Quality Problem in Software Measurement Data
    PIERRE REBOURS AND TAGHI M. KHOSHGOFTAAR
Requirements Management for Dependable Software Systems
    WILLIAM G. BAIL
Mechanics of Managing Software Risk
    WILLIAM G. BAIL
The PERFECT Approach to Experience-Based Process Evolution
    BRIAN A. NEJMEH AND WILLIAM E. RIDDLE
The Opportunities, Challenges, and Risks of High Performance Computing in Computational Science and Engineering
    DOUGLASS E. POST, RICHARD P. KENDALL, AND ROBERT F. LUCAS

Volume 67

Broadcasting a Means to Disseminate Public Data in a Wireless Environment—Issues and Solutions
    A. R. HURSON, Y. JIAO, AND B. A. SHIRAZI
Programming Models and Synchronization Techniques for Disconnected Business Applications
    AVRAHAM LEFF AND JAMES T. RAYFIELD
Academic Electronic Journals: Past, Present, and Future
    ANAT HOVAV AND PAUL GRAY
Web Testing for Reliability Improvement
    JEFF TIAN AND LI MA
Wireless Insecurities
    MICHAEL STHULTZ, JACOB UECKER, AND HAL BERGHEL
The State of the Art in Digital Forensics
    DARIO FORTE

Volume 68

Exposing Phylogenetic Relationships by Genome Rearrangement
    YING CHIH LIN AND CHUAN YI TANG

Models and Methods in Comparative Genomics
  GUILLAUME BOURQUE AND LOUXIN ZHANG
Translocation Distance: Algorithms and Complexity
  LUSHENG WANG
Computational Grand Challenges in Assembling the Tree of Life: Problems and Solutions
  DAVID A. BADER, USMAN ROSHAN, AND ALEXANDROS STAMATAKIS
Local Structure Comparison of Proteins
  JUN HUAN, JAN PRINS, AND WEI WANG
Peptide Identification via Tandem Mass Spectrometry
  XUE WU, NATHAN EDWARDS, AND CHAU-WEN TSENG

Volume 69

The Architecture of Efficient Multi-Core Processors: A Holistic Approach
  RAKESH KUMAR AND DEAN M. TULLSEN
Designing Computational Clusters for Performance and Power
  KIRK W. CAMERON, RONG GE, AND XIZHOU FENG
Compiler-Assisted Leakage Energy Reduction for Cache Memories
  WEI ZHANG
Mobile Games: Challenges and Opportunities
  PAUL COULTON, WILL BAMFORD, FADI CHEHIMI, REUBEN EDWARDS, PAUL GILBERTSON, AND
    OMER RASHID
Free/Open Source Software Development: Recent Research Results and Methods
  WALT SCACCHI

Volume 70

Designing Networked Handheld Devices to Enhance School Learning
  JEREMY ROSCHELLE, CHARLES PATTON, AND DEBORAH TATAR
Interactive Explanatory and Descriptive Natural-Language Based Dialogue for Intelligent Information
Filtering
  JOHN ATKINSON AND ANITA FERREIRA
A Tour of Language Customization Concepts
  COLIN ATKINSON AND THOMAS KÜHNE
Advances in Business Transformation Technologies
  JUHNYOUNG LEE
Phish Phactors: Offensive and Defensive Strategies
  HAL BERGHEL, JAMES CARPINTER, AND JU-YEON JO
Reflections on System Trustworthiness
  PETER G. NEUMANN

Volume 71

Programming Nanotechnology: Learning from Nature
  BOONSERM KAEWKAMNERDPONG, PETER J. BENTLEY, AND NAVNEET BHALLA
Nanobiotechnology: An Engineer's Foray into Biology
  YI ZHAO AND XIN ZHANG

Toward Nanometer-Scale Sensing Systems: Natural and Artificial Noses as Models for Ultra-Small, Ultra-Dense Sensing Systems
    BRIGITTE M. ROLFE
Simulation of Nanoscale Electronic Systems
    UMBERTO RAVAIOLI
Identifying Nanotechnology in Society
    CHARLES TAHAN
The Convergence of Nanotechnology, Policy, and Ethics
    ERIK FISHER

Volume 72

DARPA's HPCS Program: History, Models, Tools, Languages
    JACK DONGARRA, ROBERT GRAYBILL, WILLIAM HARROD, ROBERT LUCAS, EWING LUSK, PIOTR LUSZCZEK,
    JANICE MCMAHON, ALLAN SNAVELY, JEFFERY VETTER, KATHERINE YELICK, SADAF ALAM, ROY
    CAMPBELL, LAURA CARRINGTON, TZU-YI CHEN, OMID KHALILI, JEREMY MEREDITH, AND
    MUSTAFA TIKIR
Productivity in High-Performance Computing
    THOMAS STERLING AND CHIRAG DEKATE
Performance Prediction and Ranking of Supercomputers
    TZU-YI CHEN, OMID KHALILI, ROY L. CAMPBELL, JR., LAURA CARRINGTON, MUSTAFA M. TIKIR, AND
    ALLAN SNAVELY
Sampled Processor Simulation: A Survey
    LIEVEN EECKHOUT
Distributed Sparse Matrices for Very High Level Languages
    JOHN R. GILBERT, STEVE REINHARDT, AND VIRAL B. SHAH
Bibliographic Snapshots of High-Performance/High-Productivity Computing
    MYRON GINSBERG

Volume 73

History of Computers, Electronic Commerce, and Agile Methods
    DAVID F. RICO, HASAN H. SAYANI, AND RALPH F. FIELD
Testing with Software Designs
    ALIREZA MAHDIAN AND ANNELIESE A. ANDREWS
Balancing Transparency, Efficiency, AND Security in Pervasive Systems
    MARK WENSTROM, ELOISA BENTIVEGNA, AND ALI R. HURSON
Computing with RFID: Drivers, Technology and Implications
    GEORGE ROUSSOS
Medical Robotics and Computer-Integrated Interventional Medicine
    RUSSELL H. TAYLOR AND PETER KAZANZIDES

Volume 74

Data Hiding Tactics for Windows and Unix File Systems
    HAL BERGHEL, DAVID HOELZER, AND MICHAEL STHULTZ
Multimedia and Sensor Security
    ANNA HAĆ

Email Spam Filtering
    ENRIQUE PUERTAS SANZ, JOSÉ MARÍA GÓMEZ HIDALGO, AND JOSÉ CARLOS CORTIZO PÉREZ
The Use of Simulation Techniques for Hybrid Software Cost Estimation and Risk Analysis
    MICHAEL KLÄS, ADAM TRENDOWICZ, AXEL WICKENKAMP, JÜRGEN MÜNCH,
    NAHOMI KIKUCHI, AND YASUSHI ISHIGAI
An Environment for Conducting Families of Software Engineering Experiments
    LORIN HOCHSTEIN, TAIGA NAKAMURA, FORREST SHULL, NICO ZAZWORKA,
    VICTOR R. BASILI, AND MARVIN V. ZELKOWITZ
Global Software Development: Origins, Practices, and Directions
    JAMES J. CUSICK, ALPANA PRASAD, AND WILLIAM M. TEPFENHART

Volume 75

The UK HPC Integration Market: Commodity-Based Clusters
    CHRISTINE A. KITCHEN AND MARTYN F. GUEST
Elements of High-Performance Reconfigurable Computing
    TOM VANCOURT AND MARTIN C. HERBORDT
Models and Metrics for Energy-Efficient Computing
    PARTHASARATHY RANGANATHAN, SUZANNE RIVOIRE, AND JUSTIN MOORE
The Emerging Landscape of Computer Performance Evaluation
    JOANN M. PAUL, MWAFFAQ OTOOM, MARC SOMERS, SEAN PIEPER, AND MICHAEL J. SCHULTE
Advances in Web Testing
    CYNTRICA EATON AND ATIF M. MEMON

Volume 76

Information Sharing and Social Computing: Why, What, and Where?
    ODED NOV
Social Network Sites: Users and Uses
    MIKE THELWALL
Highly Interactive Scalable Online Worlds
    GRAHAM MORGAN
The Future of Social Web Sites: Sharing Data and Trusted Applications with Semantics
    SHEILA KINSELLA, ALEXANDRE PASSANT, JOHN G. BRESLIN, STEFAN DECKER,
    AND AJIT JAOKAR
Semantic Web Services Architecture with Lightweight Descriptions of Services
    TOMAS VITVAR, JACEK KOPECKY, JANA VISKOVA, ADRIANMOCAN, MICK KERRIGAN, AND DIETER FENSEL
Issues and Approaches for Web 2.0 Client Access to Enterprise Data
    AVRAHAM LEFF AND JAMES T. RAYFIELD
Web Content Filtering
    JOSÉMARÍA GÓMEZ HIDALGO, ENRIQUE PUERTAS SANZ, FRANCISCO CARRERO GARCÍA, AND MANUEL DE
    BUENAGA RODRÍGUEZ

Volume 77

Photo Fakery and Forensics
 HANY FARID
Advances in Computer Displays
 JASON LEIGH, ANDREW JOHNSON, AND LUC RENAMBOT
Playing with All Senses: Human–Computer Interface Devices for Games
 JÖRN LOVISCACH
A Status Report on the P Versus NP Question
 ERIC ALLENDER
Dynamically Typed Languages
 LAURENCE TRATT
Factors Influencing Software Development Productivity—State-of-the-Art and Industrial Experiences
 ADAM TRENDOWICZ AND JÜRGEN MÜNCH
Evaluating the Modifiability of Software Architectural Designs
 M. OMOLADE SALIU, GÜNTHER RUHE, MIKAEL LINDVALL, AND CHRISTOPHER ACKERMANN
The Common Law and Its Impact on the Internet
 ROBERT AALBERTS, DAVID HAMES, PERCY POON, AND PAUL D. THISTLE

Volume 78

Search Engine Optimization—Black and White Hat Approaches
 ROSS A. MALAGA
Web Searching and Browsing: A Multilingual Perspective
 WINGYAN CHUNG
Features for Content-Based Audio Retrieval
 DALIBOR MITROVIĆ, MATTHIAS ZEPPELZAUER, AND CHRISTIAN BREITENEDER
Multimedia Services over Wireless Metropolitan Area Networks
 KOSTAS PENTIKOUSIS, JARNO PINOLA, ESA PIRI, PEDRO NEVES, AND SUSANA SARGENTO
An Overview of Web Effort Estimation
 EMILIA MENDES
Communication Media Selection for Remote Interaction of Ad Hoc Groups
 FABIO CALEFATO AND FILIPPO LANUBILE

Volume 79

Applications in Data-Intensive Computing
 ANUJ R. SHAH, JOSHUA N. ADKINS, DOUGLAS J. BAXTER, WILLIAM R. CANNON, DANIEL G. CHAVARRIA-MIRANDA, SUTANAY CHOUDHURY, IAN GORTON, DEBORAH K. GRACIO, TODD D. HALTER, NAVDEEP D. JAITLY, JOHN R. JOHNSON, RICHARD T. KOUZES, MATTHEW C. MACDUFF, ANDRES MARQUEZ, MATTHEW E. MONROE, CHRISTOPHER S. OEHMEN, WILLIAM A. PIKE, CHAD SCHERRER, ORESTE VILLA, BOBBIE-JO WEBB-ROBERTSON, PAUL D. WHITNEY, AND NINO ZULJEVIC
Pitfalls and Issues of Manycore Programming
 AMI MAROWKA
Illusion of Wireless Security
 ALFRED W. LOO

Brain–Computer Interfaces for the Operation of Robotic and Prosthetic Devices
    DENNIS J. MCFARLAND AND JONATHAN R. WOLPAW
The Tools Perspective on Software Reverse Engineering: Requirements, Construction, and Evaluation
    HOLGER M. KIENLE AND HAUSI A. MÜLLER

Volume 80

Agile Software Development Methodologies and Practices
    LAURIE WILLIAMS
A Picture from the Model-Based Testing Area: Concepts, Techniques, and Challenges
    ARILO C. DIAS-NETO AND GUILHERME H. TRAVASSOS
Advances in Automated Model-Based System Testing of Software
Applications with a GUI Front-End
    ATIF M. MEMON AND BAO N. NGUYEN
Empirical Knowledge Discovery by Triangulation in Computer Science
    RAVI I. SINGH AND JAMES MILLER
StarLight: Next-Generation Communication Services, Exchanges, and Global Facilities
    JOE MAMBRETTI, TOM DEFANTI, AND MAXINE D. BROWN
Parameters Effecting 2D Barcode Scanning Reliability
    AMIT GROVER, PAUL BRAECKEL, KEVIN LINDGREN, HAL BERGHEL, AND DENNIS COBB
Advances in Video-Based Human Activity Analysis: Challenges and Approaches
    PAVAN TURAGA , RAMA CHELLAPPA, AND ASHOK VEERARAGHAVAN

Volume 81

VoIP Security: Vulnerabilities, Exploits, and Defenses
    XINYUAN WANG AND RUISHAN ZHANG
Phone-to-Phone Configuration for Internet Telephony
    YIU-WING LEUNG
SLAM for Pedestrians and Ultrasonic Landmarks
in Emergency Response Scenarios
    CARL FISCHER, KAVITHA MUTHUKRISHNAN, AND MIKE HAZAS
Feeling Bluetooth: From a Security Perspective
    PAUL BRAECKEL
Digital Feudalism: Enclosures and Erasures from Digital Rights Management to the Digital Divide
    SASCHA D. MEINRATH, JAMES W.LOSEY, AND VICTOR W. PICKARD
Online Advertising
    AVI GOLDFARB AND CATHERINE TUCKER

Volume 82

The Hows and Whys of Information Markets
    AREEJ YASSIN AND ALAN R. HEVNER
Measuring and Monitoring Technical Debt
    CAROLYN SEAMAN AND YUEPU GUO
A Taxonomy and Survey of Energy-Efficient Data Centers and Cloud Computing Systems
    ANTON BELOGLAZOV, RAJKUMAR BUYYA, YOUNG CHOON LEE AND ALBERT ZOMAYA

Applications of Mobile Agents in Wireless Networks and Mobile Computing
    SERGIO GONZÁLEZ-VALENZUELA, MIN CHEN, and VICTOR C.M. LEUNG
Virtual Graphics for Broadcast Production
    GRAHAM THOMAS
Advanced Applications of Virtual Reality
    JÜRGEN P. SCHULZE, HAN SUK KIM, PHILIP WEBER, ANDREW PRUDHOMME,
    ROGER E. BOHN, MAURIZIO SERACINI, and THOMAS A. DEFANTI